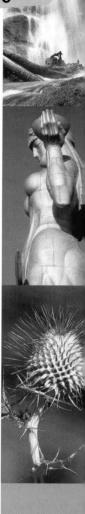

Georgia

the Bradt Travel Guide

Tim Burford

edition
3

www.bradtguides.com

Bradt Travel Guides Ltd, UK
The Globe Pequot Press Inc, USA

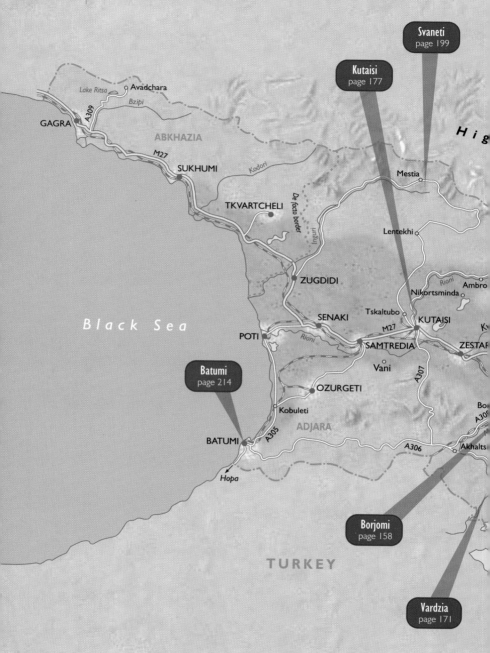

N

Bradt

Svaneti
page 199

Kutaisi
page 177

GAGRA

Lake Ritsa   Avadchara

Bzipi

A309

ABKHAZIA

Hig

M27

SUKHUMI

Kodori

Mestia

TKVARTCHELI

De facto border

Lentekhi

Inguri

ZUGDIDI

Rioni   Ambro

Nikortsminda

Black Sea

SENAKI   Tskaltubo   KUTAISI

POTI   Rioni   SAMTREDIA   M27   ZESTAF

Vani   A307

Batumi
page 214

OZURGETI

Kobuleti

Bo
A30

ADJARA

A306   Akhalts

BATUMI   A305

Hopa

TURKEY

Borjomi
page 158

0   50km
0   30 miles

Vardzia
page 171

Kazbegi
page 149

Tusheti
page 232

Davit–Gareja
page 240

Uplistsikhe
page 138

Tbilisi
page 83

KEY
Capital city
Main town
Other town
Airport
Main road
Other road
Railway
International boundary

RUSSIA

Caucasus Mountains

Rioni

Vladikavkaz

Kazbek
5033m

Alagir

Kazbegi

Roka

A301

SOUTH OSSETIA

Pasanauri

GEORGIA

TSKHINVALI

Ananauri

Omalo

Ksani

Uplistsikhe

A301

Akhmeta

M27

Aragvi

KHASHURI

GORI

Kaspi

Telavi

TELAVI

Balakan

Trialeti Ridge

Mtskheta

Iori

Sagarejo

Gurdjaani

AZERBAIJAN

Bakuriani

TBILISI

Alazani

Manglisi

A303

Chram

RUSTAVI

A302

Akhalkalaki

Bolnisi

Marneuli

Alazani

M27

Iori

Debet

Ganja, Baku

Gyumri

Tashir,
Yerevan

Alaverdi

Kur
(Kura)

Mingecevir
Reservoir

ARMENIA

Ganja, Baku

AZERBAIJAN

Georgia
Don't
miss…

Tbilisi Old Town
View of Mtkvari River and
Narikala Castle
(MB) page 83

Trekking
Hikers at Amarati
(KG)

**Borjomi-
Kharagauli
National Park**
Idyllic meadows and
mountains
(KG) page 160

Cave cities
Refectory, Cave of
Udabno Monastery
(MB) page 242

Food and wine
A typical Georgian
supra (feast)
(VG) page 72

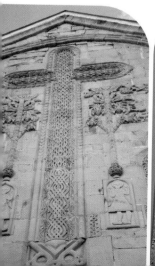

top	**Pomegranate tree** (AC)
above left	**Davit-Gareja monastery complex** (MC) page 240
above right	**Mount Kazbek, Caucasus** (MB) page 152
bottom	**Tsminda Sameba (Holy Trinity) Church, Gergeti** (AC) page 152

Author

Tim Burford studied languages at Oxford University. In 1991, after five years as a publisher, he began writing guidebooks for Bradt, firstly on hiking in East-Central Europe and then on backpacking and ecotourism in Latin America. He has now written eight books for Bradt, as well as the *Rough Guides to Romania* and *Alaska*.

DEDICATION

For Chris and Natalie, to mark over 25 years of friendship.

Spending on feasting and wine is better than hoarding our substance;
That which we give makes us richer, that which is hoarded is lost.

(Rustaveli)

PUBLISHER'S FOREWORD · *Hilary Bradt*

The first Bradt travel guide was written in 1974 by George and Hilary Bradt on a river barge floating down a tributary of the Amazon. In the 1980s and '90s the focus shifted away from hiking to broader-based guides covering new destinations – usually the first to be published about these places. In the 21st century Bradt continues to publish such ground-breaking guides, as well as others to established holiday destinations, incorporating in-depth information on culture and natural history with the nuts and bolts of where to stay and what to see.

Bradt authors support responsible travel, and provide advice not only on minimum impact but also on how to give something back through local charities. In this way a true synergy is achieved between the traveller and local communities.

* * *

It's always a pleasure to welcome another guide by Tim Burford, and *Georgia* has been one of his stalwarts. I remember a meeting at the Frankfurt Book Fair a few years ago with an Englishman who runs a bookshop in, of all places, Tbilisi. His bookshop is called Prospero's Books, and he was quite misty-eyed with praise for Tim's guide. This is what I love about publishing guides to unusual destinations. When they hit the spot they dispel a bit of magic in all directions!

Third edition published April 2007 Reprinted with amendments September 2008
First published in 1998

Bradt Travel Guides Ltd, 23 High Street, Chalfont St Peter, Bucks SL9 9QE, England.
www.bradtguides.com
Published in the USA by The Globe Pequot Press Inc, 246 Goose Lane,
PO Box 480, Guilford, Connecticut 06475-0480.
Text copyright © 2007 Tim Burford
Maps copyright © 2007 Bradt Travel Guides Ltd
Illustrations © 2007 Individual photographers and artists

ISBN-13: 9 781841 62 261 3
British Library Cataloguing in Publication Data
A catalogue record for this book is available from the British Library

Photographs Martin Barlow (MB), Tim Burford (TB), Molly Corso (MC), Anne Croquet-Zouridakis (AC), Paul Doyle (PD), Kote Gabrichidze (KG), Peter Nasmyth (PN), Marcus Stadler (MS), Visit Georgia (VG), WWF CauPo Archive (WCA)
Front cover Georgian traditional dancers, Tbilisi (PN)
Back cover Interior of Sveti Tskhoveli Cathedral, Mtskheta (AC), Statue in Alexandrov Park, Tbilisi (AC)
Title page Waterfall in Marelisi, Borjomi-Kharagauli National Park (WCA), Statue of Kartlis Deda (Mother Georgia), Tbilisi (AC), Thistle, Borjomi-Kharagauli National Park (MS)
Illustrations Carole Vincer **Maps** Alan Whitaker. Regional maps based on ITM Georgia

Typeset from the author's disc by Wakewing
Printed and bound in India by Nutech Photolithographers

Contents

LIST OF MAPS

Acknowledgements

Thanks to: Dr Jonathan Aves, Rowan Stewart, Neil Taylor, Ed Manning, Eilidh Kennedy, Arthur Gerfers, Mark Elliott, Koba & Leila, Gela & Cristina, Ana Anganashvili, Vano Vashakmadze, Remaz Rekhiashvili, Mary Ellen Chatwin, Manana Kochladze, Aleko Motsonelidze, David Tarkhinishvili and Jesse Tsinadze in Tbilisi; Tamuna & Nugzar Kvaratskhedia in Kutaisi; Natia Khordiani in Mestia; Alek & Sophiko in Zugdidi; Ramaz Georgadze in Batumi; and above all to Boris and Tsira Arhdabevsky.

Further thanks for their assistance on the second edition to: Peter Nasmyth, Amy Spurling, Hugo Greenhalgh, Eleanor O'Hanlon, Rebecca Weaver & Andrew Barnard, Polly & Susan Amos, Maka Dvalishvili, Besik Lortkipanidze, Lars Nejsig and the Javakhishvili family, Raffi Kojian and Dave Mitchell.
   Also Ben & Suki – I'm still waiting to get my Truso map back!

Additional thanks on this edition to: Amy Spurling, Boris and Tsira, Laurie Dalton, Till Bruckner, Ed Raupp, Irakli Tavartkiladze, Natia Muladze, Knut Gerber, Ramaz Gokhelashvili, Rati Jabaridze, John Graham, Inga Gotsiridze, Molly Corso, Rob Ainsley, Ian Colvin

FEEDBACK REQUEST

Please help us to keep this book up to date and to make the next edition even better by sending any comments or suggestions to: Georgia updates, Bradt Travel Guides, 23 High Street, Chalfont St Peter, Bucks SL9 9QE or send us an email at info@bradtguides.com.

Introduction

Many things in Georgia are in a poor state (the roads, hotels, postal system and electricity supply immediately come to mind), yet it's one of the most heart-warming and exciting of all European destinations. This is above all due to its people, who are some of the most hospitable and generous you could meet anywhere. In addition you'll see fantastic scenery, including Europe's highest mountains, and lovely ancient churches and cave-cities.

This does in part beg the question of whether Georgia is in Europe, Asia, the Middle East, or some other region; travellers can easily spend half their trip debating this issue. If the Caucasus is the dividing line between Europe and Asia, it's unclear which side is European and which is Asian. Armenia and Russia have international phone codes in the European 003 series, yet they are separated by Georgia and Azerbaijan which have chosen codes in the Asian 009 series. Despite this, in 2007 Georgia competed for the first time in the Eurovision Song Contest, finishing in a very creditable twelfth place. Certainly the Georgians seem to spend a lot of time squatting on their haunches in an Asian way waiting for the good times to come around, yet civil society (non-governmental organisations, pressure groups, a fair judicial system and so on) is stronger here than in the neighbouring countries.

To illustrate the joys and perils of travel in Georgia, here's an account of a cycle trip in 1995:

In a month we managed to cover 1,000km on our bikes; however, we could probably have completed it in half the time but for the Georgians taking Rustaveli to heart and insisting that we share their food with them all the time. There was the man walking by the side of the road who gave us the loaf of bread that he was carrying. There were the policemen who constantly stopped us and, when we expected to have to show our documentation, merely wished to give us a watermelon or figs. Old women would give us apples or walnuts, people driving past in cars would pass out bubble gum while on the move, the list goes on. We were constantly surprised and humbled by the generosity of everyone from the countryside to the cities. We were invited into many people's homes, by cow herders in the mountains, peasants in villages and sophisticates in towns. In every household the inevitable bottle was brought out and the toasting began. ...needless to say, on some days our cycling was seriously curtailed after such meeetings.

Ella Truscott

Part One

GENERAL INFORMATION

Location Transcaucasia, between the Black and Caspian seas, bordering the Russian Federation, Turkey, Armenia and Azerbaijan. Tbilisi, the capital, is (by rail) 3,214km from Moscow, 374km from Yerevan and 549km from Baku; 350km from the Black Sea; and 4.5 hours' flight from London.

Area 69,700km^2

Population 4 million, of whom 83% are ethnically Georgian, 6% Armenian, 6% Azerbaijani, 2% Russian, 2% Ossetian and 1% other groups

Government Presidential-parliamentary republic

Major towns Tbilisi (population 1.5 million), Kutaisi (240,000), Rustavi (140,000), Batumi (130,000), Gori (69,000)

Administrative divisions Two autonomous republics (Abkhazia and Adjara), ten regions or *mkhare* (Kakheti, Kvemo Kartli, Shida Kartli – containing the former autonomous region of South Ossetia – Mtskheta-Mtianeti, Samtskhe-Javakheti, Imereti, Racha-Lechkhumi, Samegrelo, Zemo Svaneti and Guria)

Currency Lari (GEL), divided into 100 tetri; introduced September 1995.

Exchange rate (as of March 2008) US$1 = GEL1.49; £1 = GEL2.95; €1 = GEL2.30

Language Georgian, a member of the Caucasian group of languages; Russian widely spoken

Alphabet Georgian, devised in the 4th or 5th century

Religion 70% Georgian Orthodox; Muslims, Jews and other Christian sects also present

Weights and measures Metric system

Electricity 220v 50hz (in theory), with two-prong European-standard plugs

National flag Saint George's cross (red on white), with a red cross in each quarter

Public holidays See page 74.

Background Information

GEOGRAPHY

With an area of 69,700km² (26,911 square miles), Georgia is slightly smaller than Austria or the Republic of Ireland, and under half the size of the American state of Georgia. More than half this area lies above 900m and almost 40% (2.69 million hectares) is wooded. The country's dominant feature is, of course, the High Caucasus range which forms its northern border. Although its highest peak, Elbruz (in fact Europe's highest peak at 5,642m, or 18,510ft), lies wholly within the Russian Federation, Georgia does have three peaks over 5,000m (Shkhara, 5,068m; Janga, 5,059m; and Mkinvartsveri (Kazbek), 5,033m) and ten more over 4,000m. The Caucasus is, like the Himalayas, a very young and dynamic range; it was formed just 25 million years ago, and linked about 15 million years ago to the Iranian Massif. It stretches for roughly 1,200km and contains over 2,000 glaciers, covering an area of 1,780km². The High Caucasus falls into three parts: firstly the Western Caucasus, stretching 440km from the Black Sea to Elbruz, its highest peak being Dombay (4,046m), on the border with the Russian Federation. It's composed of granite, gneiss and crystalline shales, with limestone and sandstone ridges parallel to the north and west, and is very beautiful with canyons and dense vegetation; the 100km west of Elbruz are higher and more alpine, with glaciers. The Central Caucasus covers the 180km from Elbruz, where the range is at its widest (180km), to Kazbek, where it's at its narrowest (60km), and includes all the peaks over 5,000m. Its western half is granite and shale, and its eastern half andesite and diabase, with a last small spot of granite near Kazbek; Elbruz and Kazbek are very ancient volcanoes, while the peaks between, such as Uzhba, Tetnuldi, Shkhara and Dykhtau, are younger upthrust peaks sculpted by glaciers, with gigantic north faces and lots of scree. Finally, the Eastern Caucasus, from Kazbek to the Apsheron Peninsula, is a confused mass of argillaceous slate, with outcrops of diabase, porphyrite and sandstone; its climate is far drier than to the west, with very little glaciation.

The High Caucasus forms the border with the Russian Federation, but nowhere does Georgia directly adjoin Russia itself; the Muslim peoples of the northern Caucasus, who speak at least 30 different languages, live in half-a-dozen autonomous republics: from east to west Daghestan, Chechnya, Ingushetia, North Ossetia, Kalbardino-Balkaria and Karachai-Cherkesbaijan (or Circassia).

From almost anywhere in the central valleys you'll be able to see the High Caucasus as a long white wall to the north; in many places you'll also be able to see the Lesser Caucasus, to the southwest along the Turkish border. This is a gentler, more rounded range, rising to 3,301m at Didi-Abuli; the Trialeti Ridge, covered in rich pastures and forests, stretches to the outskirts of the capital, Tbilisi. The two ranges of the Caucasus are linked by the very young Suran (or Likhi) range, which forms the watershed between the Black and Caspian seas and separates eastern and western Georgia, Kartli and Kolkhida.

3

The country is dominated by one main river, the Mtkvari (Kura in Russian; 1,364km in total), which rises in Turkey, enters Georgia near Vardzia, then flows east through Kartli and Tbilisi and then through Azerbaijan to the Caspian Sea. The main river of western Georgia is the Rioni (327km) which flows from the foothills of Racha through Kutaisi to the Black Sea; others are the Inguri (213km) which flows from Svaneti to the Black Sea, the Iori (320km) and Alazani (351km, the longest within Georgia), which flow through Kakheti and into the Mtkvari, and the headwaters of the Terek (623km in all) which flows north into Russia and eventually into the Caspian Sea.

The main centres of industry and population lie along an east–west axis, from Rustavi through Tbilisi, Gori, Zestaponi, Kutaisi, Samtredia and Senaki to Poti; the only other major cities are two Black Sea ports, Batumi, near the Turkish border, and Sukhumi, in the secessionist republic of Abkhazia.

Georgia has over 2,000 mineral springs producing 130 million litres a day, most of which is wasted. There are over 500 different waters (both hot and cold), of which most contain carbon dioxide, such as those from Borjomi, Sairme and Nabeghlavi; there are also sulphide, nitric and silicon waters (mostly hot), such as those from Tskaltubo, Tbilisi, Nunisi, Tkvartcheli and Makhinjauri, and Gagra, Sukhumi and Aspindza in Abkhazia.

At least 15% of Georgia is limestone, so it's not surprising that there are plenty of fine caves; few of them are set up properly for visitors, but there are great opportunities for exploring. The Gumistavi Cave, near Tskaltubo, is a particularly fine recent discovery, and the Pantiukhin Cave is claimed to be the second deepest in the world at 1,540m (5,050ft). The Tovliana Cave contains snow and ice far underground but has been badly polluted by cavers' rubbish, such as burnt carbide from their lamps. The people of the Tskaltubo area have unwittingly been polluting their own water supply by dumping garbage in caves; some have also been used for agricultural storage and even as hothouses.

GEORGIA'S REGIONS Georgia is much more regional and less centralised than the other Transcaucasian countries, and since independence there has been a marked increase in the power of the regions vis-à-vis the centre. The country includes the two autonomous republics of Abkhazia and Adjara, the formerly autonomous region of South Ossetia, and ten administrative regions (*mkhare*). From east to west these are Kakheti, Kvemo (Lower) Kartli, Shida (Inner) Kartli (which now includes South Ossetia), Mtskheta-Mtianeti, Samtskhe-Javakheti, Imereti, Racha-Lechkhumi, Samegrelo, Zemo (Upper) Svaneti and Guria.

Kakheti is the easternmost region of Georgia, projecting into Azerbaijan; it's known almost entirely for its vine growing and winemaking. Kvemo (Lower) Kartli lies to the south of Tbilisi, across the routes to Armenia; it's largely inhabited by people of Azerbaijani origin who produce much of the food sold in the markets of Tbilisi. Although there are secessionist tendencies and in 1992–95 there was some sabotage of pipelines and railways, both the Georgian and Azerbaijani governments are keen to keep things calm. Further west, around Lake Tsalka, is a population of Greeks raising livestock and growing potatoes. In general the people of **Kvemo Kartli** are reformist, wanting to be allowed to make money, while the Kakhetians are conservative, with plenty of old-style communists who want to be left alone with their wine.

Shida Kartli is the heartland of eastern Georgia; with a population of 343,000 it produces 5–10% of Georgia's industrial output as well as most of its fruit. It now theoretically includes the autonomous region of **South Ossetia** (also known as Samachablo, with a population of about 70,000), which has now more or less seceded.

Mtskheta-Mtianeti, to the north of Tbilisi, straddles the Georgian Military Highway, the main route to Russia; it's an agricultural area with vegetables grown in the lower region and sheep raised in the high mountains. Industry is growing in Mtskheta and Dusheti, and Georgia's main ski resort is at Gudauri.

Samtskhe-Javakheti covers the high empty volcanic tablelands of the southwest of Georgia; 90% of the population is Armenian and in many ways the area is largely autonomous. Few speak Georgian and they are not conscripted into the Georgian army; however, the Russian army base near Akhalkalaki (which closed in 2006) took recruits for the Russian army. It's a harsh area and its few agricultural products rarely reach markets due to the poor road and rail links. Javakheti, near the present border of Armenia and Turkey, was settled by Armenians in the 19th century, after the Russian conquest of the area; here and in **Meskheti**, to the west, there was also a heavily Islamicised population of largely Georgian stock, the so-called Meskhetian Turks, who were deported to central Asia in 1944 and have still not been permitted to return. There's little industry, apart from some low-grade coal and Swiss and French investment in sugar plants. There's now a road crossing to Turkey at Vale (and another planned at Cildir), and work on the 98km extension of the railway from Akhalkalaki to Kars in Turkey finally got under way in late 2007. This will link Azerbaijan with Turkey, and thus Kazakhstan and China with Europe, moving freight faster than the Trans-Siberian. It will earn Georgia about US$150 million per year in transit fees, but was held up by opposition from the US-Armenian lobby, who see it as another way to isolate their homeland.

Georgia's second city is Kutaisi, capital of **Imereti**; 10–25% of Georgian industrial production is based here, although this share is declining – it's largely dependent on the Chiatura mine (which used to produce a quarter of the Soviet Union's manganese) and the connected ferro-alloys plant at Zestaponi.

Samegrelo (or Mingrelia), in the northwest of Georgia, has historically had a considerable degree of autonomy, partly because the Mingrelian dialect is almost unintelligible to the people of Tbilisi. Politically the area is still strongly associated with Zviadism and opposition to the central government. The regional capital, Zugdidi, is now overloaded with refugees but benefits from illicit trade with Abkhazia. The subtropical climate makes tea and citrus fruits important crops, while traditionally Zugdidi has produced porcelain and Senaki carpets. Exports of tea have crashed since the end of the Soviet Union and many plantations are now being replanted with hazel trees.

To the north of Kutaisi, **Racha-Lechkhumi** and **Kvemo-Svaneti** lie in the foothills of the Caucasus; the only roads here are minor and circuitous because of the hills. Winters are harsh, with much of the population decamping to the city, but nevertheless Racha manages to produce both tea and wine. The chief towns of Racha are Ambrolauri and Oni, both little more than villages. Lentekhi, capital of Kvemo Svaneti, is even smaller. Kvemo (Lower) Svaneti was historically part of the feudal system of western Georgia, while **Zemo (Upper) Svaneti** was always self-governing and has developed a far stronger cultural identity. With its stunning Caucasian landscape, its defensive towers, its haunting music and its superb and ancient icons, Zemo Svaneti is the area to which all the more enterprising tourists to Georgia are drawn, like moths to the flame.

Guria, a small swampy region on the coast south of Poti, is known for its subtropical crops, stunningly complex polyphonic songs and the humour of its people. People usually come here *en route* to **Adjara**, which dominates Georgia's trade both across the Turkish border and through the port of Batumi. With this trade, subtropical agriculture, beach tourism and some copper and gold mining,

Adjara is a prosperous republic.

Finally, the autonomous republic of **Abkhazia**, in the extreme northwest of Georgia, has effectively seceded; its borders are closed and tourists are unable to visit, although until secession this was perhaps the most sought-after holiday area of the entire Soviet Union. Its exports are citrus fruits, hazelnuts and timber, so there is some tax revenue, and arrangements have been made to share the power produced by the Inguri hydro-electric station between Georgia and Abkhazia; but it'll be a long time before normality returns.

CLIMATE

There's quite a wide range of climates in Georgia, from the warm, humid, subtropical Black Sea coast, via the colder, wet, alpine climate of the High Caucasus, to the arid steppes of the east.

Temperatures in the mountains range from an average –4.6°C in February, to 16.4°C in July and August, with an annual average of 5.7°C. In Svaneti the winter lasts for eight months, with an average temperature of –15°C; it gets even colder on the high bare plateaux of Javakheti where temperatures drop to –30°C. On the coast of Adjara, temperatures range from 5.8°C in January to 23.8°C in August, with an annual average of 14.5°C; on the Abkhaz coast temperatures are slightly lower in winter, noticeably warmer in April and May, but virtually the same in high summer. In eastern Georgia temperatures range from 0.5°C in January to 23°C in August, with an annual average of 11.8°C, and in the south they range from –2.1°C in January to 20.1°C in August, with an average of 9.1°C.

The weather in the Caucasus is more stable than in the Alps. In June there may still be too much snow for high hikes; July and August have the best weather, but even then it can drop to –10°C at 3,000–3,500m. Lower altitudes can often be hot and humid at this time of year, and the inhabitants of Tbilisi and Kutaisi flee to the coast or the mountains.

Precipitation ranges from 2,800mm in Abkhazia and Adjara to 300–600mm in the east (with 462mm in Tbilisi), and about 1,800mm at the main Caucasian passes. There's an average of 1,350–2,520 hours of sunshine per year (four–seven hours per day) in Tbilisi.

CLIMATE IN TBILISI

| Month | Temperature | | | | Humidity % | | Rain |
	max °C	ave °C	min °C	max/min °F	max	min	mm
January	7	0.9	–1	44/30	79	60	17
February	9	2.6	0	48/32	75	53	15
March	13	6.6	3	55/37	69	50	27
April	17	11.9	8	62/46	66	49	61
May	24	17.3	12	75/53	61	47	75
June	28	21.1	16	82/60	57	42	54
July	31	24.4	19	87/66	57	40	46
August	30	24.2	19	86/66	60	42	46
September	26	19.6	15	78/59	66	49	45
October	20	13.8	10	68/50	71	53	30
November	14	7.6	5	57/41	78	60	27
December	9	2.8	1	48/33	80	65	19

Despite its small size, Georgia is ecologically very interesting. Located between the forests of northern Eurasia and the tropical deserts of Iraq and Iran, and incorporating Europe's highest mountains and a subtropical coastline, it has Europe's highest level of biodiversity and is a route for many migratory bird species. It is characterised by its complex interaction of west Asian, east European and purely local communities. There's a wide variety of plant communities, with examples of almost all the main habitat types found in Europe and some of those in Asia; many are highly valuable in terms of biodiversity, including subalpine coniferous forests, meadows, wetlands, peat bogs, and lakes; coniferous and beech forests; oak woodlands; caves and mountain gorges; unique Colchic forests with evergreen undergrowth; Mediterranean and sub-Mediterranean communities; steppe grasslands; arid light woodlands; and riparian shrub and forest vegetation along the rivers such as the Alazani and Mtkvari.

Forest covers 2.7 million hectares (36.7% of Georgia's area), of which only 59,500ha is artificially planted; around 6% of the natural forest is virgin, and 40% has avoided serious human impact.

Overall, Georgia can be split into two main biogeographical regions: firstly the Colchic and Caucasian districts, forest landscapes with plenty of autochthonous animals and plants, and others related to middle and eastern European species; and secondly the uplands of the Lesser Caucasus and the Mtkvari district, with species related in some places to Anatolia and the Middle East, and in others to the arid and semi-arid Turanian region, beyond the Caspian. Between these two main regions are mixed zones, notably the Borjomi Gorge and the Trialeti Ridge, as well as the southern slopes of the High Caucasus in eastern Georgia.

The Colchic (or Euxine) district covers most of western Georgia, between the Black Sea, the Meskhetian Mountains, the Surami Ridge and the High Caucasus; the climate is mild and humid, rarely freezing and with a metre or more of precipitation each year, and the characteristic landscape is subtropical forest with well-developed evergreen underwood consisting of many Tertiary relicts (such as *Laurocerasus officinalis*, *Ilex aquifolium* and *Rhododendron ponticum*).

The Caucasus district lies to the north at 2,000m and higher, with a severe climate and over a metre of precipitation per year. It harbours some of the most diverse and distinctive temperate coniferous and deciduous forests in Eurasia, ranging with altitude from subalpine beechwoods (half of the country's forested area), dark coniferous forests and crook-stem woods to subalpine, alpine and subnival plant communities and, above these, bare nival (ie: dominated by snow) landscapes. Its borders are fluid, with many Colchic elements in the west, and Turanian elements in the east; on the northern slopes there are many eastern European and boreal species.

The plateaux of the Lesser Caucasus are largely treeless grassland, either subalpine meadows or mountain steppes, as well as forest and semi-arid steppes. There's a severe continental climate, with annual precipitation between just 400mm and 800mm. The Mtkvari district covers much of Kartli and Kakheti, and is largely arid and semi-arid steppe, with xerophytic Turanian (or Armeno-Iranian) species predominating, and forested only along the banks of the Mtkvari. There's a warm continental climate, rarely dropping below –5°C, with under 400mm of precipitation per year.

The 'mixed' zones, at the borders of these main zones, are the most biologically fascinating regions of Georgia. There are three main mixed zones: firstly the northern slopes of the Trialeti Ridge, from the northwestern side of Tbilisi to the Borjomi Gorge, mostly dry deciduous mountain forests with a temperate climate and 400–800mm of precipitation per year – the fauna and flora are mostly Caucasian, with some Turanian and Colchic elements, and no great diversity; secondly the forests of eastern Georgia, which are relatively similar to the Trialeti forests, but with more Turanian elements – the climate is subtropical/mild, with 400–600mm of precipitation; and thirdly the smallest but most interesting is the Borjomi Gorge, which has a well-balanced range of elements from all over Georgia (although Turanian elements are scarce) with a mild temperate climate and 800–1,200mm of precipitation per year. The gorge marks the divide between the humid west and the arid east, and between Mediterranean and Turanian fauna.

Endemic species comprise about 9% of Georgia's flora, a surprisingly high proportion for so small a country, with another 5% endemic to the Caucasus. The highest proportion (for instance 87% of western Georgian scree flora) is in certain mountain areas which were turned into islands when the seas rose around 15 million years ago, in the Miocene epoch; the surrounding areas have since dried out and gone their own way biologically, while the humid subtropical forests of the mountains have survived largely unchanged, and many species there now have their closest relatives in Anatolia and Europe. Indeed the only relative of the Caucasian parsley frog (*Pelodytes caucasicus*) is *P. punctatus* in France and northern Spain, while the nearest relative of the Caucasian salamander (*Mertensiella caucasica*) and *M. luschani* (in Greece and southwest Turkey) is the gold-striped salamander (*Chioglossa lusitanica*) in Portugal and northwestern Spain. The population dynamics of the Caucasian salamander and rock lizards are particularly fascinating to scientists, with lots of more or less distinct species living together, some hybridising and some not. Some of the lizards also live in all-female colonies, reproducing by parthenogenesis (asexually). There's lots of interesting micro-evolutionary research to be done here, but the potential is almost unknown to foreign scientists. The most interesting areas are the Meskheti ridge (from Batumi to Borjomi), Lagodekhi (in northern Kakheti), and also the lower-lying Colchic forests.

FLORA Georgia boasts around 4,200 species of vascular plants (including 153 trees and 11 lianas), of which 380 are endemic to Georgia and about 600 to the Caucasus; and between 8,400 and 10,000 cryptogamous or spore-bearing plants (including between 7,000 and 21,000 fungi, 2,600 algae and seaweeds, 675 mosses, 738 lichen and 74 ferns). Ten species are extinct, notably the chickpea (*Cicer arietinum*), the Georgian elm (*Ulmus georgica*), the Transcaucasian poplar (*Populus transcaucasica*) and the Eldari pine (*Pinus eldarica*), which is now only in Azerbaijan. Fifty species are in a critical state, including the fern (*Osmunda regalis*), the Mingrelian birch (*Betula megrelica*), the Colchic water chestnut (*Trapa colchica*), and the Caucasian yam (*Dioscorea caucasica*). Around 300 species are now rare, including the Pitsunda pine (*Pinus pithyusa*), the Saguramo camomile (*Anthemis saguramica*) and a type of brassica called *Pseudovesicaria digitata*; about 140 are seriously reduced, including the joint-pine (*Ephedra distachya*), a red-berried undershrub (*Pachyphragma macrophyllum*) and the Mediterranean caper (*Capparis spinosa*). Others of interest include: *Campanula mirabilis*, found only in one gorge in Abkhazia; *Iris iberica*, only in the southeast of Georgia; *Hypericum thethrobicum*, only in Javakheti; *Senecio rhombifolius*, a Caucasian endemic found throughout Georgia; *Solidago turfosa*, in peat bogs; *Epigaea gaultherioides*, in the Colchic forests; *Heracleum sommieri*, in subalpine megaphorbias; *Rhododendron caucasicum*, in alpine habitats; and *Delphinium caucasicum*, in subnival habitats. Around 2,000 vascular species are of economic value (for timber, fruits, dyes, oils, fodder, and medicinal properties), and at least 150 fungi are edible.

Lowland Colchic forests are dominated by oak (*Quercus penduciflora, Q. hartwissiana, Q. imeretina*), chestnut (*Castanea sativa*) and lime (*Tilia sp*), while higher regions are covered by beech (*Fagus orientalis*), fir (*Abies nordmanniana*) and spruce (*Picea orientalis*), with an evergreen understorey. At subalpine levels there are crook-stem and dwarf forests of birch (*Betula litwinowii, B. raddeana, B. medwedewii, B. megrelica*) and oak (*Q. pontica*). Other trees and shrubs found in the Colchic district include hornbeam (*Carpinus caucasica*), pine (*Pinus kochiana, P. pithyusa*), juniper (*Juniperus foetidissima, J. polycarpus*), pistachio (or turpentine; *Pistacia mutica*), Colchic boxwood (*Buxus colchica*), cherry-laurel (*Laurocerasus officinalis*), holly (*Ilex colchica*), bladder-nut (*Staphylea colchica*), Colchic hazel (*Corylus colchica*), rhododendron (*Rhododendron ponticum, R. luteum, R. caucasicum, R. ungernii, R. smirnovi*), rowan (mountain ash; *Sorbus subfusca*), wing-nut (*Pterocarya pterocarpa*), Caucasian wing-nut (*P. fraxinifolia*), small-leaved elm (*Zelkova carpinifolia*) and the extremely rare strawberry tree (*Arbutus andrachne*).

The High Caucasus is also rich in endemics; on the southern slopes at lower to mid altitude there's thick deciduous forest, which on the southwestern slopes is described as 'temperate rain forest' (although it falls far short of Chilean or British Columbian standards). Then between 1,250m and about 2,300m there's mixed deciduous-coniferous forest of birch, dwarf rowan and rhododendron (the lilac-flowered *R. ponticum* below and the bright yellow *R. luteum* at the forest limit), with spectacular flowers in clearings and on the forest edges, such as the yellow Turk's cap lily (*Lilium monadelphum*), purple bellflower (*Campanula latifolia*), columbine (*Aquilegia olympica*), fragrant orchid (*Gymnadenia conopsea*), butterfly orchid (*Platanthera chlorantha*), and marsh orchids (*Dachylorhiza spp*). Around Mestia, for instance, you'll also find red helleborine (*Cephalanthera rubra*), tall pink campion (*Silene sp*), large yellow loosestrife (*Lysimachia punctata*), henbane (*Hyoscyamus niger, Datura sp*), endemic giant hogweed (*Heracleum sommieri*), hollyhocks (*Alcea sp*), as well as white foxgloves, yellow cinquefoil, and wild strawberries and gooseberries.

Above the treeline (between 1,800m and 2,400m) are subalpine meadows, which are very lush to the west: herbaceous plants include masterwort (*Astrantia sp*), maroon lousewort (*Pedicularis sp*), bistort (*Polygonum bistorta*), lilies, columbine, delphinium, ranunculus, bellflowers, orchids, campion, vetch, scabious, pansies and cornflowers. Above these you'll see the white-flowered *Rhododendron caucasicum*, and alpine meadows (up to 3,000m), home to perennials, many in rosettes or cushions. These include spring gentians (*Gentiana verna pontica*), Pyrenean gentian (*G. septemfida, G. oschtenica*), purple oxlip (*Primula elatior meyeri, P. algida, P. auriculata* and *P. bayerni*), pink cinquefoil (*Potentilla oweriana*) and yellow cinquefoil (*P. ruprechtii*); sandwort (*Arenaria sp*), chickweed (*Cerastium undulatifolium*), fleabane (*Erigeron sp*) and dwarf forget-me-not (*Myosotis sp*), Snowdon lily (*Lloydia serotina*), rock-jasmine (*Androsace villosa* and *A. albana*), whitlow grass (*Draba bryoides*) and wild pansies (*Viola caucasica, Pulsatilla aurea*), fumitory (*Corydalis conorhiza, C. alpestris*), fritillaries (*Fritillaria latifolia*), the white *Anemone impexe* and yellow *A. speciosa*, prophet flower (*Arnebia pulchra, Trollius ranunculus*), and finally, saxifrages, bellflowers and buttercups.

Many native plants have suffered from an increase in trade: in 1994, 515,000 bulbs of the snowdrop (*Galanthus ikeriae*), a species listed in Appendix II of the Convention on Trade in Endangered Species of Wild Fauna and Flora (CITES), were illegally collected in Georgia and subsequently exported by Turkish traders to western Europe. Other species have also been affected by this illicit trade, including wild cyclamen (*Cyclamen spp*) and snowflakes (*Leucojum spp*).

FAUNA There are 105–110 species of mammals (the highest number in any European country), over 350 species of birds (253 nesting), about 52 reptiles and 13 amphibians, around 160 fish, and thousands of invertebrates (including 290 molluscs, 150 homoptera and eight lepidotera). Nearly a quarter of the mammals, reptiles and amphibians are endemic to the Caucasus. Twenty-one species of mammals, 33 birds, and ten reptiles and amphibians are listed as rare, threatened or endangered; these include the goitered or Persian gazelle (*Gazella subgutturossa*) which probably became extinct in Georgia in the 1960s, though is still found in Azerbaijan. The striped hyena (*Hyaena hyaena*) and Caucasian leopard (*Panthera pardus ciscaucasia*) were thought to have met the same fate, but it now appears that a few remain in the arid steppes of southeastern Georgia. Two species are listed as critically endangered: the Kazbegi birch mouse (*Sicista kazbegica*) and the Mediterranean monk seal (*Monachus monachus*). Large mammals, such as red deer, bear, wolf, boar, lynx, golden jackal, ibex, chamois, wild goats and wild sheep (moufflon) are found almost exclusively in the High Caucasus. However, populations of many species have been halved in recent years, largely due to increased poaching; wildlife has fled from conflicts in the northern Caucasus (notably Chechnya) and from the south in Azerbaijan, then been shot in Georgia (partly by hunters from Russia).

Mammals There are four species of wild goat: the west Caucasian tur (*Capra caucasica*), the east Caucasian tur or Daghestanian goat (*C. cylindricornis*), bezoar or pasang (*C. aegragus*) and chamois (*Rupicapra rupicapra*), and all are suffering from being hunted. The bezoar has been in decline since the 19th century, and there's now a maximum of 100 on the northeastern slopes of the High Caucasus. The Daghestanian goat, endemic to the eastern Caucasus, is endangered, with its population falling from about 5,000 in 1985 to 3,500 in 2005; the west Caucasian tur, endemic to the western Caucasus, is listed as vulnerable, but its population has also been halved from around 5,000 in 1985. The chamois is endangered, its population having fallen from around 6,000 in 1985 to barely 1,000 in 1993; however, there are many more in the Carpathians and Alps.

The red deer (*Cervus elaphus maral*) is also endangered by an increase in hunting; in eastern Georgia numbers fell from 2,500 in 1985 to 880 in 1994, and an estimated total of 1,500 in the whole of Georgia. Likewise the lynx (*Felis lynx orientalis*) has fallen from over 500 in 1990 to just 100 now. The wolf is also endangered, and the bear is vulnerable, its numbers having fallen from over 3,000 in the 1980s to under 600. In fact the main hazard for hikers in the mountains is the nahgaaz or Caucasian sheepdog, used to guard sheep; this supposedly gentle giant (in medieval times visiting ambassadors would nervously ask for the lion next to the throne to be removed) is seen as a national treasure, and competitive shows (often won by Aslan Abashidze!) are very popular. Bear gall, as well as skins and horns, are smuggled to Turkey. Tougher legislation is under consideration and bounties are no longer paid for killing animals that attack flocks, while reintroduction programmes are underway for wolves and other large mammals.

Mid-sized mammals in the mountains include the badger (*Meles meles*), pine marten (*Martes martes*), stone marten (*M. foina*), marbled polecat (*Vormela peregusna*), wild cat (*Felis silvestris*), fox (*Vulpes vulpes*), hare (*Lepus europaeus*) and weasel (*Mustela nivalis*), which here fills the niche of the marmot, scavenging in campsites. Other endangered species include the jungle cat (*Felis chaus*) whose range stretches from here to Indochina, the European otter (*Lutra lutra*), the Caucasian mink (*Mustella lutreola caucasica*) and golden jackal (*Canis aureus*). The Persian squirrel (*Sciurus anomalus*) is suffering from an invasion by the European squirrel (*S. vulgaris*).

Twelve species of small mammals are endangered or vulnerable, largely due to over-grazing or agricultural expansion; these include the red-backed vole (*Clethrionomys glareolus ponticus*), the Transcaucasian golden hamster (*Mesocricetus brandti*), the pygmy or grey hamster (*Cricetulus migratorius*), the shrew (*Sorex volnuchini*), the birch mice (*Sicista caucasica, S. kluchkorica, S. kazbegica*) and the

Prometheus mole vole (*Prometheomys shaposhnikowi*), most of which have been split up into isolated groups. Many of these are endemic to the Caucasus: the Transcaucasian golden hamster; the black-chested hamster (*M. raddei*); the shrews (*Sorex volnuchini, S. raddei, S. caucasica*) and the water shrew (*Neomys schelkownikowi*); birch mice (*S. caucasica, S. kluchorica, S. kazbegica* and *S. armenica*); the Prometheus vole; the Caucasian moles (*Talpa caucasica, Terricola daghestanicus* and *T. nasarovi*); the yellow-breasted mouse (*Apodemus fulvipectus*), as well as *A. ponticus*; and hybrids with the house mouse (*Mus musculus*).

Cetaceans There's been little research on the cetaceans of the Black Sea, but the harbour porpoise (*Phoecoena phoecoena*), bottlenosed dolphin (*Tursiops truncatus*) and common dolphin (*Delphinus delphis*) are all present.

Reptiles There are around 52 species of reptiles in Georgia (the total keeps changing as lizards are reclassified), 25% of which are endemic to the Caucasus. The dominant lizard species is *Lacerta praticola*, while *L. rudis, L. derjugini, L. parvula, L. mixta, L. valentini, L. unisexualis, L. clarcorum, L. valentini* and *L. mixta* may or may not be separate species. Much the same applies to the *Vipera (pelias) kaznakovi* complex. Threatened species include Schneider's skink (*Eumeces schneideri*), the lidless skink (*Ablepharus pannonicus*), the leopard snake (*Elaphe situla*) – perhaps the most beautiful in Europe – and the Transcaucasian ratsnake (*E. hohenackeri*), the dwarf snake (*Eirenis collaris*), the boigine snake (*Malpolon monspesulanus*), the racerunner (*Eremias arguta*), the turtle (*Clemmys (Mauremis) caspica caspica*), the snake-eyed lizard (*Ophisops elegans*) – the commonest lizard in the Anatolian steppes, the javelin sand boa (*Eryx jaculus*), the garter snake (*Natrix megalocephala*), the Caucasian viper (*Vipera kaznakovi*), the Transcaucasian long-nosed or sand viper (*V. ammodytes transcaucasiana*), the Levantine viper (*V. lebetina obtusa*) – the *giurza*, up to 1.8m in length, *V. dinnicki* and *Lacerta dahli*.

Amphibians Georgia's amphibians consist of four species of Caudata: the Caucasian salamander (*Mertensiella caucasica*), the banded newt (*Triturus vittatus ophryticus*), the smooth newt (*T. vulgaris lantzi*), and the southern crested newt (*T. cristatus karelini*) and nine species of Anura – the frogs and toads (*Pelobates syriacus syriacus, Pelodytes caucasicus, Bufo viridis viridis, B. verrucosissimus, Hyla arborea shelkownikowi, H. savignyi, Rana macrocnemis, R. camerani,* and *R. ridibunda*). A quarter of these are endemic to the Caucasus (*Mertensiella caucasica, Pelodytes caucasicus, Bufo verrucosissimus,* and hybrids of *Rana macrocnemis* and *Hyla arborea*). The Caucasian salamander is in fact found only in the Lesser Caucasus of Georgia and Turkey, not the High Caucasus. *Pelobates syriacus, Mertensiella caucasica,* and probably *Hyla savignyi* are threatened, and *Pelodytes caucasicus, Bufo verrucosissimus* and *Rana macrocnemis* are in decline.

Fish A quarter of fish species are also endemic to Georgia: the sturgeon (*Accipenser nudiventris*) is probably extinct in Georgia, while *A. guldenstadti* and *A. sturio* are endangered. Eastern European fish have been introduced into the lakes of the Javakheti Plateau, virtually wiping out local fish species; the Crucian carp (*Carassius carassius*) is also harming newt populations.

Birds Georgia acts as a 'funnel' for birds migrating from their breeding grounds in Siberia and northern Europe to their winter homes, so it's hardly surprising that very few are endemic to the Caucasus, and even these are subspecies rather than distinct species. Twenty species are endangered: the lammergeyer or bearded vulture (*Gypaetus barbatus*), the black or cinereous vulture (*Aegypius monachus*), the griffon vulture (*Gyps fulvus*), the Egyptian vulture (*Neophron percnopterus*), the peregrine (*Falco peregrinus*), the lanner falcon (*F. biarmicus*), the short-toed eagle (*Circaetus gallicus*), the marsh harrier (*Circus aeruginosus*), the Imperial eagle (*Aquila heliaca*) and lesser-spotted eagle (*A. pomarina*) – the Georgian populations of both are under 85 pairs, the golden eagle (*A. chrysaetos*), the booted eagle (*Hieraaetus pennatus*), the Caucasian snowcock (*Tetraogallus caucasicus*), the black francolin (*Francolinus francolinus*), the grey partridge (*Perdix perdix*), the black stork (*Ciconia nigra*), the spoonbill (*Platalea leucordia*), the crane (*Grus grus*), the demoiselle crane (*Anthropoides virgo*) and the glossy ibis (*Plegadis falcinellus*), as well, probably, as some woodpeckers and passerines. Certainly the Syrian woodpecker (*Dendrocopus syriacus*) is vulnerable, as, amazingly, is the pheasant (*Phasianus colchicus*); having taken over the world it is suffering in its land of origin from loss of forest and increased hunting.

Many raptors migrate along the flyway down the Black Sea coast; lammergeyer live year-round in the High Caucasus, but the population has dropped from 40 pairs to 20 pairs in the last 50 years. Others nest in the mountains but can often be seen hunting in the semi-desert of Davit-Gareja; other mountain species include the Caspian snowcock (*Tetraogallus caspius*) – from the Eastern Caucasus to Iran, the Caucasian snowcock (*T. caucasicus*) – more to the west, and the Caucasian black grouse (*Tetrao (Lyrurus) mlokosiewiczi*) – typically Caucasian, and probably a relict species. There's an isolated population of the alpine finch or great rosefinch (*Carpodacus rubicilla*), which otherwise lives in central Asia; the scarlet grosbeak (*C. erythrinus*) breeds from Sweden to Japan and passes through to winter between Iran and China. An endemic subspecies of the rock partridge (*Alectoris graeca*) (which is kept as a domestic fowl in Armenia) can be seen near the snowline.

Other species found in the High Caucasus include Kruper's nuthatch (*Sitta kruperii*), the white-winged or Guldenstadt's redstart (*Phoenicurus erythrogaster*), Radde's accentor (*Prunella ocularis*), the red-fronted serin (*Serinus pusillus*), the grey-necked bunting (*Emberizia buchanani*) and rock bunting (*E. cia*), the alpine accentor (*Prunella collaris*), the redwing (*Turdus iliacus*) – only in winter – and a subspecies of jay (*Garrulus glandarius krynicki*).

In the deserts you may find the trumpeter bullfinch (*Rhodopechys sanguinea*), the rufous bush robin, or tugai nightingale (*Cercotrichas galactotes*), the chukar (*Alectoris chukar*) and, in winter, great bustard (*Otis tarda*) and little bustard (*O. tetrax*).

Perhaps the most important bird habitats are the wetlands of the Black Sea coast and the Javakheti Plateau, where you may see migratory birds such as white spoonbills (*Platalea leucorodia*), red-breasted geese (*Rufibrenta ruficollis*), red-necked grebe (*Podiceps grisigena*), white pelican (*Pelecanus onocrotalus*), Dalmatian pelican (*P. crispus*), squacco heron (*Ardeola ralloides*), great white egret (*Ardea alba*), little egret (*Egretta garzetta*), white stork (*Ciconia ciconia*), black stork (*C. nigra*), glossy ibis (*Plegadis falcinellus*), ruddy shelduck (*Tadorna ferruginea*), ferruginous duck (*Aythya nyroca*), and other ducks, herons, geese and cormorants.

CONSERVATION Royal hunting reserves known as *korugi* (similar to Britain's New Forest) are first mentioned in the *Law Book of Vakhtang VI* (1709). Georgia's first nature reserve in the modern sense was created in 1912 to protect the wolves of the Lagodekhi Gorge; by the end of the Soviet era there were 15, totalling 168,800ha (1,680km^2, or 2.4% of the country's area), in addition to forests and other protected zones, now covering a total of 4.4% of the country. The WWF (now the Worldwide Fund for Nature) set up an office in 1989, and started to create a Western-style system of Protected Areas, with a hierarchy from Protected Landscapes through Nature Reserves to National Parks; in March 1996 Parliament declared the law on Protected Areas, creating the first National Park, at Borjomi. This replaces the Soviet *zakaznik* system of totally closed reserves with a flexible system allowing sustainable use of many areas. President Shevardnadze has announced a 'Gift to the Earth' which will increase protected areas to 20% of the country's area. Georgia also signed the International Convention on Biodiversity in 1994, and the CITES agreement in 1996. Land privatisation began in 1992; by mid 1995, 38% of arable land (around 20% of all agricultural land) had been privatised, and in 1999 a land-registration programme made farmers the official owners of their land. Since 1996 hunters have required permits, but this has generally been ignored. In 2005, an Environmental Protection Inspectorate (or the ecological police) was set up, but initially had no budget except what was provided by international donors.

The WWF has also set up an environmental education programme: teaching the teachers, making TV programmes, and opening Ecocentres for school groups in Kazbegi (1995), Bakuriani (1996) and, in 1999 and 2000, Tbilisi, Telavi and Batumi. More are to follow in Lagodekhi, Akhmeta and Vashlovani, and later in Kintrishi, Sataplia, Chacuna and Iori.

There's an active 'green' movement in Georgia, which grew out of a 1989 campaign against a planned dam in Svaneti; the Georgian Greens are now affiliated to Friends of the Earth, and Zurab Zhvania, ex-speaker of parliament, was first elected as a member of the Green Party. Since 1991 they have been campaigning against the truly dreadful pollution of the Black Sea and for a sustainable forestry industry; the government imposed a tax of US$46 per m^3 of timber, but the IMF forced its withdrawal. Nuclear issues have a high profile, even though the research reactor in Mtskheta was closed in 1990, and plans for a second nuclear power station in Armenia were abandoned in 1996 after big protests. In 1997, 11 servicemen on the Red Army's former Lilo base near Tbilisi developed skin burns, which after three months (and no help from the Russians) were diagnosed as radiation burns; eventually nine radiation sources were found, including stores of depleted uranium bullets and capsules from Geiger counters. Around 300 radiation sources were found at the former nuclear missile base of Vaziani, 30km east of Tbilisi. Russia has been unable or unwilling to provide any information, which led to large demonstrations at the Russian embassy in 1998. In addition, strontium fall-out from Chernobyl in Ukraine caused illness in western Georgia. The oil pipelines across Georgia have undergone surprisingly strict and detailed Environmental Impact Assessments, but there's scepticism about the standards in Azerbaijan and the central Asian states.

Georgia has inherited many environmental problems, largely due to Soviet industrialisation, with pollution by oil, heavy metals and fertilisers, disrupted water-catchment areas, and erosion due to uncontrolled logging and over-grazing. The numbers of sheep in the mountains are still 2.5 times optimum levels, and 30% of pastures are affected by erosion, silt from which covers spawning beds. Forests and wetlands continue to be converted to farmland, causing serious ecological damage.

However, what foreigners notice at once is the amount of litter strewn around, especially along main roads (Georgians don't even notice it).

HISTORY

It can be said that the history of Georgia goes back to the dawn of time. Noah's son Thargamos settled in the land of Japhet, somewhere between the Ararat and Caucasus mountains; the Georgians claim descent from him via his great-grandson Karthlos (while the Armenians claim descent from his brother Haik), and therefore still call themselves Karthians, or Kartvelebi, and their country Sakartvelo. Protohuman remains about 1.8 million years old and human remains about 200,000 years old have been found (at Dmanisi) as well as Paleolithic artefacts. By the 2nd millennium BC, tribes were on the verge of statehood, and

In Greek mythology, Jason was the son of Aeson, King of Iolcus, near Volos in Thessaly. After his uncle Pelias seized the throne Jason was reared by the centaur Chiron on Mount Pelion (the concept of the centaur has its origin on the steppes to the north of the Caucasus, where men were first seen riding horses). When Jason grew up, Pelias ordered him to bring him the legendary Golden Fleece from Colchis, expecting never to see him again. Jason built a ship called the *Argo*, and assembled a crew of 50, including such heroes as Hercules, Orpheus, Theseus, Castor and Pollux. After overcoming storms, monsters and seductive women, they at last reached Colchis, where the king, Aetes (son of Helios and brother of Circe and Phaethon), agreed to give Jason the fleece if he succeeded in further trials such as yoking two fire-breathing bulls to a plough and sowing the dragon's teeth of Cadmus (which sprouted as armed men). He won the love of Medea, daughter of Aetes and a sorceress who gave her name to the science of medicine; she secretly helped him win the fleece and escape from Colchis. They returned to Iolcus, supposedly sailing up the Danube and carrying the *Argo* overland to the Adriatic. Pelias was killed but his son drove Jason and Medea from the city; they took the fleece to Orchemenus in Boetia, and settled in Corinth, living there for many years. Jason abandoned Medea when he fell in love with King Creon's daughter Glauce; Medea took revenge by making a magic robe that burned to death both father and daughter. For breaking his vow to Medea, Jason was condemned to be a wanderer until, as an old man, he at last returned to Corinth and was killed when the prow of the *Argo* fell over and crushed him.

The Jason myth dates from around 1400BC but the definitive compilation came only in the 4th century BC with the *Argonautica* of Apollonius of Rhodes, who worked out their actual route; it was a great success and Apollonius became director of the great Library of Alexandria, one of the Seven Wonders of the Ancient World.

The first voyage myth, it is in part a metaphor for the expansion of Greek trade, the fleece and Medea's gifts of magic oil and stone being exchanged for technology, represented by harnessing bulls and ploughing. The legend of the fleece itself arose from the use of sheep fleeces to trap particles of gold from mountain streams in the countries around the Black Sea, as witnessed by the writers Patrick Leigh Fermor in Romania and Tim Severin in Georgia.

Medea and her father King Aetes probably did live between the 14th and 13th centuries BC on the Black Sea coast. Certainly the state of Colchis (Kolkhida or Egrisi) existed here by the 9th century BC, when tribute was demanded by Assyria, with Greek trading ports by the 6th century BC. The oldest (and somewhat lurid) account of Georgia is by Xenophon who retreated from Persia at the end of the 5th century BC. In the east of the country the state of Kartli (known to the Greeks as Iveria) was created by one of Alexander the Great's generals, overthrown in 335BC by King Parnavaz I. In the 1st century BC it was an ally of Rome, ruled for a time by Mithridates IV Eupator, King of Pontus, who turned against Rome and also seized Colchis. He was finally beaten in the Third Mithridatic War (66–65BC) by Pompey, who incorporated Colchis into the Roman Empire, although few traces remain. Iveria continued as a Roman satellite state until AD298, when Rome signed a treaty with Persia, recognising the Persian-born Mirian III as King of Iveria; he founded the Chosroid dynasty which ruled for two centuries. In the 4th and 5th centuries Colchis (now known as Lazika) also came under Persian influence. In AD337 Mirian, following his wife Nana, was converted to Christianity by Nino, a slave from Cappadocia. Thus Georgia became the world's second Christian state, preceded only by Armenia. By the end of the 5th century the Chosroid King Vakhtang Gorgasali (AD442–502) ruled a feudal state which included Abkhazia, Ossetia and much of Armenia; he moved the capital of Kartli from Mtskheta to Tbilisi, and secured autocephalous (self-governing) status for the Church. However, from the mid 6th century the Persians took control again, followed by the Byzantine Empire, and then the Arabs who had conquered Georgia by the mid 7th century, leaving its kings in power as long as they acknowledged the supremacy of the caliphs: their dominance lasted until the 9th century. The Armenian family of the Bagratids (who claimed descent from David and Bathsheba via Bagrat or St Pancras) had moved to the Georgian borderlands by the late 8th century; Ashot Bagration became chamberlain to the Byzantine emperor and soon de facto ruler of Kartli and, in AD866, Adarnase IV took the title of king; their dynasty ruled until the Russians took over in the 19th century.

MEDIEVAL GEORGIA Bagrat III became King of Kartli in AD975, and united east and west Georgia by 1008 (excluding Tbilisi); in 1068 the Seljuk Turks under Alp Arslan came out of central Asia, creating havoc and finally defeating the Byzantine Empire at Manzikert in 1071. However, the kings were again allowed to keep their thrones, although Georgia remained a backwater till it was again united under King Davit IV Agmashenebelis (David the Builder). Born in 1073, he took over from his father Giorgi II in 1089, annexed Kakheti in 1105 and, in 1121, drove the Seljuks out of Tbilisi, making it his capital the next year. He made Georgia the most powerful state in the Near East, and economic strength led to a cultural Golden Age in the 12th century. Davit died in 1125, and was succeeded by his son Demetre I (1125–56) and then Giorgi III (1156–84).

Georgia's favourite monarch remains Davit's great-granddaughter Queen Tamar (*Tamar Mepe* in Georgian – this is sometimes mistranslated as King Tamara, as *mepe* simply means monarch), who was born in 1154 and who ruled jointly with her father Giorgi III after crushing a revolt in 1178, and then alone from 1184 to 1213. In 1185 she married Prince Giorgi Bogoliubskoi of Suzdal, a vicious drunken adventurer (a typical Russian in the eyes of many Georgians) who was soon divorced and expelled for sexual (perhaps homosexual) misconduct; after the fiasco of this political union she married the far more suitable David Soslan, an Ossetian prince, who led her armies and fathered Giorgi IV Lash and his sister and successor Queen Rusudan (said to have been 'fearless only in her lusts'). Tamar extended Georgian rule from the Black Sea to the Caspian, defeated the Turks at the battles of Shamkhori (1195) and Basiani (1202), and after the sack of Constantinople by the Fourth Crusade in 1204 she set up a new Byzantine Empire in Trebizond (now Trabzon) under her kinsman Alexius Comnenus, who had been brought up in Georgia. The Golden Age was brought to an abrupt end in 1220 by Chinghiz (Genghis) Khan and his Mongol hordes, followed by the Black Death from 1366, and by Temur Lang (Tamerlane) who invaded six times between 1386 and 1403. The last king of a united Georgia was Alexander I (1412–43); on his death the country was divided between his three sons, with the oldest taking Kartli (with his capital in Tbilisi), the second Imereti (based in Kutaisi), and the third Kakheti (based in Telavi). As the centralised state fell apart, other noble families took control of smaller areas, such as the Dadianis in Mingrelia, the Gurielis in Guria, and the Gelovanis in Svaneti. After the fall of Constantinople in 1453, Persia and the Ottoman Empire vied for control of the area in a protracted and destructive struggle – Georgia was split between them, although the kings were left on their thrones as long as they did what they were told. Shah Abbas (ruler of Persia from 1587 to 1629) established his rule over Kakheti and Kartli, punishing an uprising in 1615–16 by killing 60,000–70,000 and deporting 100,000.

RUSSIAN RULE The 18th century saw the rise of a third power in the region: Russia, which claimed to protect the Orthodox from Islamic oppression. It began the process of conquering the northern Caucasus in 1722 under Peter the Great, who died three years later. The enlightened Vakhtang VI of Kartli fled into exile in Russia in 1723; fortunately he had constructed irrigation channels and other public works (and written the history of Georgia) before he left. In 1744 the Persians installed Irakli (or Heraclius) II as King of Kakheti, and his father (who had ruled Kakheti since 1733) as King of Kartli; Irakli (1720–98) also ruled Kartli from his father's death in 1762 until his own death, but despite heroic efforts to resist Persian dominance finally had to call for Russian help. Nevertheless Frederick the Great of Prussia saw him as an invincible equal due to his youthful exploits with Nadir Shah on his campaign in India. In 1768 the first Russo-Turkish war began, and in 1769 the Russian General Todleben crossed the Caucasus, taking Tbilisi and Kutaisi, but was recalled before he could capture Poti; in the Treaty of Kutchuk-Kainardji of 1774, the Turks gave up their claims to western Georgia, and agreed not to help the Muslim tribes of the Caucasus against Russia, though in fact they continued to do so.

In 1783 Persia's new shah, Ali Murad, tried to reimpose his sovereignty, and Irakli II was forced to ask for Russian aid; the Treaty of Protection was signed in Gurgievsk Castle on 24 July 1783, and Count Paul Potyomkin (cousin of the Russian empress Catherine the Great's lover, Grigori Potyomkin) reached Tbilisi later that year, becoming the first viceroy of the Caucasus in May 1785. Also in 1785 the Chechens of the north Caucasus rose in a revolt that lasted until 1791; to deal with this Russian troops were withdrawn from Tbilisi in 1787, and in 1795 the city was razed by Shah Aga Mohammed Khan of Persia, who killed 50,000 and took 20,000 slaves. Catherine refused to help, even though there had been plenty of warning (much like Stalin refusing to help the Warsaw uprising), but the Russians then attacked Persia, thus seizing Azerbaijan. However, Catherine died the next year and her successor, Paul I, withdrew to the river Terek. In December 1800 George XII died in Tbilisi, and in March 1801 Paul was assassinated; his successor, Alexander I, at once violated the Treaty of Gurgievsk and abolished the Georgian monarchy; eastern Georgia (Kartli and Kakheti) was annexed as the province of Tiflis. In 1802 Alexander installed a new viceroy, Prince Paul Dmitrovich Tsitsianov (Georgian born and Russian educated), who deported the remnants of the royal family to Russia and in 1804 occupied Imereti.

Russia was at war with Persia from 1804 to 1813, and with Turkey from 1807 to 1812, and in 1812 Napoleon invaded Russia; amidst all this confusion Russia was still able to crush revolts in Kakheti (1802 and 1812–13) and Imereti (1819–20), the last Georgian king, Solomon II, fleeing in 1810. Tsitsianov was killed in Azerbaijan in 1806, but by 1813 Persia had been forced to give up its claims to Georgia and Daghestan. In 1825 Nicholas I became tsar and in 1827 appointed as viceroy Prince Alexander Paskevich, who on the tsar's behalf captured Yerevan and Tabriz. In 1828 Russia made peace with Persia (retaining eastern Armenia) then began another war with Turkey; Paskevich captured Kars, Akhaltsikhe, Erzurum and Poti. The Treaty of Adrianople (now Edirne) in 1829 restored Erzurum and Kars to Turkey (prompting many Armenians to flee), but Guria was reunited with Georgia. In 1856 the Crimean War ended and Prince Alexander Baryatinski (a veteran of the never-ending campaigns against the Muslim tribes of the northern Caucasus) became viceroy; in 1857 he occupied Mingrelia and Svaneti, and by 1859 he had been able to defeat the Chechen leader Shamyl who had led a very effective guerrilla revolt since 1837. In 1864 the Circassians of the north Caucasus were crushed (and 600,000 fled to Turkey), and the next year Abkhazia was also incorporated into the Russian Empire. Another Russo-Turkish war followed in 1877–78, with Russia capturing Kars and Batumi (both reoccupied by Turkey in 1918).

Under Russian rule economic development proceeded apace, but the Georgian populace did not benefit greatly. By the late 19th century 58% of Georgia's area was owned by Russians and by the government, and the merchant class was overwhelmingly Armenian. Ilia Chavchavadze (1837–1907) and Akaki Tsereteli (1840–1915) led the group of intellectuals known as 'the men of the '60s', or *Tergdaleulebi*, who began to infuse a sense of national consciousness in the Georgian people; in the 1890s another wave of Russian-educated men returned to their homeland, including Noe Zhordania (1868–1953). Political unrest grew in Georgia as elsewhere in the Russian Empire, with the various strands of Marxist thought as influential as elsewhere. On 28 October 1905, 60 were killed when Cossacks broke up a Social Democrat meeting in Tbilisi, and in 1907 Ilia Chavchavadze was killed; this was long blamed on tsarist agents, but the feeling now is that in fact the Bolsheviks wished to remove his persuasive voice for moderation.

After the Russian revolutions of 1917 Georgia briefly regained independence, but found itself the pawn of larger countries competing for access to the Caspian oil fields. In April 1918 Transcaucasia (Georgia, Armenia and Azerbaijan) declared itself an independent federal state, but on 26 May 1918 Georgia broke away, having been persuaded by Germany that it would provide protection against the Bolshevik threat from north of the Caucasus. German troops helped to drive the Turks, supposedly their allies, out of Batumi; a week after the defeat of Germany and Turkey at the end of 1918, 15,000 British troops landed in Batumi to occupy Transcaucasia (stopping fighting between Georgians and Armenians in the Akhalkalaki area after Turkey's withdrawal). Britain and its chief commissioner, Oliver Wardrop, wanted to maintain Georgia as a buffer against Bolshevism, but the Social Democrat (Menshevik) government led by Zhordania from June 1918 refused to form an alliance with Denikin's White Russians, the last tsarists. Zhordania's government introduced universal suffrage, health insurance and some nationalisation and land redistribution; but this wasn't enough for the Bolsheviks in Russia who imposed a blockade, leading to food shortages. In May 1920 a Bolshevik coup attempt in Tbilisi and a revolt in South Ossetia failed; in January 1920 the Allies granted de facto recognition to all three Transcaucasian republics, and a year later Britain and France granted full *de jure* recognition. Zhordania felt

BERIA

Lavrenti Pavlovich Beria, born in 1899 near Sukhumi, was involved in undercover revolutionary activities in Baku and elsewhere before the revolution, and it's likely that he was an agent for the British as well. He only joined the Bolshevik Party in 1917; in 1921 he became head of the Cheka (secret police) in Transcaucasia, where he implemented Stalin's purges so effectively that in 1938 he became head of the secret police of the whole Soviet Union. He also became a politburo member and deputy chairman of the Council of Ministers in 1946; suspected of involvement in Stalin's death and of planning to take power himself, he was arrested and executed on 23 December 1953. He probably didn't kill Stalin but may have given him warfarin which brought on other complications.

Although he has a terrible reputation in the West, he was by no means the worst of the purgers (reaching the top only after the 1936–38 terror), and he began to empty the Gulag camps after Stalin's death. He was surprisingly pragmatic and might well have been a better leader than the more idealistic Khrushchev, leading a faster and more thorough process of de-Stalinisation. His downfall came because he had no party base and so was isolated after Stalin's death.

Josef Vissarionovich Djugashvili probably had more influence on people's lives than anyone else in the 20th century, bringing between 45 and 66 million of them to a premature end. Nazism killed around 25 million and Chinese communism about 65 million. Yet he did have charm and charisma and 45 years after his death one Russian in six calls him their greatest leader (which admittedly is not saying much).

He was a Georgian, born in the Russian quarter of Gori. Although his birthdate was officially given from around 1922 as 21 December 1879 (9 December by the Old Style calendar), it seems he was born a year earlier and may have changed it once he had absolute power in order to have a nationwide celebration of his 50th birthday. His mother did laundry, and his father was an alcoholic cobbler. He was born with a webbed left foot, was pockmarked by smallpox from the age of six, and acquired a crooked left arm when he was run over by a cart; it seems likely that these deformities in some way fuelled his ruthless ambition, together with his mother's obsessive desire for him to succeed as a priest and beatings from his father which made him hate authority. He was a star pupil at the church school in Gori, and won a scholarship to study at the seminary in Tbilisi in 1894. In 1895 and 1896 seven of his poems were published in *Iveria* (edited by Ilia Chavchavadze) and sang in the opera chorus, but he was soon involved in revolutionary politics. He was expelled from the seminary in 1899, and worked as an accountant and record-keeper at the Tbilisi Meteorological and Geophysical Observatory until March 1901.

After the violent demonstration of May Day 1901 he was expelled from Mesame Dasi and went underground in Batumi and Baku. He was arrested in 1902 after strikes in the Rothschild oil plants and sent to Siberia, escaping in 1904 and returning to Batumi and then Tbilisi. At this time he first met Nadezhda Alliluyeva, then aged three, whom he was to marry 16 years later, and who was to shoot herself in 1932. In 1903 the Social Democrats split into two groups, the Bolsheviks and Mensheviks; Koba, as he then called himself, supported the more radical Bolsheviks and their leader, Lenin, and took a new *nom de guerre*, Stalin, suggesting 'Man of Steel' in Russian. From this time on his loyalty was to Russia and to international communism, rather than to Georgia; although he had no oratorical skills or charisma, he had plenty of energy, organisational talent and a retentive memory. He roamed the Caucasus, fomenting strikes and spreading the message of socialism, as well as staging robberies to raise funds, together with Simon Ter-Petrossian (known as Kamo), who was also from Gori, although Armenian.

Between 1902 and 1913 he was frequently arrested and sent to Siberia, but he always escaped. In 1912 he founded the party newspaper *Pravda* ('Truth') and Lenin rewarded Stalin's loyalty by appointing him to the Bolshevik Central Committee; he began to gain influence in the party, but was arrested again in 1913 and this time had to stay in Siberia until the March revolution of 1917.

IN POWER In the Bolshevik government Stalin served as commissar of nationalities (fomenting trouble in Baku), and in 1920 as commissar of the army heading for Berlin,

protected by the League of Nations, but Lloyd George was more interested in a deal with Moscow; the British troops left early in 1920, and on 16 February 1921 the Red Army invaded, occupying Tbilisi nine days later.

The takeover was engineered by the Soviet ambassador Sergei Kirov and Sergo Ordjonikidze (a Georgian Bolshevik, who in 1937 'committed suicide at Stalin's urgent suggestion, being granted in return a state funeral', as Fitzroy Maclean, then a diplomat in Moscow, put it) on Stalin's instructions and against Lenin's wishes; in Moscow it was denied that it was happening and Lenin was very unhappy with the brutality used. A Russo-Turkish treaty restored large areas of historically being blamed by Trotsky for its defeat in the Battle of Warsaw. In 1922 he became general secretary of the party's Central Committee, and on Lenin's death in 1924 used all the levers of power to crush his rivals as he manoeuvred into a position of absolute power, despite Lenin having specifically instructed the party to beware of him.

Initially he advocated moderate economic policies and an end to world revolution, which aroused the opposition of the leftists led by Trotsky, Kamenev and Zinoviev; by 1928 he had driven them from any position of power, and then adopted leftist policies such as rapid industrialisation and agricultural collectivisation, arousing the opposition of the rightists. By the end of 1929 Stalin was the undisputed master of the Soviet Union, and communism died in any meaningful sense.

Having seized the land of the *kulaks* (bourgeois peasantry) in 1928, Stalin was able to fund industrialisation by exporting their grain stocks, and continued collectivisation despite dogged resistance from the peasants and a famine in 1932 which may have cost over 10 million lives. Sergei Kirov, the Leningrad party secretary, protested, and was murdered in 1934; Stalin used this as a pretext for his first purge, arresting virtually all his senior colleagues and staging the Moscow show trials between 1936 and 1938. Only 41 of the 139 deputies elected to the Central Committee in 1934 survived, and millions more died as he purged the party, the professions and intellectuals throughout the Soviet Union. By 1938 there was no doubt that this was a dictatorship.

By concluding a non-aggression pact with Nazi Germany in 1939 (including a secret clause agreeing to a joint attack on Poland) Stalin bought time for further industrialisation and rearmament before the Nazi attack in June 1941. The Soviet people made immense sacrifices in what they know as the Great Patriotic War, but its huge reserves of manpower (expended extravagantly by Stalin) and industrial power, coupled with ferocious winter weather and the contributions of the Allies, finally brought victory. Stalin (now a generalissimo) was far more of a hands-on commander than any of the other Allied leaders, while also out-manoeuvring them diplomatically.

There was no relaxation after the war; the imposition of communist rule on eastern and much of central Europe led to further waves of repression and the outbreak of the Cold War with his former allies. In 1953 his health failed but he claimed to have discovered a plot by his doctors to kill him; a massive new purge seemed imminent, but he died on 5 March 1953. In 1956 his successor Nikita Khrushchev denounced his crimes and in 1961 his body was moved out of the Red Square mausoleum. Under Brezhnev criticism of Stalin was muted, but again in 1987 Gorbachev told a party congress that his crimes were 'enormous and unforgivable'. The huge death toll of the purges and collectivisation was finally revealed, and with the opening of the Soviet and KGB archives more and more is being revealed.

Nevertheless he is widely seen, particularly in Georgia, as a 'strong man', the sort of leader who might pull the country out of the morass, and his crimes are widely overlooked as a price worth paying.

Georgian territory to Turkey (where they remain today), while Georgia retained Akhalkalaki, Akhaltsikhe and Batumi. Georgia became a Soviet socialist republic, but in December 1922 was absorbed into the Transcaucasian Soviet Federative Socialist Republic; this was dissolved in 1936 (with the adoption of the USSR's second constitution), and Georgia became a Union Republic. The Soviets closed around 1,500 churches and monasteries, leading to a revolt in 1921–22; in August 1924 there was another uprising and General Mogilevski was killed when his Georgian pilot deliberately crashed. This was brutally suppressed by Stalin and Ordjonikidze and 7,000–10,000 were killed, followed by widespread emigration.

There were further purges in 1936–37 and 1953. Nevertheless, communism brought some social and material advances and the Georgians fought bravely in World War II (although some fought in the SS against the Soviet Union). Stalin died in 1953, and in 1956 Khrushchev's speech denouncing his crimes led to anti-Russian (and pro-Stalin) riots which were crushed on 9 March by tanks, with more than 100 being killed.

THE END OF THE SOVIET UNION In 1972 Eduard Shevardnadze, then the republic's interior minister, was appointed First Secretary of the Georgian Communist Party, and followed the Brezhnevite line of the time, although he took action against corruption. In 1985 Mikhail Gorbachev became leader of the Soviet Union and Shevardnadze became his foreign minister. Although there had already been some surreptitious glasnost pre-Gorbachev, from 1985 political agitation escalated (with 80% of Georgian men avoiding their military service). In February 1989 the Abkhazian campaign for secession (begun in the 1970s) was renewed, followed by counter-demonstrations in Tbilisi and then hunger strikes against Russian involvement. On 9 April 1989 (a date now commemorated by street names in many towns) tanks were sent on to the streets of Tbilisi and special troops of the Interior Ministry attacked the demonstrators (using sharpened entrenching tools and gas), killing 21 of them (mostly young women), who at once became martyrs. Jumber Patiashvili, First Secretary of the Georgian Communist Party, resigned and Shevardnadze flew in from Moscow to calm things down. As the Soviet Union began to fall apart, the Georgian Supreme Soviet declared Georgian law superior over USSR law in November 1989, and then declared Georgia 'an annexed and occupied country' in February 1990; in March the Communist Party's monopoly on power was abolished.

In August the statue of Lenin in Lenin Square (now Freedom Square) was removed (supposedly to permit 'repairs' to the square), and multi-party elections were held in October and November 1990. These were won by a coalition of nationalist parties known as the Round Table-Free Georgia, with 64% of the vote and 155 of 250 seats; the Communist Party (now also pro-independence) won 64 seats. The Round Table was led by Zviad Gamsakhurdia, a university lecturer and translator of French and English poetry and son of the writer Konstantin Gamsakhurdia (most of Georgia's Gamsakhurdia Streets are named after him, not Zviad); he had co-founded Georgia's Helsinki monitoring group in 1976, was jailed for five years but controversially was released after two after recanting on TV. (Merab Kostava, who co-founded the Helsinki group and did not recant, stayed in prison from 1977 to 1987 and was killed in October 1989 when his car supposedly hit a cow.)

Georgia was the first Soviet republic to elect a non-communist government, Gamsakhurdia becoming chair of the new Supreme Soviet. He was a naïve and charismatic nationalist, working on the assumption that the Georgians had long been a persecuted minority in their own country and set out to rectify this injustice (proposing, for instance, to limit the franchise to Georgian speakers); this led to the worst outbreak of messianic nationalism in any of the former Soviet republics. From the beginning, some political groups had refused to recognise the legitimacy of a legislature elected under the Soviet system and of Gamsakhurdia's government; these groups organised public demonstrations and hunger strikes, which Gamsakhurdia met with repression. He had no understanding of democracy, believing that winning an election gave him absolute power and the right to treat all criticism as an attack on the nation; it was soon clear that he was succumbing to clinical paranoia. He also nearly bankrupted Georgia by isolation both from Russia and the Commonwealth of Independent States (CIS), and from the West.

In January 1991 the National Guard was founded as a new army and Jaba Ioseliani, a playwright and expert on theatrical history and folklore, who had founded a paramilitary body known as the *Mkhedrioni* (Horsemen) after the 1989 massacre, was arrested with the help of Russian troops after failing to disarm. The referendum on the future of the Soviet Union in March 1991 was boycotted, except in South Ossetia, Abkhazia and Red Army barracks, which all turned out, unsurprisingly, to be strongly pro-Union. On 31 March the Georgian government held its own referendum in which 93% (of a 95% turnout) voted for independence. In April (on the anniversary of the 9 April 1989 killings) the Soviet declared independence and in May Gamsakhurdia was elected president with 86% of the vote. He had significant rural and working-class support, but was strongly opposed by the urban and professional intelligentsia. Things went very wrong after the August 1991 Soviet coup attempt which Gamsakhurdia at first failed to condemn; Tengiz Kitovani (formerly a sculptor) was sacked as leader of the National Guard, before Gamsakhurdia declared a state of emergency in Tbilisi and clamped down on the media. Ioseliani was jailed, followed in September by Georgi Chanturia, leader of the opposition National Democratic Party, whose wife Irina Sarishvili-Chanturia began a hunger strike outside parliament. Demonstrations gathered momentum, turning in December to fighting. Gamsakhurdia was besieged in the parliament building by the National Guard and *Mkhedrioni*, who released Ioseliani and Chanturia and also about 8,000 common criminals whom they equipped with Kalashnikovs.

Between 113 and 200 people were killed in street fighting, which wrecked a few buildings near the parliament and Freedom Square; on 6 January Gamsakhurdia fled to Armenia (soon reappearing in his home town of Zugdidi and being driven out again to Chechnya). A military council went through the pretence of approaching the royal family in Spain, but it was soon clear that Eduard Shevardnadze would be invited to return from Moscow to save his country. He returned in March 1992 and was designated chair of the State Council, which replaced the Military Council; Ioseliani was deputy chair and Kitovani was minister of defence.

POLITICS

In October 1992 elections (boycotted in South Ossetia, Mingrelia and parts of Abkhazia) were held for the State Council (formerly the Supreme Soviet). The largest party won just 29 seats out of 235, giving free rein to Shevardnadze, who became chair of parliament; the State Council wanted to abolish the post due to Gamsakhurdia's excesses, but Shevardnadze was convinced of the need for a strong executive leader. However, he struggled to control the National Guard and *Mkhedrioni*, who by now were running the country as one massive protection racket, controlling petrol and cigarette distribution and setting up roadblocks to 'tax' motorists; for most of 1992–93 the interior minister (in charge of the police) was Temuraz Khachishvili, a convicted criminal put in place by the *Mkhedrioni*. Economic policy was chaotic, with a disastrously loose credit policy and pyramid investment scandals.

Throughout 1992 unrest had continued in the west, stronghold of the Zviadists (supporters of Gamsakhurdia); in June they seized Tbilisi's TV tower, recaptured only with the loss of 40 lives. In August Kitovani precipitated fighting in Abkhazia by his recklessness when the interior minister was kidnapped; he was finally forced to resign in May 1993. In August the Council of Ministers resigned after parliament rejected the 1993 budget, and Shevardnadze also resigned when parliament refused to let him declare a state of emergency; crowds blockaded the government building and his resignation was rejected by the parliament. A state of emergency was declared in September, but already the country seemed ungovernable; in October Abkhazia was lost (see below), and Zviadist rebels captured Poti and Samtredia, and began advancing east. The only way out, as in the 18th century, was to call for Russian help; Georgia finally agreed to join the Commonwealth of Independent States, Russian troops arrived in late October and within weeks defeated the Zviadists. Gamsakhurdia himself was surrounded by government troops in January 1994 and committed suicide; he was buried (eventually) in Chechnya, but in 2006 there was talk of moving his remains to the new Sameba Cathedral in Tbilisi. Russia was given permission to maintain four bases in Georgia (Vaziani near Tbilisi, Akhalkalaki, Batumi and Gudauta in Abkhazia) for 25 years. In 2005 Russia agreed to close its bases by 2008, later brought forward to the end of 2006, although it wants to replace them with 'anti-terrorist centres'.

The winter of 1993–94 saw the start of large-scale operations against organised crime, particularly the National Guard and Zviadist groups; the *Mkhedrioni* were largely left alone, being nominally incorporated into the army as the 'Rescue Corps' until they were finally disarmed in May 1995. By the summer of 1994 basic law and order had been re-established, but there then followed a wave of political assassinations, of which the most prominent victim was Giorgi Chanturia, gunned down in December 1994; his widow Irina took his place as leader of the NDP. Some land and housing were sold in 1993, but economic reform really began with price liberalisation in September 1994, with gas prices increasing five times, electricity ten times, and bread up to 280 times.

In January 1995 Kitovani and his followers set out in an attempt to 'liberate' Abkhazia but were arrested (Kitovani was eventually jailed for eight years). A new constitution was approved by parliament in August, virtually as drafted by Shevardnadze; it established a presidential republic governed by a 235-seat Republican Council (it should also have a Senate once agreement has been reached on the representation of territorial units such as Abkhazia and South Ossetia). The prime minister was replaced by a minister of state, acting as adviser to a president directly elected for a maximum of two five-year terms.

The militia leaders were unhappy at being marginalised, and on 29 August a car bomb exploded in the courtyard of parliament – the closest of the many attempts on Shevardnadze's life since 1992; Ioseliani, Igor Giorgadze (the state security minister and son of the leader of the revived Communist Party), and his deputy were accused, together with an unholy alliance of mafia and pro-Russian forces. Ioseliani was jailed for 11 years in 1998 but Giorgadze fled to Russia, where he has remained in comfortable exile to this day. Shevardnadze, the 'silver fox', had been very cunning, playing the gangsters off against one another until all were in jail and gradually bringing reformers into government.

A new currency, the lari, was successfully introduced in September 1995, and elections were held under the new constitution in November. The results were something of a surprise, with only three parties over the 5% barrier for 150 party-list seats: the Citizens' Union of Georgia (CUG or SMK), set up by Shevardnadze as a personal vehicle, won almost half these seats with a quarter of the vote, and over 60% of the electorate voted for parties which polled under 5%. With further seats filled by a first-past-the-post system, the CUG won a total of 107 seats, followed by the National Democratic Party with 34 seats and the Union for Georgian Revival (led by the Adjaran strongman Aslan Abashidze) with 31 seats. In the presidential election Shevardnadze won 75% of the votes, with the nearest of his five rivals being Jumber Patiashvili (communist first secretary of Georgia from 1985 to 1989, running as an anti-reform independent), with 19%. Parliament elected the moderniser Zurab Zhvania to be its chair or speaker; trained as a biologist, he was leader of the Greens before joining the CUG. Real structural economic reforms began at long last, with an IMF stabilisation programme, a Partnership and Co-operation Agreement with the European Union, and similar deals with neighbouring countries. The reformers won the election but this was not reflected in the makeup of the government, and the overlap continued of law enforcement and criminal gangs involved in drug- and arms-trafficking, and then in kidnapping.

In February 1998 Shevardnadze survived another assassination attempt when grenades were fired at his motorcade, killing two bodyguards. This was blamed on the remaining Zviadists, 13 of whom were convicted in 2001. Lurking behind them is the ogre of Russia, which has a permanent interest in destabilising its newly independent neighbours and former colonies. Nevertheless Russia agreed to remove its troops from Georgia's borders, to be replaced by a Georgian border force; however, they left a booby-trap in their headquarters, which was defused.

In July 1998 Shevardnadze dismissed most of his ministers in a bid to revive reform and root out corruption, but in fact many were simply reappointed. An army mutiny in October, caused by lack of pay and poor conditions, also damaged the government (in 2001 another mutiny showed that nothing had improved).

In March 1999 the NDP and the Republican Party joined forces as the Third Way; then the Socialist and Traditionalist parties formed the Revival of Georgia bloc with Abashidze, and the new Industry Will Save Georgia party (Mretsveli) was formed by Georgi Topadze, owner of the Kazbegi brewery. In October 1999, soon after the Russians launched their latest Chechen war, inadequately clean parliamentary elections were held: the CUG won 42% of the vote and 132 seats (56% of the total), Revival won 25% of the vote and 58 seats, and Industry Will Save Georgia won 7% and 15 seats, all other parties being eliminated from parliament. Another set of businessmen, including Levan Gachechiladze, founder of the GWS wine company, and David Gamkrelidze, founder of Georgia's largest insurance company, soon split from the CUG to form the New Rightists Party, which remained loyal to Shevardnadze. In April 2000 the presidential election (again less than fully free and fair) was won by Shevardnadze with 80% of the vote (Stalin's grandson Evgeni Djugashvili was refused registration when it was decided that he was not a Georgian citizen). In January 1999 Georgia was admitted into the Council of Europe, and in June 2000 into the World Trade Organisation (in both cases well ahead of Armenia and Azerbaijan).

THE STRUGGLE FOR THE SUCCESSION In August 2001 the justice minister Mikheil Saakashvili proposed confiscating luxury houses built by ministers and senior officials, unless they could prove they were built with legitimate funds (many are worth US$200,000 or more, though even cabinet ministers earned only US$200 a month), but Shevardnadze refused to overturn the principle of the presumption of innocence. (The houses on Sairmis Gora are now something of a tourist attraction – see page 116.) Saakashvili specifically accused three ministers of corruption. He vowed to push his proposals through, but resigned on 19 September, two days after Shevardnadze had announced that he planned to relinquish the leadership of the CUG and wouldn't seek a third term as president in 2005. Also in August Minister for Taxes and Revenues Mikhail Machavariani resigned in protest at the draft 2002 budget; like Saakashvili, he was a leading member of the CUG's 'young reformers', with Finance Minister Zurab Noghaideli, Nino Burjanadze, head of the parliament's foreign relations committee, and as a rule Zhvania, although it was usually impossible to tell what game the last was playing. Their showdown with the Soviet-era old guard led by Interior Minister Kakha Targamadze became increasingly bitter as it turned into a battle for the succession to Shevardnadze (it's far simpler in Azerbaijan, where President Aliev's son was groomed to take over in 2003). Shevardnadze himself seemed as incapable as ever of taking sides; his perpetual balancing-act worked when he was popular, but was less effective once he sank to just 6% in the polls. Suffering from diabetes, he was seen as ageing, tired and confused, and simultaneously weak and heavy-handed in Abkhazia, where an outbreak of fighting was a real blow to him. The CUG halved in size, from 98 to 50 deputies, with at least two new factions forming; the opposition likewise realigned itself, although Aslan Abashidze's Union for Georgian Revival remained the dominant force. The rump of the CUG consisted of hardline conservatives, the former *nomenklatura* (Soviet bureaucrats) and those benefiting from corruption.

Shevardnadze parroted his commitment to rooting out corruption but achieved little; an anti-corruption commission came up with superficial recommendations such as abolishing police checkpoints. Georgi Sanaia, an outspoken journalist on the Rustavi-2 TV channel, was shot dead in July, presumably for attacking corruption, which led to protests on the streets. In October Rustavi-2 was raided by tax inspectors; demonstrators again took to the streets, accusing Targamadze and also Shevardnadze of trying to suppress free speech; Shevardnadze was forced to sack the state security minister, but said he'd resign if deputies voted to force out Targamadze (generally supposed to know some dirty secret about Shevardnadze, perhaps dating from the Abkhaz war of 1993). Then Zhvania claimed Targamadze and associates were planning to stir up unrest as a pretext to arrest him and his supporters, and declared that he would resign to force Targamadze out; they both resigned on 1 November, and Shevardnadze, with his support now almost non-existent, had no choice but to dismiss the whole government. He was still unable to have a proper clean-out and the 'power' ministries and security apparatus remained entangled with organised crime. Shevardnadze created a new alliance, For A New Georgia, out of his faction in the CUG plus the National Democratic Party, the Socialists and the Greens, as well as unions and business groups. Zhvania was not popular but boosted his reputation in the resignation crisis; he was now clearly opposed to Shevardnadze, leaving the CUG in early 2002 and forming his own party, the United Democrats; likewise, the more confrontational Saakashvili (who became Mayor of Tbilisi in November 2002) created the National Movement, forming a coalition with the Republicans and Conservatives. Local elections in June 2002 were the first major setback for the CUG, followed by parliamentary elections in November 2003 which were marred by fraud, leading to demonstrations by up to 15,000 people calling for Shevardnadze's resignation after exit polls and independent observers showed that Sheverdnadze, who claimed victory, had in fact lost. Saakashvili and his associates insisted on peaceful protest, backed up by a sharp statement from the US ambassador complaining that many people had been 'denied their constitutional right to vote' – presumably not what Shevardnadze expected. After almost three weeks the results were finally validated, Shevardnadze's For a New Georgia being given 21.3% of the vote, Revival 18.8%, and Saakashvili's National Movement 18%. Busloads of protestors came to Tbilisi to prevent the new parliament from meeting, and the head of the Security Council admitted fraud and called for new elections (but not Shevardnadze's resignation); Aslan Abashidze sent his supporters to Tbilisi for pro-Shevardnadze counter-demonstrations. When the parliament met protesters stormed in as Shevardnadze was in the middle of a speech declaring a state of emergency; he was rushed away by bodyguards and Nino Burjanadze, reformist speaker of parliament, declared herself temporary president. The next day, 23 November (St George's Day), Shevardnadze resigned, having been abandoned by the army and police. Due to the roses carried by the protesters, this became known as the **Rose Revolution**; it followed the similar upheaval in Serbia, and itself inspired the Orange Revolution in Ukraine at the end of 2004 and the Tulip Revolution in Kyrgyzstan in 2005. All were largely orchestrated by youth movements funded and guided by George Soros's Open Society Institute and other American groups.

Zhvania became prime minister and in January 2004 Saakasahvili, the only opposition candidate, won a presidential election with 88% of the vote. In parliamentary elections in March the National Movement-Democrats (uniting Saakashvili's, Zhvania's and Burjanadze's supporters and the Republicans) took 67% of the vote and 135 of the 150 party-list seats; the Rightist Opposition (the New Rightists and Industry Will Save Georgia) was the only opposition grouping over the threshold, with 7.6% and 15 seats (Revival and the Labour Party each took 6% of the vote). With the addition of constituency members elected in November 2003, the government had the support of at least 150 of 235 deputies, but in the summer of 2004, when Saakashvili changed the constitution to allow the president to dismiss parliament, the Republicans (the most liberal party in Georgia) left the government coalition to form the Democratic Front faction with the Conservatives.

Saakashvili soon fell out with Aslan Abashidze, who suppressed protests and in May 2004 had three bridges linking Adjara to the rest of Georgia destroyed; Saakashvili gave him ten days to disarm and return to constitutional rule, sending the army to conduct a major exercise just across the border, while activists were smuggled in to lead protests and seduce Abashidze's guard away from him. Fortunately he was also persuaded to go peacefully and was flown to Russia, and Adjara returned to being a normal part of Georgia.

Zhvania was found dead of carbon monoxide poisoning in February 2005; this was not exactly unprecedented in Georgia, but many people assumed he'd been murdered, probably by the Russians. He was replaced by Finance Minister Zurab Noghaideli, although he has less power than the interior and defence ministers. In May 2005 President George W Bush visited Tbilisi and was greeted with great enthusiasm (although an Abashidze supporter did throw a grenade at him, which failed to explode). The opposition boycotted parliamentary sessions from March 2006, after Republican deputy Valeri Gelashvili was suspended for mixing business and politics, but this was crumbling by October.

Igor Giorgadze lives comfortably in Russia but has set up the Justify Party (run in Georgia by Abashidze's former police minister) and the Giorgadze Foundation (run by Irina Sarishvili-Chanturia, who also leads the Imedi or Hope Party). His father, Panteleimon Giorgadze, once a Soviet general, who speaks Russian better than Georgian and often visits his son in Russia, is leader of the minuscule United Communist Party of Georgia. Former Security Minister Irakli Batiashvili set up the Forward Georgia Party and was implicated in Emzar Kvitsiani's revolt in the Kodori Gorge (see below). All of these tiny groups and the Anti-Soros Party (really) are basically a Russian fifth column.

The French-Georgian Salome Zourabichvili arrived as French ambassador in 2003 just before the Rose Revolution, and in 2004 became foreign minister of Georgia (though still paid by the French government) but was soon forced out, establishing her own party, Sakartvelos Gza or Georgia's Way. This soon merged with the Freedom Party, founded by Zviad Gamsakhurdia's son Konstantin (Koko). The Labour Party, founded in 1995 and led by Shalva Natelashvili, won the 2002 Tbilisi city council elections and has a few MPs; however, it lost a lot of popularity by not supporting the Rose Revolution, seeing it as a mere palace coup.

The Rose Revolution was great PR but many feel there's been little change except new sports facilities (including cunning combined basketball/mini-soccer pitches). However, corruption was tackled vigorously and tax collection rates rose sharply; tariffs have been cut from a maximum of 30% to 5–12% and from 16 to three bands. The government aims to be the third nation (after Hong Kong and Singapore) to have no tariffs, from January 2008.

In January 2006 banker Sandro Girgvliani was murdered after an argument in the Sharden Bar, apparently on the orders of the wife of Interior Minister Vano Merabishvili; four men were jailed but there were widespread accusations of a cover-up and calls for Merabishvili to resign. In February a former policeman was shot, possibly because he had information on the involvement of some in the Interior Ministry in drug smuggling. In March a prison riot, that the government claimed was part of a nationwide plot by the 'criminals-in-law' (the top dogs who control Georgia's prisons as well as much criminal activity outside), was put down with seven deaths; the opposition parties suspected a cover-up but demands for an investigation have always been voted down.

However, Merabishvili remains in office, and it seems that the 'power ministries' still see themselves as unaccountable, undermining Saakashvili's reforms and his credibility. Saakashvili's popularity has also fallen due to his constant publicity-chasing – on the ski slopes, opening the new Rustavi prison several times, and similarly the tunnel to Batumi (first at one end, then the other…). More substantially, he has managed relations with Russia very badly, causing massive damage to Georgia's economy.

THE RUSSIAN CRISES Externally, despite Saakashvili's efforts to move towards the West and specifically NATO and EU membership, Georgian politics is dominated by relations with Russia, which has always sought to dominate is neighbours. Since the outbreak of the latest Chechen war in 1999 Russia has tried even harder to manipulate Georgia, wanting Russian troops to be allowed in to seal the border with Chechnya; this was refused (although Russian jets and helicopters did drop bombs on the Georgian side of the border), so since 2000 Russia has required visas for Georgians (about a million of whom work there), though not for Abkhazians and Armenians. Russia accused Georgia of harbouring Chechen terrorists (and even al-Qaeda guerrillas) in the Pankisi Gorge in Kakheti, an enclave populated by Kists or Christian Chechens plus 7,000 Chechen refugees. In 2001 various foreigners were kidnapped and held in Pankisi; this was linked to just about every possible political faction, but was simple criminality and they have now been freed. British banker Peter Shaw was kidnapped in June 2002 and held with a chain around his neck in a tiny cellar in the Pankisi Gorge until his release in November; the Georgian special forces tried to claim credit but it seems to have been due to high-level political pressure. Less happily, the brother of the AC Milan footballer and Georgian captain Kakha Kaladze was kidnapped and eventually murdered.

In 2002 Georgia (backed by the US) twice accused Russia of bombing Pankisi, but Russia accused Georgia of staging it. In August 1,000 Georgian Interior Ministry troops, trained by US special forces, went into Pankisi and arrested a few criminals, failing to find any al-Qaeda camps. Even so, in September Russia accused the Georgian government of being 'fellow travellers' of international terrorism and threatened economic sanctions and even an 'anti-terrorist' operation across the border.

Since the Rose Revolution Russia has been determined to block Georgian entry to NATO by keeping the Abkhaz and South Ossetian conflicts alive; Saakashvili has retaliated by blocking Russian entry to the World Trade Organisation. In January 2006 Russia doubled the price of gas supplied to Georgia and later that month, during a particularly cold spell, an explosion (presumably sabotage) cut the gas pipeline from Russia to Georgia, leaving most of the population without heat or power for a week (gas supplies had also been briefly cut off in the winter of 2000 due to Georgia's 'lack of co-operation on Chechnya'). Russian aircraft flew over Senaki and Kazbegi and their consulate stopped giving visas to Georgians, and in March Georgian wine was banned by Russia, supposedly due to impurities, soon followed by Georgian mineral water and fruit. The quantity of Georgian wine sold in Russia is far greater than that actually produced, and any health risks are entirely due to the fake wine produced in Russia; this is a country in which 35,000 people a year die due to bad booze, and the ban hurts Russian retailers and consumers as much as it does Georgia. Saakashvili blithely said 'What doesn't kill you makes you stronger', and sought new markets for Georgian wine in Asia, but he is widely blamed for provoking the crisis.

The US backs Georgia, partly from gratitude for the few Georgian troops in Iraq (and Kosovo), and NATO began an intensified dialogue with Georgia in 2006, although membership is still many years off.

In July 2006 Russia's only border crossing to Georgia was suddenly shut 'for repairs'. In September there was apparently a pathetic attempt at a coup by the minor Russian-backed parties, and four Russian military intelligence officers and 11 Georgians were arrested for spying; this was seen as very obvious grandstanding in the run-up to local elections, but the Russian response was furious, withdrawing the ambassador and staff and families from the embassy in Tbilisi and ceasing to issue visas to Georgians. The Russians were released after three days but Russia stepped up the punishment, suspending transport and postal links, expelling at least 5,000 Georgians from Russia (with two dying in the process), raiding Georgian-owned restaurants and casinos for 'tax irregularities' and encouraging a xenophobic hysteria in which some schools expelled children with Georgian names. It was estimated the crisis could cut Georgian economic growth by 1.5%, but in fact the economy continued to grow, and the government did indeed do well in the local elections. The ambassador returned in January 2007, but flights to Russia were still suspended in March 2008.

As Russia becomes sure of its stranglehold over European gas supplies, it is increasingly willing to offend the West and is taking a harder line with Western-minded neighbours. Lithuania, for instance, decided in early 2006 to sell Eastern Europe's largest refinery (Mazeiku Nafta) to a Polish company rather than Russia's supposedly independent Gazprom. That summer the Russians 'found a leak' in the oil pipeline and it has been closed ever since. In June 2006 Georgia's hydro-electric power stations and distribution system were sold for US$132 million (plus a promise of US$200 million investment) to the Czech company Energo-Pro in preference to a Russian company; however there are strong suspicions that this was actually a stalking-horse for Russia's UES anyway. In November Gazprom announced that the price of Georgia's gas would double again in January 2007; a few days later it suggested it could leave the price unchanged if Georgia sold it the pipeline instead, a proposal greeted by the sound of Georgian jaws hitting the ground at the sheer brazenness of the blackmail attempt. In the end Georgia agreed to pay the higher price, but can now buy most of its gas from Azerbaijan.

In September 2007 former defence minister Irakli Okruashvili accused Saakashvili of corruption and was himself arrested two days later on corruption charges. The opposition for once formed a united front and organised mass protests; after demonstrators had blocked Rustaveli Avenue for four days they were brutally driven away by police, sparking international outrage, and a state of emergency was declared. However the next day Saakashvili was forced to call early elections for January 2008, in which the main opposition candidate was Conservative leader Levan Gachechiladze; Saakashvili was declared winner with 53% of the vote, sparking claims of vote-rigging. Almost at once Badri Patarkatshishvili (see page 198), who had won 7% of the vote for president after his

Imedi TV station had been closed down in the state of emergency, was charged with plotting a coup; he died in England in February from what seems to have been a genuine heart attack.

ABKHAZIA Under Georgia's 1921 constitution Abkhazia was virtually autonomous; Stalin made Abkhazia an autonomous republic in 1930, but he also encouraged large numbers of Georgians to immigrate; by 1989 the population of 450,000 was 46% Georgian, 18% Abkhaz, 14% Armenian, 14% Russian and 3% Greek. Perestroika encouraged the growth of secessionism and in July 1989 demands for teaching at the University of Sukhumi to be in Georgian rather than Abkhazian led to fighting and 14 deaths. In August 1990 the Abkhaz Supreme Soviet voted for independence as a Union Republic within the Soviet Union, but was persuaded to reverse this; in the referendum of March 1991 virtually the whole non-Georgian population of Abkhazia voted in vain to stay in the Soviet Union, seeing it as less of a threat than being part of an independent and nationalist Georgia.

Although the 1921 constitution was restored in 1992, the Abkhaz were convinced that Tbilisi was bent on denying them autonomy and saw no choice but independence; therefore a Republic of Abkhazia was declared in July 1992 (though without the required two-thirds majority). The next month Shevardnadze's defence minister, Kitovani, sent the National Guard into Abkhazia, ostensibly to protect transport links with Russia, and full-scale conflict broke out. The Abkhaz leader, Vladislav Ardzinba (a historian in Moscow until 1987), retreated to the Russian army base at Gudauta; with help from Russia and Muslim paramilitaries from the northern Caucasus he had regained control of northern Abkhazia by October. By spring of 1993 the front line seemed stable along the river Gumista, north of Sukhumi, although the city was largely destroyed by the Russians bombing Georgian troops. Shevardnadze flew to Moscow to urge Yeltsin to bring his generals under control, but he soon saw that Russia was determined to bring the former Soviet Republics under its domination. In May Kitovani was sacked; by July there was a ceasefire and UN observers arrived in August; however, the Abkhazians launched a surprise attack in September and soon 'liberated' Abkhazia (Shevardnadze went to Sukhumi vowing to defend it himself, but had to flee ignominiously by air). Around 8,000 people were killed between August 1992 and October 1993.

Between 200,000 and 350,000 Georgians and others fled, about 400 dying in the mountains on the border with Svaneti. Talks in Geneva produced an agreement on refugee repatriation; in July 1994 3,000 CIS (mainly Russian) peacekeepers moved in, and in August the first 5,000 refugees returned. The Georgians exiled from Abkhazia have considerable political influence in Tbilisi, and they and other nationalists are pushing for a (totally unrealistic) military solution; in January 1995, when Russia was distracted by its disastrous war in Chechnya, Kitovani attempted to invade with just a thousand fighters, but ended up in a Georgian jail.

Gali, the district of Abkhazia bordering Mingrelia, was virtually unscathed in 1993–94 and has been a demilitarised zone since mid 1994; but in May 1998 Georgian paramilitaries killed between six and 20 Abkhaz militiamen, before being driven out of Gali, with between 60 and 200 deaths, and at least 30,000 refugees took to the roads again. Over 2,000 buildings were burnt down by the Abkhaz in the buffer zone patrolled by the Russian peacekeepers (which even Russian officials later admitted was too close to turning a blind eye to ethnic cleansing). Many of the Georgian refugees began crossing by day to work fields in Gali, returning to sleep in Zugdidi, and in 1999 they began to return to their homes. The Abkhazians claim that 70,000–90,000 have returned, but Georgia claims the total is far lower.

The youngest of five children, Eduard Shevardnadze was born in Mamati, Guria, in 1928. His parents wanted him to become a doctor but he chose politics, joining the Communist Party at 20 and working his way up to be Georgia's Minister of Internal Affairs, ie: head of the secret police. In 1972, aged just 44, he was appointed Secretary-General of the Georgian Party, with a mission to cut corruption. At his first politburo meeting, it's said that he asked those present to raise their hands if they agreed that corruption should be eliminated; naturally they all agreed, and he asked them to keep their hands up while he went round the table; all those with foreign watches were sacked. After this, however, he failed to make much impact in this area, but his reforming economic and political policies presaged perestroika, and when Gorbachev became Soviet leader in 1985 he appointed Shevardnadze foreign minister. He is still especially popular in Germany where he is seen as having brought about the fall of the Berlin Wall and German reunification more or less single-handed. In 1989 he resigned in protest at Gorbachev's repressive attempts to slow the break-up of the Soviet Union, although he did serve again as foreign minister during the Soviet Union's final days, before returning to Georgia.

As chair of parliament from 1992 he had no formal executive powers but rapidly built up a semi-presidential apparatus while parliament was too fractured to play a real role; in 1995 he became president. Although backed by his own party, the Citizens' Union of Georgia, which dominated parliament, Shevardnadze ruled outside formal political structures, preferring an informal network of contacts and cronies, which is very much part of Georgian culture and a fertile breeding-ground for corruption.

The CUG comprised both progressive 'greens' and reactionary 'reds', and its political identity was unclear (this applied equally to the opposition parties, with the Communist and Zviadist parties supported by both right- and left-wingers). Some reformers, such as Zurab Zhvania, established themselves in positions of power, but without being allowed to rival Shevardnadze. This helped him effectively to blackmail the electorate, saying 'it's me or it's chaos'. Shevardnadze was re-elected president in 2000; in September 2001 he announced that he was relinquishing the chair of the CUG, and began to plan the transition to post-Shevardnadze politics – rather than simply finding a successor (or allowing someone else to seize power), he seemed to prefer to hand over the business of the state slowly to a prime minister who would become an heir apparent, if successful. He followed a classic 'divide and rule' strategy, giving hope to both the 'young reformers' led by Zhvania and the conservatives led by Targamadze. It all came unstuck when the country tired of his fence-sitting and swept him from power; however, he is still in his palace and often appears on TV to give his opinions.

Although most people accepted that Shevardnadze was clean of corruption himself, he was seriously tainted by the activities of his nephews, particularly Nugzar Shevardnadze who dominated the cigarette and kerosene trades; he may not have directly used access to the president, but he certainly assumed that his name made him untouchable.

The two sides continue to talk, with Abkhazia insisting on equal confederal status with Georgia, and Georgia insisting on an asymmetric arrangement with more power for Tbilisi. Nor can Georgia accept Abkhazia staying in the rouble zone. Russia came in for a lot of international criticism for its role; the general commanding the Russian peacekeepers claimed in 1994 that Abkhazia had always been an integral part of Russia, and the economic blockade of Abkhazia has only been enforced half-heartedly. As discussed on page 66, Russia is thought to be fomenting instability in Georgia to boost its own Caspian–Black Sea pipeline and keep it out of NATO. It is claimed that the Russian airfield at Vaziani (just east of Tbilisi) was the base for the 1995 attempt to assassinate Shevardnadze, and Moscow has failed to extradite Igor Giorgadze and Guram Absandze, both of whom are accused of involvement in the plot; Giorgadze appeared regularly on TV but Russia's police responded to an Interpol warrant by denying it knew where he was, until he was granted asylum in 2006. In mid 1999 Russia opened its border with Abkhazia (although it had been very porous for a long while).

In October 1999 Abkhaz presidential elections produced a 99% vote for Ardzinba, the only candidate, and a referendum on independence was approved by 97%; a week later the Abkhaz parliament formally declared independence, and the new Abkhaz premier Anri Jergenia spoke of applying to join the Russian Federation, though this was still a step too far for Putin. Russia failed to withdraw in July 2001 (as agreed in 1999) from Gudauta, the base for the CIS peacekeepers and also for dodgy Russian arms sales worldwide. After the terrorist attacks of 11 September 2001 Russia expected a free rein to strike at Chechen 'terrorists', yet continues to support Abkhazian separatism, and no-one now expects Gudauta to be relinquished.

The upper part of the Kodori Gorge, adjoining Svaneti, still in Georgian hands, became a flashpoint; in 1999 first Georgian government officials and then UN observers were kidnapped there, with armed clashes in July 2001. In October 2001 Georgian guerrillas, reportedly aided by Chechen fighters, launched raids here resulting in at least 30 deaths, and a few days later a UN helicopter was shot down near the Kodori Gorge, killing five UN military observers, three Ukrainian crewmembers, and a Georgian interpreter – it seems likely that Russian missiles from Gudauta, and possibly Russian personnel, were involved. Russian jets also flew over Svaneti and dropped bombs in the Kodori Gorge. The Georgian parliament voted 163-1 for Russian peacekeepers to withdraw, and talked of leaving the CIS. In July 2006 Georgian special police were sent to the Kodori Gorge to arrest the renegade governor turned warlord, Emzar Kvitsiani, and disperse his paramilitary Hunter battalion. There was some skirmishing in the villages of Azhara and Omarishi, and one civilian was killed but order was soon established, and, apparently, some slaves were freed. The Abkhazian government-in-exile was moved from Tbilisi to the Kodori (renamed Upper Abkhazia), and Saakashvili and Burjanadze visited.

Saakashvili pledged to reunite Abkhazia and South Ossetia with the rest of Georgia by 2008, and there were alarming signs that a military solution might be attempted; Russia has granted citizenship to most residents of the two republics and has said it will protect them if Georgia uses force. Saakashvili is pushing, so far in vain, for Russian peacekeepers to be replaced by an international force. The separation of Kosovo from Serbia is being used by Russia as a precedent for separating Abkhazia and South Ossetia from Georgia (but oddly not for separating Chechnya from Russia), and in March 2008 Russia lifted its sanctions on Abkhazia.

Meanwhile, the economy is doing well under Prime Minister Sergey Baghapsh; tourism from Russia is booming and there's lots of development.

SOUTH OSSETIA There has also been conflict in Samachablo (South Ossetia), although less fierce and relatively well patched up. The Ossetians are ethnically totally distinct from all their neighbours and, as the majority population in South Ossetia (an autonomous region since 1922), felt entitled to protection from an

The idealistic young man who drove Shevardnadze from power was born in Tbilisi in 1967, his father a well-known doctor and his mother a historian at Tbilisi State University. He studied international law in Kiev, Strasbourg and Columbia Law School in New York, acquiring fluent English, French, Ukrainian and Russian along the way, as well as a Dutch wife, Sandra Saakashvili-Roelofs, with whom he has two sons.

In 1995 he was persuaded by his old friend Zurab Zhvania, who had been commissioned by Shevardnadze to recruit talented young Georgians, to return to Georgia and enter politics. Together with current Republican Party leader David Usupashvili and Conservative Party founder Koba Davitashvili, they were leading members of the Georgian Young Lawyers Association, which became a pro-reform pressure group. Saakashvili and Zhvania both entered parliament in December 1995 for Shevardnadze's CUG and were soon noticed. Saakasahvili was successful as chair of the parliament's judiciary committee and in January 2000 he was appointed vice-president of the Parliamentary Assembly of the Council of Europe.

In October 2000 he became justice minister and implemented major reforms, but was unable to root out top-level corruption, despite producing documents at a cabinet meeting that showed some colleagues had built huge houses with illicitly gained cash.

He was finally ground down by the 'power' ministries (notably Kakha Targmadze's Interior Ministry), or else decided he had to provoke a showdown, and resigned in September 2001, founding his own party, the National Movement, in the social-democratic mould.

In June 2002, with the backing of the Labour Party, he became Mayor of Tbilisi, home to a third of Georgia's population, and, already one of the country's most popular politicians, he built a strong power base by delivering local services and fixing roofs and drains. As a crusader against corruption and poverty, he built a populist bandwagon that clearly won more votes than Shevardnadze's For a New Georgia in November 2003's elections, and harnessed the general indignation to bring up to 100,000 people onto the streets in non-violent protests for two weeks, until Shevardnadze was forced to resign and was replaced by the speaker of parliament. Saakashvili had to wait until the elections of January 2004 to become Europe's youngest president. He was forgiving of his predecessor, saying: 'History will judge him kindly.'

He immediately replaced the country's flag with a new one, and set out vigorously to tackle corruption. These efforts and a new tax code have had considerable effect in increasing government revenues and thus expenditures too; Georgia was named the world's leader in economic reform and one of the best to do business in, well ahead of its neighbours. However, his populism has often tipped into demagoguery and authoritarianism, for instance in a new media law in 2004 and the favouritism shown to some TV stations (notably Rustavi-2) and pressure on others.

independent and nationalist Georgia. Demands in 1989 for unification with North Ossetia, within the Russian Federation, were rejected heavy-handedly by Georgia, but in 1990 South Ossetia declared independence within the Soviet Union. This was confirmed by a referendum and in December the Georgian Supreme Soviet abolished the autonomous region and declared a state of emergency in the capital, Tskhinvali.

The new Shevardnadze government blamed Gamsakhurdia's runaway nationalism for all the preceding problems and released the chair of the South Ossetian Supreme Soviet from prison. However, another referendum called for integration with the Russian Federation and in 1992 Georgian troops attacked Tskhinvali; 400 Georgians and over 1,000 Ossetians were killed before a ceasefire was arranged in June. Monitors from the Organisation for Security and Co-operation in Europe (OSCE) and Russian peacekeeping troops have managed to maintain this, and refugees have returned home. However, many South Ossetians are unable to forgive the brutality of the Georgian military. Lyudvig Chibirov was elected president in 1996 and South Ossetia seemed to have effectively seceded (with its budget entirely financed by Moscow) until North Ossetia rejected the idea of unification. In 1999 relations worsened after Chibirov's party lost elections (held illegally, according to Georgia) to Russian-oriented communists, who won more than 80% of the seats, and the Georgian government cut the electricity supply to just 30 minutes per day. In 2001 Chibirov himself lost a presidential election (also unrecognised by Georgia), to the more radical Eduard Kokoiti, a 37-year-old Moscow-based businessman, and in March 2002 the South Ossetian parliament asked the Russian Duma to recognise its independence. Saakashvili's rapid success in bringing Adjara back into the fold led him to try for the same result in South Ossetia, leading to rapid militarisation there. It's claimed that the Ergeneti market in Tskhinvali handles US$120 million a year of trade, with no tax paid except for the rake-off taken by the Russian generals. Saakashvili claimed Russia was using the market to undermine Georgia's economy and in 2004 sent in Interior Ministry troops to close it down, resulting in several dozen deaths. In 2005 he offered an autonomous parliament and government, but this was dismissed by Kokoiti. Russia claims South Ossetia needs more protection from them than the Kosovar Albanians did from NATO, but it seems that trust in Moscow (which refuses to absorb South Ossetia) is ebbing, and Kokoiti has asked for a non-aggression pact with Georgia. In July 2006 Oleg Albarov, secretary of South Ossetia's National Security Council, was killed by a bomb while opening his garage door, allegedly murdered for being willing to talk to Georgia – but the attack was blamed by South Ossetia on Georgia. Five days later a bomb exploded in front of the home of South Ossetian MP Bala Bestaev; he was unharmed, but two teenagers were killed and four passers-by were wounded. In September missiles were fired at two Georgian helicopters, one carrying Georgia's defence minister, and one Georgian and three South Ossetian policemen were killed in a clash outside Tskhinvali.

In November 2006 Kokoiti was re-elected president with 96% of the vote, and another referendum called for independence – Georgian passport-holders were not allowed to vote and only South Ossetia and Russia took the results seriously. Georgia set up a parallel administration under Dimitri Sanakoyev in the village of Kurta.

ECONOMY

During the Soviet period, Georgia's industry was, of course, state-owned and directed from Moscow; it was a major supplier of electric locomotives and jet fighters to the Soviet Union, and the city of Rustavi was founded in 1948 to supply metallurgical products. Although there was more private production in agriculture, it was also excessively oriented to the production of tea, citrus fruit, grapes and wine for the rest of the Soviet Union, leaving Georgia dependent on imported grain and meat. Nevertheless Georgia had a higher standard of living than most other republics. Naturally there has been major restructuring since independence, and coupled with the energy crisis (see pages 34–5) and the collapse of the Russian market this has meant that much of Georgia's industry simply closed down, with production virtually halving in 1992.

In July 1993 Georgia withdrew from the rouble zone, introducing a temporary coupon currency, and then in 1995 its own currency, the lari (meaning 'scales', as in *libra* or *lire*), at GEL1.3 to the US dollar. By the end of 1993 a combination of pyramid savings frauds, the Abkhazia war (which cost 50 million roubles a day) and a disastrous policy of printing money had caused hyperinflation (just 7% of credits were used for their designated purpose; Demur Dvalishvili, governor of the National Bank in 1992–93, committed suicide in 1994 while under investigation). Consumer prices rose by 15,606% in 1994: savings were wiped out, industry shut down, half the economy went underground and the tax base fell from 40% of GDP to under 10% – the lowest in the former Soviet Union. This led to Georgia applying to the IMF for help, and committing itself to the required reforms. From September 1994 prices were freed, and privatisation began in 1995. By 1997, 90.4% of retail turnover was private, and by April 1998 11,492 of 11,593 small businesses (with under 50 staff) had been privatised (mainly by insider sales), as had 884 of 1,149 medium and large businesses, although there was little progress in Adjara. The electrical supply industry was split up and privatised in 1998, and land, water supply, ports and telecommunications followed; and at last there is an effective bankruptcy law in place.

The economy turned around in 1995; Georgia soon had the fastest-growing economy in the Newly Independent States, with GDP growth over 11% for 1996 and 1997 (admittedly from a very low base), but 1998 was a bad year, with a harvest 20% below 1997's, and an appallingly low rate of tax collection; the lari had to be devalued in the wake of the Russian economic collapse. GDP grew by 3% in 1998 and 1999, and by just 1.9% in 2000 (to US$4.8 billion), after a drought hit agriculture again. Nevertheless manufacturing output rose by 10%, and mining by 75%, and services have grown steadily as a share of the economy. Foreign Direct Investment fell 18%, largely due to the completion of the 'early oil' pipeline (see page 66). Inflation in 2000 was 4.6%, below target. Average incomes crept above the subsistence level, but in fact expenditure was 36% above reported income on average, indicating that people were rather better off than they let on. In 2002 GDP grew by 5.4% to US$3.3 billion (US$674 per head), and inflation was 6%. Tax collection improved slightly, with some high-profile raids to spread the message, but customs was still corrupt and inefficient; in 1998 excise stamps, printed by the German company that is also printing the euro notes, were introduced on alcohol and tobacco, to reduce evasion. As a result of the shortfall in tax revenues, IMF loans were delayed and public spending was cut across the board, except for social spending.

The retirement age was raised by five years, to 65 for men and 60 for women; now there are 785,000 pensioners in a population of 4.5m, supported by 743,000 working. A State Social Allowance was introduced in 1998, intended mainly as a top-up for lone pensioners, of GEL9 a month, in addition to the basic GEL15; unemployment benefit of GEL12–15 per month is now paid for six months.

Since the Rose Revolution the Saakashvili government has produced remarkable economic achievements, with an anti-corruption drive yielding big increases in tax revenue and privatisations also boosting the state coffers. The civil service has been cut and the tax code simplified, persuading international lenders to restructure Georgia's debt and provide more aid. This has allowed the government to pay, and increase, pensions, to refurbish transport and energy infrastructure, and to strengthen the military. Since 2007 there has been less privatisation income, the big construction projects (notably pipelines, worth US$195 million, the new terminal at Tbilisi Airport, worth US$65 million, the Khulevi oil terminal, worth US$45 million, and hotels in Adjara, worth US$100 million) have been completed, and energy prices have risen; on the other hand the pipelines are starting to earn substantial transit fees.

The economy has doubled in size in six years, from GEL6.7 billion in 2001 to GEL13.8 billion (US$7.9 billion – US$1,800 per capita) in 2006. GDP grew by

In 1985 Georgia produced 14.4GW of energy (6.2GW of hydro-electric power and 8.2GW of thermal power; however, in 1996 total production was just 7.2GW (6.1GW hydro-electric and just 1.1GW thermal). This was largely due to Turkmenistan cutting off supplies of natural gas (due to unpaid bills of US$465 million) and to a lack of funds to buy fuel elsewhere, but it also illustrates the rottenness of the Georgian state as a whole. During the civil war and the period of chaos that followed, gas supplies and other utilities simply ceased to function; gas was restored by 1995 in a few cities, such as Gori, where the administration could be bothered; in Tbilisi it began to be restored from 1996, but effectively was only restored in 2000. On New Year's Eve 2000 gas supplies from Russia were cut off, partly due to unpaid debt, but more as cynical political bullying. By 2007 energy production had grown to just 8.3GW (80% hydro-electric and 20% thermal).

Less than half of households have gas heating, others relying on kerosene or electric heaters. In the 1990s only a third of domestic energy bills were paid, consumers preferring to bribe the collector to mark them off as paid, with him then paying his superior to do the same. The system was close to melt-down, domestic users receiving about six hours of shuki (power) a day in winter, but the situation has now normalised.

The monopoly gas supplier is the Russian firm Itera (closely linked to Gazprom), which owns half of Sakgazi, the Georgian national distributor, and Shevardnadze supported its bid to take over Tbilgazi, the local supplier in Tbilisi; this was in fact bought in 2006 (after eight years of delays) by the Kazakh company KazTransGas, for US$12.5 million (including US$232 million of debts). Already gas cost three times as much as north of the border, and it was rightly assumed this would get worse: prices doubled in the first half of 2006 and again in January 2007. The American company AES took over electricity supply in Rustavi, installing new meters and insisting on payment in return for reliable power 24 hours a day; this was highly controversial at first but did work. AES was then allowed to take over Telasi, the Tbilisi electricity supplier, at the end of 1998; AES-Telasi claims to have invested US$275 million in the local economy, including US$45 miiion in meters and over US$200 million in the rehabilitation of Tbilisi's electricity distribution

9.3% in 2005, and probably would have grown by a bit more in 2006 until the Russian economic sanctions knocked it back to 8% (about GEL13 billion); growth was 11% in 2007 and will be 7–9% for 2008–10.

In 2005 state revenues increased significantly and were GEL110 million more than budgeted; social spending accounted for the largest share of expenditure (19% or GEL529 million), followed by 'other expenses' (transparency has a long way to go) at GEL460m, and then defence at GEL390m. In the 2007 budget, revenue from taxes is expected to grow by 14% and there is still a lot of room for improvement in tax collection, with only 40% of tax being paid voluntarily. Budgeted revenue for 2007 is GEL3.4 billion with expenditure GEL400 million less than in 2006 and a budget deficit of GEL426 million; Georgia has agreed with the IMF to cut the fiscal deficit from 4% of GDP (GEL550 million) to 2% (GEL340 million), which should keep inflation to around 10% at the end of 2006 (although it was up at 14.5% in July). Inflation rose to 11% in 2007 and is still rising, due to growth in government spending and in remittances from abroad (mainly Russia).

In April 2006 12% of the labour force was unemployed (26% in Tbilisi), many of them actually working in the shadow economy; however it's estimated that 22% of the economy is in the untaxed shadow sector, down from 53% in 2003.

network, but big businesses, ministries and officials in particular continued to avoid paying their bills and AES-Telasi couldn't make money. In 1999 the tariff was increased from 6 tetris (US$0.03) per kilowatt to 9.8 tetris, and in 2001 AES-Telasi asked to increase it to 17 tetris, with 13.8 tetris finally being permitted, after AES threatened to pull out of Georgia. In July 2003 AES finally quit, selling its Georgian interests, including its 75% stake in Telasi, the 600MW Mktvari power station and the 240MW Khrami power stations, to Russia's electricity monopoly UES, owned by Anatoly Chubais. The government blamed AES, the leading Western investor in Georgia, for failing to manage its business properly, but there's little doubt that the Shevardnadze government itself was to blame for failing to uphold laws protecting foreign investors or to tackle the corrupt inside interests that totally undermined the business. In addition, until 2002 AES was taxed on the electricity it produced rather than on the payments it received, and in 2003 a court reversed the tariff increase. The failure of AES, coupled with kidnappings of Western businessmen, was a major blow to hopes of increasing Western investment. UES has a better understanding of Georgian culture and the ability, with Gazprom, simply to shut off Georgia's gas and power if things don't go their way.

In 2006 the government decided to sell six hydro-electric power stations and two other distribution companies, covering 70% of the country (see page 27).

Georgia's hydro-electric potential is 100–160 billion kWh, but under one-tenth of this is actually produced; a new approach is needed, as the gigantism of the Soviet approach leads to dams that soon silt up and cause all kinds of erosion and other environmental problems. There's a huge potential for reducing consumption with elementary energy efficiency measures, but until bills have to be paid there will be no interest in this. Georgia has reserves of 350 million tonnes of relatively poor coal (in the Tqibuli, Tkvartcheli and Akhaltsikhe areas), with a maximum annual output of three million tonnes; oil reserves of around 12 million tonnes are known, though there may be far more.

As for alternative energy sources, Georgia produces 200–250 million m^3 per year of geothermal hot water, enough to provide heating for half a million people. Wind energy has huge potential, with Mount Saboueti in the Likhi range (north of Surami) receiving over 7,000 hours a year of wind at 4m per second or stronger.

Trade is growing with Turkey (now US$405 million) and western Europe, but Russia is still Georgia's main trading partner, due to increasing gas prices, at US$538 million. Exports were worth US$867m in 2005 (up from US$648 million in 2004), but imports continue to rise faster (to US$2.5 billion), with the trade deficit growing to US$1.6 billion in 2005. In 2007 imports were an estimated US$5.2 billion, and exports US$1.24 billion. In 2004 the main export was scrap metal, just ahead of wine and ferroalloy; the main imports were oil and gas (20%) and cars.

In the future one of the best sources of foreign exchange should be **tourism**; in the Soviet era four million tourists a year (and 47% of all foreign visitors to the Soviet Union) came to Georgia, almost all to the Abkhazian coast. The loss of Abkhazia, coupled with the occupation of Georgia's hotels by refugees from Abkhazia and the general economic crisis, almost wiped out the tourist industry. However, it's now doubling every year, from a very low base, so Tbilisi guesthouses can charge absurdly high prices, while elsewhere rooms are very cheap (when you can find them). The top end of the business is over-regulated (with plenty of scope for corruption in the administration of sanitary controls), but there's also a huge number of rooms available informally. In 2005 there were 542,428 foreign visitors (40% above 2005), and almost one million in 2006.

Agriculture suffered as much as the rest of the economy, with production in 1995 half that of 1990; but the 1997 and 2001 harvests were good, thanks to privatisation, foreign technical aid and credit, and agriculture offers promise for the future (although agriculture's share of GDP has fallen from 38% in 1995 to under 25% in 1998, under 20% in 2003 and under 13% in 2007). This was the only Soviet Republic where farmers were able to keep some of their land, and privatisation of collectivised land began in 1992. Only 13.2% of agricultural land (although over half the better-quality land) had been privatised by 1998; progress is slow due to the lack of a land registration system (which the World Bank estimates will take several years and cost US$42 million).

Oil and gas are important, though mainly in transit (see page 66); however, some oil is produced in Samgori and Ninotsminda, east of Tbilisi, and the American firm Arco is exploring on the Black Sea shelf. Oil production is at best 100,000 tonnes per annum (2,000 barrels per day) against consumption of 13,000 barrels per day; gas production is around 60 million m^3 a year, against consumption of 1.7 billion m^3.

PEOPLE

With 15 major ethnic groups (and up to 80 in Tbilisi), Georgia is the least homogenous of the Transcaucasian states. The population is probably under four million, although statistics are unreliable, due to population movements since the 1989 Soviet census, when the population was 5.5 million, including Abkhazia and South Ossetia; many Russians, Armenians, Jews and Greeks have left the country, some Georgians have returned home but maybe 600,000 (or a million including those with Russian citizenship) are living and working in Russia. It is estimated that 83% of the population was Georgian, 6% Armenian, 6% Azeri, 2% Russian, 2% Ossetian and 1% other groups, including 95,000 Kurds, 52,000 Ukrainians, 12,000 Jews, 8,600 Belarussians, 6,000 Assyrians and 4,000 Tatars. Germans, invited to come as colonists in the 1780s by Potemkin, first viceroy of Caucasus, were deported to central Asia in 1941 but then left for Germany. There are about 270,000 Internally Displaced Persons or refugees, mainly from Abkhazia. Life expectancy is 73 on average (69 for men and 77 for women), and the population is ageing, 12% now being over 65 years old. The birth rate is falling, due to economic disruption and the fact that many of those of working age are abroad. The population density is 78 per km^2 overall, and up to 300 per km^2 in the fertile plains; 56% of the population is urban (one-third of them in Tbilisi).

Overall, the Georgians are marked by what the historian W E D Allen called 'aesthetic irresponsibility'; or as the writer Laurens van der Post put it, they and the Irish both 'realise the positive creative uses of irresponsibility'. They are impulsive and passionate people for whom hospitality and having a good time are the highest aims. Unlike the more serious Armenians who have suffered from genocidal attacks more than once, the Georgians have managed to dance their way through history and come out laughing. The Georgians grew out of a blend of Neolithic and Bronze-Age cultures, and the present-day nation is still a mix of very different types – the Megrels or Mingrelians in the west who are quick, smart, boastful, and can't be stopped from feeding guests, the naïve and funny Svans, the extremely hospitable and talkative Imeretians, the slow and careful Rachvels, the political and humorous Gurians, the calm wine-loving Kakhetians, not to mention the Karts, Khevsurians, Pshavians, Mokhevians and Meskhians. As for the Adjarians, they are said to have all the above qualities; they are ethnically and linguistically Georgian but mostly Muslim in religion.

Other groups share ethnicity and religion with the majority population but are linguistically distinct: these include the million or so Megrels, the Svans, and the Laz, most of whom (around 200,000) live across the border in the Hopa region of Turkey. Related to the Megrels, the Laz are very extrovert and humorous, and tend to have reddish hair.

MINORITY COMMUNITIES The **Armenians** form the largest ethnic minority in Georgia and are found all over the country; however, the vast majority live either in Tbilisi (200,000) and in the Akhalkalaki and Ninotsminda regions, known to them as Javakhk, where they form a majority of the population. Their ancestors settled here as refugees from western Anatolia during the 19th-century Russo-Turkish wars, and also just before and after World War I. It's a bleak area with poor infrastructure, and there is some discontent with the bad conditions here. Tbilisi, on the other hand, has always been a major centre of Armenian culture and continues to produce many leading figures in Armenian life. Their lingua franca has always been Russian, and few in the rural areas speak Georgian. The Armenian government is not particularly interested in changing its borders, but it takes an interest in the well being of the Armenian population in Georgia.

Russians are scattered thinly across Georgia, apart from small groups of religious dissidents such as Molokans and Doukhobors, mainly in the centre and south. The families of some arrived in the 19th century, but the bulk arrived in the Soviet period, settling mainly in urban and industrial areas such as Tbilisi and Rustavi as well as in Abkhazia. These later arrivals still tend not to speak Georgian and many are trying to emigrate, mainly to Russia but also to Canada and elsewhere. This is draining away many of Georgia's skilled workers and technicians. However, Georgians see Russian men as drunks and the women as sexually easy ('sleep with Russians, marry a Georgian' is the Georgian male's credo).

The **Azeri** population occupied the southeastern corner of the country, around Marneuli, Bolnisi and Gardabani, in the early 17th century when it was depopulated by the Persian wars. This is an underdeveloped area and life is harder than these hard-working farmers deserve, although they are relatively well off. They are mostly Shia Muslims, although not too fervently so. Between 1926 and 1989, when the national population doubled, their population quadrupled. Not all are ethnically Azeri in the purest sense, but it's generally accepted that all the Turkophone Muslims in Georgia can be included in this category, and the government of Azerbaijan does take a certain degree of responsibility for them.

Until recently the majority of the 165,000 **Ossetians** in Georgia lived outside the then autonomous region – mainly in Tbilisi and Rustavi, and also in some rural areas. An Indo-European people, speaking an Iranian language, they are unrelated to the other peoples of the Caucasus. They are held to be the descendants of the Alans, one of the many nomadic peoples who came out of Asia and settled in the north Caucasus. During the last two centuries they have increasingly moved into the highlands on the south of the Caucasus, living peacefully (and inter-marrying) with the Georgians. Now many have moved to South Ossetia, and there's a tendency towards learning Russian rather than Georgian, and strengthening cultural ties with the north Caucasus. Most are Orthodox Christians, although some of the later arrivals are Sunni Muslim; in fact, paganism still plays a strong part in their religious lives.

The **Abkhaz** are considered to be one of the aboriginal peoples of the Caucasus, entitling them to an autonomous republic under Stalin's scheme for ethnic relations (while the South Ossetians, having arrived relatively recently, were entitled only to an autonomous region). Even before secession, they almost all lived in Abkhazia, but they formed just 18% of the republic's population; since secession they form all of 25% of its population, due to other groups leaving. Closely related to the Adigh peoples of the northern Caucasus, they have preserved their traditional culture and their highly prized oral literary heritage. They are both Christians and Sunni Muslims, although many Muslims emigrated to Turkey after the Russian conquest in the 19th century.

Greeks live in the Tsalka and Tetri-Tskaro areas of Lower Kartli (the so-called Anatolian Greeks, or Rums), and on the Black Sea coast (the Pontian Greeks); although it's tempting to assume that the latter have been there ever since the classical Greeks established trading ports there, in fact they arrived from 1829, fleeing persecution in Turkey. Although most are Orthodox Christians, some in fact converted to Islam. There's a steady flow back to Greece, although some speak Pontian Ancient Greek rather than the modern language, and most of those in Lower Kartli (a poor isolated community) speak Turkish; many have also moved to Tbilisi.

Most of the **Kurds** in Georgia are Yezidi (Mithraist pagans), descended from refugees from Ottoman persecution. They live mainly in Tbilisi and Rustavi, but although fairly well integrated socially, they preserve their distinct ethnic identity, language and cultural traditions. There was also a small rural (Muslim and Turkish-speaking) population living in southern Georgia, which was deported to central Asia in 1944.

It's a proud boast in Georgia, and largely true, that **Jews** have lived there for 2,600 years without suffering persecution (ironically, yet another way for Georgians to show their superiority to the Russians). It may have helped that they have the same appetite for wine as the Georgians. The population is divided into about 10,000 Ashkenazim (European or Russian Jews) and 14,000 Georgian Jews (Georgian-speaking, and considered as Sephardim due to their religious ritual); over half live in Tbilisi, with many of the rest in the west of the country. As a rule they feel very attached to Georgia, and although over 17,000 have emigrated to Israel they maintain close links with Georgia and preserve Georgian cultural traditions.

Finally, a group that currently is scarcely represented in Georgia are the so-called **Meskhetian Turks**. Under the Ottomans, Javakheti was heavily Islamicised from 1624, producing a population of mixed Georgian and Turkish ethnicity; in November 1944 all 70,000–120,000 of these people were deported to central Asia, for supposedly pro-Turkish (and thus possibly pro-Axis) sentiments – even though most of their menfolk were serving in the Red Army. Unlike most other deported groups they were not allowed to return after the Stalinist era, and struggled to establish themselves in their new homes. After the break-up of the Soviet Union, and mob violence against them in Uzbekistan in 1989 (officially ascribed to a dispute over the price of strawberries), they began demanding to return home, moving to the northern Caucasus and Azerbaijan. Now they number around 300,000, of whom 100,000 live in camps in northern Azerbaijan. Georgia is reluctant to take them back, due to its lack of resources, but in 1996 agreed to a plan for 5,000 to return, subject to their learning the Georgian language and other conditions. Nothing happened, and in September 1998 a demonstration in their support in Tbilisi met with a heavy-handed response; due to international pressure an initial 5,000 should soon return. The government is still procrastinating, as it is already struggling to cope with the Abkhazian IDPs.

LANGUAGE

While the Turks and Azeris speak Turkic languages, and the Armenians, Ossetians and Russians speak Indo-European languages, **Georgian** is the most important of the Caucasian group of languages. This is divided into three families: the South Caucasian or Kartvelian – comprising Georgian (Kartuli), Megrelian, Laz and Svan, spoken by 3.5 million people in all – and the relatively similar northeastern and northwestern Caucasian families, spoken by about a million people each. These comprise about 40 languages in an area the size of France, although Strabo recorded that in the 1st century BC the Romans needed no fewer than 70 interpreters in the Dioscurias (Sukhumi) area alone. Just in Daghestan there are 14 ethnic groups and 29 languages, and it's no surprise that the name Caucasus derives from the Arabic for 'mountain of languages'.

Efforts have been made to place the Caucasian languages in a 'super-group' with the Indo-European, Turkic, Semitic, Finno-Ugric and even Chinese languages, but no links have been proved. Nor has it been possible to prove links with Basque, although some scholars speak of an Ibero-Caspian group.

The Caucasian languages are all grammatically complex; the northwestern languages have verbs with a huge variety of inflections, while the northeastern ones have simple verbs, but complex nouns, with up to eight grammatical classes (such as male, female, animal, and mass noun), and up to 46 cases. The southern languages, ie: Georgian, have both a large case system for the noun and complex verbs. Likewise, they all have complex sound systems. The northwestern languages have only two distinct vowels, but highly complex consonant systems. The northeastern languages have fewer consonants, but large numbers of vowels. The southern languages are simpler but still have enormous clusters of consonants, 'back-of-the-throat death-rattles' that utterly baffle foreigners. Georgians love to test foreigners with tongue-twisters such as '*Baqaqi tskalshi kikinebs*' (the frog is croaking in the water), and a similar one about the duck (*ikhwi*) going quack (*khaadha*) in the water. Just to make things even harder, there are no capital letters.

Naturally, **Russian** is used as the *lingua franca* of the area; everyone in Georgia is bilingual from an early age, and no-one has any hang-ups about using the colonisers' language. However, it is proposed to replace Russian by English as the second language in schools. **Turkish** may be useful in Batumi and also Kutaisi.

The Georgian alphabet has five vowels and 28 consonants, and looks like nothing else on earth, except the Armenian alphabet. An alphabet may have existed in the 3rd century BC but was supplanted by Greek and Aramaic; the present alphabet may have begun to evolve with the arrival of Christianity, and was certainly in use by AD450; after the 10th century a more cursive script was adopted that was smaller and easier to read. There's a variety of forms of many letters, but at least there's no upper or lower case. The Abkhaz language uses an extended Cyrillic (Russian) alphabet.

See *Appendix 1*, page 249 for vocabulary and other practical information.

RELIGION

Christianity was introduced to Georgia in the 1st century by the apostle Andrew the First-Called, who travelled around the Black Sea before becoming the first Patriarch of Constantinople, and also by the apostles Simon and Matthew. Armenia was converted to **Christianity** in AD301 (or perhaps AD314); in AD313 the Roman Emperor Constantine granted freedom of worship to Christians and it became the most favoured religion in the empire. However, it didn't become the sole official religion until AD380, while Georgia was converted in AD337, making it the world's second Christian nation. St Nino, a slave from Cappadocia, cured a child by placing her hair shirt on him and praying; Queen Nana heard of this and Nino cured her by prayer of some unknown malady, and converted her to Christianity. King Mirian followed his wife in converting when Nino was able to cause a thunderbolt to destroy the pagan idols, followed by an eclipse of the sun which didn't lift until he agreed to convert. However, Christianity was not firmly established until the 6th century, when the Syrian Fathers came from Antioch; it's uncertain whether they were Georgians or Chalcedonians, but it's clear they could speak the language before they arrived. They founded several monasteries in Kartli and Kakheti, such as Shiom-ghvine, Zedazeni, Samtavisi, Alaverdi, Nekresi and Davit-Gareja, and spread the gospel throughout the country. Between 790 and 861 more monasteries were founded by St Gregory of Khantza. In the 10th century classical texts such as Zeno's *On Nature* and Porphyrius were preserved in Georgian monasteries, and the texts of Buddhism were first translated by St Euthymius in the Georgian monastery on Mount Athos, in Greece. Bachkovo, the second most important monastery in Bulgaria, was founded in 1083 by the Georgian Grigorii Bakuriani, who renounced the governorship of Smolyan and Edirne to be a monk, and his brother Abasius.

For centuries the Orthodox Church was split by theological disputes and heresies: firstly Arianism, which denied the full deity of Jesus claiming that he was created by God, and 'there was a time when he was not', and then from the 4th century Monophysitism, the doctrine that Jesus had only one nature, rather than two, divine and human. Finally, in the 5th century, Nestorianism argued against the Virgin Mary being called 'mother of God', claiming she was mother of Christ only in his human aspect. Monophysitism was popular in the monasteries of Davit-Gareja and it survives as official doctrine of the Armenian Church; however, the Georgian Apostolic Autocephalous Church has followed the official Orthodox line. It was granted autocephaly or self-governing status in AD466; this was abolished in 1811, when authority was transferred to the Moscow patriarchate.

Stalin repressed religion here as elsewhere, but by 1943 he felt he'd broken its back and recognised autocephaly. In the post-Stalinist period there was a limited revival in the Church's fortunes, and from 1988 some churches were reopened. However, it never played the sort of role in the nationalist movement that the Roman Catholic Church did in Poland and Lithuania, partly due to its conservative hierarchical nature and its addiction to being allied with authority, and partly due to the Catholicos, Ilia II, having been selected by the KGB.

While the Orthodox Church may seem utterly conservative, many monks are extremely fundamentalist and regard the Catholicos and priests as dangerously liberal. In particular, the decision to join the World Council of Churches was seen as virtually heretical (Orthodox doctrine being that there are no other legitimate churches), and Ilia was forced to reverse this in 1997. Nevertheless the next year he celebrated the 20th anniversary of the election of the Pope, who then visited Georgia in 1999. The True Orthodox sect, which also exists in Russia and Greece, is also active here, and has links with extreme nationalist groups such as the Zviadists. Fundamentalist groups such as Jvari (the Cross) and the Society of Saint David the Builder have been accused of orchestrating attacks on Baptists, Pentecostalists and Jehovah's Witnesses; but Saakashvili has tackled harassment of those following non-traditional faiths, for instance sending police to break into a church and arrest a priest blamed for attacks on Jehovah's Witnesses. There is widespread discrimination against the 14,000-odd **Jehovah's Witnesses** in particular, due mainly to their pacificism. The tiny **Roman Catholic** congregation is due largely to Turkish oppression of Orthodox believers in the 17th century, mainly in Meskheti.

As described above, there are various **Muslim** communities (mostly Shia) and a very long-established **Jewish** presence (see page 38), with synagogues in Tbilisi, Kutaisi and Batumi. Most of the Kurds are Yezid or openly **pagan** rather than Muslim, but in fact pagan influences can be found throughout Georgia, and above all in the remoter mountain areas. Decorative motifs are often derived from nature worship, and fertility rites and offerings can be found in many places, notably trees with pieces of cloth tied to the branches, as at a Cornish holy well. This is especially so in Svaneti – see page 199 for more details.

There are also many premature deaths in Svaneti – see page 201 for the elaborate funeral rites there. Georgian cemeteries are usually fenced plots on the edge of the fields, rather than next to a village church; in the west of the country the graves can be very elaborate, often roofed and with benches, and sometimes a family plot will be more like a *dacha* or summerhouse. Easter in particular is a time for feasting at the graveside. Weddings are also big events in Georgia, traditionally lasting for two or three days, with brain-damaging quantities of alcohol consumed. On summer and autumn Saturdays (the Tbilisoba weekend seems particularly popular in Tbilisi) you'll see many convoys of over-excited people rushing to and from churches, hooting and yelling and driving even worse than usual. Women in particular should dress respectfully to enter churches, and cover their heads; in Tbilisi there is less need for this.

CULTURE

Lovers of **architecture** will already be aware of Georgia's churches. On a compact groundplan they combine simple and efficient forms with attractive proportions and perfect harmony with their setting. The oldest, dating from the 4th to 6th centuries, are basilicas derived from the law courts of Rome and Byzantium, a tradition transmitted via Syria and Asia Minor. These are relatively long straight buildings with a semi-circular apse at the east end for the altar and priest. In Georgia they take two forms: firstly triple-aisled with a common ceiling and no transepts, and then from the late 6th century a uniquely Georgian form known as the triple-naved basilica, which has longitudinal walls and doors rather than arches, and again no transepts. Bolnisi Sioni is the only survivor of the first type, with later and less pure forms at Anchiskhati and Urbnisi.

Domed churches derive from the form of eastern Georgian homes since the 3rd or 4th millennium BC; from the 6th century AD these developed into cruciform churches, with a central cupola at the centre of a cross. In a cruciform church the central area becomes the liturgical focus of the church, under a dome that symbolises the sphere of heaven. Again there are two types: firstly with a semi-circular apse at the east end and the other ends square (such as Samtsevrisi), and secondly the tetraconch form, with apses on all four arms of the cross. This developed fast around the turn of the 7th century, when the Jvari church at Mtskheta, with smaller chambers filling the spaces between the arms, became the prototype for many others such as Ateni Sioni, Dzveli-Shuamta, Martvili and Dranda. This architectural flowering was stopped by the Arab invasion in the second half of the 7th century; however, the Georgian Renaissance brought a new climax in the 11th and 12th centuries, with much bigger churches such as Svetitskhoveli (Mtskheta), Bagrati (Kutaisi) and Alaverdi. In these churches too the interior seems unexpectedly large, since the compact proportions of the groundplan keep the volumes tightly packed.

Many of the churches are decorated with **frescoes**, which are also largely based on Byzantine traditions. Until the mid 9th century the church discouraged the painting of human images, and in the Great Iconoclasm of AD726–843 all religious art other than images of the cross and symbolic birds and plants was destroyed. However, Byzantine art then entered a Golden Age, named after the ruling Macedonian dynasty, in which the development of the cruciform church was matched by the flowering of fresco and mosaic art. This was now organised thematically with Christ Pantocrater (Lord of All) in the central dome, the Virgin in the apse over the altar, and the Life of Christ and the saints painted elsewhere.

In the Greek tradition the figures portrayed in religious art were strongly modelled but unemotional, with a calm dignity and stern grandeur. However, Georgia was also marked by the much freer and more humanistic tradition of Antioch and Alexandria, in which figures were portrayed more naturalistically and with concern for their emotional impact. There are few ancient mosaics in Georgia, but fresco art reached its peak between the 11th century and the first half of the 13th. The best are those preserved in the churches of Ateni Sioni, Kintsvisi, Timotesubani and Ubisi; and in the cave monasteries of Bertubani and Udabno (at Davit-Gareja) and Vardzia, as well as in Svaneti; others worth looking at are in the churches of Nekresi, Zemo Krikhi and Gelati.

Icons (religious images) were also produced, of three types: silver, painted on wood, and combined (silver and painting), the silver surface of the icon being generally covered with gilt. The images, of Christ, the Virgin and saints, followed the same stylistic patterns as the frescoes. The standard of metalwork in Georgia is amazing – see pages 123–5.

The sack of Constantinople by the Fourth Crusade was closely followed in Georgia by the Mongol invasions, bringing an end to the high period of Georgian religious art. However, in the secular sphere (illuminated manuscripts, for instance), Persian influence later led to much fine work in Georgia.

Perhaps it's unfortunate that Georgia's best-known **paintings** are those of Pirosmani, as his charming naïve works have nearly hidden from foreign view the country's many other fine artists. Many of these worked in Paris in the 1920s and 1930s and were well known at the time. Perhaps the best known was Elena Akhvlediani (1901–75), who was born in Telavi. Her mother was a princess but her father was poor; however, they managed to send her to Tbilisi's Second Gymnasium in 1911 and then to the Tbilisi Art Academy. She spent two years in Italy, and three in Paris, where she exhibited in the Salon des Indépendents, before returning to Georgia in 1927, where she worked for Koté Marjanishvili as a stage designer. After a long and varied career, she was declared a People's Artist of Georgia in 1960, and awarded the Rustaveli Prize in 1971. She had a wide range of styles, none especially challenging, and was the most romantic of the Georgian painters, with a great interest in traditional rural life. She also produced designs for films, and many illustrations for books, by Longfellow and Mark Twain among others, and for some children's stories.

David Kakabadze was born to a peasant family near Kutaisi in 1889, studied science in St Petersburg until 1918, but was then able to change to an artistic career, going to study in Paris in 1920 before living in Tbilisi from 1927 until his death in 1952. Lado Gudiashvili was born in Tbilisi in 1896 and lived in Paris from 1920 to 1925 and then in Tbilisi until his death in 1980. He toed the party line during the Stalinist period (although for some reason his characters have no ears), but also produced bitterly ironic graphics for private consumption. Niko Pirosmani (once known as Piroshmanvili) was born in 1862 and moved to Tbilisi when he was orphaned; he worked as a self-taught sign-painter, earning drinks with his quirky portraits. He was 'discovered' in 1912 by three artists down from Moscow on their holidays, but despite increased earnings his lifestyle did not change. In 1918 he was found unconscious in a basement and taken as an unknown beggar to hospital, where he died. Only 200 of possibly 2,000 paintings survive; quite a few can be viewed on the websites www.parliament.ge and www.steele.com. A new website selling Georgian art is www.Georgian-Art.com. The contemporary art scene is surprisingly lively; two of my favourites are Gogi Lazarishvili and Irakli Sutidze.

There's also a strong tradition in Georgia of public art, most notably monumental **sculpture** and mosaics that somehow managed to avoid being totally derailed by communist dogma (there are also quite a few surviving Stalin busts across the country). The best-known sculptor is Elgudja Amashukeli, whose Mother Georgia (1958–63), King Vakhtang Gorgasali (1967) and Pirosmani (1975) in Tbilisi, and King David the Builder (1995) in Kutaisi, are all characterised by stylised monumentalism and muscularity. His contemporary Merab Merabishvili was responsible for the statues of Griboedev (1961) west of Saarbrücken Platz in Tbilisi, and of Irakli II in Telavi. A possible successor is Merab Berdzenishvili who created the statues of the poets Galaction Tabidze and David Guramishvili (1966) near Chavchavadze Avenue 21, of Paliashvili (1973) outside the Opera House, and of King David the Builder (1997) outside the Hotel Iveria, all in Tbilisi. In Moscow the 'monstrous creations' of Zurab Tsereteli are impossible to avoid (thanks to his schoolboy friendship with Mayor Luzhkov) – freakish iron reanimations of Russian folk tales and other high kitsch. A recent project was a 100m-high statue of Columbus to be erected in Puerto Rico to commemorate the 'discovery' of America in 1492. When he saw it the client cancelled the deal, but Tsereteli swiftly arranged for the city of Moscow to buy the statue, calling it 'Peter the Great' (as founder of the Russian navy); Dervla Murphy described its 'monumental kitsch ... a grotesque agglomeration of ships and sails and rigging seeming to rise out of the river, dwarfing every building in sight'. Although he has a house with a very strange and wonderful garden in the hills outside Tbilisi (just visible to the left of the Manglisi road soon after the Vake cemetery), there's very little of his work to be seen in the city, except for the psychedelic mosaic façade of the Israeli embassy (1977), another on the Ortachala bus station (1973), and the statue of St George and the Dragon now being installed in Freedom Square.

A uniquely Georgian style of **theatre**, stylised but emotionally powerful, has developed, which is rightly seen as one of its national treasures. Under great directors like Robert Sturua (who runs the Rustaveli Theatre in Tbilisi), this style is turned loose on foreign classics as much as on Georgian texts. Shakespeare is a particular favourite, with very successful world tours of plays such as *Richard III*, which oddly is seen as his greatest work. ('It's magnificent, but it's not Shakespeare,' was the comment of the Royal Shakespeare Company's director Adrian Noble.) It's remarkable how many Shakespearean references Georgian journalists use.

GIFT, the Georgian International Festival of the Theatre, was founded in 1997 with a bravura publicity campaign and made a great impact, with many highly renowned international artists and companies appearing for next to nothing; the 1998 festival was smaller, due to funding problems, but future festivals, in or around September each year, based at Tbilisi's Marjanishvili Theatre, should be well worth seeing.

The Georgian National **Ballet** is usually abroad nowadays, thanks to a worldwide reputation for athleticism and spectacle, including sabre dances and knife-throwing. The State Ballet, now run by Nina Ananiashvili, ex-prima ballerina of the Bolshoi and American Ballet Theatre, is undergoing a remarkable revival; the ballets of George Balanchine (see page 183) are of course very important to them.

Georgia also had a highly successful **cinema** industry, based at the Gruzhia film studios in Tbilisi's Digomi suburb. Sandro Akhmetil worked with the Rustaveli Theatre from 1928 to 1935 before directing films to such effect that he now has a metro station named after him. Koté Marjanishvili also worked at the Rustaveli, and the main square on the left bank of the Mtkvari is named after him. Both men were shot in Stalin's reign of terror. Sergei Paradjanov was born to an Armenian family in Tbilisi and lived in Kyiv until his death in 1990, so, although he filmed quintessentially Georgian subjects such as *The Surami Fortress*, he's not generally thought of as a Georgian director. Misha Chaiureli, Stalin's favourite director and a personal friend, made historical and propaganda films, and his daughter Sophiko Chiaureli starred in Paradjanov's masterpiece *The Colour of Pomegranates*. The successful biopic *Pirosmani* was directed by Eldar Shengelaia, son of the director Nikoloz Shengelaia and the actress Nato Vachnadze, after whom the *Nato*, the Georgian equivalent of the Oscar, is named. The most successful Georgian film of recent years is *Repentance* (*Monanieba*; 1986, directed by Tenghiz Abuladze), about a dictator who was a thinly veiled composite of Stalin and Beria; it won six prizes. Temur Babluani's *The Sun of the Sleepless* (1991) won a Silver Bear at the Berlin Film Festival. The director Nana Jorjadze, meanwhile, earned an Oscar nomination for *Chef in Love* (with the French comic star Pierre Richard) in 1996 and was elected a member of the Academy of Motion Picture Arts and Sciences.

The Georgian industry has more or less collapsed, but fine directors such as Jorjadze, Otar Iosseliani, Mikheil Kobakhidze, Dino Tsintsadze and Irakli Kvirikadze are doing well abroad (especially in France), as well as actors such as Dato Bakhtadze, Nutsa Kukhianidze and Merab Ninidze.

The classic work of Georgian **literature** is *The Knight in the Panther's Skin*, by Shota Rustaveli, who was Queen Tamar's treasurer; the writer Fitzroy Maclean described it as 'a fine allegorical poem of great breadth of vision, harmoniously fusing the currents of neo-Platonist philosophy and eastern romance.' It foreshadows the literature of courtly (Platonic) love of the European Renaissance, but was only translated into English after World War I by Marjory Wardrop, whose brother Oliver was then Britain's chief commissioner of Transcaucasia. In the 19th century there was a fine crop of romantic poets, led by Alexander Chavchavadze (1786–1846), a friend of the Russians Pushkin and Griboedov (who married his daughter); others included Nikoloz Baratashvili (1817–45) and Akaki Tsereteli (1840–1915), who is not to be confused with the radical journalist Georgi Tsereteli (1842–1900). Galaction Tabidze (1892–1959) is the most popular of Georgia's 20th-century poets, whose suicide is still bitterly regretted. His less famous cousin Titsian Tabidze (born 1895) was shot in the purge of 1937 (he was a close friend of Boris Pasternak, who translated his work into English, and whose genuine love of Georgia probably helped save him in the purges; many of his translations of Georgian poetry were done in Tabidze's flat on Griboedov kucha in Tbilisi). Currently Russia's hottest novelist is Grigori Chkartishvili (under the un-Georgian pseudonym Boris Akunin) whose books about his fictional 19th-century detective Fandorin are aimed at the middle class and not at all trashy.

GEORGIAN MUSIC Georgia has a wonderful and highly distinctive tradition of polyphonic **singing**, which developed several hundred years before it appeared in western Europe. Instrumental music and music for dancing are also quite common, but as later developments from the vocal tradition. Folk songs span many genres, with women singing traditional lullaby and healing songs, while men, often accompanied by large quantities of wine, sing war and feasting songs; some festival songs may have been sung by men and women together.

Igor Stravinsky said that Georgian polyphony was 'more important than all the discoveries of new music'. This was recognised when it was named part of humanity's intangible cultural heritage by UNESCO in 2001 and the Research Center for Traditional Polyphony of Georgia was founded at Tbilisi State Conservatoire. Its website (*www.polyphony.ge/en/homepage/home.php*) is a great source of information on Georgian song.

Georgians sing in a tuning all their own, which baffled the 19th-century musicologists who first tried to transcribe Georgian folk songs and church chants into Western notation. Georgian folk music is modal and often breaks out of simple 'major' or 'minor' classifications, being characterised more by the dissonance and resolution of close harmony. This produces a rich sonorous flow of sound stabbed from time to time by startling disharmonies, often repeated, before returning to the smooth flow. Parallel firsts, fifths and octaves, long 'banned' in the West, still predominate in Georgia; minor and major thirds are both considered dissonant, hence the frequent use of non-resolving fourths and sevenths.

Polyphony and harmony are both supposed to have existed in Georgia when both Orient and Occident were still monodic. It's easy to see the roots of polyphony in Georgian choral song, in which a single melody was supported by an organ-point or plain chant, to keep the lead singer in pitch; in Georgia the plain chant is usually sung by the middle part. This very strong drone may have evolved for the church acoustic. The 11th-century scholar Ioanne Petrisi explained the nature of the Trinity in terms of the harmonic and melodic functions of the three voices – the *mzehekri mazkhr* or top voice (in fact a mid tenor), *zhir*, a middle voice or low tenor, and *bam* or bass. The various genres of folk song include *mushuri* (working songs), *supruli* (table songs, including toasts), *satrpialo* (love songs) and *sagmiro* (epic songs – a long solo from the oral tradition or from a 19th-century writer such as Chavchavadze). Songs are mostly in the form of a strophic rondo, with or without a refrain, with syllabic setting as a rule. Rhythmically, there's often a swift alternation of 3/4 and 6/8 in the same phrase, accounting for the 'bouncy' nature of Georgian secular song.

The most complex polyphony is to be found in the western regions, above all in Guria, where the composer Honegger was defeated trying to notate a seven-part song; every voice is given a special degree of freedom, with even the bass improvising freely and taking solos. *Naduri* songs (from *nadi*, voluntary co-operative labour for harvesting or house-building) are unique to Guria, with two choruses of four voices alternating; the top voice (*gamkivani* or *krimanchuli*) simply indulges in yodel-like wordless cries, the tenor or *damtskebi* carries the poetic text, the third voice or *shemkmobari* carries the organ-point, and the bass or *bani* sings a wordless melodic counterpoint to the tenor. The Mingrelians also excel in weaving voices, with 'composed' *ritenuti* and *accelerandi*. Mingrelia is the only place where you may find mixed choruses of men and women. Wordless (glossolalic) phrases (like 'hey-nonny-no' in an English madrigal) are especially common in the west of Georgia.

Svaneti, high in the Caucasus, has kept alive a primeval and ethereal style of three-part singing, with pentatonic harmonies (unlike the rest of Georgia). This is often accompanied by the *changi*, the Svan harp, which looks as if it's come straight off a Greek vase, or the lute-like *chianuri* or *panduri* (which can only be played by men). Svaneti is also rich in round-dances called *perkhuli*, which gradually accelerate to end in fantastic male dance solos, and in female mourning songs. The funeral traditions here and in Racha combine pre-Christian wailing traditions with Christian singing, mainly by women though sometimes by men, but not together.

In eastern Georgian songs the bass often sings a long steady wordless drone, over which the heroic tenors sing ornamented tunes with words in close harmony; church chants show similarities to the region's secular music, although all parts sing words. Some of the richest, most sonorous and wine-soaked songs predictably come from Kakheti, while further south you find the long, lyrical *orovel*, a rare example of a solo song originally sung while ploughing or riding an oxcart. These are closely related in name and sound to the *horhovel* songs of Armenia.

Church music, which shows a direct line of descent from Byzantium, is slower and softer than secular music with harmonies and melodic patterns more interwoven, and a static rhythm. Hymns are sung with great intensity and voices overlapping to give continuous moving harmonies, as if the singers are not breathing. The unique Orthodox chant tradition of medieval Georgia survives in the form of manuscripts from the 10th century onwards and from handwritten transcriptions from the early 20th century into Western musical notation. Chant developed as Byzantine texts were translated in Palestine and Mount Athos in the 9th and 10th centuries by Georgian monk scholars such as Giorgi Mtatsmindeli and Grigol Khandzteli.

Three-part homophonic chant is believed to have begun at this period, as academies were founded to propagate church traditions such as chanting, centred on Gelati monastery near Kutaisi. Students spent up to seven years learning their craft from *sruligalobeli* (master chanters) before being initiated as chanters themselves.

The *neumas* (musical notation) was gradually lost from the 17th century, and only deciphered in the mid 20th century, although local styles were passed down verbally, while medieval neumatic notation is still undeciphered. A hymn to the Virgin by King Demetre I (1125–56), 'You are the Vine' (*Shen Khar Venakhi*), has also been sung at weddings for a century or more. The mixture of a strong secular singing tradition and the professional school of church chant yielded a genre of 'folk-sacred' songs such as *chona*, fertility songs performed just before Easter, and *alilo*, carols sung around the village on Christmas Eve (5 January). Though group singing is the dominant traditional form of music, **instruments** abound in Georgia, the oldest yet found being a 3,000-year-old bone shawm (*salamuri*) from near Mtskheta. The *doli*, a round skin-covered drum, beat out 5/4 rhythms to accompany ancient Georgians into battle (as attested by Xenophon, writing about the Mossynoeci tribe). Common instruments today include the *panduri*, a three-stringed lute from eastern Georgia, the *chonguri*, a four-stringed plucked lute from western Georgia, and from Svaneti and Racha the *chianuri*, a viol-like three-stringed bowed instrument employing harmonics, and the *changi*, a hand-carved wooden harp. There are two traditional bagpipes, the *chiboni* from Adjara and the *gudatsviri* from Racha. Introduced instruments include the clarinet-like *duduki* and the oboe-like *zurna*, both from Armenia (see below).

From the 19th century Western harmonies have combined with Georgian three-part singing to form a popular genre known as 'urban music', which can now be heard in every car and bar of Georgia. It has catchy tunes and sentimental lyrics, sung in simple harmony and sometimes accompanied by guitar or piano. The most famous example is *Suliko*, a song of homesickness by the poet Akaki Tsereteli, which as everyone will remind you was Stalin's favourite.

In the communist period, the Rustavi Choir was the best known of Georgia's professional ensembles, and produced some fine recordings, now on CD, which serve as a good introduction to Georgian song. Similarly the Tsinandali Choir produced an enjoyable collection, *Table Songs of Georgia*, in fact all from Kakheti. As ever, French companies such as Ocora have produced some good compilations of field recordings, including a fine collection from Svaneti. However, in post-communist Georgia it's the Anchiskhati Choir (*www.anchiskhati.org*) and a group called Mtiebi ('Morning Star') who have emerged as the leaders in rediscovering and preserving the most authentic examples of Georgian song; Mtiebi's CD is available from Edition Musikat, Charlottenstasse 12, 70182 Stuttgart, Germany (✆ +49 71 124 0709; f +49 711 2360 816; e *julius@buch-julius.de*). The Anchiskhati Choir's five CDs are available from Marika Lapauri-Burk, Max-Brauer-Allee 68, 22765 Hamburg, Germany (✆f +49 40 389 2222; e *info@lile.de; www.lile.de*). Their first CD, *Anchiskhati Choir – Sacred Music from the Medieval Ages – Georgian Polyphonic Singing*, is a great introduction. Others to look out for include Zedashe, Elesa and the women's choir Mzetamze; Georgian choirs have also appeared in the West, such as the London Georgian Singers, the Canadian groups Kavkasia and Darbazi (*www.argosoft.com/darbazi*), and in the USA Iveria (*www.iveria.org*), which has released a CD, *Songs from the Republic of Georgia*.

In addition, *99 Georgian Songs, a work book for singers* by Mtiebi's founder, the late Edisher Garakanidze, is published by the Centre for Performance Research at the University of Wales, 6 Science Park, Aberystwyth SY23 3AH (*www.performancebooks.co.uk*). Songbooks are available online from Northern Harmony in Vermont (*www.northernharmony.pair.com/store/GEsongbooks.html*). If you read German, see also *Musik aus Georgien* by Thomas Houssermann (Erka Verlag, 1993). If addicted, you could join the Georgian Harmony Association (*c/o Michael Bloom, 5 Alder Lodge, 292 Bury St West, London N9 9LL;* ✆ *020 8360 9991;* e *michaelbloom1@compuserve.com*), or the Maspindzeli choir in London (*http://maspindzeli.org.uk*). There should soon be detailed information on Georgian music on www.geofolk.net.

In the field of **classical music**, the great bass Paata Burchuladze (born 1955) is Georgia's main claim to fame; he's very much in the Western operatic tradition rather

Katie (originally Ketevan) Melua has put Georgia on the map for a whole generation of Westerners. However, as a folk-jazz-bluesy singer-songwriter inspired by Eva Cassidy, Ella Fitzgerald, Freddie Mercury, Nick Drake, Joni Mitchell and Bob Dylan, she seems an unlikely candidate for chart success, even with her classically Georgian good looks and her lack of ego.

Born in Kutaisi in 1984, she came to Britain in 1992 when her surgeon father took a job in Belfast, moving to Surrey in 1997. As a student at the Brit School for Performing Arts, she was discovered by producer Mike Batt; fortunately Melua was unaware of his earlier career as creator of *The Wombles*.

Her first album, *Call Off The Search*, was released in 2003, with songs by Melua, Batt, John Mayall and Randy Newman; it sold 1.7 million copies in the UK, making her the country's best-selling female artist two years running, and three million abroad. Her debut single, 'The Closest Thing to Crazy', written by Batt, was a top-ten hit in the UK. Her follow-up album *Piece By Piece*, released in 2005, was darker but just as successful.

In 2005 she became a British citizen, partly so as to be able to travel without needing visas almost everywhere, but she retains Georgian citizenship. She's never been seen as a turncoat in Georgia – probably because few over the age of 16 recognise the name, and those who do think of her as 'half-Georgian' – and returned in early 2005 to record with a traditional male-voice choir. She gave her first concert there in November 2005 and says she'd like to do an album of Georgian folk songs. A year later she performed the world's deepest gig on a Norwegian oil rig, a record 303m underwater.

Melua's sense of humour came to the fore after a tongue-in-cheek media debate about the scientific accuracy of some lyrics in her song 'Nine Million Bicycles'. She duly produced a spoof 'corrected' version which went: 'We are 13.7 billion light-years from the edge of the observable universe. That's a good estimate with well-defined error bars and with the available information, I predict that I will always be with you.'

For more information see www.katiemelua.com.

than the Russian, and is in great demand worldwide. Less well known are the conductors Jansugh Kakhidze and Evgeni Mikeladze, the pianist Eliso Virsaladze, and the violinists Elizabeth Batiashvili and Marina Iashvili. The Tbilisi opera house is named after the composer Zakaria Paliashvili (1871–1933), who established classical music in Georgia with his operas *Abessalom and Eteri* (1918, a monumental tragedy), the lyric-dramatic *Daisi* (1923, prefiguring Khachaturian but with a 'Georgian' tone in its peasant crowd scenes) and the heroic-patriotic *Latavra* (1927). Mikhail Ippolitov-Ivanov (1859–1935), a student of Rimsky-Korsakov, was conductor of the Tbilisi Symphony Orchestra for a decade, and his *Caucasian Sketches* (1895) is based on Georgian folk tunes. It may be interesting to know that Stravinsky based *Les Noces* on Georgian harmonic and melodic patterns. The leading Georgian composer of the 20th century was Gia Kancheli (born 1935), whose violent early symphonies have given way to increasingly subdued, wistful later works.

Armenia, by contrast, is known for lively instrumental music (derived from the Islamic world) with drums and the *duduk*, like a reedy clarinet (usually played in pairs, with the second instrument providing a drone). The other traditional style is that of the *ashugs* or troubadours, who were poets and storytellers as well as musicians. The most famous was Sayat Nova (1712–95) who was based in Tbilisi, at the court of Irakli II.

2

Practical Information

WHEN TO VISIT (AND WHY)

Firstly, for as long as Georgia remains at risk of energy shortages, winter is not the smartest time to visit, except for Tbilisi and the ski resorts. High summer can be too hot and humid, but spring and autumn are ideal times to visit; in particular the golden autumn colours can be spectacular, and the wine harvest makes this a great time to visit Kakheti.

HIGHLIGHTS

Given the difficulties and unpredictabilities of travel in Georgia, many visitors will confine themselves to Tbilisi, with brief excursions to places such as Mtskheta and Davit-Gareja. However, the rewards for venturing outside the capital are great for those prepared to make the effort. To the east, Kakheti is ideally placed for an outing of two to four days, sampling wines and churches, and to the north the Georgian Military Highway leads into the heart of the High Caucasus. The country's main axis is the highway from Tbilisi to Kutaisi and on to Poti or Batumi, or to Zugdidi and Abkhazia; this begins by following the Mtkvari and then crosses into the Rioni Basin in the west of the country. Batumi is one of the most pleasant and laid-back cities in Georgia, although the Black Sea's beaches are not really worth visiting. From Zugdidi it's also possible to head north into the heart of the Caucasus, to the region of Svaneti where unique architecture and semi-pagan customs are preserved.

i TOURIST INFORMATION

There's no system for providing tourists with information in Georgia (although a tourist information centre is planned in Tbilisi, probably on Pushkin Square), so you should try to get all the information you think you'll need before departure. The **Department of Tourism and Resorts** (*Kazbegi Av 12A, 0160 Tbilisi;* ℄ *+995 32 381535/54;* f *+995 32 294052;* e *georgia@ tourism.gov.ge; www.tourism.gov.ge*) may answer specific questions, but they have just one general brochure and a map to mail out. The mobile phone company Geocell has an information number (℄ *7099; US$0.17/min*) where there should be an English-speaking operator.

Your best bet is probably to use the internet, although searches for 'Georgia' always produce vast amounts of material on the US state – try 'Tbilisi' or 'Caucasus' instead. See page 254 for useful websites.

If venturing anywhere outside Tbilisi, you should pick up the third edition of the 1:625,000 map of Georgia, published by International Travel Maps of Vancouver BC and available in major stores such as **Stanfords** (*12 Long Acre, London WC2E 9LP;* ℄ *020 7836 1321;* f *020 7836 0189;* e *sales@stanfords.co.uk*). A superior 1:800,000 version of this is produced in Germany by ERKA-Verlag, called *Georgien – Reisekarte* (ISBN 3-929184-07-9). There's also a 1:1,000,000 map of the entire Caucasus which includes parts of Russia, Turkey and Iran: this is published by GiziMap of Budapest and is also available through Bartholomew's at Stanfords and other shops, or through Caucasus Travel, who have put their own cover on it.

TOUR OPERATORS

UK

Exodus 9 Weir Rd, London SW12 0NE; ℡ 020 8675 5550, 0870 950 0039; f 8673 0779; e info@exodus.co.uk; www.exodus.co.uk. In the past this company has also operated hiking trips to Georgia but is not currently doing so. It may be worth contacting Exodus, however, to see if this has changed.

Explore Nelson Hse, 55 Victoria Rd, Farnborough GU14 7PA; ℡ 0870 333 4001; f 01252 391110; e info@explore.co.uk; www.explore.co.uk. This company offers hiking trips. Their £1,229 Land of the Golden Fleece tour spends 6 days in Armenia & 10 in Georgia, with a bit of walking at Gudauri, Kazbegi & Davit-Gareja.

Regent Holidays 15 John St, Bristol BS1 2HR; ℡ 0870 499 0911; f 0117 925 4866; e regent@regent-holidays.co.uk; www.regent-holidays.co.uk. Regent is the leading British operator, offering tailor-made tours to suit any budget or interest. It can book as much or as little as required of accommodation, transport, guides or other services. Long weekends cost from £535 in Tbilisi; their nine-day Classic Georgia tour costs from £1,190 low season or £1,250 high pp. All prices include flights.

Ride World Wide Staddon Farm, North Tawton, Devon EX20 2BX; ℡ 01837 82544; f 01837 82179; e info@rideworldwide.com; www.rideworldwide.co.uk. Offers a 10-day horseback trip for £1,370, exploring the little-touristed area south & southwest of Tbilisi including the 12th-century monasteries of Gudarekhi & Pitareti.

Silk Road and Beyond 371 Kensington High St, London W14 8QZ; ℡ 020 7371 3131; f 020 7602 9715; e sales@silkroadandbeyond.co.uk; www.silkroadandbeyond.co.uk. Offers a 9-day private tour from £1,190 (sharing) or £1,590 sgl; a 5-day break in Tbilisi costs £695/795.

Steppes East 51 Castle St, Cirencester, Wilts GL7 1QD; ℡ 01285 651010, 880980; f 01285 885888; e east@steppestravel.co.uk; www.steppestravel.co.uk. Steppes East also arranges trips to Georgia as well as Armenia & Azerbaijan; these are custom-made but a 16-day tour inc Svaneti & Kazbegi would cost £1,650.

The Traveller & Palanquin 92 Great Russell St, London WC1B 3PS; ℡ 020 7436 9343; www.the-traveller.co.uk. This company offers a Caucasian Traveller cultural tour (covering Georgia, Armenia & Azerbaijan) which costs US$2,550 for 17 days; it also runs 11-day trips to Georgia, though not every year.

Wild Frontiers Adventure Travel 6 Townmead Business Centre, William Morris Way, London SW6 2SZ; ℡ 020 7736 3968; f 020 7751 0710; www.wildfrontiers.co.uk. This company offers adventurous trips such as the Short Walk in the Caucasus or Land of Myths & Mountains, both 9 days for £1,050 (plus £400 for flights from the UK), visiting Gudauri & Kazbegi, plus Bakuriani & Vardzia on the Land of Myths & Mountains tour. It also combines Georgia with Azerbaijan & Armenia, a 14-day trip costing £1,400 (plus flights), as well as skiing at Gudauri.

Cruising

Noble Caledonia 2 Chester Close, London SW1X 7BE; ℡ 020 7752 0000; f 020 7245 0388; info@noble-caledonia.co.uk; www.noble-caledonia.co.uk. Offers a Black Sea circuit inc a stop in Batumi, with excursions as far afield as Gelati, from £1,995.

US From the United States there are more expensive trips on offer.

MIR 85 South Washington St, Suite 210, Seattle, WA 98104; ℡ +1 800 424 7289, 206 624 7289; fax +1 206 624 7360; e info@mircorp.com; www.mircorp.com. MIR offers a 13-day cultural tour running weekly through the summer, for US$3,395.

Mountain Travel Sobek 1266 66th St, Suite 4, Emeryville, CA 94608; ℡ +1 888 687 6235, 510 594 6000; f +1 510 594 6001; e info@mtsobek.com; www.mtsobek.com. Similar to Wilderness Travel (see below).

Wilderness Travel 1102 9th St, Berkeley, CA 94710; ℡ +1 800 368 2794; f +1 510 558 249. This company offers 14-day trips for about US$3,600, inc strenuous hiking in Tusheti.

AROUND THE WORLD

Adventure Centre Toronto; ☎ +1 416 922 7584, & Adventure Center, Emeryville, California; ☎ +1 800 227 8747. Offers the Explore trip (see UK).

Adventure World Australia; 5 branches inc Sydney; ☎ +61 02 8913 0700. Offers the Explore trip (see UK).

ERKA Reisen Postfach 4240, Robert Stolz Str 21, 76626 Bruchsal; ☎ +49 7257 930390; f +49 7257 930392; e service@erkareisen.de; www.erkareisen.de. This German company offers tours for Germans,

GEORGIA

Alioni Travel Services Kazbegi St; ☎ 922993; f 380666; e alionitour@gol.ge; www.alionitour.ge. Offers car tours, hiking & camping trips, homestays & cultural trips, including to Tusheti, Kakheti & Davit-Gareja.

Argotour Paliashvili 28/8; ☎ 292706, 292779; f 220422; e argotourism@gol.ge; www.argotour.com. Marjanishvili 5; ☎ 952634, 953985. Shevchenko 10; ☎ 921780. Shartava 7; ☎ 388708. This company's branches are open 7 days a week (Mon–Sat 09.30–19.00, Sun 10.00–18.00); it also has a desk in the Courtyard by Marriott Hotel, Freedom Square 4; ☎/f 999042; e argotour_hotel@service.net.ge.

Caucasus Travel Leselidze 44/11, 0105 Tbilisi; ☎ 987400; f 987399; e online@caucasustravel.com; www.caucasustravel.com. Set up in 1991 by some of Georgia's leading climbers as Caucasian Travel, the company was renamed when it was found that this could give offence; now it's the leading agency dealing with incoming tourists & has associated companies offering car hire, business consultancy & adventure tours. Service is superb & they're totally reliable regarding what is possible & safe; their website is an excellent reference tool. Their city tour costs US$50–95 depending on numbers; day trips to Davit-Gareja cost US$70–160.

Ex-Caucasus m 899 782718. This company specialises in paragliding.

Explore Georgia Barnov 1; ☎ 921911; e info@exploregeorgia.com; www.exploregeorgia.com. This company has a full range of hiking, climbing, horseriding, mountain-biking & caving trips.

Georgian Adventures Barnov 42; ☎ 250491; e info@gata.ge; www.gata.ge. This company offers trips to Lagodekhi & Khevsureti & 14 weekend tours for expats (costing US$224–312 for 2 nights).

Georgian Discovery Tours Chavchavadze Av 74; ☎ 294953; f 204070; e info@gdt.ge; www.gdt.ge. This Georgian-Swiss company offers boutique tours.

naturally, inc climbing, riding & farm stays.

Kaukasus Reisen Janjgava 14, Tbilisi; ☎ +49 170 337 7228; e info@kaukasus-reisen.de; www.kaukasus-reisen.de. This German-run company offers adventure tours, inc a 14-day introductory tour for €1,380 (land-only); trekking or riding in Borjomi-Kharagauli National Park from €450 for 3 days; or a 12-day trek in Khevsureti for €1,250.

Trek Holidays Canada; toll-free ☎ +1 888 456 3522. Offers the Explore trip (see UK).

Georgian Travel Guide Digomi 2, 19–30; m 893 937751, 899 554335; f 371977; e gtg@geo.net.ge; www.travelguide.ge. Particularly useful for trips to Davit-Gareja (about US$100 for 1–3 people) or for skiing & wine tours.

GeorgiCa Travel Shanidze 22; ☎ 252199; f 985607; e georgica@caucasus.net; www.georgicatravel.ge. This company offers cultural tours, trekking, horseriding, cycling & climbing. They can book accommodation & car hire, & can offer combined trips with other Caucasian & Silk Road countries.

Intourist Caucasia Louis Pasteur 14; ☎ 910656; f 910646; e intourism@yahoo.com; http://itour.8m.com

John Graham ☎ +995 99 365372; e jagraham@wesleyan.edu. John runs music courses in Signaghi, & also offers occasional tours such as Discovering Medieval Monasticism in Georgia, at US$1,200 for 11 days.

Sky.Georgia Rustaveli 19; ☎ 922581; e tour@sky.ge; www.sky.ge. This is an amalgamation of 4 companies offering air & hotel reservations, car & bus rental & other travel services; it offers day tours of Tbilisi (US$90), Mtskheta & Gori (US$110), Davit-Gareja (US$110) or Kazbegi (US$115), or 2 days in Kazbegi (US$300), Kakheti (US$270) or Imereti (US$290).

Sunny Travel ☎ 233062; e info@discovergeorgia.net; www.discovergeorgia.net. Offers adventure & cultural tours, including day tours of Tbilisi & Davit-Gareja.

Sustainable Tourism Centre (STC) Paliashvili str 17, Tbilisi; ☎/f 224962; f 226030; m 899 578449; e stc@gol.ge; www.osgf.ge/stc. The Centre's Georgian Explorer programme offers guided ascents of Mounts Kazbegi & Uzhba (from US$95 per day) & Chaukhi (from US$95 for 2 days), as well as hiking & ski-mountaineering trips.

Tbilisi Tourist Centre Akhvlediani Str 5; ☎ 985075; e ttc@wanex.net; www.ttc.ge. Offers general &

cultural tours mainly for Germans, such as 8 days in the Borjomi-Kharagauli National Park (€ 570) or the High & Low Caucasus (15 days for € 940). **Visit Georgia** Nishnianidze 14; \f 996829; e visitgeorgia@geo.net.ge; www.visitgeorgia.ge. Offers a wide range of tours; prices vary with the standard of hotels. However, using a 2-star hotel in Tbilisi, the 9-day In Search of the Golden Fleece tour of western Georgia costs US$710–960 depending on numbers; the 12-day World of Mountains tour costs US$860–1,130; Climbing Kazbegi costs US$610–890 for 9 days; a 7-day wine tour of Imereti & Kakheti costs US$620–720; & a 7-day birding tour costs US$560–740.

If you want to do it yourself, **Tariel Tabashidze** (\ 648928; m 899 648928; e tariel_tabashidze@yahoo.com) is a good guide who speaks German and English, and has a Subaru 4x4 car, for US$40 per day plus petrol (US$50 for a Niva jeep). You can find similar contacts on the noticeboard at **Prospero's Books**, (see page 109) such as Dato (m 899 766890, 899 197815), charging just US$15 per day with your car, or more with his.

RED TAPE

Since June 2005 citizens of the European Union, USA, Canada, Japan, Israel and Switzerland have not required visas for visits to Georgia of up to 90 days; nevertheless most tour company websites still indicate that visas are required by all visitors. You should have a full passport with three months of validity remaining. Most others can buy a single-entry one-month visa on arrival at either Tbiilsi or Batumi airports for US$10. Visas are not issued at land borders, so if any Australians, New Zealanders and others planning to enter at Sarpi will have to call at one of the Georgian consulates in Trabzon, Istanbul and Ankara, which issue visas on the spot. You can, of course, apply in advance: visa application forms can be downloaded from www.georgiaemb.org/vizisblanki.pdf; you'll also need to send your passport, a colour photo, a money order or certified cheque (no cash or credit cards) and paid self-addressed envelope. Fees are US$10 or £7 for a month (US$15 or £11 for double entry), or US$30/45 (£21/32) for a three-month stay. A transit visa costs US$5 (£3.50) and a one-year multiple-entry visa US$100 (£70).

Visa extensions are no longer given as such; if expecting to overstay you should go to the Civil Registration Agency offices at Budapest 2, Saburtalo, or Irakli Abashidze 68, Vake, and ask for a temporary residence permit. For further information contact the Ministry of Foreign Affairs (*Chitadze 4, Tbilisi;* \ *284747;* f *284761;* e *inform@mfa.gov.ge; open Mon–Fri 10.00–14.00*). It's better not to overstay – on exit you will pay three times the cost of your visa plus a fine for each day overstayed. It's not possible to cross from Georgia to Abkhazia; however, there's no problem visiting Adjara and Batumi, or South Ossetia and Tskhinvali, although the British and US embassies still advise against the last.

There has been a great deal of petty corruption and grafting at Georgia's borders, with officials demanding a few dollars from travellers, but this has largely been cleaned up since the Rose Revolution.

GEORGIAN EMBASSIES ABROAD

Armenia Arami 42, Yerevan; \ +374 2 523674, 564183; f + 374 2 564357; e georgia@arminco.com, geoemb@netsys.am
Austria Marokanegasse 16, 1130 Vienna; \ +43 1 710 3611; f +43 1 710 3610; e georgia@magnet.at, georgia@nextra.at

Azerbaijan Asafa Zeinalli 24, Icheri Shekher, 370004 Baku; \ +994 12 497 455860; f +994 12 497 4561; e emb@georgian.baku.az, embgeo@azeurotel.com
Benelux & EU Av Orban 58, 1150 Brussels; \ +32 2 761 1190/1; f +322 2 761 1199;

e mdgadc@skynet.be; consulate: Square Charles Wiser 2, 1040 Brussels; ☏ +322 2 732 8550; f +322 2 732 8547;
e sconsulaire.georgie@skynet.be
France Av Poincaré 104, 75116 Paris; ☏ +33 1 45 02 16 16; f +33 1 45 02 16 01; e sophieko@cybercable.fr, ambgeo@22noos.ge
Germany Heinrich Mann Strasse 32, 13156 Berlin; ☏ +49 30 484 9070, 90715, consulate +49 30 484 90741–3; f +49 30 484 90720;
e geobotger@aol.com, info@botschaftvongeorgien.de
Iran 8th Alley 9, Shahid Qalandari (Dastoor-e Jonoobi) St, Sadr Expressway, Tehran; ☏ +98 21 260 9765; f +98 21 260 154; e lia_ch2004@yahoo.com
Italy Corso Vittorio Emanuele II 21 scala A, 00186 Rome; ☏ +39 06 6992 3298, 6993 2508; f +39 06 6994 1942; e amgeorgia@libero.it
Russian Federation Mali Rzhevskii Lane 6, 121069 Moscow; ☏ +7 095 290 4657, 921787; f +7 095 291 2 2136; e ineza@got.mmtel.ru
Turkey Hilal Mahallesi, Hollanda Cad 31, Çankaya, 06680 Ankara; ☏ +90 312 442 6508–10; f +90 312 442 6507; e geoemb@ada.net.tr; & consulates

in Elmadağ: Cumhuriyet Caddessi 169, Belvı i Apt Elmada, Şişl, Istanbul 34373; ☏ +90 212 296 9006; f +90 212 343 9258; e istanbul.con@mfa.gov.ge, sakons@superonline.com & Trabzon Ertev Pasha 10, Trabzon; ☏ +90 462 326 2226; f +90 462 326 2296; e trabzoncons@gul.net.tr
Ukraine Melnikova 83D, 04119 Kiev; ☏ +380 44 451 4353/57; f +380 44 451 4356; e posta@georgia.com.ua; www.georgia.org.ua; consulate Tolstoy 30, 65045 Odessa; ☏ +380 48 726 4727; f +380 48 731 0695; e geoconsulate@paco.net
United Kingdom 4 Russell Gardens, London W14 8EZ; ☏ +44 20 7603 7799; f +44 20 7603 6682; e geoemb@dircon.co.uk; www.geoemb.org.uk (Kensington Olympia station; open Mon, Tue, Thu & Fri 10.00–13.00 except British & Georgian holidays)
United States, Canada & Mexico 1101 15th St NW, Suite 602, Washington DC 20005; ☏ +1 202 387 2390, consulate +1 202 393 6060, 387 9150; f +1 202 393 4537; e embassy@georgiaemb.org, consulate@georgiaemb.org; www.georgiaemb.org (consulate open Mon–Fri 14.00–17.00, mornings by appointment)

GETTING THERE AND AWAY

✈ **BY PLANE** Travelling directly from western Europe or North America, you have little choice but to **fly**; however, almost all the schedules are inconvenient in the extreme.

From Britain the only direct flights are with bmi (once British Midland), which in February 2007 bought BMed (formerly British Mediterranean Airways), which for ten years had been flying from London Heathrow to Tbilisi as a British Airways franchise operator. Currently bookings can still be made through BA as well as through bmi and its Star Alliance partners, although this may change. They continue to fly A320 Airbuses, leaving Heathrow in the early afternoon on Wednesday, Fridays and Sunday and arriving four and a half hours later, late in the evening local time – you'll be unable to change money or catch a bus at the airport, although there are ATMs, taxis and trains. Return flights are more convenient, leaving mid-morning on Monday, Thursday and Saturday and arriving in the early afternoon.

Other Star Alliance airlines serving Tbilisi are Lufthansa and Austrian Airlines – Lufthansa has flights from Munich five nights a week, arriving at 04.00 (with connections from Heathrow at 17.15). Austrian fly three times a week, leaving Vienna at 22.30 on Monday, Wednesday and Friday, returning at 05.45 on Tuesday, Thursday and Saturday, ideal for connecting flights – Austrian fly from Heathrow four times a day.

There's also Turkish Airlines (THY), which flies four days a week from Istanbul, with a connection from London Stansted at 13.20 which gets you to Tbilisi at 02.30 (returning at 06.00). The no-frills Germania Express flies from Cologne/Bonn on Saturday night at 21.00, arriving at 04.15 and returning at 05.15 on Sunday; it's cheap (€280 one-way, €420 return) but offers no connections and is not wholly reliable. Air Baltic also offers cheap flights from Riga, at about 23.00 on Tuesday, Thursday and Sunday, arriving in Tbilisi at 04.00 and returning at

04.50; but flights from London or Manchester (£290 return including taxes) require at least a 24-hour stopover in Riga. Return fares from London start at about £325–550 including taxes, depending on season.

From New York, return fares to Tbilisi usually start at about US$570 plus taxes; from California they start at US$700 plus taxes. It's worth noting that quite often there's a substantially cheaper fare to Yerevan. Far cheaper fares are available to Istanbul (little more than £40 return with EasyJet from Britain, with luck), from where you can travel overland (see below).

The main Georgian operator is **Georgian Airways** (still sometimes referred to as Air Zena). In 1991 the Georgian division of Aeroflot became Orbi Georgian Airlines; it flew ancient Soviet planes and maintained them so badly that US embassy staff were not permitted to use the airline; in 1999 the charter line Airzena bought the bankrupt Georgian Airlines, as it now is, and Air Georgia, and the state now holds just 20% of the company. In 2000 it leased two Boeing 737s (it now has a third), which fly to Almaty, Astana, Amsterdam, Athens, Dubai, Frankfurt, Kiev, Minsk, Paris, Vienna, Teheran and Tel Aviv. Georgian Airways also flies daily to Moscow Domedodovo, from where there are connections to anywhere in the CIS and, indeed, the world (although you'll usually have to transfer to Sheremetyevo Airport).

There's also **Georgian National Airlines** which has a single CRJ regional jet flying from Tbilisi to Almaty, Kiev, Odessa, Prague, Mineralni Vody and St Petersburg, and via Kutaisi to Moscow (Vnukovo).

The Russian companies Aeroflot, S7 (Siberian Airlines) and AviaExpressCruise also fly between Tbilisi and Moscow. UM Air (Ukrainsko-Sredizemnomorskiye Avialinii or Ukrainian-Mediterranean Airlines) flies four times a week from Kyiv to Tbilisi and Batumi, and Azal flies daily from Baku (with either a Tupolev or an Airbus). Tickets for flights within the CIS are most easily bought at *Aviakassa* counters, in all major towns. Fares from London to Moscow start at about £250/US$400 return, and from Moscow to Tbilisi at about £90/US$140 each way.

Airline addresses

Air Baltic (UK) ☎ 0911 598 0599, 01293 555700 (London Gatwick Airport), 0161 489 8811 (Manchester Airport); www.airbaltic.com

Austrian Airlines 10 Wardour St, London W1D 6BQ; ☎ 020 7434 7300, 0845 601 0948; f 020 7434 7363; www.austrianairlines.co.uk, www.aua.com/ge/eng; & ☎ +1 800 843 0002 in North America

bmi Donington Hall, Castle Donington, Derby DE74 2SB; ☎ 0870 6070 555; f 01709 314993; www.flybmi.com

Georgian Airways (Air Zena) Rustaveli 12, Tbilisi; ☎ 772797, 934732, 785551; e info@airzena.com; www.airzena.com, www.georgian-airways.com. Also at the Maidan Business Centre on Gorgasali Square; ☎ 922020, Davit Agmashenebelis 164; ☎ 342280, & Bakradze 6; ☎ 355801/2; Parkring 12A, 1010 Vienna; ☎ +43 1 214 7877; f +43 1 218 3080; e airzenavie@aon.at; Pfälzer Weg 11, D-65474, Germany; ☎ +49 6 144 402 408; f +49 6 144 402 9958; Bd Bonne Nouvelle 12, 75010 Paris;

☎ +33 1 48 01 67 24; f +33 1 48 01 67 58; Air Support, Evert van de Beekstraat 35, PO Box 75569, 1118 CL Luchthaven Schiphol, Netherlands; ☎/f +31 20 316 4240; f +31 20 316 4241; www.airsupport-gsa.nl; Syngrou Ave 7, 11743 Athens; ☎ +30 1 921 2470; f +30 1 921 3385; c/o Special Fares Ltd, 1151 K St NW, Suite 503, 20005 Washington DC; ☎ +1 800 220 3106; f +1 301 325 2386; e spclfres@pop.erols.com; c/o Panorama Travel, 156 Fifth Av, Suite 1019, 10010 New York; ☎ +1 800 204 7130, 212 741 0033; f +212 645 6276; e mail@panoramatravel.com; www.panoramatravel.com

Georgian National Airlines Rustaveli 5, Tbilisi; ☎ 936595, 355802; e info@national-avia.com; www.national-avia.com

Germania Express ☎ +49 01 805737; www.gexx.de

Lufthansa (UK) ☎ 0870 837 7747; www.lufthansa.com

Turkish Airlines 125 Pall Mall, London SW1Y 5EA;

020 7766 9300; f 020 7976 1733; e info@
turkish-airlines.co.uk; www.thy.com; & ✆ +1 800

874 8875; f 020 7247 5425; e info@tknyc.com in
the USA

Ticket agency addresses

Air Travel Guide 38 Riding Hse St, London W1W
7ES; ✆ 020 7927 7555; f 020 7636 9672;
www.airtravelguide.com
Levon Travel 1132 North Brand Bd, Glendale, CA
91202; ✆ +1 818 552 7700, 800 445 3866; f +1
818 552 7701; e sales@levontravel.com;
www.levontravel.com; & 7083 Hollywood Bd, Los
Angeles, CA 90028; ✆ +1 323 871 8711, +1 800
445 3866; f +1 323 462 7410;
e levontravel@msn.com

Regent Holidays 15 John St, Bristol BS1 2HR;
✆ 0117 921 1711; f 0117 925 4866; e regent@
regent-holidays.co.uk; www.regent-holidays.co.uk
STA Across the UK; ✆ 0870 163 0026;
www.statravel.co.uk; across the USA; ✆ +1 800 781
4040; www.statravel.com
TravelCUTS 187 College St, Toronto M5T 1P7; ✆ +1
866 246 9762, +1 888 359 2887, +1 416 979
2406, USA +1 800 592 2887; f +1 416 979
8176; www.travelcuts.com/english

🚋 **BY RAIL** It's also feasible to reach Georgia by train: services from Moscow ran via
Baku (Azerbaijan) to Tbilisi (3,214km, taking three days) until the opening in the
late 1930s of a line along the Black Sea coast. This became the main route
(2,509km, taking 41hrs), but is now closed due to the secession of Abkhazia; the
Baku route was also closed by the Chechen war. However, the opening in 1997 of
a new link through Daghestan (avoiding Chechnya) allowed Moscow–Baku
services to resume. The through service to Tbilisi via Baku was restored in May
2006, and suspended in October as Russia cut transport links with Georgia. There
have been various attempts at building a direct route through and under the
Caucasus, but all were abandoned and it seems unlikely to be tried again. (The
writer Fitzroy Maclean records how it used to be announced in Tbilisi that 'the
train to the Soviet Union will leave from platform such-and-such ...')

Currently the train from Moscow runs to Baku, where you have to re-book; it
leaves Moscow at 21.30 on Tuesday, Thursday and Sunday, arriving at 09.00 on the
third morning; coming back it leaves Baku at 16.45 on Monday, Thursday and
Saturday, arriving at 05.00 on the third morning. However, fares, currently starting
at around US$83 one-way, are about half the air fare.

Continuing from Baku, the train to Tbilisi is liable to serious delays, with
perhaps a couple of hours at the Georgian border post and the same at the Azeri
border. Leaving Baku at 20.30, it takes around 18 hours for 549km, and fares start
at about US$20. In 2000 the luxury SI Express train (*http://express.sialliance.com/eng*)
was introduced, running between Tbilisi and Baku (with a stop at Ganja); it's very
expensive at US$168–380 (including two meals and insurance) but usually full,
and passport checks are taken care of by staff during the two half-hour border
stops. It runs five days a week, leaving at about 20.00 and reaching Tbilisi at 07.00
and Baku at 08.00. Tickets can be bought from American Express (*Davit
Agmashenebelis 67, Tbilisi;* ✆ *940364, 941069;* f *941706;* e *vip@btc.com.ge*) or
GeorgiCa (*Shanidze 22, Tbilisi;* ✆ *252199;* f *985607;* e *georgica@caucasus.net*). In
Baku go to SI Travel (*Nizami 111;* ✆ *(994 12) 970800, 970900;* f *971902;* e
amex@amex.baku.az; www.si-travel.com).

The train from Yerevan (Armenia) to Tbilisi is less subject to delays; in theory
it takes 12 hours to cover 374km, but allow two to three hours more for delays.
It leaves Yerevan for Tbilisi at 19.00 on Tuesday, Thursday and Saturday,
returning at 15.20 on Wednesday, Friday and Sunday; it's slow and run-down,
but it does save the cost of a hotel. However, women travelling alone have found
it a frightening experience. One-way fares are between US$17 and US$25,
depending on class; the best class, SV, can be a very civilised way to travel, if
you're in no rush.

See the Thomas Cook Overseas Timetable, in all major libraries, for the current timings (not their European Timetable).

BY BUS Coming from Turkey, you're most likely to travel by bus (a rail link is to be built from Kars to Akhalkalaki, perhaps by 2010). There are two routes, along the Black Sea coast to Batumi, and by the Vale border crossing to Tbilisi; a third crossing is planned at Cildir.

For the first route, fly, sail or take a bus to Trabzon (there are no-frills airlines plus several buses per hour from Istanbul, taking around 18hrs for the 1,110km journey and costing US$25–38); from here buses run east to Hopa every half-hour, taking three hours to cover the 165km (US$10). From Trabzon Airport head south (with the sea behind you) to the main road; just to the right is the stop for minibuses to the bus terminal and town centre, while 200m to the left (at an overpass) is a stop for buses to Hopa. There are a couple of decent hotels, and various flea-pits, in Hopa, which is also served by one or two buses a day from Erzurum, which is five hours to the south and can be reached from Istanbul (via Ankara) by the *Dogu Ekspresi* sleeper train. The border crossing at Sarpi, another 20km to the northeast, is effectively a huge bazaar, and there's plenty of transport on both sides of the border. It costs US$2 in a minibus, US$4 by shared taxi or US$15 by private taxi from Hopa to Sarpi, and GEL1 (US$0.50) by minibus or GEL9 by taxi onwards to Batumi; remember to put your watch forward two hours. Avoid the through bus which leaves Trabzon at 16.00 and Hopa at 19.00, as this can take between four and eight hours to cross the border, due to the large amounts of merchandise to be negotiated through customs, and it'll get you to Batumi in the middle of the night; but if you want to go all the way to Tbilisi, it'll get you there in the morning for US$20. However, there are direct minibuses from Trabzon to Batumi (and on to Tbilisi) from midday onwards, leaving from just outside the Trabzon Otogar, which are a better bet.

To reach the Vale crossing, take a train or bus to Kars, then a minibus to Posof (4hrs), then a taxi or minibus via Türközü and Eminbey to the border (30mins) and finally a taxi (on a very bad Georgian road) to Akhaltsikhe (US$25). The Posof crossing is open daily from 08.30 to 18.30. The Vale route is used by through buses from Istanbul and Ankara to Tbilisi (and on to Baku), costing US$25 from Ankara and US$40 from Istanbul. It's a 42-hour marathon, but these are very comfortable air-conditioned Turkish vehicles. The main operators are Turkish companies:

AST Turizm In Tbilisi: ☎ 334396; m 899 507032, 899 962564. In Istanbul: Aydede Caddesi 24/2; ☎ 212 254 5830, 212 254 1616
Mahmudoglu Turism www.mahmudoglu.com. In Tbilisi: Shartava 7; ☎/f 380475; and Ortachala; ☎ 754434. In Istanbul: at the Otogar, office 3B; ☎ 212 658 3834/5
Nako Göktaş Ardahan In Tbilisi: Gogol 1; ☎ 724417, 959175. In Istanbul: ☎ 212 658 3476/7, 212 656 3648. In Ankara: ☎ 312 224 0057. In Posof: ☎ 478 511 2277, 511 2465. In Trabzon: ☎ 462 352 5522

Öz Gölen In Tbilisi: in the low level of the Sport Palace plaza; ☎ 334396; m 899 174847, 899 507032. In Istanbul: Küçük Haydar Efendi Sk Demiröz Center 15 and Beyazit 36; ☎ 0212 638 1046/518 9201
Ulusöy www.ulusoy.com.tr. In Tbilisi: Ortachala bus terminal. In Istanbul: Otogar, office 128; ☎ 212 658 3000/1; f 212 658 3010; and İnönü Caddesi 59, Taksim; ☎ 212 444 1888. In Ankara: in the Otogar; ☎ 242 331 1310. In Trabzon: ☎ 462 325 2201, 321 1281

Buses from Greece to Tbilisi are run by:

Elas Travel In Tbilisi: ☎ 788000; m 899 410000, 899 759338. In Athens: ☎ 2100 286268. In Thessaloniki: ☎ 231 522 5194

Iveria In Tbilisi: ☎ 750605. In Athens: ☎ 210 523 4406
Kakheti Tur In Tbilisi: ☎ 724417, 451112; m 899

There are also buses between Yerevan (Armenia) and Tbilisi, as well as minibuses and shared taxis, and a train (see above). The buses are slow, taking seven to eight hours for about 250km, and cost US$10 (in Tbilisi buy tickets at Kassa No 3 at Ortachala). There are about six a day, leaving between 08.00 and 15.30 and at 19.00. Hourly *marshrutka* minibuses are a better bet, taking five to seven hours and costing US$15; you can also go to the bus station and wait till a shared taxi is full. This will take five or six hours and cost about US$30, as long as all four seats are taken. The road via Sadakhlo is in a poor state, but allows you to stop at Sevan *en route* to Yerevan; buses usually take the route to the west via Bolnisi and Tashir, which has less traffic and a quicker border crossing. These roads should be rebuilt as part of an international project to improve infrastructure in the Armenian-populated areas of Georgia.

A few buses run from Vanadzor and Gyumri (in Armenia) to Tbilisi. There's also a daily bus from Yerevan to Akhalkalaki (8hrs, US$6), continuing three times a week to Batumi (15hrs, US$22). Take your own food and drink.

From Baku to Tbilisi there's less traffic so you're less likely to find a taxi; the train is slower and far more erratic than the Yerevan service. There are a few buses (14hrs), mostly coming through from Turkey; ask at the offices of the Turkish companies at Ortachala. There's also a daily bus via Kazbegi between Tbilisi and Mineralni Vodi in the Russian Federation, continuing several times a week all the way to Moscow (US$60); however, Westerners are not allowed to use this border crossing (although flying to Min Vodi or Moscow is fine, with the required visa).

🚢 BY SEA Another option which is now increasingly possible is to arrive by **ship**; with the completion of new docks, train-ferry services were introduced in 1999 from Varna (Bulgaria) and Ilichevsk (Ukraine) to Batumi and Poti, also carrying cars, trucks and passengers. The route from Ilichevsk in Ukraine to Poti is served by the *Greifswald*, a large and comfortable ferry; built in Germany in 1988, it carries trucks and railway wagons and has a restaurant, non-smoking lounge, playroom and conference room as well as a swimming pool and sauna. Leaving on Tuesday at 23.00 (check in at the office of Euro-Asian Transport Company by the ferry terminal entrance), it takes around 40 hours to Poti, returning in principle on Friday evening, although this can be delayed until noon on Saturday. Tickets can be booked through Ukrferry-Tour in Odessa (✆ +380 482 347995 or 346708; e *nvg@ukrferry.com or welcome@ukrferry-tour.com*). A two-bed cabin costs US$150 per passenger, including three meals; a car costs US$315.

From the resort of Sochi (in Russia, near the border with Abkhazia), the ferry *Mikhail Svetlov* sails at 17.00 on Monday, Wednesday and Friday (less often out of summer), taking ten hours to Poti (US$48) and 13 hours to Batumi (US$53); there's also a hydrofoil or *kometa* which leaves on the same days in summer at 13.00, taking 4½ hours to Poti (US$60) and six hours to Batumi (US$65). Tickets can be booked from 09.00 the previous day at Kassa No 3 in the terminal (✆ 609816; *www.sochiclub.narod.ru/info.htm*).

Other services are from Burgas (Bulgaria), Novorossiysk and Kavkaz (Russia) and Rize (Turkey) to Poti, and from Novorossiysk, Istanbul (and perhaps soon Trabzon) in Turkey to Batumi. These are all a bit haphazard so you'll probably have to see what's available at the time; contact Blasco (*Black Sea Shipping Company;* ✆ 212 252 4600) or Bumerang Travel (✆ 212 215 7373), both in Istanbul.

Finally, if you need to send goods or equipment to Georgia your best bet is either the Belgian company Nomad Express (*Belcrownlaan 23, 2100 Deurne;* ✆ +32 3 360 5506; f +32 3 360 5579; e *info@nomadexpress.be; http://gcca.gosselinwwm.com;* in Georgia:

2

e *move@nomad.com.ge*), or Georgian Express (*Avlabari Square, Metekhis 22, Tbilisi;* ✆ *273311, 273372;* m *889 578457;* e *tbilisi@georgia-express.com; www.georgia-express.com*).

✚ HEALTH with Dr Felicity Nicholson

Reform and privatisation of Georgia's corrupt and run-down health service began in 1995; now a State Medical Insurance Company and 12 health funds are funded by a payroll tax of 3% on employers and 1% on employees. The health service is still corrupt and run-down, but slowly improving as the economy recovers, though the share of GDP spent on health is still under 1%. Although British citizens are covered by a reciprocal agreement and need only proof of UK residence (ie: UK passport) for free treatment, they will still have to pay cash for drugs and many other services; as a rule US health insurance is not valid in Georgia without paying a substantial premium. Treatment is expensive (US$600 for a hernia operation), and even if you can pay for it there is a shortage of basic medical supplies, such as hypodermic needles, anaesthetics and antibiotics. There are plans for major investment in new hospitals from 2007. Embassies have lists of good English-speaking doctors in Tbilisi.

BEFORE YOU GO You are advised to be up to date with vaccinations against **tetanus, diphtheria** and **polio**, now available as an all-in-one ten-year vaccine (Revaxis). You should also be covered for **hepatitis A** and possibly **typhoid**. For trips over four weeks you would also be advised to have a course of **hepatitis B** and **rabies** injections. A hepatitis B vaccination is essential if you are working in a medical capacity or with children, regardless of the length of stay. Having the pre-exposure rabies jab is particularly important as there's a shortage of the rabies vaccine used for treatment following bites, scratches or licks over open wounds from any warm-blooded mammal. The courses for rabies and hepatitis B comprise three injections over a minimum of 21 days, so you should go to see your GP or travel clinic specialist well in advance of your trip. **Tuberculosis** (TB) is spread through close respiratory contact and sometimes through infected milk or milk products. Experts differ over whether a BCG vaccination against tuberculosis is useful in adults: discuss with your travel clinic.

HEALTH HAZARDS

Tick-borne encephalitis This viral illness is spread through the bites of infected ticks which are usually picked up in forested areas with long grass. Anyone liable to go walking in late spring or summer when the ticks are most active should seek protection. Although the vaccine is not licensed in the UK it can be obtained by some GPs or travel clinics on a named patient basis. It is unavailable in the USA. If you can locate the vaccine then a course of three vaccines given over 21 days should suffice. However, taking preventative measures is also very important. When walking in grassy and forested areas, ensure that you wear a hat, tuck your trousers into socks and boots, have long-sleeved tops and use tick repellents. It is important to check for ticks each time you have been for a long walk. Don't forget to check the head and behind the ears in children as they are more prone to getting ticks in this area of the body. If you find a tick then slowly remove it by using special tweezers, taking care not to squeeze the mouthparts. Go as soon as possible to a doctor as tick immunoglobulin should be available for treatment.

Malaria The risk of malaria in Georgia is solely in the benign form (*Plasmodium vivax*), and only occurs from July to October in some villages in the southeastern part of the country beyond Signaghi and Davit-Gareja. Malaria had been eradicated

European ticks are not the prolific disease transmitters they are in the Americas, but they may spread Lyme disease, tick-bite fever and a few rarities. Tick-bite fever is a non-serious, flu-like illness, but still worth avoiding. If you get the tick off whole and promptly, the chances of disease transmission are reduced to a minimum. Ticks should ideally be removed as soon as possible as leaving ticks on the body increases the chance of infection. They should be removed with special tick tweezers that can be bought in good travel shops. Failing that you can use your fingernails by grasping the tick as close to your body as possible and pull steadily and firmly away at right angles to your skin. The tick will then come away complete as long as you do not jerk or twist. If possible douse the wound with alcohol (any spirit will do) or iodine. Irritants (eg: Olbas oil) or lit cigarettes are to be discouraged since they can cause the ticks to regurgitate and therefore increase the risk of disease. It is best to get a travelling companion to check you for ticks and if you are travelling with small children remember to check their heads, and particularly behind the ears. Spreading redness around the bite and/or fever and/or aching joints after a tick bite imply that you have an infection that requires antibiotic treatment, so seek advice.

in Georgia in 1970, but reappeared in 1996, with numbers increasing until 2003. From 2004 it has been largely dealt with and since these regions are seldom visited by travellers, taking antimalarial medication is not recommended. However, should you be going to these areas it is wise to seek advice from a travel expert. Malaria is transmitted by mosquitoes that emerge from dusk till dawn. Even if antimalarial medication is not recommended it is sensible to use insect repellents, wear trousers and long-sleeved tops and ensure that your accommodation is as mosquito proof as possible when travelling in these remote areas.

Dentistry Some dental treatment should be provided free under the UK's reciprocal agreement – in Tbilisi Denta Plus at Vazha-Pshavelas Ave 38 (✆ 395406; www.dentaplus.ge) has been recommended. Pharmacies (aptiaki in Georgian) are usually marked in Cyrillic (Аптека) and are plentiful and easy to find, and many are, in theory, open 24 hours. The Aversa and PSP chains have modern shops in many towns and all over Tbilisi.

Drinking water Tap water is generally safe, but you may prefer to drink bottled water for the first few weeks while your system adapts to new strains of E. coli; meat and other foodstuffs are also safe, though care should be taken over milk and other milk products if there is doubt as to whether it has been pasteurised (see risk of TB above). About a third of the former Soviet Union's spas are in Georgia, and it's easy to find mineral waters such as Borjomi.

Smoking More likely health hazards include passive smoking and car crashes. Georgia has among the highest levels of **tobacco** use in the world, with most men smoking most of the time, as well as 28% of pregnant women and 35% of breast-feeding women. An average 8.9 billion cigarettes are consumed every year in Georgia, 2,200 per capita, against a world average of 1,600 per capita, and the 11,000 smoking-related deaths per year account for about 24% of mortality. The excise on tobacco is relatively high at GEL0.70–0.90 per pack (three-times Russia's) so 60–70% of the market is contraband and the excise is to be cut to GEL0.50. Men now live a surprisingly long time but generally in poor health. Georgians spend GEL1.5 million (US\$0.7 million) per day on cigarettes, but there's so much tax evasion and smuggling that US$34 billion a year of sales goes untaxed. However, when the Ministry of Health tried a poster campaign in Tbilisi all the billboard sites were bought up at once by Philip Morris, manufacturers of Marlboro cigarettes.

In September 2005 smoking was banned in public places, but no-one expects this to have any effect. Thankfully, at least the metro, theatres and parliament are smoke-free. There is smoking on buses and trains, but these are fairly well ventilated and smokers often congregate either by the driver or at the rear of buses, and in the corridors of trains. It's acceptable for women to smoke in restaurants, but only prostitutes smoke on the street.

Driving The death toll on the roads is particularly terrible on certain roads such as that to Svaneti (see page 201), but, given the appalling road surfaces, the undisciplined and excessively macho approach to driving, and the refusal to wear seat belts, it's not surprising that it's high everywhere. Pedestrians are at risk too, as drivers assume they'll get out of the way – bad luck if your sight or hearing aren't too good. Take care at twilight, too.

HIV/AIDS HIV does not so far seem to be a big problem here (unlike in Russia); by the end of 2004 there had officially been 638 cases, but the estimated total for the country was 3,000–5,600, and growing fast, due to injecting drugs. Occasionally immigrants or long-term expatriates may be asked for proof that they are free from HIV infection. Check if you need this when applying for visas or work permits.

Other dangers Accidental death rates are surprisingly low in Georgia, at 118 per 100,000 for men and 23 per 100,000 for women, under half the rates in Russia and the Baltic States. This is undoubtedly linked to the low rates of vodka consumption; yet Primakov's solution to Russian economic meltdown in 1998 was to increase official vodka production by 60%! In 1989 alcohol-related illness rates in the Russian Federation were 191 per 100,000, and just 16 per 100,000 in Georgia.

TRAVEL CLINICS AND HEALTH INFORMATION A full list of current travel clinic websites worldwide is available from the International Society of Travel Medicine on www.istm.org. For other journey preparation information, consult www.tripprep.com. Information about various medications may be found on www.emedicine.com.

UK

Berkeley Travel Clinic 32 Berkeley St, London W1J 8EL (near Green Park tube station); ✆ 020 7629 6233

Cambridge Travel Clinic 48a Mill Rd, Cambridge CB1 2AS; ✆ 01223 367362; e enquiries@travelcliniccambridge.co.uk; www.travelcliniccambridge.co.uk. *Open Tue–Fri 12.00–19.00, Sat 10.00–16.00.*

Edinburgh Travel Clinic Regional Infectious Diseases Unit, Ward 41 OPD, Western General Hospital, Crewe Rd South, Edinburgh EH4 2UX; ✆ 0131 537 2822; www.link.med.ed.ac.uk/ridu. Travel helpline (0906 589 0380) open weekdays 09.00–12.00. Provides inoculations & advises on travel-related health risks.

Fleet Street Travel Clinic 29 Fleet St, London EC4Y

1AA; ✆ 020 7353 5678; www.fleetstreetclinic.com. Vaccinations, travel products & latest advice.

Hospital for Tropical Diseases Travel Clinic Mortimer Market Bldg, Capper St (off Tottenham Ct Rd), London WC1E 6AU; ✆ 020 7388 9600; www.thehtd.org. Offers consultations & advice, & is able to provide all necessary drugs & vaccines for travellers. Runs a healthline (✆ 0906 133 7733) for country-specific information & health hazards. Also stocks nets, water purification equipment & personal protection measures.

Interhealth Worldwide Partnership House, 157 Waterloo Rd, London SE1 8US; ✆ 020 7902 9000; www.interhealth.org.uk. Competitively priced, one-stop travel health service. All profits go to their affiliated company, InterHealth, which provides health care for overseas workers on Christian projects.

MASTA (Medical Advisory Service for Travellers Abroad) Moorfield Rd, Yeadon LS19 7BN; ✆ 0870 606 2782; www.masta-travel-health.com. Provides travel health advice & vaccinations. There are over 25 MASTA pre-travel clinics in Britain; call or check online for the nearest. Clinics also sell mosquito nets, medical kits, insect protection & travel hygiene products.

NHS travel website www.fitfortravel.scot.nhs.uk. Provides country-by-country advice on immunisation, plus details of recent developments, & a list of relevant health organisations.

Nomad Travel Store/Clinic 3–4 Wellington Terrace, Turnpike Lane, London N8 0PX; ✆ 020 8889 7014; travel-health line (office hours only) ✆ 0906 863

3414; e sales@nomadtravel.co.uk; www.nomadtravel.co.uk. Also at 40 Bernard St, London WC1N 1LJ; ✆ 020 7833 4114; 52 Grosvenor Gardens, London SW1W 0AG; ✆ 020 7823 5823; & 43 Queens Rd, Bristol BS8 1QH; ✆ 0117 922 6567. For health advice, equipment such as mosquito nets & other anti-bug devices, & an excellent range of adventure travel gear.

Trailfinders Travel Clinic 194 Kensington High St, London W8 7RG; ✆ 020 7938 3999; www.trailfinders.com/clinic.htm

Travelpharm The Travelpharm website, www.travelpharm.com, offers up-to-date guidance on travel-related health & has a range of medications available through their online mini-pharmacy.

Irish Republic

Tropical Medical Bureau Grafton St Medical Centre, Grafton Bldgs, 34 Grafton St, Dublin 2; ✆ 1 671 9200; www.tmb.ie. A useful website specific to

tropical destinations. Also check website for other bureaux locations throughout Ireland.

USA

Centers for Disease Control 1600 Clifton Rd, Atlanta, GA 30333; ✆ 800 311 3435; travellers' health hotline 888 232 3299; www.cdc.gov/travel. The central source of travel information in the USA. The invaluable *Health Information for International Travel*, published annually, is available from the Division of Quarantine at this address.

Connaught Laboratories PO Box 187, Swiftwater, PA 18370; ✆ 800 822 2463. They will send a free list

of specialist tropical-medicine physicians in your state.

IAMAT (International Association for Medical Assistance to Travelers) 1623 Military Rd, 279, Niagara Falls, NY 14304-1745; ✆ 716 754 4883; e info@iamat.org; www.iamat.org. A non-profit organisation that provides lists of English-speaking doctors abroad.

International Medicine Center 920 Frostwood Drive, Suite 670, Houston, TX 77024; ✆ 713 550 2000; www.traveldoc.com

Canada

IAMAT Suite 1, 1287 St Clair Av W, Toronto, Ontario M6E 1B8; ✆ 416 652 0137; www.iamat.org
TMVC Suite 314, 1030 W Georgia St, Vancouver BC

V6E 2Y3; ✆ 1 888 288 8682; www.tmvc.com. Private clinic with several outlets in Canada.

Australia, New Zealand, Singapore

IAMAT PO Box 5049, Christchurch 5, New Zealand; www.iamat.org
TMVC ✆ 1300 65 88 44; www.tmvc.com.au. Clinics in Australia, New Zealand & Singapore, including:
Auckland Canterbury Arcade, 170 Queen St, Auckland; ✆ 9 373 3531

Brisbane 6th floor, 247 Adelaide St, Brisbane, QLD 4000; ✆ 7 3221 9066
Melbourne 393 Little Bourke St, 2nd floor, Melbourne, VIC 3000; ✆ 3 9602 5788
Sydney Dymocks Bldg, 7th floor, 428 George St, Sydney, NSW 2000; ✆ 2 9221 7133

South Africa and Namibia

SAA-Netcare Travel Clinics P Bag X34, Benmore 2010; www.travelclinic.co.za. Clinics throughout South Africa.
TMVC 113 D F Malan Drive, Roosevelt Park,

Johannesburg; ✆ 011 888 7488; www.tmvc.com.au. Consult website for details of other clinics in South Africa & Namibia.

Switzerland

IAMAT 57 Chemin des Voirets, 1212 Grand Lancy, Geneva; www.iamat.org

SAFETY

Georgia is in general a safe country, with too few tourists for them to be targeted by thieves. You should not attempt to visit Abkhazia, which has effectively seceded, and the bordering area around Zugdidi is also risky. South Ossetia is less of a problem politically, but crime levels are higher than elsewhere, partly due to the wide availability of guns; the same applies to Svaneti, where tourists may be robbed. It's wiser to organise accommodation in Tbilisi or elsewhere before going to Svaneti, not to go there alone and not to go walking outside Mestia without a local guide. The British embassy advises against travelling to Svaneti. Tusheti and Khevsureti are safer options – they were closed to tourists due to the Chechen war but there's no problem now. In Tbilisi, you should take the same common-sense precautions as anywhere else. There's little public drunkenness in Georgia, and there are usually plenty of people on the streets, even late at night; however, there have been vicious muggings of foreigners, usually in the dark entrances to apartment blocks. Otherwise, there is some pickpocketing, particularly in the metro, but few other problems. The days of Kalashnikov-toting *Mkhedrioni* running the whole country as one big protection racket are long gone!

The police force was incompetent and corrupt, but in 2004 numbers were cut by three-quarters and the survivors properly paid at last, and its popularity has risen from 2% to 75% in polls. In particular the new 'patrol police' (who should salute when they pull your car over) have a good reputation – but the 'balaclava police' (part of the Security Ministry), who stage dramatic raids on tax dodgers and the like, often with TV cameras in attendance, are seen as out of control.

Sexism in Georgia is as bad as anywhere in the world, but as a rule foreign women see only the positive, chivalrous side of the Georgian male's distorted world view. Half of Georgia's judges are women, and many leading politicians (including speaker of parliament Nino Burjanadze, leader of the government caucus Maia Nadiradze, chair of the parliament's committee for human rights Elene Tevdoradze, and leaders of small Russian-backed parties Irina Chanturia-Sarishvili and Maia Nikoleishvili, not to mention the French-born former foreign minister Salome Zourabichvili). Nevertheless the proportion of women in parliament has fallen from 30% in Soviet times to 17% now, and in the 2004 local elections only 11% of those elected were women.

Men may actually have a bit of a raw deal (it's not fair that when they dress in black they're said to look like gangsters while women in black are said to look like Medea) – but they've foolishly kept the bad jobs for themselves (manual labour, driving trucks and so on), as well as the mind-rotting ones like sitting around smoking in hotel lobbies, supposedly supervising or providing security, so it's no surprise the women are the ones getting ahead, especially in public service.

US citizens can request the brochure *Tips for Travelers to Russia and the Newly Independent States*, available from the Superintendent of Documents, US Government Printing Office, Washington DC 20402.

Emergency phone numbers are 01 (fire), 02 (police) and 03 (ambulance).

WHAT TO TAKE

Given the risk of power cuts, it's sensible to bring a torch (flashlight) or candles. In addition, outside Tbilisi it's wise to have some toilet paper and soap or shower gel; a sheet sleeping bag may be a comfort in some hotels. You should also consider bringing presents for people you stay with (see page 79).

$ MONEY AND BANKING

The unit of currency is the lari (GEL), which is divided into 100 tetri. The lari derives its name from the Latin *libra* or scales, while tetri simply means 'white'. As of March 2008, the exchange rate is about GEL1.49 to the US dollar (GEL2.95 to the pound sterling, GEL2.30 to the euro).

Banking hours are from 09.30 to 17.30 Monday to Friday. The main banks will change travellers' cheques, although they are choosy and erratic in the brands they accept; Thomas Cook and American Express are the most widely accepted. The US dollar, euro and Russian rouble are the preferred currencies; other currencies are of less interest. You should carry some of your money as travellers' cheques for security, but you should also bring some cash dollars (carried in a moneybelt or some other secure place, of course). Sterling can only be changed in a few places in Tbilisi and Batumi (and only at poor rates), and other currencies are useless. It's far easier to exchange cash than travellers' cheques, with exchange counters all over the place, especially around markets and bus stations.

The first 24-hour ATMs (Automatic Teller Machines, or cashpoints; known as *bancomat*) were installed in 1999, and can now be found in most major cities (not necessarily at the actual bank offices); they are safe and reliable and the obvious way to fund your travels. Some banks also have swipe machines (available only in office hours) to give advances on MasterCard and VISA cards (for a 3% commission). VISA and MasterCard are accepted by the more expensive hotels, restaurants and supermarkets. Western Union (*www.westernunion.com*) and MoneyGram (*www.moneygram.com*) have lots of agents in Georgia, all prominently signed, so it's easy but expensive to have money sent to you from abroad.

Costs are generally low. In restaurants, cafés and taxis, it's normal to tip by rounding up the total rather than by adding a percentage. It's usual to haggle in markets, where you can get up to 30% off.

GETTING AROUND

BY BUS The main system of public transport is the **bus**; there are fairly frequent departures between major towns, and at least one or two a day to most villages. Cities have fairly substantial bus stations, while smaller places may just have a yard by the rail station or in the centre of town. Departure bays will have the destinations served written in Georgian, but if you look at the rear of this sign you may find the same information in Cyrillic or even Latin script. Comfortable modern buses run from Tbilisi to Kutaisi and Batumi. Local services are often worked by 20-seat yellow Paz vehicles, usually with a large area at the back cleared for luggage, as people take immense quantities of agricultural produce or building materials by public transport. The last bus from a town to a nearby village often leaves at about 17.00 or earlier, and the last service inbound to town may well be even earlier. Fares are generally about GEL1 per 20km, eg: GEL8 to Lagodekhi, GEL18 from Tbilisi to Batumi or GEL10 from Kutaisi to Batumi.

In addition to the public buses, there are also many private minibuses or shared taxis, known as marshrutka services, which operate both local and inter-urban routes and also offer fast, virtually non-stop services between Tbilisi and, for instance, Batumi. These charge up to double the bus fare, and have less luggage space. While long-distance buses tend to set off in the mornings, these leave later and some may also run overnight, for example from Tbilisi to Batumi. Some marshrutkas leave only when they're full, but others now run to a timetable.

Any bus or marshrutka with spare space (which doesn't necessarily mean a seat) will stop for anyone who flags it down; this can be tricky as it's hard to read the destination boards (only rarely in Cyrillic script as well as Georgian) until the last moment. Therefore (once you've learnt to read 'Tbilisi') heading towards the capital is an easier business than heading away from it! In most cases you'll pay as you get off at the front of the bus (where small change is kept stuck to a magnet), so you should remember the name of the place where you boarded. If you have a ticket you'll be expected to hand it in as you get off.

🚗 **BY CAR Driving** is difficult, given the awful state of the roads and the excessive urgency of the other drivers. Self-drive car hire is not yet common, and the cost of a driver is not high, so this may be the easiest solution; in Tbilisi it's easy to hire a taxi (including 4x4 vehicles) at the Didube bus station. You'll pay about US$25 a day for a car with driver in Tbilisi, and US$50 a day outside Tbilisi (plus fuel, and food and accommodation for the driver). The only major international car-hire chains represented in Tbilisi are Avis and Hertz, whose agents are Caucasus Travel (see page 51). A licence from almost any of the developed Western countries is valid in Georgia. Speed limits range from 50km/h in cities to 90km/h on highways, although these are universally ignored. Not even police motorcyclists wear helmets.

Contrary to general belief, Georgians are not totally lunatic drivers. They have some concern for life and limb, and perhaps more for their vehicles, skirting very carefully around pot-holes and taking bends at fairly reasonable speed. Problems also arise with laws and signals, which are widely ignored – I've hardly ever seen a Georgian wear a seatbelt, though it's now required on major roads. Problems also arise in relation to other cars; a Georgian's manhood (we can leave women drivers out of the discussion, as they are so few and they only drive locally as a rule) requires him to overtake at once; so drivers in both directions try to make a two-lane road into a three-lane one, with inevitable consequences. They also drive on the horn, not the brake, as it's always the other guy who is wrong or incompetent.

BICYCLE TOURING IN GEORGIA

Alex Tilson

Having toured throughout North America, Asia, Europe and Australia, I am convinced that there is no place on the planet as well suited for bicycle touring as Georgia. Georgians are the world's most hospitable people and there is no better way to be embraced by that hospitality than to arrive on a bicycle. Unlike any other method of travel, if you arrive as a 'velotourist' you will immediately command both curiosity and respect, and you will be welcomed with consistently open arms. We literally had multiple people grabbing us, pulling in different directions, begging us to stay with them – not for financial gain, but out of a genuine spirit of hospitality. It is awesome and will deeply touch the way you deal with guests for the rest of your life. In addition, Georgian food is amazing, a joyous celebration of life itself.

Georgia has a unique history that makes it a fascinating place to travel. This history is alive at every corner, discussed at every table, a veritable feast for the mind as much as food is for the belly, hospitality to the soul and scenery to the eyes. Now is an excellent time to travel before it is forever changed by the inevitable throngs of Western tourists.

Nevertheless, Georgia is not for the faint of heart. Though the human spirit is thriving, the infrastructure is not and the roads vary from bad to truly awful. Bring all of your own gear, tools and spare parts.

There are 20,000km of asphalt roads (93.5% of the total), although it can often be hard to tell the difference as most roads are in poor condition. Fuel costs GEL0.90–1 a litre for normal, GEL1.20–1.30 for super, and GEL0.65 for diesel; there's little lead-free fuel, so it would be foolish to bring your own car. Hitching is not really a practicable option except on roads that have next to no bus service, but it may be helpful to know that older cars with registration numbers beginning with A are fom Tbilisi, those with B from Batumi, C from Sukhumi, D from Kutaisi, L from Poti, N from Borjomi, O from Gori, R (and now TEL) from Kakheti, KZY from Racha, and PZY from Kazbegi. Now there are many private plates such as VIP, BMW and TIT; all are in Latin script, as is an increasing number of road signs. In Svaneti and other remote areas there are still lots of cars with Soviet-era Cyrillic number plates, and in Kazbegi and South Ossetia there are now many Russian-registered cars, as these are cheaper than Georgian ones.

Distances are not great: by road it's about 85km from Tbilisi to Gori, 128km to Khashuri, 230km to Kutaisi and 384km to Batumi (349km by rail).

₩₩ BY TRAIN There has been a remarkable revival of Georgia's railways, which were neglected and pounded by heavy trains transporting oil from Baku. Now the pipelines are open and new trains have been introduced, in addition to the long-distance overnight trains – although there are still enough oil trains to cause delays. The main line from Tbilisi to Senaki is double-track, and all Georgia's railways are electrified, though at one time power cuts were causing US$30,000 of damage a month to delicate traction equipment, and causing oil trains to take an average of 35 hours from Baku to Batumi instead of the scheduled 21 hours. Now new day trains run from Tbilisi to Batumi (taking 7hrs 20mins), Poti (7hrs 30mins), Ozurgeti (6hrs) and Zugdidi (7hrs 15mins), and there are now 14 trains a day from Tbilisi to Gori and nine to Samtredia.

However, it has to be said that there is a near-total lack of information about services. There's also a very poor service to Kutaisi, the country's second city, which is bypassed by the main line; you can use Rioni station, just south, as a sort of parkway station, especially coming from the west. The overnight train from Tbilisi to Batumi is one that is particularly worth considering: for the same price as being crammed in a minibus for a day (currently GEL18), you can enjoy a comfortable berth with clean sheets and good service.

The ticket offices are computerised, so you can go to any window; you'll have to give your name so have a passport or credit card handy. The maximum fare is currently GEL15 for a first-class (SV) sleeper berth from Tbilisi to Batumi. The day trains are spacious, with overhead lockers and TV in some; the seat numbers are hidden by curtains. There's also a luxury express between Tbilisi and Baku (see page 55).

There are three classes of accommodation on the night trains: *platzkart* is a hard seat, *coupé* is a four-bed compartment, and *esveh* (SV) is a two-bed compartment. Fares from Tbilisi to Batumi range from GEL5/US$3 for *platzkart* to GEL15/US$7 for *esveh*. The local *electrotreny* have only hard seats, and you simply pay the conductor on board; these are cheap but dreadfully slow and infrequent, and there's very rarely any reason to use one. In Tbilisi it's possible to get rail information by phoning 351003, 566119, 564717 or 883 952527; only Georgian and Russian are spoken; the Georgian Railways website (*www.railway.ge*) gives a brief outline of services in English.

CITY TRANSPORT City transport is also mainly by bus and marshrutka, although there are also a few trolleybus lines, and in Tbilisi there's a metro. Marshrutka fares are usually shown in the windscreen; pay the driver when you get off. City buses

The programme known as Traceca (Transport Corridor Europe–Caucasus–Asia) was set up at a conference in Brussels in 1993 by Georgia, Azerbaijan, Armenia and five central Asian states, and has since been joined by Ukraine, Mongolia and Moldova. It's a sort of re-creation of the Silk Route, with substantial funding from the European Union, which has mainly gone into refurbishing railways and ports and introducing new train-ferries across the Caspian and Black Seas. Shevardnadze was a great enthusiast, rightly seeing Georgia as an essential link in any new Silk Route, which was both an economic opportunity and a way of reinforcing Georgia's international standing.

For cotton exports from central Asia, a route via Georgia and a train-ferry from Poti to Varna (Bulgaria), Constanţa (Romania) or Ilichevsk (Ukraine) is around 2,000km shorter than the one through Russia to the Baltic ports. However, Russian Railways are still faster, and the Baltic States have uniformly low tariffs. Even so, traffic along the Traceca route rose from one million tonnes through Georgia in 1997 to 12 million tonnes in 2001 and was perhaps double that in 2004. You'll read quite a bit about Traceca in the papers, but its real significance is as a measure of Georgia's international status and its integration into the world.

Similarly, in 1995 the major companies involved in the extraction of oil from the Caspian and beyond announced that their 'early oil' would be moved through improved pipelines through both Georgia and Russia (which both opened in 2001), while continuing to debate the route to be taken by the larger modern pipeline needed for bulk flows. The best route is through Georgia to Ceyhan on Turkey's Mediterranean coast (as it removes tankers from the Bosphorus, which is 700m wide at its narrowest, with nine sharp bends, and faces a possible five-fold increase in tanker traffic); however, Russia did all it could to promote its route to Novorossiysk, even though this passes through Daghestan and close to Chechnya. This promotion may have included fomenting instability in neighbouring countries, perhaps going so far as abetting an assassination attempt on Shevardnadze. Iran has also offered a route to the sea, but this was of course vetoed by the USA. The Ceyhan route is of course the longest, at 1,700km, and most expensive. Its viability was thrown into doubt by the oil price plummeting from around US$20 a barrel to US$10 in a year. The Caspian oil reserves have also been reassessed, and may be 'only' 25–30 billion barrels (3.7–4.5 billion tonnes), not 200 billion barrels (30 billion tonnes). However, Turkey managed to halve its estimate of the construction

take a long time at each stop; drivers won't open the rear doors (for boarding) until everyone has got off (and paid) at the front, but even so some people always wait to slip off at the rear, or to board at the front. Nevertheless, the buses will get you to your destination in the end, and they are very cheap indeed. There are also plenty of taxis; in Tbilisi these come in two types, the official red ones, and unofficial ones, which are less trustworthy. Outside Tbilisi there are only semi-official taxis at best.

ADDRESSES Many street names have changed since independence, as communist figures such as Lenin have gone out of fashion; new signs have replaced worn and faded old ones, but these are often only in Georgian whereas the old ones were also in Cyrillic script. Latin-script signs may indicate there's a guesthouse or embassy on the street. In any case many people still use the old names. There are also grammatical differences between Georgian and Russian even where the names have survived unchanged. Likewise, streets named after people often have an 's' tacked on the end in Georgian. Taxi drivers are often more likely to recognise the old names than the current official ones. It's worth noting that street names are cost, claiming that it had been using German labour costs and hadn't realised that Turkish wage rates could be used.

The oil price rose again and, in 2001, BP finally committed itself to the US$3 billion Ceyhan Project (in which it has a 30% share), after three years' hesitation; this was perhaps linked to BP's shift from being a British company to being an American one. The 'early oil' or Western Route Export Pipeline (also 34% owned by BP), a refurbished Soviet pipleine from Baku to Supsa, now carries 150,000 barrels a day (three million tonnes a year); the BTC (Baku-Tbilisi-Ceyhan) pipeline, opened in 2005, carries around a million barrels per day.

The BTC pipeline was followed the next year by a parallel pipeline to take Azeri gas from the Shah-Deniz field to Erzurum via Tbilisi, breaking the Russian monopoly of supplies to Georgia. In fact, Georgia is entitled to 5% of the seven billion m³ of gas passing annually through the pipeline, which will supply half its needs. The 3,300km Nabucco pipeline, opening in 2013, will carry the Azeri gas on from Erzurum to Austria. The proposed GUEU (Georgia–Ukraine–Europe) gas pipeline, under the Black Sea, would offer another route around Russia.

Georgia is also the route for most of Armenia's trade, as Armenia's borders with Turkey and Azerbaijan are closed. Most of this also takes the main railway line to Batumi; Armenia is particularly keen to see a resolution of the Abkhaz conflict, allowing its exports to go by train directly to Russia. Armenia is also keen on an Iran–Armenia pipeline project, to secure Armenia's fuel supply and possibly carry gas from Iran to Europe.

In parallel with Traceca, from 1996 Georgia, Ukraine, Azerbaijan and Moldova began to form a bloc of nations seeking to escape Russia's overpowering influence; Uzbekistan also joined, and the GUAM charter was adopted in June 2001, followed by a free trade pact (without Uzbekistan) the next year. In May 2006 Saakashvili again antagonised Russia by meeting the presidents of Ukraine, Azerbaijan and Moldova to revive GUAM and discuss the potential for new pipelines from the Caspian avoiding Russia. It has received new impetus from the US-led anti-terrorism campaign since 11 September 2001; oil was already crucial to Bush's foreign policy (indeed the 'multiple pipelines' policy dates from the Clinton administration), but secure supplies have become even more important, and so Azerbaijan and the countries through which pipelines could run are seeing more American support. However, Russia has also gained in importance; the US has embraced it as an ally in the war against terrorism and is adopting a see-no-evil policy to human rights abuses in Chechnya and to bullying of Georgia.

often shown not at the street corners but on house numbers, and many city buildings are very long, so that you may be told to go to, for example, No 20, 3rd entrance; you may also be given a floor to go to (the ground floor counts as the first) as well as an apartment or office number. Six-digit Soviet postcodes beginning with 38 have been replaced with four-digit ones.

Remember that 'street' is *kucha*, 'avenue' is *gamziri*, and 'square' is *moedani*.

ACCOMMODATION

Finding somewhere to sleep can be a problem in many towns. Many hotels have been used to accommodate Georgian refugees from Abkhazia, many of whom have now settled in for the duration as they pay just GEL8 (US$4) per month. However, some of the hotels now have a few rooms available once again for travellers, and some have been totally emptied of refugees to allow renovation. You might want to bring a (sheet) sleeping-bag, earplugs, towel and head torch, if you expect to use these half-wrecked places; there'll be no loo seat or hot water and you may not be able to lock the door. However, there are now many new better hotels, especially in Tbilisi. In any case this problem has given Georgia the chance to start again on a small-scale sustainable basis, with many family homes opening as guesthouses. Many of those on the Black Sea, in resorts such as Kobuleti, are well up to European standards, while those in remoter areas such as Svaneti and Tusheti are more basic, although this is compensated for by the ambiance.

There are plenty of guesthouses in Tbilisi, but these evolved as upmarket abodes for businesspeople and offical visitors. Some really are luxurious, and all are amazingly pricey for a country in which the standard of living is so low. There are very few truly affordable alternatives in Tbilisi, but I list what I can on page 93. In hotels a single room often in fact has a double bed, and you may just be able to pay a bit more for a second breakfast; but a double room often has twin single beds.

The biggest problem is simply finding out what's available, in the absence of any tourist information system; I give what information I can here, and the Agroturism Association (*Davit Agmashenebelis 150A, 380012 Tbilisi; on the eighth floor of the block at the rear by the river embankment;* \f *967437;* e *toto@levontravel.ge*) has a list of 400 families offering homestays, mostly around Borjomi, along the Georgian Military Highway and in Khevsureti – they'll probably only speak Georgian and Russian, but the welcome will be warm. The Sustainable Tourism Centre (see page 51) also hopes to act as an information hub. If in doubt, you can simply ask a taxi driver if he knows anyone who has a room free; in villages you'll never be allowed to go without a bed. Georgian hospitality is renowned, and you'll usually find liberal amounts of alcohol included in the cost of a homestay, as well as food. Although hotel beds can be absurdly soft, in homes they're usually firm enough, and washing facilities, which are clean enough in hotels, tend to be even more so in homes. The Worldwide Fund for Nature (WWF) plans to provide training for guesthouse owners in Borjomi, Poti and Tusheti, as part of a broad strategy for sustainable use of resources; other NGOs such as Horizonti have similar projects. The Woman's Initiatives Supporting Group (m *899 223295;* f *331917;* e *i_inaridze@hotmail.com; http://agrotourism.iatp.org.ge*) lists rural homestays (in French) on its website, but without precise locations or contact details.

Value-added tax of 20% is added by more expensive hotels; the smaller ones either don't pay or include it in the quoted rates.

✗ EATING AND DRINKING

Georgian cuisine is far closer to that of Turkey and Iran than that of Russia, with plenty of garlic, walnuts, cumin and coriander; huge feasts are traditional, though not as huge as in the Brezhnev years, when food was absurdly cheap. Meat is central, but a Georgian meal is served with many dishes, including vegetable ones, on the table at once and everyone helping themselves to whatever they want. It's best to pace yourself, as it's likely to be a long evening with plenty of wine.

Traditional meat dishes include *kharcho* (a spicy soup of mutton with garlic, rice and vegetables); *jigari* (a stew of liver, heart, kidney, onion and parsley); *ostri* (a stew of beef, tomato and onion); *chakapuli* (a stew of lamb, scallions and greens in their own juices with tarragon); *chakhokhbili* (a drier but equally tasty stew, originally of pheasant, but now usually chicken, with herbs, diced tomatoes, garlic and onion); *kupati* (kidney stuffed with minced meat and spices); *chanakhi* (lamb with tomatoes, greens, garlic and green peppers, baked in a clay pot); and *abkhazuri* (a meat puree with onion, garlic, pomegranate, herbs and spices). Chicken is also much used, in the form of *satsivi*, pieces of chicken (or turkey) in a sauce of walnut, cornflower, garlic and saffron (a traditional New Year dish); *tabaka*, pressed fried chicken; *chikitma*, chicken soup with egg; and *shkmeruli*, roast chicken in garlic sauce.

Mtsvadi or mutton grilled on a vinewood fire (also known as *shashlik*) is very popular for outdoor feasts, although pork can also be used. *Basturma* (ie: pastrami, as used in New York delis) is air-dried pressed mutton. Fish is also popular, notably of course sturgeon and trout, such as *kefalia*, small fried trout from the mountains of Adjara. Finally in the meat department, *khinkhali* are pasta envelopes of dough (shaped like little money bags) stuffed with minced meat (or cheese), which are associated especially with villages near the Georgian Military Highway such as Dusheti.

Vegetable dishes include several with aubergine, for instance fried with walnuts, stuffed with hazelnut paste, or as *ajapsandali*, stewed with tomato and peppers. Bean dishes include *lobio* (kidney beans stewed with coriander), *karabakh loby* (green beans in sour cream and tomato sauce) and *mtsvane lobio niguzit* (a bean salad in a walnut dressing). *Pkhali* is a generic term for walnut and vegetable pâtés such as minced spinach with walnuts, spices, garlic and a topping of pomegranate seeds; similarly, shredded beetroot tops are served with red peppers and pomegranate seeds, and red beans with walnuts, garlic, celery and coriander. *Phklovani* is spinach and cheese; *soko ketze* is mushroom and cheese. Beetroot is also served with walnuts, or mashed with garlic. Salads include *tarkhun* (long green leaves with an aroma of aniseed, eaten with kebabs), and raw cabbage salad with walnuts, as well as the ubiquitous tomato and cucumber salad. Bunches of coriander (*kinza*) are used for sprinkling water over produce in markets, to keep it fresh, and it is eaten raw (for long life) as well as in cooking; dill is also popular. Food is spicier in western Georgia, and better for vegetarians, with more use of maize and nuts. Saying (*me*) *khortss ar v-ch'am* means *I don't eat meat*.

There's a range of pastes and sauces eaten with *shashlik* and other dishes; the best known is *tkemali*, a sour plum sauce. Others are *adjika* (a hot red pepper and coriander paste from the west of Georgia, which also comes in a green variety), and *bazha* (a sauce of crushed walnuts with a combination of spices with garlic and saffron known as *tkhmali-suneli*). *Masharaphi* is a pomegranate dressing.

CHEESE AND BREAD There are various cheeses, divided into *brindza*, the bog-standard salty factory cheese found in shops everywhere, and far more interesting local and largely homemade cheeses. *Sulguni* is a mozzarella-like cheese associated with Mingrelia and Svaneti, and *sulguni shebolili* is a smoked version; *imeruli* is a curd cheese and *gudiskweli* is a very salty cheese made of sheep's milk in Tusheti in a bag (*guda*) of sheepskin (with the wool inside). *Nodun* (or *naduri*) is whey curd (like cream cheese) with mint (or tarragon), *matsoni* is yogurt, and *kefir* is the equivalent of the central Asian buttermilk known as *kumiss*.

Breads are also excellent; in addition to *zavatskoy* or regular 'Georgian bread', there are also various types produced in the *tone* or oven set in the floor, like an oversized tandoor (now often with electric elements rather than wood fuel). These include the spear-shaped *shoti*, and the flat, unleavened Armenian bread known as *lavash*. In Kakheti you'll find thin flattened loaves, a bit like unleavened baguettes. In the west of the country maize is used rather than wheat, both for *chadi*, a heavy but delicious crusty cornbread, and for *ghomi*, a form of polenta served with *sulguni* cheese; in Svaneti *elargi* is like *ghomi*, a mix of maize flour, cheese and milk. The national snack is *khachapuri*, which takes many forms: when made at home it's usually a cheese-filled bread, while on stalls nationwide (especially in bus stations) it's a cheese-filled pastry. Cooks will tell you that there are four varieties: *imeruli*, like a cheese calzone, which is made in homes and restaurants; *pelovani*, like a *millefeuille* cake (especially associated with Tbilisi but found in bus stations nationwide); *achma*, made of thin layers of filo-like pastry (boiled then baked) interleaved with goat's cheese and folded into a square; and *adjaruli* (ie: Adjaran),

Oliver Moss

On 22 July 2006, I set off from the familiarity of London's Hyde Park along with 200 other cars, on the road trip of all road trips: the Mongol Rally. The purpose of the rally is to make your own way from London to Mongolia's capital Ulaanbaatar to raise money for various charities, in a car with an engine size below 1,000cc (eg: Nissan Micras, Fiat Pandas, Ladas, Minis, Ford Escorts) which would normally be deemed wholly unsuitable for such a journey. The route you take is largely up to you.

After reaching Prague on the second night, the teams started to head off in different directions according to their planned route. Some headed north through Scandinavia, St Petersburg, across the Urals and down into Mongolia; others headed across Poland to Moscow and through Kazakhstan; others through Ukraine and central Asia; and others down through the Balkans, across Turkey, the Caspian and central Asia. I, with my team of four Fiat Pandas, decided to take the last of the described routes. We spent a total of three days in Georgia, which under normal circumstances would barely seem sufficient. But the innate sense of hospitality and friendliness for which Georgians are well known, and the fact that we crossed the entire country from the western border with Turkey to the eastern border with Azerbaijan, meant we left this compact and stunning country with huge reluctance and a longing to return in the future.

On our first day, after a long wait at the border, we sat down to a late lunch in a beachside café overlooking the Black Sea. Having heard of the banquets that are the average Georgian meals, and the local wines of which they are so proud, we had to ask the staff to halve the dozen or so courses they were trying to lavish on us. The food was superb and very filling, with enormous amounts of cheese and meats and wine: it seemed rude to turn them down when they attached such devotion and pride to their meals.

boat-like with a lightly fried egg on top swimming in molten butter. In Kazbegi they make *khabajini*, a potato khachapuri, and in Svaneti khachapuri is stuffed with greens; *kubdari* is the Svan national dish, bread stuffed with meat. *Chebureki* are pies (like the Ukrainian and Russian *pirozhi*) of unleavened dough and filled with spiced mutton; *lobiani* are similar but with beans. *Kartushki* are greasy potato rolls found in bus stations, though the most popular snack is sunflower seeds (*semichki*), which probably use more energy than they provide.

DESSERTS AND FRUIT Desserts such as *halva* and *baklava* show influence from the south; walnuts are also used in many ways, such as in cakes, crushed and wrapped in a flour and honey paste, and best of all as *nigozis muraba*, picked green, marinated in slaked lime and water, and boiled in the shell with sugar, until you can easily bite through the shell and the nut is the texture of marron glacé. Also quintessentially Georgian is *churchkhela*, made by threading walnuts or hazelnuts, almonds and raisins on a string, covering them in flour, dipping them repeatedly in simmering grape juice and hanging out to dry; made at the grape harvest each year, they look like brown candles. The definitive version comes from Kakheti, where it's made with wheat flour and walnuts (*k'ak'ali*); in Imereti they use maize flour and hazelnuts (*tkhili*).

Fruit is also excellent; in addition to the citrus fruits grown by the Black Sea, there are various relatives of the persimmon (*Diospyros lotus*), such as the *karalioke* (Russian for 'royal fruit'), similar to the Israeli sharon fruit, which can be eaten hard, with no need to peel; and the *khulma*, which looks similar but must be soft when eaten. November is the season for these, producing the striking effect of trees with

The first night we spent in the port city of Batumi, an interesting place rather than beautiful, with colourful markets set against crumbling grey Soviet apartment blocks, and dilapidated buses pushing their way through the thronging streets. The next day we embarked on a memorable journey to Tbilisi, crossing mountain passes where medieval castles overlooked long-abandoned Soviet factories, driving through stunning, green, wooded valleys with crystal-clear rivers winding and roaring their way down from the Caucasus Mountains, and passing through villages where pony and trap and horse and plough were still in widespread use.

When we got to Tbilisi, we were taken out on a city tour by a contact of mine, proud to show off his city and culture. Unlike the other major cities, Tbilisi is a beautiful old city, the jewel of the Caucasus, with grand buildings, windy cobbled streets, and ancient castles nestled in a deep valley. We went out for another traditional Georgian feast complete with toasts every few minutes, before heading to our hotel.

The main concern before entering Georgia were the reports of potential violence surrounding the disputed breakaway republics within Georgia. However we never felt unsafe – in fact, we were made to feel so welcome that the image we had before we arrived was quickly forgotten, and we forged a new one of a beautiful, welcoming and fascinating country.

Unfortunately not all of our cars made it to Mongolia, as was perhaps expected. The first burst into flames on a particularly dodgy Azeri road, the second finally gave up the ghost in northern Kazakhstan, but the final two limped over the line some five weeks after setting off from London: battered, dusty and falling to pieces, but covered in hundreds of good luck messages from people along the way who had helped us to complete such an incredible journey.

For more information visit www.mongolrally.co.uk.

no leaves but large numbers of golden fruit. The pomegranate (*Punica granatum*) grows wild between the Caucasus and the Middle East and bears many-seeded red fruit up to 13cm in diameter. In addition to being eaten fresh, its seeds and dark red juice are used in cooking. It's associated with the goddess of love, fertility, spring, youth and eternity, and does in fact contain lots of antioxidants while the seeds are high in potassium, vitamin C and polyphenols, which protect the heart. The medlar (*Mespilus germanica*) is a small tree up to 6m in height, with brown acidic fruit, like apples, up to 5cm in diameter. The fruit remains hard until frost, after which it is picked and kept in a cool dry room until soft, when it is eaten raw or in preserves. Figs and soft fruits are used for conserves, served with tea after dinner.

While some restaurants serve fine Georgian food, others serve European food, and yet others haven't changed from the communist era, when all any restaurant offered was *cotlet* and potatoes, with a tiny cucumber salad if you were lucky. Unfortunately, menus are never displayed outside restaurants. In Tbilisi there are also fast-food joints selling burgers, hot-dogs and a poor approximation to pizza. Cafés everywhere sell *khachapuri* and other traditional snacks. Street sellers, who also come onto buses, sell *marozhni* (ice cream) and *semichki*, the sunflower seeds which are chewed and spat out everywhere.

Foodies may wish to see the Georgian food web page at www.angelfire.com/ga/Georgian/cousine.html.

WINE There's been wine in Georgia almost as long as there have been Georgians: around 6,000–7,000 years. Stone wine presses and clay containers have been found dating from the 3rd millennium BC, and vine leaves and stems have been found in

The set-piece Georgian feast is known as the *supra*, meaning literally 'tablecloth', from the Arabic *sufratun*; it's a marathon of food and drink in which men will drink up to four litres of wine over three to five hours. In theory they're not allowed to leave the room, but in practice an excuse can usually be found.

The key feature of the supra is the ceremony of toasting, led by a *tamada* or toastmaster (assisted by a *merikipe*, who fills the glasses and stokes the conversation but stays sober; both, of course, are always male). It's almost sacramental, with the first dozen or so toasts (of 20 or more) following a prescribed order. The first will be proposed by the master of the house to the tamada (unless he's playing this role himself), then the tamada will propose toasts to the person being celebrated, if any (for example, for a homecoming or a birthday), to his family or the host family, to the elderly (if any are present), to siblings, to the ancestors, to the dead, to children (ie: the future), to the parentland, to women and mothers, to the winemaker, and to 'our son' (any local hero, which could include Stalin or Tamar). For the toast to the dead, wine is poured onto bread, or onto the ground, and men may stand; for the toast to women those slaving in the kitchen will emerge to join in for a few minutes. After this, things become more flexible, with toasts to specific people, present or not, and guests may ask for permission to propose a toast themselves (a sure way for a foreigner to win approval). In regions such as Svaneti the pattern differs slightly, with, for instance, a toast to St George. Between the toasts there may well be singing.

Each *sadghegrdzelo* or toast is in fact a speech of ten to 15 minutes, during which it's not permitted to touch your wine (although water or soft drinks are always available); when it's done the tamada will drain his glass, or ideally a horn, and turn it upside-down, everyone says '*gaumarjos*' (victory), and you will have to drain your glass in one swallow too. Never have I drunk so much and tasted so little as at a Georgian supra; it's largely irrelevant whether Georgian wine fits contemporary Western tastes when so little of it makes contact with the taste buds. When it gets too much for you, ask permission to propose a toast, toast the host family, and leave.

Most meals are, of course, informal family affairs, but wine will be produced for a guest, and one-line toasts will be proclaimed: 'To Britain!', 'To Georgia!', 'To Thatcher!', 'To Stalin!' being a hardly atypical exchange. As at a supra, you should not drink wine outside toasts, and you must then, at least initially, drain your glass in one. Wine is never drunk without toasting, while beer is never drunk with toasting (except for a toast to 'the police and the president'), except in remote places like Khevsureti where they have to drink beer instead of wine.

Bronze-Age tombs. Wine is absolutely central to the Georgian lifestyle and to their self-image, and everyone (especially men) drinks large quantities and will want you to do the same. In theory Georgians drink red wines in winter, and whites in summer, but in practice it's hard to tell the difference, as even 'red' (literally 'black' or *shavi*) wines may in fact be straw-coloured. Most families make their own, storing it in *kvevri*, large sealed clay vessels set into the floor of a room known as the *marani*. In every ancient site you visit, such as Vardzia or Uplistsikhe, there'll be a *marani* or three. It seems that our word 'wine' derived from the Georgian *ghvino*.

There are at least 500 varieties of grape in Georgia, with up to 38 in common use, and more or less every village produces its own wine, effectively semi-organic – draught wine accounts for 80–90% of the domestic market. Farmers will sell theirs in Tbilisi markets for GEL1.20 a litre (bring your own container), but a regular bottle will cost you about GEL4–6 (US$2–3). Despite its antiquated production methods, Georgia has great potential for producing wine of reasonable quality for export; but it has to be admitted that Georgian wine is not easy going for consumers accustomed to the rounded fruity flavours of New World wines. Exports have doubled in the last couple of years, from 26 million bottles in 2004, but are mainly to Russia; in 2006 exports were expected to reach 65 million bottles until Russia imposed its vindictive ban on Georgian wine, fruit and mineral water. There's also a large amount of private production for home consumption.

Several joint ventures – such as Chalice Wines and Georgian Wines & Spirits (*GWS; www.gws.ge*) – are having a go at reviving the industry, mostly in Kakheti. They are installing bottling lines at the wineries, rather than sending it off in tankers to Tbilisi for bottling, and are introducing other new-fangled techniques such as computer control, stainless-steel vessels, and membrane filters. In particular **GWS**, set up in 1993 and taken over in 1999 by Pernod-Ricard, produces wine in a New Worldish style, not typically Georgian; these are mostly made with the Saperavi grape, which has deep colour, rich plummy flavours and crisp natural acidity, but GWS plans to introduce Cabernet Sauvignon and Chardonnay, alas. GWS now uses two umbrella brands, Tamada and Old Tbilisi, which includes semi-dry red and white Alaverdi, semi-sweet red and white Alazani, the dry red Sareavi Dzelshavi and dry white Rkatsiteli Mtsvane. The reds are blends of Saperavi and Rkatsiteli, the whites almost wholly Rkatsiteli. In Britain Safeway supermarkets sell Tamada Saperavi – the 1998 vintage was described as a 'fresh gluggy red, reminiscent of a thirst-quenching Barbera'. Some would say that their semi-sweet wines are perhaps more impressive, such as the red Tamada Pirosmani (from the Saperavi grape) and white Tvishi (Tsolikauri), which avoid the sticky oiliness of many dessert wines. GWS has introduced three new products – draught white wine, *chacha* and restored Georgian cognac. *Chacha*, something like Italian grappa, and Gremi brandy, are both sold mainly as gifts.

Perhaps the best-known wine from Kakheti is Tsinandali, a white made since 1886 from Rkatsiteli and Mtsvane grapes which are left for weeks to macerate with their skins, as for red wine, giving a strong tannic flavour. For three years it matures in oak barrels in the cellars of the Tsinandali winery, and when ready it's a pale-straw colour, with a fine fruity bouquet. Gurdjaani is a light-gold wine with a unique subtle, bitter taste, first produced in 1887. It also is made from Rkatsiteli and Mtsvane grapes grown in the Gurdjaani, Signaghi and Sagarejo districts of Kakheti, and matures in oak for three years in the cellars of the Gurdjaani winery.

Other contenders are Rkatsiteli, 'rich and full-bodied, making up for its very dry aftertaste', and Sameba, seen by some as 'the grape of the Georgian future'. Other dry wines from Kakheti include Tibaani, Manavis Mtsvane and Vazisubani; sweet red wines include Kindzmarauli and Mukuzani.

Two fortified white wines are also produced in Kakheti. Kardanakhi is made from Rkatsiteli grapes grown in the Kardanakhi vineyards near Gurdjaani, and matures in oak barrels for three years. The amber-coloured wine has a pleasant specific bouquet with a typical port wine flavour and a fine honey fragrance. Anaga is made in the Gurdjaani, Signaghi and Tsiteltskaro areas from Rkatsiteli, Khikhvi and Mtsvane grapes. It's light-golden to dark-amber in colour with a Madeira-like taste.

At the other end of the country, in Imereti, they make lighter, more flowery wines using the Aladasturi, Otskhanuri Sapere and Odzhaleshi grapes for red wines and Tsitska, Tsolikouri and Krakhuna for whites; here vines are allowed to grow high on trees and the grapes are collected in a pointed basket known as a *gideli* which is lowered down on a rope. This doesn't affect the taste, but does give rise to a specific genre of worksongs. The red wine from Kvanchkara, in Racha, is famed as Stalin's favourite (and costs twice as much as other wines). Sparkling

2

wine ('Georgian champagne' or *champanska*) is produced in factories nationwide rather than in homes; it's inexpensive and ranges from more or less dry to ultra-sweet in taste.

OTHER DRINKS The national beer is Kazbegi, a nice tangy German-style brew which has been produced in Tbilisi since 1881; Argo, a premium beer, is produced by the same company, as well as a porter, ice tea and a version of *kvass* (supposedly a weak malted rye beer), which tastes more like a bitter cola. Founded in 2005, the Natakhtari brewery produces Chekhuri (Czech-style) beer, which is better than the Kazbegi brews; Russian beers such as Baltika are also available, as well as German Krombacher, Czech Staropramen and so on at high prices.

Vodka is drunk in Georgia, but far less than in Russia and the other Slav countries; the national spirit is *chacha*, a firewater made at home, as a rule from grain, although in Svaneti, where grain doesn't grow, they use bread instead! It's intriguing to wonder whether there's any linguistic connection with *chicha*, the fermented maize drink of the Andes. Although the Georgians love to drink, there's very little public drunkenness and few of the alcohol-related problems that are found north of the Caucasus.

Soft drinks are easily available, both the ubiquitous Coca-Cola and Fanta, and local fruit juices, which are slightly cheaper as well as rather healthier. Borjomi mineral water is also sold almost everywhere, costing a bit more at GEL0.70 (US$0.35) for a half-litre bottle (for some reason a poster was produced entirely in Georgian except for the words 'Borjomi 0.5L not returnable'!); the milder Borjomi Light was introduced in 2001. Nabeghlavi and Sairme are other excellent mineral waters. Coffee (instant or Turkish) is available in cafés, and you'll usually be able to find tea – it's generally from Sri Lanka, as while Georgia produces tea, it's all green tea for the Russian samovar market.

PUBLIC HOLIDAYS AND FESTIVALS

1 January	New Year's Day
7 January	Christmas (Orthodox Church)
19 January	Epiphany (Orthodox Church)
3 March	Mothers' Day
8 March	International Women's Day
9 April	Remembrance Day
April	Easter Sunday and Monday (Orthodox Church): falling between 4 and 27 April until 2012.
26 May	Independence Day
28 August	Assumption of the Virgin (Mariamoba) (Orthodox Church)
14 October	Sveti-tskhovloba (Mtskhetoba) – Mtskheta town festival
23 November	St George's Day (Giorgoba), now also celebrated as the anniversary of the Rose Revolution, and of Aslan Abashidze's departure from Adjara a year later

SHOPPING

Larger shops open from 09.00 to 20.00 Monday to Saturday, with state-owned ones closing for lunch. Kiosks and house-front groceries are usually open from 08.00 at the latest until in some cases midnight or later, and are usually open on Sundays too.

In Tbilisi there are quite a few 'antique salons', in which you can buy items such as ceramics, wood- and metalwork, and carpets. An export permit (and attached photo) is needed from the Ministry of Culture (*Rustaveli 37, 3rd floor, room 16;* ⤵

990285) to export carpets and some other items. You may find it simpler to take wine to your loved ones, or, if you really want to perplex them, sticks of *churchkhela*.

Among the more interesting items are the male national dress, the *chokha* and *akhalukhi*, a sort of frock coat with a row of pockets across the chest to hold cartridges, and a silk inner coat. More exotic perhaps is the *nabadi* or *burka*, the shaggy sheepskin cape worn by mountain shepherds. A dagger or *khandzali* is always worn by men with the national dress: it should have an elaborately decorated side, for weddings, and a plain one, for funerals. A winehorn or *khantsi* is another possible present. See page 109 for suitable shops in Tbilisi.

PHOTOGRAPHY

You should aim to bring enough film or memory cards with you; although standard brands of film are available in Tbilisi, you won't find slide film or any of the new types of digital film. Similarly you should carry a spare battery. For photography tips, see box on pages 76–7.

ʃ MEDIA AND COMMUNICATIONS

Three English-language **newspapers** are published in Tbilisi: *The Messenger* appears Monday to Friday and costs GEL3; *Georgia Today* appears on Fridays and costs GEL2.50 and *The Georgian Times* appears daily Monday to Friday, costing GEL2. All three have websites that are updated most days. The amount of world news you'll find in them is minimal, but they're a useful window onto Georgian life, politics and business. Subscriptions are available for *The Messenger* at Barnov 28, Tbilisi (↘ 996045; f 939169; e gtze@messenger.com.ge; www.messenger.com.ge); *Georgia Today* at Georgi Tsereteli 1, 0162 Tbilisi (↘ 227196/7; f 251075; e info@georgiatoday.ge; www.georgiatoday.ge); the *Georgian Times* is at Kikodze 125, Tbilisi (\f 934405; e times@gtze.com.ge; www.geotimes.ge). Friday's *Messenger* is good for culture and what's on; in addition it produces *Tbilisi Pastimes*, a cultural (in the broader sense) magazine that appears monthly at GEL3. There's also *Financial (formerly Georgian Business Week; www.b2b.ge)*, available free in the top hotels on Mondays.

In Tbilisi there are eight Georgian **TV** channels plus two Russian ones; in addition Ayeti relays 24 channels from its satellite station on top of Mtatsminda, including MTV, EuroNews, Eurosport, NBC and CNN; they have invested in a fibre-optic network in Tbilisi to give high-quality internet access as well as cable TV. The only truly nationwide channel is the state-owned Channel 1, which is hardly neutral politically. The independent Rustavi-2 TV station earned a good reputation towards the end of the Shevardnadze era, especially for its hard-hitting investigative programme *Sixty Minutes*, but is now tediously pro-government.

TELEPHONES The telephone system has traditionally been so decrepit that most people ignore it, using mobile (cell) phones instead. However, there has now been investment in modern equipment, with Siemens, Alcatel and Daewoo installing new exchanges and Alcatel laying a 280km fibre-optic line underwater from Sochi to Poti, now extended across Georgia to Azerbaijan, *en route* to Shanghai. In Tbilisi in particular there are now good connections for broadband internet, but some villages still don't have phone lines. The number of lines has risen to over 526,000 (around 20 lines per 100 people in urban areas, around four per 100 in rural areas).

Public phones are in a dreadful condition and you'll need a token, available from kiosks; in Batumi 'PTT' signs indicate shops and kiosks where you can make local calls for cash. In Tbilisi there are now a few good modern card phones, from which you can make international calls. Unfortunately phonecards (up to GEL100 or

2

Ariadne Van Zandbergen

EQUIPMENT Although with some thought and an eye for composition you can take reasonable photos with a 'point-and-shoot' camera, you need an SLR camera if you are at all serious about photography. Modern SLRs tend to be very clever, with automatic programmes for almost every possible situation, but remember that these programmes are limited in the sense that the camera cannot think, but only make calculations. Every starting amateur photographer should read a photographic manual for beginners and get to grips with such basics as the relationship between aperture and shutter speed.

Always buy the best lens you can afford. The lens determines the quality of your photo more than the camera body. Fixed fast lenses are ideal, but very costly. A zoom lens makes it easier to change composition without changing lenses the whole time. If you carry only one lens, a 28–70mm (digital 17–55mm) or similar zoom should be ideal. For a second lens, a lightweight 80–200mm or 70–300mm (digital 55–200mm) or similar will be excellent for candid shots and varying your composition. Wildlife photography will be very frustrating if you don't have at least a 300mm lens. For a small loss of quality, tele-converters are a cheap and compact way to increase magnification: a 300 lens with a 1.4x converter becomes 420mm, and with a 2x it becomes 600mm. Note, however, that 1.4x and 2x tele-converters reduce the speed of your lens by 1.4 and 2 stops respectively.

For photography from a vehicle, a solid beanbag, which you can make yourself very cheaply, will be necessary to avoid blurred images, and is more useful than a tripod. A clamp with a tripod head screwed on to it can be attached to the vehicle as well. Modern dedicated flash units are easy to use; aside from the obvious need to flash when you photograph at night, you can improve a lot of photos in difficult 'high contrast' or very dull light with some fill-in flash. It pays to have a proper flash unit as opposed to a built-in camera flash.

DIGITAL/FILM Digital photography is now the preference of most amateur and professional photographers, with the resolution of digital cameras improving the whole time. For ordinary prints a 6 megapixel camera is fine. For better results and the possibility to enlarge images and for professional reproduction, higher resolution is available up to 16 megapixels.

Memory space is important. The number of pictures you can fit on a memory card depends on the quality you choose. Calculate in advance how many pictures you can fit on a card and either take enough cards to last for your trip, or take a storage drive on to which you can download the content. A laptop gives the advantage that you can see your pictures properly at the end of each day and edit and delete rejects, but a storage device is lighter and less bulky. These drives come in different capacities up to 80GB.

US$50) can be bought only at central post offices (don't get a mobile top-up by accident). Otherwise international calls can be made by operators in central phone offices, usually in or by post offices, and will cost about US$2 per minute.

Mobile phones work on a GSM system using Siemens-Motorola kit that is compatible with Western systems. Probably the most reliable supplier is Magticom, a joint venture with the American company Telcell that was run by Shevardnadze's son-in-law, Georgi Jokhtaberidze. After the Rose Revolution he was arrested at the airport and only freed after paying US$15 million to the state treasury, allowing it to pay salaries and pensions on time at last. They offer WAP and Motorola GPRS, and promise 3G. The main alternatives are Geocell and Beeline.

Dialing is not simple: mobile codes are 877 or 893 (Geocell) or 899 (Magticom)

Bear in mind that digital camera batteries, computers and other storage devices need charging, so make sure you have all the chargers, cables and converters with you. Most hotels have charging points, but do enquire about this in advance. When camping you might have to rely on charging from the car battery; a spare battery is invaluable.

If you are shooting film, 100 to 200 ISO print film and 50 to 100 ISO slide film are ideal. Low ISO film is slow but fine grained and gives the best colour saturation, but will need more light, so support in the form of a tripod or monopod is important. You can also bring a few 'fast' 400 ISO films for low-light situations where a tripod or flash is no option.

DUST AND HEAT Dust and heat are often a problem. Keep your equipment in a sealed bag, stow films in an airtight container (eg: a small cooler bag) and avoid exposing equipment and film to the sun. Digital cameras are prone to collecting dust particles on the sensor which results in spots on the image. The dirt mostly enters the camera when changing lenses, so be careful when doing this. To some extent photos can be 'cleaned' up afterwards in Photoshop, but this is time-consuming. You can have your camera sensor professionally cleaned, or you can do this yourself with special brushes and swabs made for the purpose, but note that touching the sensor might cause damage and should only be done with the greatest care.

LIGHT The most striking outdoor photographs are often taken during the hour or two of 'golden light' after dawn and before sunset. Shooting in low light may enforce the use of very low shutter speeds, in which case a tripod will be required to avoid camera shake.

With careful handling, side lighting and back lighting can produce stunning effects, especially in soft light and at sunrise or sunset. Generally, however, it is best to shoot with the sun behind you. When photographing animals or people in the harsh midday sun, images taken in light but even shade are likely to be more effective than those taken in direct sunlight or patchy shade, since the latter conditions create too much contrast.

PROTOCOL In some countries, it is unacceptable to photograph local people without permission, and many people will refuse to pose or will ask for a donation. In such circumstances, don't try to sneak photographs as you might get yourself into trouble. Even the most willing subject will often pose stiffly when a camera is pointed at them; relax them by making a joke, and take a few shots in quick succession to improve the odds of capturing a natural pose.

Ariadne Van Zandbergen is a professional travel and wildlife photographer specialising in Africa. She runs The Africa Image Library. For photo requests, visit www.africaimagelibrary.co.za or contact her on ariadne@hixnet.co.za.

– 77 or 99 from abroad; pause after the 8 and 99 for a tone. To call a Tbilisi number from a mobile, dial 832 then six digits; to dial any other fixed line, dial 8 and the code and the number.

Bring your own phone, and buy a SIM card for GEL10, including GEL5 credit, from a corner shop. In truly remote areas such as Khevsureti there's no mobile (or fixed) phone coverage, but some satellite phones are available, at GEL9 per minute.

Georgia's country code is 995, and the code for Tbilisi is 32, so that from most countries you'll dial 0099532, followed by the number. Other codes are 222 for Batumi, 231 for Kutaisi, 293 for Poti, and 250 for Telavi; calling from abroad, however, you must change the initial 2 to 3.

Special numbers include:

Fire 01	Long-distance operator 07
Police 02	Taxi 008
Ambulance 03	Directory enquiries for Tbilisi 09, elsewhere 05

You'll need to speak Georgian or Russian to use any of these.

Charge-card and Home Country Direct services are available, but only through the operator; for British Telecom, ☎ 8 0200; for MCI, ☎ 8 024995; for AT&T, ☎ 8 0288; and for Sprint, ☎ 8 0100.

✉ **POST AND COURIERS** The state postal service is unreliable, particularly for international mail. Whether to or from Georgia, you should stick to postcards if possible. Airmail to western Europe costs GEL1.20 (US$0.60) and takes about ten days; it's possible to buy pre-stamped envelopes for internal mail for just GEL0.05 at cigarette kiosks. Letter boxes are blue, but you should always hand your mail in at a post office and check that the stamps are cancelled. Incidentally, the first Georgian stamp was the 'Tbilisi Unica' of 1857, which was the first in the Russian Empire; now it survives nowhere in the former Soviet Union, and only in two collections in the world. It's featured on a new GEL0.80 stamp, against a photo of 19th-century Tbilisi.

The courier companies DHL, TNT, UPS and FedEx all have offices in Tbilisi (see page 107) and they offer the only decent international mail service.

BUSINESS

Georgians are known as wheeling-dealing businessmen, and Russians in particular also associate them with organised crime – unfairly, as most of the gangsters in Moscow are in fact Chechens and indeed Russians. Laws and accountancy norms are being brought into line with Western (especially German) standards; but to do business here you will have to come to terms with a culture of corruption, which is locally described more in terms of networks of loyalties.

Economic data can be obtained from the Economist Intelligence Unit, 26 Red Lion Square, London WC1R 4HQ (☎ *020 7576 8181;* f *020 7576 8476;* e *london@eiu.com*); 111 West 57th St, New York, NY 10019 (☎ *212 554 0600;* f *212 586 1181;* e *newyork@eiu.com; www.eiu.com*); and from Georgian Economic Trends, c/o Georgian-European Policy and Legal Advice Centre (GEPLAC), Chitadze 3A, 0108 Tbilisi (☎ *921371;* f *931716;* e *office@geplac.org; www.geplac.org*).

Business information is available from the US government's Business Information Service for the Newly Independent States (BISNIS) (*US Department of Commerce, USA Trade Center, Stop R-BISNIS, 1401 Constitution Av, NW, Washington, DC 20230;* ☎ *800 872 8723, 202 482 4655;* f *202 482 2293;* e *bisnis@ita.doc.gov; www.bisnis.doc.gov*). In Tbilisi, the Georgian Chamber of Commerce and Industry is at Chavchavadze Ave 11 (☎ *230045;* f *235760;* e *ktm@ean.kheta.ge; www.gcci.org.ge*). AmCham, the American Chamber of Commerce in Georgia, is at Nutsubidze 1, Tbilisi (☎ *312110;* f *312105;* e *amcham@amcham.ge; www.amcham.ge*); they have an online database of businesses in Georgia, and publish the useful and interesting *AmCham News* every two months (available free online). The Georgian National Investment Agency runs a free helpline (☎ *933095*) (in Georgian, English and Russian).

For **casual work**, about your only option is teaching English – try International House Tbilisi, Centre for Language Studies (*Dolidze 2, 0171 Tbilisi;* ☎ *940515;* f *001127;* e *schoolih@access.sanet.ge; www.ihworld.com*); The Byron School (*Griboedov 2, Tbilisi;* ☎ *983478;* e *byronschool@hotmail.com*); The English Language Centre (*Barnov 51A, Tbilisi;* ☎/f *222326*); and others listed at www.britishcouncil.org/ge-education-english-language-schools.htm.

CULTURAL ETIQUETTE

CULTURAL DOS AND DON'TS Perhaps the most important rule is to learn to accept a drink even when it's the last thing you want. Restaurant bills are never split; they're always paid by one person, almost always a man.

Adult Georgians don't wear shorts. In churches shorts and low-cut dresses are unacceptable, and this is true in general in the remoter mountain areas. Women cover their heads in church (though not always in Tbilisi). Queues are surprisingly orderly.

INTERACTING WITH LOCAL PEOPLE Georgians, though poor, are fantastically hospitable people; this is in some cases a form of subconscious domination or possession rather than pure generosity, but you still have to deal with the question of how to pay them back. Payment with money will never be accepted and may be seen as offensive, but presents for children are usually welcome (postcards or picture books about your home country, coloured pencils, toys, chocolate, etc). American cigarettes will usually be accepted by men, but the hardest problem is to find suitable gifts for the women who work so hard for so little in the way of thanks; in the remoter villages even make-up is inappropriate, but headscarves, napkins and tablecloths are much appreciated.

GIVING SOMETHING BACK

The best way to find out what's going on in the Georgian NGO scene is by reading the excellent newsletters published (on paper and online) by the Caucasus Environmental NGO Network (CENN). Details for the CENN and other organisations are listed below.

Caucasus Environmental NGO Network (CENN)
Betlemi 27, Tbilisi; ℸ 751903/4; e cenn@
access.sanet.ge; www.cenn.org
Georgian Center for the Conservation of Wildlife
7 Nutsubidze Plateau 3/1, Tbilisi; ℸ 326496,
537478; e office@gccw.org; www.gccw.org
**The Noah's Ark Centre for the Recovery of
Endangered Species (NACRES)** Abashidze 12A, 0179
Tbilisi; ℸ 233706; f 537124; e administrator@
nacres.org; www.nacres.org

Sustainable Tourism Centre Paliashvili str 17, Tbilisi;
⅄f 224962; f 226030; m 899 578449;
e stc@gol.ge; www.osgf.ge/stc. Arranges volunteer
summer camps.
World Vision Georgia Gogebashvilis 33, Tbilisi;
ℸ 292955; e gib_brown@wvi.org;
http://georgia.worldvision.org. Working mainly with
children of poor families.
WWF-Georgia Aleksidze 11, 0193 Tbilisi;
ℸ 330154/5; e office@wwfcaucasus.ge;
www.panda.org/caucasus

OTHER PRACTICALITIES

TIME Georgia is four hours ahead of GMT, but since October 2005 has been on permanent summer time, ie: GMT +3. Georgians are not early risers, but can be lively well into the night.

PUBLIC TOILETS Public toilets are few and far between. Where you do find one, the doors are likely to be marked with Cyrillic symbols, M for men and Ж for women.

ELECTRICITY Electrical power is supplied in theory at 220V 50Hz, using two-prong European-standard plugs; however, it's subject to surges, and in winter there may be power cuts.

No.1
to Eastern Europe

With 45 destinations and over 550 connections per week Austrian is the number one carrier to Central & Eastern Europe. We have 5 flights a week to Tbilisi and offer a complimentary food service in all classes. You can even travel Business Class for full fare economy prices by taking advantage of our Silver Ticket promotion. When you plan your trip to Georgia visit **www.austrian.com** and travel with the experts to Central & Eastern Europe.

Austrian

Earn miles with **Miles & More**

www.austrian.com

A STAR ALLIANCE MEMBER

Part Two

THE GUIDE

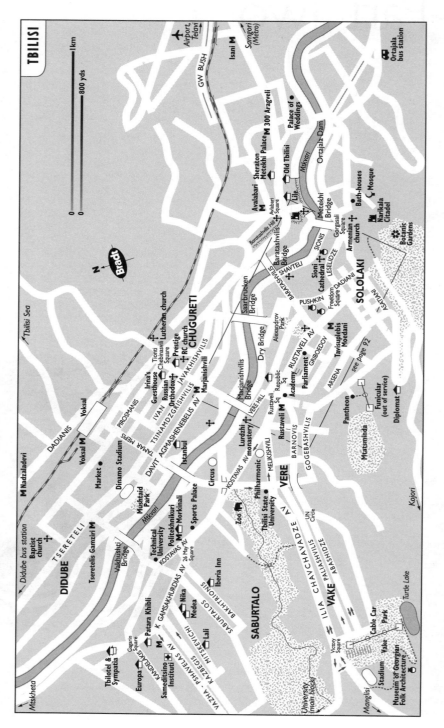

TBILISI

1km
800 yds

Bradt

3

Tbilisi თბილისი

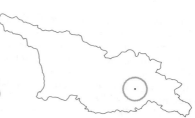

Tbilisi lies at about 380m altitude, on the same latitude as Rome, Barcelona, Boston and Chicago. It stretches for 20km along the river Mtkvari (the Kura in Russian), with mountains on three sides: Mtatsminda to the southwest, Mount Tabori and the Solalaki Ridge to the southeast, and the low undulating Makhat Ridge to the northeast, beyond which is the so-called Tbilisi Sea, now a reservoir, and then the Samgori steppe.

The average temperature in Tbilisi is 13.2°C (24.4°C in July, and 0.9°C in January), and average annual precipitation is 505mm (the wettest months are May with 75mm, and April with 61mm). A damp spring is followed by a summer which can be oppressively hot and stuffy, then a fine autumn with lower humidity; the first snow appears on the mountains in mid October, but winter in the city tends to be damp and misty with minimal snowfall. This is a seismically active zone: seismologists reckon that the strongest earthquake likely to occur here will be of magnitude 4.5, and this was tested in April 2002 when a quake of magnitude 4.3 (Richter 4.8) struck. Six people died (two from heart attacks) and over 2,000 buildings were damaged in the old city, but none actually collapsed. Some roads are still closed with public transport diverted, especially in the Chugureti district.

Perhaps the most evocative accounts of Tbilisi come from the 1930s, because of the contrast it offered to the rest of the USSR: the author Arthur Koestler said:

> I loved Tbilisi more than any other town in the Soviet Union, perhaps because it was still so untouched by the drabness and monotony of Soviet life. The town has an irresistible charm of its own, neither European nor Asiatic, but a happy blend of the two.

Fitzroy Maclean, who came here a dozen times or more, called it 'one of my favourite towns anywhere'. Of his first visit he wrote:

> Immediately the town took my fancy. It had a graceful quality, a southern charm, an air of leisure, which I had so far found nowhere else in the Soviet Union. In the old city the houses, crazy structures with jutting verandas, hang like swallows' nests from the side of a hill. Beneath them a mountain stream tumbles its rushing waters and more houses cluster on the far side.

HISTORY

The city's name derives from *tbili*, meaning warm, referring to the 30 hot springs on the northeastern slopes of Mount Tabori – which produce three million litres a day, at between 24°C and 46.5°C – and in the 12th century supplied 65 bath houses. *Tiflis* is the Persian name, also used by Russians and Armenians; the locals (or *Tbilisebi*) just say *kalaki* or the town.

Legend has it that King Vakhtang Gorgasali ('Wolf-Lion'; AD446–502) went hunting from his capital in Mtskheta, and wounded a deer or pheasant, which was miraculously cured (or alternatively cooked) by a hot spring. Vakhtang decided to move his capital to this health-giving spot (the water is even said to restore eunuchs), though it was his son King Dachi who completed the walls of the new city and moved the capital here. In fact there's evidence of habitation since at least 3000BC, and it's not surprising given the combination of defensible hills with the hot springs. The city suffered 40 invasions between AD627 and 1795, by Persians, Byzantines, Arabs, Khazars and Seljuk Turks (many of them several times); in 1121 King Davit IV (the Builder) recaptured the city and rebuilt it (allowing the Muslims to stay), building his palace across the river in the Isani ('fortified place') district. The next year Tbilisi became capital of the most powerful state in the Near East, and then centre of Georgia's cultural flowering under monarchs such as Tamar. Then the invasions recommenced, with the Mongols in the 13th century, Temur Leng in the 14th, and the Ottomans in the 15th. Georgia was divided into weak principalities, and from 1632 Tbilisi was governed by imposed Shahs (including Khusran-Mirza, an illegitimate member of the Bagratid family who had converted to Islam and who ruled for 26 years as King Rostom I). In 1744 they were driven out by King Teimuraz II and his son Irakli II, and in 1762 it became capital of eastern Georgia. In 1795 the Shah of Persia, Aga Mohammed Khan, utterly destroyed Tbilisi (almost nothing survived; the churches you see now were rebuilt afterwards) and drove out the entire population.

After this disaster Irakli appealed for protection to the tsar and Georgia entered the Russian Empire. Tiflis (as the Russians know it) recovered but was soon largely inhabited by Armenians and Russians, with Georgians mainly in the Avlabari quarter, across the river beyond the Metekhi church, which had been the Armenian quarter in Tamar's time, and is again now. The Russians developed the Garetubani area (the present centre, around Freedom Square and Rustaveli Avenue) only in the 1850s, when merchants' villas began to creep up the foothills of Sololaki and Mtatsminda. Across the river, towards the railway station, the Chugureti district was settled by Poles and Germans; the latter were invited to settle in the Russian Empire in 1817, and their influence can perhaps still be seen in the popularity of Doberman pinschers in Tbilisi. At this period it was the capital of the entire Transcaucasus, and many great figures came here. In 1829 Pushkin passed through on his way to Erzurum, in 1851–54 the young Tolstoy wrote his first significant stories here, and Gorki also wrote and published his first story here in 1892; he called Tbilisi his second home. The city was also visited by Tsar Nikolai I in 1837.

There are some fine Art Nouveau buildings (known as Moderne here), notably the National Library; in 1933–41, under Stalin and Beria, the Circus, Dinamo stadium and Rustaveli cinema were built, and the first high-rise apartment blocks appeared; from 1951 the so-called 'attractive new housing developments' of Digomi, Varketili, Avchali and Gldani were built. Varketili is an extremely deprived area which has developed a particularly good community organisation to tackle its problems; if you should happen to go there, note block No 303, the Leaning Tower of Tbilisi, which has a cant of 1m. A few buildings in the Freedom Square/Rustaveli area were destroyed in the civil war of 1991–92, but most gaps have been filled by new developments, such as the Courtyard by Marriott Hotel. The city's population was 71,000 in 1865, 120,000 in 1900, 194,000 in 1913, and 519,000 in 1939; it reached a million in 1977, and now has about 1.4 million inhabitants, 40% of whom are not ethnically Georgian.

GETTING THERE AND AWAY

BY AIR Tbilisi's **Lochini** (formerly Novo-Alexeyevka) **Airport** (code: TBS) is 18km east of the centre, reached by bus or taxi along the Kakheti highway; there are signs in English and a tall monument of a woman holding a sun at the turn-off. From the air, see if you can spot the *kurgans* (Bronze-Age burial mounds) near the airport, or the Tbilaviamsheni factory that produces Sukhoi fighter-bombers. The old arrivals terminal is a very small but attractive Modernist building from the Stalinist epoch. In February 2007 a new international terminal opened, and one of the old terminals is to become a hotel; the airport can now handle aircraft as large as A330 and A340 Airbuses, and 2,000 passengers an hour. There's now an Avis car-rental counter and ATMs, but the exchange desk is unlikely to be open when most planes from western Europe arrive; those on the departure side are open by 05.30, however.

For **departures** check-in is 60–90 minutes before departure and flights within the CIS can suffer spectacular delays. Information (of sorts) is available by phoning 997613 or 410403. There's a bar selling foreign beers and Georgian wines, and a duty-free shop (☏ *947302*) selling over-priced Georgian wines, various whiskies and a range of perfumes, cigarettes, sunglasses and electrical goods.

Airline offices
Aeroflot Gamsakhurdias 1; ☏ 943896, 372111; f 373796; e tbstosu@aeroflot.ru Tickets for **Air Baltic** flights via Riga can be booked through Berika International (see page 87).
Austrian Airlines Sheraton Metechi Palace Hotel, Telavi 20; ☏ 774506/10; f 770912; www.aua.com/ge/eng
Avia ExpressCruise Rustaveli 2; ☏ 988734, 988271
Azerbaijan Airlines Chavchavadze 28; ☏ 251669, 251301
Belavia Davit Agmashenebelis 95; ☏ 956890
bmi GMT Plaza, 4 Freedom Sq; ☏ 940719/20; f 940725; e tbs.sales@flybmi.com
Georgian Airways (still sometimes referred to as Air Zena) Rustaveli 12, Tbilisi; ☏ 772797, 934732, 785551, 999730; f 999660; e info@georgian-airways.com; www.airzena.com, www.georgian-airways.com. The national airline also has outlets at the Maidan Business Centre on Gorgasali Sq; ☏

922020, Davit Agmashenebelis 164; ☏ 342280 & Bakradze 6; ☏ 355801/2.
Georgian National Airlines Rustaveli 5; ☏ 936595, 355802; ☏ (airport) 947677; e info@national-avia.com; www.national-avia.com. Don't confuse this with the more useful Georgian Airlines.
Germania Express Sheraton Metechi Palace Hotel, Telavi 20; ☏ 773171; f 744171; www.gexx.de
Lufthansa Sheraton Metechi Palace Hotel, Telavi 20; ☏ 273301; f 273302
S7 (Siberian Airlines) G Abesadze 5; ☏ 920021, 983029
Turkish Airlines (THY) Davit Agmashenebelis 147; ☏ 959022, 940703; f 940704; e thytbs@access.sanet.ge; www.turkishairlines.com
UM Air (Ukrainsko-Sredizemnomorskiye Avialinii or Ukrainian-Mediterranean Airlines) Ingorovka 12;

Airport transfer Bus route 37 (a yellow midi bus) runs every 20–30 minutes from the airport along the Kakheti highway to Samgori (where an underpass leads to railway, metro and bus stations), Avlabari, the Baratashvilis bridge, Freedom Square, Rustaveli, Kostavas and Tamar avenues, giving a handy tour of the central area, and after half an hour reaching the Voksal (railway station), where they leave from a relatively obvious stop on the down ramp road. It costs just GEL0.50 (US$0.25), but (as you only pay when you get off) a dollar bill (worth over GEL2) would doubtless satisfy the driver if the exchange desk is still shut. It operates from 07.30 to 20.30 (07.00–20.00 from the city); alternatively, take a taxi, costing around GEL20 (US$11) by day or GEL30 (US$17) at night, usually after 20.00 (confirm the price before departure). A train station opened in 2007, with departures from the city at 08.00, 09.00 and 10.00, six between 17.15 and 23.15, and four more in the early hours, all returning half an hour later. Alternatively it's under 2km to the highway; the decent Hotel Meridiani is beside the highway into town, named after George W Bush when he visited in 2005.

BUS AND RAIL TERMINALS International buses from Azerbaijan, Armenia, Turkey and Greece arrive at Ortachala, southeast of the centre, in theory the main bus station, with exchange desks but no ATM. In fact, the main terminal is at Didube, to the north; emerging from the metro station (where the crush of stalls and traders should have been cleared away) you'll find in front of you a yard full of minibuses and shared taxis – marshrutkas for Akhaltsikhe and Gardabani wait just to your left, with taxis to Davit-Gareja, and marshrutkas and buses for Mtskheta are about 50m ahead and to the right. Beyond them you can find buses and marshrutkas to Kazbegi (sometimes with signs in Latin or Cyrillic scripts). The bus station proper is several hundred metres to the right, first the new *Autovoksal Okriba*, which is just as chaotic as the rest of the site, with what should be ticket offices rented out as shops, and then the old terminal, where you'll find vile toilets and left-luggage and exchange facilities. Buses to Gori and Kaspi leave every 30 minutes or so, and the really quite decent coaches to Kutaisi run hourly. Marshrutkas to Borjomi leave on the hour from near the Okriba terminal, with others to Tqibuli (the 09.00 departure continuing to Oni) and elsewhere.

Buses for destinations in the west of the country, and north to Kazbegi, leave Didube in the mornings; in the early afternoon there'll still be some minibuses and shared taxis leaving from here, but later on you're best off going to the Voksal (main rail station). At the station's rear (or north) side, to the left buses leave for Batumi (bay 1), Zugdidi (bay 2), Senaki (bay 3), Kutaisi (bay 4), Samtredia (bay 5) and Poti (bay 6), etc; to the right minibuses wait for passengers, leaving when full, with the last departures at about 19.00. Overnight buses to Batumi take about nine hours and cost GEL9 (US$4.50); minibuses take about seven hours but are twice as expensive. A few minibuses also leave from the south side of the station. A daily bus to Vladikavkaz and Mineralni Vodi (in Russia) via the Georgian Military Highway also leaves from here, although Westerners are not allowed to cross the border; tickets from International Service Ltd at Kassa No 18 (✆ 993522), or from Kassa No 5 at Samgori bus station (✆ 716629). This bus usually continues to Rostov or Moscow, with connections at Kropotkin to Odessa, and at Rostov to Kiev; other buses, and also shared taxis, run from Didube. There are also buses to Yerevan, at 11.00 and 17.00, with tickets (GEL25) sold from Kassa 18 or 24 (✆ 943554, 993522).

Likewise at the Ortachala bus terminal, tickets for Moscow, St Petersburg and Kiev are sold at Kassa No 2 (✆ 753433; m 893 642021). Buses to Turkey and Greece (a very long haul) leave from Ortachala; see page 56 for details of operators. Heading for Trabzon, buses leave the Ortachala terminal in Tbilisi at about 17.00 and take about 16 hours; it's best to buy tickets a day ahead. Buses eastwards to Kakheti leave from the Samgori (also known as Naftlugi) metro and rail station, east of the centre (local buses to Sagarejo, for instance, from right outside, and longer-distance buses from a small terminal to the right). Marshrutka minibuses for Kakheti leave from the square just behind (north of) Isani metro station, and also from outside the Samgori station. For Telavi, there are between eight and 12 buses a day (09.00–18.20), costing GEL6; marshrutkas cost about the same, and are significantly preferable. The occasional bus to Tsiteli Khidi (the Krasni Most or Red Bridge, the main border crossing to Azerbaijan) also leaves from Samgori and others run from opposite the Isani metro station; they connect with minibuses on the far side of the border. Buses for Manglisi and Akhalkalaki leave from Victory Square (Gamarjvebis Moedani), Bagebi. Marshrutkas to Marneuli and Bolnisi leave from the Ortachala roundabout.

Buses to Rustavi leave from the Dinamo stadium; a surprisingly frequent train service runs from the Samgori station. The Voksal handles mainly long-distance and international **trains**, while local services to the west often leave from the so-called Borjomski platforms, to the southwest. The main hall is to the south, with computerised ticket machines; it may be easier to buy local tickets on the north side, reached by a footbridge to the west. Left-luggage is in the underpass, which leads only to the central platforms. For tickets for the regular train to Baku go to the international counter, which has a computer printout of the schedule in English posted in the window. For rail information, try phoning 351003, 566119, 564717 or 883 952527, or see www.railway.ge which gives a brief outline of services. There's no information in English at the Voksal except some screens which don't mention intermediate stops. The Voksal is to be renovated by 2008, in theory, with a new hotel upstairs. Long-distance trains leave for Batumi at 08.50 and 21.00, for Poti at 09.20 and 23.00, for Zugdidi at 09.15 and 21.30, for Ozuregti at 09.15 and 21.00 and for Senaki at 14.45, although precise times may change. Others head west to Nikosi (Tskhinvali) and Borjomi, giving a fairly frequent service to Mtskheta and Gori.

Ticket agencies For flights to CIS destinations, you can buy tickets over the counter at the *Aviakassas* (air ticket agencies) all over town; one of the best is **Aviaservice** at Rustaveli 36; others are at Rustaveli 19 and Leselidze 30. The leading Georgian agency is **Sky.Georgia**, an amalgamation of four companies offering air and hotel reservations, car and bus rental and other travel services; they're at Rustaveli 19 (↘ 922581, 999662; e tour@sky.ge; www.sky.ge; open Mon–Fri 10.00–17.30, Sat 10.00–14.00). **Levon Travel** (*Chavchavadze Av 20;* ↘ 250010; f 232399; e levont@access.sanet.ge, sales@levontravel.ge; www.levontravel.com) and the slightly less slick **Berika International** (*Kostava 14;* ↘ 932829; fax; 982283; e berika@caucasus.net; www.berika.ge) are travel agencies that deal more with residents than visitors but can book flights with all major airlines. **Intertour** (*Tamar Mepis 7;* ↘ 339966; f 942880; e ticketing@intertour.ge) and **Ultratour** (*Metekhi Business Center, Metekhi 22 at Avlabari Sq;* ↘ 778680, 776202; m 877 409007) also have links with Western airlines.

CGTT Voyages (*on the third floor of the closed Hotel Sakartvelo, Melikishvili 12;* ↘ 221425; f 221426; e cgtt@voyages.com.ge; www.cgtt-tbilissi.ge) is a French-owned company, operating across the CIS.

American Express have an office (operated by VIP-BTC) at Davit Agmashenebelis 67 (↘ 940364, 958810; f 941706; e contact@amexgeorgia.com; www.amexgeorgia.com; open Mon–Fri 10.00–13.30 & 14.30–18.30, Sat 11.00–16.00), but they can't change their own travellers' cheques or do anything particularly useful, other than selling tickets for the very expensive luxury train to Baku.

See pages 51–2 for tour operators.

GETTING AROUND

METRO Tbilisi has a two-line metro system, as well as trolleybuses, buses, and swarms of private marshrutka minibuses. Public transport runs from 06.00 to midnight.

The **metro** (*www.metro.ge*) opened in 1965 and now extends for 24km, with 21 stations. There are two lines, mostly underground, meeting at the Voksal (Vagzalis Moedani), and trains run roughly every five minutes. Local residents can use a swipe card for access, but otherwise you'll have to pay GEL0.40 for a plastic token (buy enough for a day or two) which you put into a turnstile a few metres away. Crime is not really a problem, although some embassies warn against using the metro.

The principal line runs largely parallel to the Mtkvari from north to southeast, from Akhmeteli to Didube, Voksal, Marjanishvilis, Rustaveli Square, Freedom

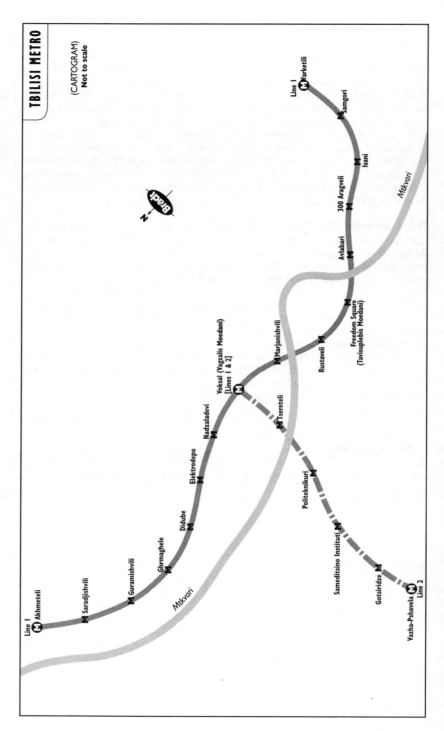

TBILISI METRO

(CARTOGRAM)
Not to scale

Square, Avlabari, Isani, Samgori and Varketili; there's a free transfer to the other line, which runs westwards from Voksal to Universiteti, with just five intermediate stops mostly along Vazha-Pshavelas Avenue. Signs are only in Georgian and the system can seem challenging to foreigners at first; but the last word of the pre-departure announcement is the name of the next station, which is also the first word on arrival. The system seems to have been built on the cheap, with stations unusually far apart and platforms only five carriage-lengths long (and four-carriage trains); however, the trains and four central stations were refurbished in 2006.

TAXIS The most reliable taxis are red Mitsubishis (as a rule) found at the red-and-white Georgia Bus and Taxi Company ranks (for instance, along Rustaveli and at the airport) or by phoning 327849. You may have to remind them to turn the meter on, and you shouldn't pay more than GEL5 (US$2.50) around town (fares double late at night). Other taxis are less reliable and are unlikely to have a meter; even so the maximum fare shouldn't be more than GEL6 (double that late at night).

MARSHRUTKAS AND BUSES Marshrutkas are a phenomenon which barely existed under the Soviet Union: the franchise for each line is owned by someone (often a member of parliament, for some reason), whom minibus owners/drivers pay for the right to work. They run from dawn to 23.00 (later in summer). Fares (clearly displayed) are between GEL0.40 and GEL0.80, compared with GEL0.20 for trolleybuses. A fleet of 500 relatively new yellow Dutch **buses** has recently arrived, and the marshrutka minibuses have been summarily banned from the main axis of Rustaveli, Kostavas and Chavchavadze Avenues. The marshrutkas (which should have been reorganised to be feeders to the metro and the new buses) simply moved to the inadequate parallel streets, with no information available about where they can be found or where they go.

Then there's not much information about where the buses go either, and their route numbers clash with those of the marshrutkas. The new shelters at bus stops carry advertising only, not information, but you could try phoning 723433 for information. The buses have fixed stops on Rustaveli, Kostavas and Chavchavadze, but elsewhere they stop where the driver wants, like marshrutkas; however, they are much more sedate and comfortable than the marshrutkas. Some pointless and dangerous bus contraflows have also been introduced. Bus route 87 is a handy loop, from Freedom Square along Rustaveli Avenue, Kostavas, Gamsakhurdias Avenue and Vazha-Pshavelas Avenue to Delisi metro, then around by the university to Chavchavadze Avenue and back along Rustaveli to Freedom Square. Get on in the middle of the new buses, get off and pay (GEL0.40) at the front (unless you have a season ticket).

A few decrepit **trolleybuses** still run on a couple of routes, having been trounced by the marshrutkas; they are slow but very cheap and have plenty of space for baggage. Trolley 7 starts west of Baratashvilis Bridge, also on the left bank, and runs via Avlabari Square and Ortachala to Gorgasali Square; trolley 15 follows the same route to Avlabari, continuing to Samgori and Isani metro stations. Trolley 16 links Samgori and Ortachala.

There is also a cable car from Vake Park to Turtle Lake (working at weekends), but the cable car and funicular up to Mtatsminda are both out of action.

Ortachala bus terminal is served by marshrutkas 8, 10, 13, 24A, 45, 46, 48, 48A, 94, 108, 121, 132, 140, 149, 150, 161, 198 and 213, buses 5, 10, 19, 16, 50 and 55, and trolleys 7, 16 and 21; some of these terminate at the roundabout just to the west. The Didube bus station is best reached by metro, but many marshrutka routes pass it, notably 6, 32, 40, 41, 51, 61, 92 and 100.

1 Samgori metro, Isani metro, Kakheti Highway, Lilo
2 Chichinadze, Kindzmaraulis, Moscow Avenue, Ketevan Tsamebulis, Avlabari, Baratashvilis, Rustaveli Avenue, Kostavas (back by Varaziskhevis, Melikishvilis), Tamar Mepis Avenue, Voksal
3 Akhmeteli Metro, Mukhiani, Temka, Anapa, Sarajishvili metro
5 Aviation factory, Bogdan Khmelnitskis, Cholokashvilis, Ortachala, Gorgasalis, Metekhi Bridge, left bank, Baratashvilis, Rustaveli Avenue, Kostavas (Back: Kostavas, Varaziskhevis, Melikishvilis) Saakadze Square, Buluchauris, Vazha-Pshavelas (Back: Kazbegis), Kavtaradze, Tbilisi State University 'Maglivi' building
10 Varketili, Kaloubanis, Javakhetis, Samgori metro, Ketevan Tsamebulis, Ortachala, Gorgasalis, Baratashvilis
12 Avlabari metro, Baratashvilis, Rustaveli Avenue, Kostavas (Back: Kostavas, Varaziskhevis, Melikishvilis) Gamsakhurdias Avenue, Vazha-Pshavelas Avenue
14 Didi Digomi, Davit Agmashenebelis, Gagarin Square, Shartava, Kostavas, Varaziskhevi, Rustaveli Avenue, Baratashvilis
16 Baratashvilis, Gorgasalis, Rustavi Highway
17 Voksal, Tamar Mepis Avenue, Varaziskhevis, Melikishvilis, Rustaveli Avenue, Baratashvili, Gorgasalis, Rustavi Highway, Upper Ponichala
18 Avlabari metro, Meskhishvilis, Bukhaidze, Gorkis, Khetagurovis, Davit Agmashenebelis, Tamar Mepis Avenue, Voksal
19 Vazisubani, Varketili metro, Javakhetis, Moscow Avenue, Samgori metro, Ketevan Tsamebulis, Navtlugis, Baghdadis, Ortachala, Rustavi Highway, Upper Ponichala
21 Tbilisi State University Maglivi building, S Eulis, Vazha-Pshavelas, Kazbegis, Tamarashvils, Chavchavadze Avenue, Melikishvils, Kostava St (Back: Varaziskhevis), Heroes Square, Tamar Mepis Avenue, Central Market, Tseretelis, Robakidze Avenue, Ljubljana, Mioni factory, Automobile market, Didi Digomi
24 Gldani, Akhmeteli metro, Children's Hospital #2, Ljubljana, Robakidze Avenue, Gelovanis, Gagarini Square, Vazha-Pshavela Avenue, (Back: Kazbegis), Kavtaradze St, TSU 'Maglivi' Building
25 Vazisubani, Varketili metro, Javakhetis, Moscow Avenue, Samgori metro, Isani metro, Baratashvilis
27 Voksal, Tamar Mepis Avenue, Davit Agmashenebelis Avenue, Tsabadze, Tseretelis, Robakidze, Gelovanis, Godziashvilis, Vashlijvari
29 Gotsiridze metro, I Vakelis, Lisis, Oncological Hospital
30 Varketili, Sukhishvilis, Javakhetis, Moscow Avenue, Ketevan Tsamebulis, Saarbrucken Square, left bank, Tamar Mepis Avenue, Voksal
31 Aviation factory, Cholokashvilis, Bogdan Khmelnitsks, Baghdadis, Ketevan Tsamebulis, Avlabari, Baratashvilis, Rustaveli Avenue, Kostavas (Back: Varaziskhevis, Melikishvilis), Tamar Mepis Avenue, Voksal
33 Gldani, Vekua, Kerchis, Guramishvilis, T Eristavis, Tseretelis, Davit Agmashenebelis, Marjanishvilis, Elbakidze, Rustaveli Avenue, Freedom Square, Baratashvilis. Back: Rustaveli Avenue, Kostavas, Tamar Mepis Avenue, Davit Agmashenebelis, etc.
34 Tskneti, Bagebi, Chavchavadze Avenue, Melikishvilis, Rustaveli Avenue, Republic Square, Elbakidze, Marjanishvilis, Davit Agmashenebelis, Tamar Mepis Avenue, Voksal. Back: Voksal, Tamar Mepis Avenue, Varaziskhevis, Chavchavadze Avenue, Bagebi, Tskneti
37 Voksal, Tamar Mepis Avenue, Varaziskhevis, Melikishvilis (Back: Kostavas), Rustaveli Avenue, Baratashvilis, Ketevan Tsamebulis, Black Sea St, Kakheti Highway, Airport

CAR RENTAL Caucasus Travel have the franchise for **Hertz**, the first of the big chains to reach Georgia; contact CT Car Service, Metekhi Business Centre, Metekhi 22 on Avlabari Square (✆ *999100;* e *hertz@georgia.com.ge),* who offer both self-drive and chauffeur-driven cars. They also have a desk at the airport (✆ *995003;* f *995122; open Mon–Sat 09.00–18.00).* **Avis** are at Freedom Square 4 (✆ *923594;* f *923591;* e *reservations@avis.ge; www.avis.ge)* and at the airport, with cars costing around US$70 per day, plus insurance waivers etc. A cheaper option is **T & T International Ltd** (*Chavchavadze Av 9;* ✆ *553033;* f *233074),* who have Kia

39 Nutsubidze Plateau, Nutsubidze, Marijanis, Kavtaradze, Kazbegis (Back: Vazha-Pshavelas) Tamarashvilis, Chavchavadze Avenue, Melikishvilis (Back: Kostavas, Varaziskhevis), Rustaveli Avenue, Baratashvilis, Avlabari Metro, Isani Metro, Samgori Metro, Moscow Avenue, Javakhetis, Sukhishvilis, Varketili

40 Akhmeteli metro, Mukhiani, Temka, Guramishvilis, T Eristavis, Tseretelis, Davit Agmashenebelis, Heroes Square, Gamsakhurdias, Vazha-Pshavelas (Back: Kazbegis) Kavtaradze, TSU 'Maglivi' Building

42 Voksal, Tamar Mepis Avenue, Kostavas, Dolidze

46 Gigomi market, Beliashvilis, Tseretelis, Tsabadze, Davit Agmashenebeli, Heroes Square, Varaziskhevis, Melikishvilis (Back: Kostavas), Rustaveli Avenue, Baratashvilis, Avlabari metro, Isani metro, Gulia Square, Rustavi Highway, Kvemo Ponichala

48 Gotsiridze metro, Nutsubidze

49 Gotsiridze metro, Tavadze, Nutsubidze St, Dzotsenidze St, Nutsubidze Plateau

50 Vazisubani, Varketili metro, Javakhetis, Samgori metro, Isani metro, Baghdadis, Ortachala, Gorgasalis, Freedom Square

54 Mioni factory, Digomi, Tseretelis, Davit Agmashenebelis Avenue, Tamar Mepis Avenue, Voksal

55 Aviation factory, Bogdan Khmelnitskis, Cholokashvilis, Ortachala, Gorgasali, Metekhi Bridge, left bank, Baratashvilis, Rustaveli Avenue, Kostavas, Varaziskhevis (Back: Melikishvilis), Chavchavadze Avenue, Tamarashvilis, Gotsiridze metro, Kavtaradze, TSU 'Maglivi' building

56 Samgori metro, Isani metro, Kakheti Highway, Orkhevi

57 Voksal, Tamar Mepis Avenue, Kostavas, Gamsakhurdias, Bakhtrionis, Ikalto Hill

59 Vake Park, Chavchavadze Avenue, Melikishvilis (Back: Kostavas, Varaziskhevis), Elbakidze, Marjanishvilis, Davit Agmashenebelis, Saarbrucken Square

61 Bagebi, Chavchavadze Avenue, Melikishvilis (Back: Kostavas, Varaziskhevis), Rustaveli Avenue, Freedom Square, Baratashvilis

64 Agrarian University, Davit Agmashenebelis, Gagarin Square, Shartava, Kostavas, Varaziskhevi (Back: Melikishvilis, Kostavas), Chavchavadze Avenue, Bagebi

65 Dolidze, Kostavas, Rustaveli Avenue, Baratashvilis

69 Didube metro, Robakidze Avenue, Davit Agmashenebelis, Mukhatgverdi

71 Varketili plateau, Kakheti Highway, Isani metro, Avlabari metro, Baratashvilis, Rustaveli Avenue, Kostavas, Varaziskhevi (Back: Melikishvilis), Chavchavadze Avenue, Tamarashvilis, Vazha-Pshavelas Avenue, TSU 'Maglivi' Building

74 Didube metro, T Eristavis, Tsotne Dadianis, Chitaia, Chikobava, Nekrasov, Saarbrucken Square, Orbeliani Square (former US embassy)

76 Samgori metro, Moscow Avenue, Kakheti Highway, Lilo market

78 Voksal, Tamar Mepis Avenue, Heroes Square, Varaziskhevis, Melikishvilis, Chovelidze, Gogebashvilis, Rcheulishvilis, Zemo Vake

83 Gotsiridze metro, Nutsubidze, Nutsubidze Plateau

84 Digomi, Davit Agmashenebelis, Robakidze Avenue, Tseretelis, Dinamo Stadium

85 Vake Park, Tamarashvilis, Kazbegis, Gamsakhurdia Avenue, Kostavas, Heroes Square, Varaziskhevis, Chavchavadze Avenue, Vake Park (circular)

87 Freedom Square, Rustaveli Avenue, Kostavas, Gamsakhurdias, Vazha-Pshavela Avenue, Tamarashvilis, Chavchavadze Avenue, Melikishvilis, Rustaveli Avenue, Freedom Square

cars from US$50 per day or US$300 per week. **S&N** (*Chavchavadze Av 2;* ↘ *224958;* e *sandn.co@caucasus.net, sandnco@yahoo.com; www.snmotors.ge*) has bigger American cars for US$100–175 per day, US$150–175 per weekend or US$575–725 per week, with drivers available.

A far cheaper option is to look on the noticeboard at Prospero's Books (*Rustaveli Av 34*) where drivers offer themselves and their cars from US$15 per day. There are 24-hour petrol stations at the airport junction, Ortachala, and on the Mtskheta highway, and there are plenty of others on the river embankments.

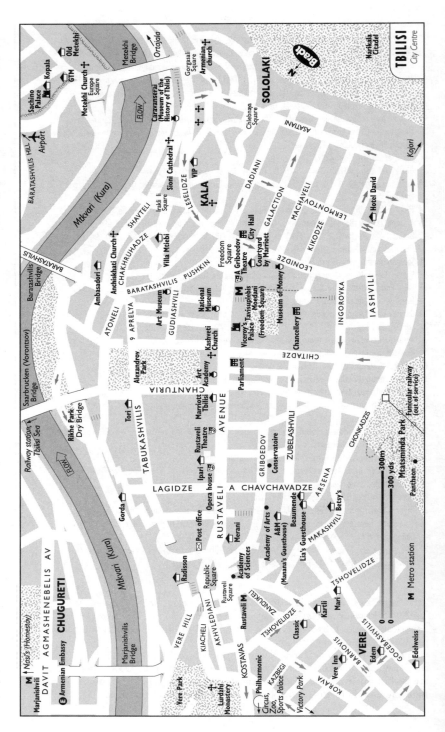

TBILISI
City Centre

92

After the Abkhazian war the Soviet-era block-hotels in Tbilisi and across Georgia were taken over by refugees and for a while there was almost nowhere to stay; soon a crop of small, pricey guesthouses sprouted up for businessmen; these often have no sign on the street (both for security and for tax evasion), and should be booked in advance. In the last couple of years a new generation of backpacker-oriented homestays have appeared, and there are also plenty of new small hotels, as well as a couple of new Marriotts for the business market. Now the refugees have been relocated from some hotels and these are being rebuilt as modern facilities: Radisson, Novotel, Intercontinental and Hyatt hotels are due to open in 2008–09, as well as an airport hotel. 'Kempinski plan to open a hotel on Rustaveli Avenue by 2010.

Most hotels cater for Georgian tastes with huge (cold) rooms and echoing apartments; a few, such as the Kartli, have smaller, snugger European-style rooms. All but the very cheapest have their own generator; few have lifts. Remember that you'll have to pay an extra 18% tax in many cases.

HOSTELS

Nasi Gvetadze Marjanishvilis 30/92; 950594. Just north of the Marjanishvilis metro station, to the right inside a courtyard to the left of Marjanishvilis St, this was for a long time the nearest thing to a backpackers' hostel. Nasi speaks German & acts like the retired schoolteacher she is, with strict rules such as no hanging towels to dry & being in bed by midnight. There are now some better alternatives, in the same area not far from the Voksal. *Shared rooms US$10 pp, with showers for US$1 more.*

Dodo Kevlishvili (3 rooms) Marjanishvilis 38; 954213. This is 2 blocks north (on the same side after the church) of Nasi Gvetadze's place. Dodo speaks English & has 3 rooms with beds. *Rooms GEL15 pp inc showers.*

Irina Japaridze Ninoshvilis 19; 954716; m 899 111669. This is the first street on the left after the Russian church (taking Marjanishvilis north from the metro); it's the top flat in the third building on the right. It's clean & spacious, with TVs & great views over the city, plus free internet access & 2 kitchens & a washing machine (GEL5 for a full load). It's very popular with Israelis & even hosts celebrations of major Jewish holidays. *Beds GEL15 pp.*

Khatuna's Chitaya (formerly Sovietskaya) 12, on the main road from the Dry Bridge to the rear of the Voksal; turn left at the top of Marjanishvilis, & it's on your left. From the Voksal, turn hard left (east) to take Pirosmanis, which leads into Chitaya. Long known to Japanese travellers. *Beds GEL8.*

Muradashvili Homestay Sulkhan-Saba 5; 935898; m 893 959947. This is on the other side of the river, right at the rear of the Marriott Courtyard Hotel. Tina works at the National Museum & Zviad is a taxi driver, so excellent & affordable tours can be arranged. *The cost is € 10 pp, inc a filling b/fast.*

Otherwise, for budget travellers looking for something slightly better than the Ortachala Hotel, the best bet is probably a private room; these are still in short supply, but can be booked through GeorgiCa (US$28 pp, with b/fast and shared bathrooms) – see page 51. For longer stays you might want to rent an apartment – see www.realestate.ge.

The hotels below are listed broadly from east to west, on the left/north bank and then the right bank. To book from abroad prefix phone numbers with +99532.

EAST OF THE CITY

Meridiani Kakheti Highway 69; 767563. On the left heading in from the airport, this is an acceptable stopover for one night, but too far from the city.

Ortachala In the international bus terminal (one flight up, sign in English); 724636. Nearer the Old Town. *Simple but good value at GEL20 pp (plus US$2 for a shower).*

AVLABARI (HANDY FOR THE AIRPORT)

⌂ **Sheraton Metechi Palace Hotel** (140 rooms) Telavi 20; ⟍ 772020; UK 0800 960501; f 772120; e smph@access.sanet.ge, smpth@sheraton.com; www.sheraton.com/Tbilisi. The city's premier hotel for many years, this has packed a lot of living into its short life. In 1994 it was taken over by Kalashnikov-toting *Mkhedrioni*, supposedly there to guard the place; instead there were lurid stories of shootings in the bar & drug dealing in the corridors. The US embassy banned its officials from going there (although the EC office was there), & its general manager fled back to Austria. Famously, a sign at the door read 'Handguns allowed, semi-automatics to be left at reception'. In 1997 the Marco Polo group sold it to Sheraton, never having made any profit. Now, of course, it's like any other international business hotel, with its 7-storey atrium & 3 gold & glass internal lifts, 24hr business centre, gym, indoor, outdoor & children's pools, jacuzzi & sauna, & is home to the Dutch embassy, Lufthansa, Austrian Airlines & Germania Express; nevertheless it's been overtaken by the Marriott downtown. Some rooms are non-smoking, which is seen as a strange Western affectation elsewhere in Georgia; the top 3 floors have been refurbished as executive rooms, with a lounge, office space, fax & free internet access. *Rooms from US$190 sgl or US$220 dbl, inc tax.*

⌂ **Old Tbilisi** (24 rooms) Ketevan Tsamebuli 27; ⟍ 773840–3; f 773844; e hoteloldtbilisi@yahoo.com; www.info-tbilisi.com/oldtbilisi. On the main road to the airport, this is a new & very nouveau hotel that is not really aimed at Westerners, although English is spoken. *Rooms US$95–100 sgl, US$125–130 dbl, & US$140–170 for a suite, inc b/fast & 3hrs internet access, on a PC or your laptop.*

⌂ **GTM** Metekhi Rise 4; ⟍ 273348; f 273349; e hoyel-gtmkapan@mail.ru; www.gtmkapan.ltd.ge. A modern business-style hotel in a prime location, with views over the river & Old Town; rooms are good & clean with cable TV & free laptop internet access, but English is not really spoken. There's a restaurant, conference hall, swimming pool, sauna, gym & billiards. *From US$50 sgl, US$60 dbl inc b/fast.*

⌂ **Dzveli (Old) Metekhi** (15 rooms) Metekhi 3; ⟍ 990536; f 997843; e oldmetekhi@yahoo.com; www.oldmetekhi.ge. A historic building set on the cliffs of the Mtkvari River, 10 of the 15 rooms have balconies with a view of the city. All rooms have AC, minibar, safe & satellite TV; there's also a good restaurant, which offers a 10% discount for hotel guests. *Rooms sgl US$50–90, dbl/twin US$60–100, apts US$120, all inc b/fast & tax.*

⌂ **Kopala** (11 rooms, 8 suites) Chekhov 8; ⟍ 775520; f 775590; e hotel@kopala.ge; www.kopala.ge. In a fantastic setting above the Metekhi church, but the views are best enjoyed from the rooftop terrace rather than the restaurant, which serves small portions of average food. The rooms are nice, with AC, satellite TV, minibar, internet access, safe & hairdryer; there's a gym, sauna & business centre. *Sgl from US$90, dbl from US$105, apts US$240, with b/fast.*

⌂ **Lile** (8 rooms) Gvinis Agmarti 19; ⟍ 773856; www.hotellile.ge. On the south side of Avlabari Sq, this has 8 rooms (1 en suite), in a good slick modern style, with cable TV & AC. It's clean & friendly, with some English spoken, although cheaper rooms can be a little noisy. Note that the hotel is above the café, through the door next to the double ones; they also offer cheap tours with their own 4x4 & minibus & guides who charge US$5 per hr, about half the tour agencies' rate. *Twins US$35–45; tax is inc, plus b/fast after 2 days.*

⌂ **Istanbul** (14 rooms) Davit Agmashenebelis 148; ⟍ 911182–4; f 911185; e istanbul@wanex.ge; www.istanbul.ltd.ge. In a former military school on the Turkish section of Davit Agmashenebelis, this new hotel has a cramped staircase & lift, but decent rooms with TV, minibar, free laptop connection & good bathrooms. English is spoken & a restaurant is opening in mid 2006. *Rooms US$50–120 inc b/fast.*

⌂ **Prestige** (25 rooms, 5 suites) Marjanishvilis 51; ⟍ 940505, 942974; f 965656; e hotelprestige@wanex.ge; www.hotelprestige.ge. Fairly handy for the Voksal, this small new hotel has AC rooms with satellite TV & minibar plus a restaurant-bar & parking. *Sgl US$50–60, dbl US$70, suites US$80–120.*

THE OLD TOWN

⌂ **VIP** (7 rooms, 1 suite) Leselidze 31; ⟍/f 920040, 989809; e hotel@vipmail.ge. In a courtyard without a sign, this hotel is accustomed to international business visitors & good English is spoken. *There are 4 sgl rooms at US$50, 3 twins at*

US$60, & a suite (with jacuzzi) at US$100, inc b/fast & tax; dinner can be ordered, & there's free internet access.

⌂ **Ata** (5 rooms) Leselidze 17; ⟍ 987715; f 986026; e info@hotelata.com; www.hotelata.com.

A modern block in fact on a side road off Leselidze, the adequate large rooms have small TVs, metal doors & electric water-boilers; Nana speaks fair English. *Sgl US$45, twin US$60 inc b/fast.*

⌂ **Dzveli Ubani** (15 rooms) Dumas 5; ☎ 922404; f 922464. Also just off Leselidze. This is an older building; rooms have cable TV, AC, fridge & rather oldish bathrooms. Very clean & friendly, with some English & good German spoken. *4 sgls at US$40, 9 dbls at US$50 plus a semi-suite at US$60 & a suite at US$80, all inc b/fast; dinner is available to order.*

⌂ **Courtyard by Marriott** (118 rooms) Tavisuplebis Moedani (Freedom Square) 4; ☎ 779100; f 779110; e tbilisi-marriott@caucasus.net; www.marriott.com/tbscy. Opened in 2002, this 4-star sidekick to the Marriott proper offers all necessary amenities at a slightly more affordable price. All rooms have 2 phone lines & dataport, voice mail, cable/satellite TV, AC, safe, hairdryer & iron. There's a health club, swimming pool & sauna, & a bar & brasserie, notable for its Sun brunch (12.00–16.00).

THE NEW TOWN

⌂ **David** (11 rooms) Iashvili 16A; ☎ 935006, 931685; f 982719; e giafbi@yahoo.com. Opened in 2001, rooms are a little Soviet-style, but bathrooms have tubs & the corridors are spacious & airy. Rooms have satellite TV, fridge & internet access for laptops, & there's a functional little restaurant. *Sgls (with dbl bed) US$50, dbl (with twin beds) US$70 & suites US$80, all inc b/fast but not tax.*

⌂ **Diplomat** (9 rooms, 1 suite) Bolo Agmarti 4; ☎/f 923746, 922088; e hoteldip@hotmail.com; www.qartuli.com/diplomat. A very comfortable modern hotel at the upper edge of the Old Town, the Diplomat's rooms are AC with satellite TV & minibar. There's a business centre with internet access & a sauna, gym & pool are available. Take marshrutka 12 or 196 to the first hairpin on the Kojori highway. *6 sgls at US$50–75, 3 twins at US$60–85, & a suite at US$70 (although unusually this only has a shower & no bath). Prices inc tax & b/fast.*

⌂ **Dea** (7 rooms) Mtkvari 3; ☎ 997045. Between the old central market & the river (just behind an old tower), marked by a bar/café sign, this is in fact a new hotel with good modern design, though a bit misapplied in places. Staff are friendly but don't really speak English. There is a sauna (GEL30 per hr), with a plunge pool & direct phone to the bar. *Twin rooms, with fans & shower, cost US$30–60 (the most expensive rooms inc b/fast).*

Deluxe (ie: regular) rooms cost from US$150, superior rooms from US$200, up to US$235 for a junior suite, all plus US$10 for b/fast, & tax.

⌂ **Villa Mtiebi** (8 rooms, 1 suite) Chakhrukhadze 10; ☎ 920340–2, f 923247; e tbilisi@hotelmtiebi.ge www.hotelmtiebi.ge. In a discreet & beautifully restored 19th-century building, with a lovely b/fast hall/winter garden, rooms all have AC, satellite TV, CD player, minibar, laptop access, free umbrella, hairdryer & orthopaedic mattress plus a large bathroom. There's also free internet access, gym, sauna & small swimming pool. *The 4 sgl rooms cost US$85, the 4 dbls US$100 & the suite US$130, all inc b/fast but exc tax.*

⌂ **Ambasadori** (42 rooms) Shavteli 13; ☎ 920403, 921627, reservations 998199; f 931740; e info@ambasadori.ge; www.ambasadori.ge. The grandest of Tbilisi's locally owned hotels, with a rooftop swimming pool, lift & business centre. *The AC rooms cost from US$110 sgl, US$160 dbl or twin, & up to US$250 for a suite with b/fast in the 4th-floor terrace café (open to 02.00).*

⌂ **Tori** (33 rooms, 6 suites) Chanturia 10; ☎ 923765; f 923822; e tori@access.sanet.ge. A gift from the Turkish army, this is run by Georgia's Ministry of Defence, but is in fact a perfectly normal hotel in a good location on the west side of the Alexandrov Park. Billiards, table-tennis & a Turkish bath are also available. There's a café-bar on the 3rd floor plus a full restaurant, & a business centre with internet access. *Twin US$100, a few sgls (US$80), suite (US$170–240), inc tax, b/fast, & use of the gym.*

⌂ **Gorda** (8 rooms) Sanapiro 8A; ☎ 934746; f 995523; e hotel_gorda@yahoo.com; www.welcome.ge/hotel_gorda. On the river embankment, with car parking at the rear. English, French, German & Italian are spoken, apparently. *Sgl US$50, dbl US$70–80, inc b/fast; 2 rooms have huge bathrooms, & some have balconies.*

⌂ **Marriott Tbilisi** (127 rooms) Rustaveli 13; ☎ 997200, toll-free UK 0800 221222, US 1 888 236 2427; f 997210; www.marriott.com/tbsmc. Built in 1915 as the Majestic & reopened in 2002, this is Tbilisi's only 5-star hotel. Innovations include Tbilisi's first wine bar, the Patio open-air summer restaurant & ice machines on each floor (one of which is smoke-free). *Deluxe (ie: standard) rooms cost from US$195 plus b/fast (US$15) & tax, executive rooms from US$285, & a presidential suite a mere US$995!*

🏠 **Ipari** (10 rooms) V Abashidze 4; 📞 996799; f 990751; e ipari@gol.ge; www.ltd.ge/ipari. Just off Rustaveli, east of the opera house, this family-run hotel is in a prime location & not too noisy. 4 rooms are 'luxe' with a balcony & a bath (although the boilers are a bit basic). *Sgl US$60, twin US$80, & 'luxe' US$100–120, inc b/fast & tax.*

🏠 **Merani** (7 rooms) Rustaveli 42; 📞 932378;

VERE

🏠 **Beaumonde** (11 rooms) Chavchavadze St 11; 📞 986003, 921172; f 996246; e bali103@hotmail.com. This is a comfortable friendly place with an atrium sitting area (with fireplace), free beer & wine, both European & Russian billiards tables, & big fish in a tank in the dining area. *US$80–100 with b/fast, plus dinner at US$10.*

🏠 **A and M** (Manana Skhirtladze's guesthouse) (6 rooms) Zubelashvili 51; 📞 936397; f 923435. Manana claims to have been the first to open a guesthouse in Tbilisi although she has now moved a block downhill to this building, with en-suite rooms, as well as meeting rooms, jacuzzi & a terrace with a good view. There's free use of a PC with scanner & printer. *Sgl US$90sgl, dbl US$100–135, both HB, inc laundry.*

🏠 **Mtis Kalta** Arsena 46; 📞 936397; f 923435. Manana Skhirtladze's original guesthouse, still a very comfortable & convenient place with TVs in the rooms & a video lounge with a huge Russian billiards table (which has bigger balls than the standard version, only just fitting into the pockets). There's one bathroom for every 2 rooms. *Sgl US$90, dbl US$100, both HB, inc laundry.*

🏠 **Lia's Guesthouse** (4 rooms) Arsena 35; 📞 920858; f 984443; e arsena35@yahoo.com. Opposite Manana's, her 'pupil' (15 years ago). Rooms at Lia's have ornate antique-style furniture (& TV). *Dbl US$70–80 inc b/fast; dinner is available if required.*

🏠 **Mari** Gogebashvilis 21; 📞 989551; f 989553; e ghousemari@internet.ge; www.g-housemari.ge. Once, as Betsy's Guesthouse, this was a Tbilisi institution, & although Betsy has retired there's still a very snug guesthouse there at the corner of Tamriko Tshovelidze (still better known as Belinskis) & Gogebashvilis, although externally it looks unfinished. Inc b/fast, laundry & internet access, & there's a roof terrace with great views. *Sgl US$80, twins US$90, plus tax.*

🏠 **Kartli** (5 rooms) Barnov 32; 📞/f 982982; e hot_kartli@gol.ge. German-owned, this is one of the more switched-on places in town; tours & airport transfers are available. *Sgl US$40, dbl*

f 934675; e hmerani@iberiapac.ge. A modern place with good service in a location that's hard to beat. The better rooms have a view of Rustaveli, although these are noisier. There's a snack bar that can provide simple meals, but there are plenty of restaurants nearby. It has its own generator, hot water & air-conditioning, & satellite TV. *Sgl US$60, dbl up to US$140, inc b/fast.*

US$80–100 (less in winter or for a week or more) inc b/fast but not tax.

🏠 **Vere Inn** (3 rooms) Barnov 53; 📞 294733; f 291252; e maiko_baratashvili@yaho.com; www.makler.com. Lovely dbl rooms, with sauna, plunge pool, a small bar, AC & satellite TV. *Dbl US$60–100 inc b/fast.*

🏠 **Classic** (8 rooms) Gogelia 18; 📞/f 227415, 251280; e info@classic.ge; www.classic.ge. Down an alley formerly known as 2nd Barnov Lane at Barnov 43, the Classic has AC & a friendly family atmosphere; English is spoken. *Sgl US$40, twin US$50 inc b/fast.*

🏠 **Kolkhi** (30 rooms) Shanidze 31; 📞 290936, 226679; f 234093; e info@hotelkolhki.ge; www.hotelkolhki.ge. One of the bigger & more reliable hotels in this area, there's internet access, a lift, a conference hall, & a restaurant on the 5th floor, with a great view; good English is spoken. *Twins US$50 sgl/dbl US$60, inc b/fast but not tax. A new block 2 doors away has nicer rooms with balconies for US$70 sgl, US$80 dbl.*

🏠 **Edem** (5 rooms) Shanidze 34; 📞 220160, 252712; e hoteledem@hotmail.com. A new family-run hotel; all rooms have shower, cable TV & AC; dinner is available to order, & good English is spoken. *US$60–80 per room inc b/fast.*

🏠 **Edelweiss** (9 rooms) Petriashvili 42; 📞 251235; f 294450; e edelweiss@wanex.ge; www.edelweiss.ltd.ge. A glitzy new hotel; all rooms have cable TV & balconies. There's a small garden, sauna & plunge pool, gym, massage & PC with internet access, but no restaurant, although b/fast is included (but not tax). Good English spoken. *Sgl US$70, dbl US$90.*

🏠 **Primavera** (19 rooms, 1 suite) Kuchishvili 8; 📞 251146; f 251147; e primavera@primavera.ge www.primavera.ge. An American-Georgian joint venture, this is a fine modern building on a less fine street. There's a swimming pool, gym & jacuzzi on the 5th floor & a Georgian-Italian restaurant, & there's free WiFi internet access on the top floors. *Dbl US$100, suite US$120–140, inc b/fast & tax.*

Vere Palace Hotel (17 rooms) Kuchishvili 24/8 (entry on Nikoladze); ☎ 253340–2; f 221298; e hotelvp@verepalace.com.ge; www.verepalace.com.ge. A modern block where the Pope stayed; there's a business centre & WiFi internet access, a bar & restaurant, & from 2007 a swimming pool. *Sgl US$90, dbl US$120 , suite US$140–200; prices inc b/fast but not tax.*

Demi (7 rooms) Ananauri 10; ☎ 220619; f 252321; e demi@access.sanet.ge; http://demi.myweb.ge. A nice friendly guesthouse; all rooms are dbl, with a tiny balcony. There's AC, satellite TV, & English is spoken. *Sgl US$70–120, dbl US$80–130, inc b/fast & tax.*

Iliani (24 rooms) Anjaparidze 1 (at Nikoladze); ☎ 234086, 335710; f 225676; e inrecenter@iliani.com; www.iliani.com. A modern block has rooms with AC, balcony, cable TV & minibar. Internet access is available in the business centre; the friendly staff speak English, but the lift & corridors are cramped. An extension includes conference facilities & a roof-top terrace. *Sgl (with a queen bed) from US$100, dbl from US$120 & suites from US$140, all inc b/fast & tax.*

VAKE

Morkinali (18 rooms, 4 suites) 26 May Sq 1; ☎ 221512; f 333356. This is a modern Turkish hotel just off the square behind a casino. Little English is spoken, but the facilities are pretty decent. *Twin GEL70, or GEL100 for half-luxe, GEL160 for luxe, inc b/fast.*

Iberia Inn (8 rooms) Bakhtrionis 10A;

SABURTALO

Bomond (or Beaumonde) **Garden Hotel** Marshal Gelovani 6; ☎ 303030, 532016; f 532092; www.mgroup.ge/bomond.php. Opened in 2006 on the western outskirts of the city, it has large AC rooms with terraces & a garden with open-air swimming pool plus sauna & a bar & restaurant, serving a Swedish buffet b/fast. *Dbl $120–140, suites $160.*

Nika (6 rooms) Mitskevich 38; ☎ 382931, 899 974266; e nick-ko@mail.ru. Reached by marshrutkas 22 & 171, this friendly guesthouse is popular with Peace Corps Volunteers visiting Tbilisi. All rooms have TVs, some English & German are spoken, & there's a nice garden with safe car-parking. *It has 3 rooms with facilities across the corridor, at US$40 for 2 or US$60 for 4, exc b/fast, & 3 newer en-suite rooms, 2 smaller ones at US$40 for 2, & a bigger one at US$30 for 1 or US$50 for two, inc b/fast.*

Varazi (44 rooms) Kostavas 45; ☎ 931161, 921630; f 921161; e hotelvarazi@yahoo.com. Opened in 2004, this aims to rival the Marriott & Ambasadori, but realistically cannot compete; still, it is a very affordable alternative. All rooms have AC, satellite TV & hairdryer; there's a café-bar in the foyer & 2 restaurants plus a 24hr business centre (plus laptop connections in some rooms) & 24hr laundry service. *Sgl US$90, dbl US$110, suite US$140–150, inc b/fast but exc tax.*

Betsy's Hotel (26 rooms) Makashvili 32; ☎ 931404, 923996; f 001237; e besty@2121.ge; www.betsyshotel.com. For many years Betsy's Guesthouse in Vere was a Tbilisi institution & Betsy herself Georgia's best-known expat; now she has retired but the name lives on. The hotel is used more by NGO workers than by business visitors or tourists; most rooms have with balconies & views across the city. Some are office suites with free fibre-optic broadband. There's a lift, spa, sauna & outdoor pool, plus a restaurant. *Sgl US$140, dbl US$165, suiteUS$175, plus tax.*

☎ 366835, 366827; f 366842. This looks like a particularly intimidating fortress, but inside it has huge rooms with tasteful grey décor. It seems almost deliberately disabled-unfriendly, with steps to the lift even on the ground floor. All rooms have satellite TV, minibar, hairdryer & so on. *Dbl US$100 B&B.*

Medea (6 rooms) Mitskevich 40; ☎ 370125; f 371243; e hotelmedea@posta.ge. A pleasant suburban house with a friendly spacious feel, perhaps not the most slickly managed of places. There are 6 rooms, with dbl beds (as well as the more usual twin singles), balcony, satellite TV & bath; laundry & car service are available, & a minimum of English is understood. *Sgl US$45–50, dbl US$55–60 inc b/fast, tax & internet access.*

Bu Mitskevich 40A; ☎ 381739, 380230; e hotelbu40@yahoo.com. This is a viable alternative if the others on Mitskevich are full; they're friendly but don't speak English. *Dbl $40.*

Lela Mitskevich 60; ☎ 371174; f 379933. Less good value than the Medea, despite unlimited fruit & drinks. They have off-street parking & a generator, but speak little English. *Sgl US$75, twin US$100 (discounts for longer stays).*

🛏 **Lago** (10 rooms) Kandelaki 27; \/f 380517;
e hotellago@hotmail.com; www.tbilisi-info.net/hotels/lago. A luxurious house with antiques & marble fireplaces & stairs (without banisters – beware!); rooms have balconies & AC. English is spoken, & dinner can be ordered. US$60–120 per room inc b/fast, free fruit, drinks, & use of the pool.

🛏 **Europe** (15 rooms) Kandelaki 23; ☎ 233432, 380696; f 969777; e hoteleurope@gmail.com; www.hoteleurope.ge. Formerly the Tamuna, this is a big, brightly lit place catering to the nouveau riche. There's a satellite phone as well as satellite TV. There's a restaurant & a business centre (with internet access), & some English is spoken, but it's still not very tourist-friendly. AC rooms cost from US$50 sgl, US$70 dbl, inc b/fast & tax.

🛏 **Patara Khibli** (5 rooms, 1 suite) Gamsakhurdias 44; ☎ 379421. A good budget option, the 'Little Khibli' (aka Tela) is hidden behind the Khibli proper, now filled with refugees; on Gagarin Sq, it's well served by public transport, inc the Sameditsino Institut (Medical Institute) metro station. B/fast is extra, & there's also laundry & car service. English not spoken, but staff are friendly. It has just 4 twin rooms (GEL40 with shared shower, GEL50 en suite), 1 trpl at GEL60, & 1 suite at GEL100.

🛏 **Tbilotel** (7 rooms) 1st Alley Gagarin Sq 8; ☎ 387804–6. A well-run place with good English spoken at reception, 24hr internet access (with a PC or your own laptop) & lift. The 5 'single' rooms take 2 people for US$70, & the 2 'doubles', with a dbl & a sgl bed, cost US$90, both inc b/fast plus AC & satellite TV.

🛏 **Sympatia** (14 rooms, 12 suites) 1st Alley

Gagarin Sq 4, Saburtalo; ☎ 995588; f 376263; e info@sympatia.com.ge; www.sympatia.com.ge. A big modern hotel, mostly aimed at 'biznessmen' ie: mafiosi, with a lift (but lots of steps to reach it), billiards, gym, sauna, jacuzzi, & a roof terrace with indoor & outdoor pools. All rooms have AC, satellite TV & minibar. Sgl from US$100, dbl US$120, with suites from US$210, all inc b/fast & tax.

🛏 **Khedi** ('View'; 16 rooms) Vedzisi 63; ☎ 380416; f 376263. Owned by the same group as the Sympatia, this is a big new building on the hillside above Saburtalo, best reached by car or their minibus – go to the northern end of Tashkent & then to the right up the hill. Sgl US$45, dbl US$55, inc b/fast, minibar, satellite TV & terrace.

🛏 **Villa Berika** (12 rooms, 5 suites) Dzotsenidze 9, Nutsubidze, III Microrayon; ☎ 942506; f 933562; e villaberika@access.sanet.ge; www.villaberika.com.ge. This is the most prestigious (or at least the most self-promoting) of Tbilisi's guesthouses, although it now calls itself a boutique hotel. It's run by the wife of the actor Ramaz Chkhikvadze, famous as Richard III, Lear & in Brecht's *Caucasian Chalk Circle* (a berika is a travelling mountebank); she also runs a travel agency & is a chum of Shevardnadze. Plenty of marshrutkas run to the Nutsubidze Plateau, & it's a short walk down to the bus on Kandelakis. Rooms have satellite phone & TV, free WiFi internet access, a minibar & Russian antique furniture. There's also a sauna, gym, billiards & garden, city view, laundry. Good English is spoken, & you can order lunch or dinner. Sgl US$80, dbl US$140, inc b/fast, plus tax.

✖ WHERE TO EAT

As with the hotels, these are listed from east to west, with the right bank first.

THE RIGHT BANK
Old Town

✖ **Olimpic** Leselidze 9; ☎ 935596. Khinkali is a speciality of the house. See page 69.
✖ **Thailand Kitchen** Leselidze 31; ☎ 988940. This restaurant is passable, though pricey & a bit slow at times; good vegetarian options. Mains GEL8–10.
✖ **Maidan** Rkinis Rigi 6 (on the embankment; entry on Sharden); ☎ 751188. Deceptively rustic, Maidan serves expensive Georgian food, with music from 20.00; it's owned by the same group as the nearby China Town.
✖ **China Town** Leslidze 44 (entry on Sharden);

☎ 751014/114. The grandest of Tbilisi's Chinese restaurants, specialising in seafood.
✖ **Kala** Irakli II 8; m 899 799737; www.cafekala.info-tbilisi.com. A good café, typical of the pedestrianised Irakli II, often with live jazz, but poor food.
✖ **Ars Longa Vita Brevis** Irakli II (opposite Kala). A French-style pavement café.
✖ **Bio Shop** Irakli II 10; ☎ 985013. Organic coffee, tea, juices & jams, plus soaps & shampoos. Closed Mon.

✗ **Agora** Irakli II II; **m** 877 488082. Sushi in the basement & European cuisine upstairs, but it's badly run & nothing special.

✗ **Argo** Irakli II 17; ✎ 999723. The ground-floor restaurant is furnished with Greek busts, while the basement bar is something like a single-deck trireme, with round portholes & a walkway over a fishpool. *Closed Mon.*

✗ **Prego** Irakli II 19; ✎ 999723. An adequate Italian restaurant-pizzeria.

✗ **Ar Idardo** (or Don't Worry; also known as the Sans Souci or Gabriadze's) Shavteli 13; ✎ 986594. A nice stylish place with a few interesting dishes such as sturgeon *shashlik*, although it's best for a drink on the balcony overlooking the church.

Near Freedom Square

✗ **Mukhrantubani** Baratashvilis Av 23; ✎ 997474. One of the best & most expensive restaurants in Tbilisi; it has an English-language menu & private rooms, making it ideal for business meals. There's also a German *Biergarten* here, & a converted tramcar in front selling *shashlik*, or kebabs.

✗ **Zur Glocke** Baratashvilis Av 17; ✎ 921916. This is a German *Bierstube*.

✗ **Narindji** Baratashvilis Av 9; ✎ 995308. West Georgian food a speciality.

✗ **The Golden Fleece** Vertskhli 55; ✎ 977877. At the top end of Baratashvilis, this specialises in Mingrelian food, inc *gebjalia* (cheese in mint), & both *elargi* & *ghomi*, 2 forms of polenta.

✗ **Tbilisuri** Pushkin 19 & 23; ✎ 988191. A good restaurant offering Georgian food, fast food & a nightclub/bar.

✗ **Lotos** Freedom Sq 7; ✎ 515342. Tbilisi's best (& only) vegetarian restaurant, especially busy in Lent; it serves hot dishes such as khinkhali, pakoras, samosas & pizza, as well as sweets & juices.

✗ **Racha** Lermontov 12 (at Dadiani). Serves food & wine from Racha, of course.

✗ **Gratsi** (Graz) Lermontov 9 (at Dadiani); ✎ 923613. In a 19th-century cellar built of 400-year-old bricks, this restaurant serves Austrian food as well as international & Georgian cuisine.

Rustaveli Avenue

✗ **Nikala** Rustaveli Av 22; ✎ 997075. A slick café (one of a chain), affordable & busy with ordinary Georgians enjoying kebab, chips & beer, for instance.

✗ **Lagidze** Rustaveli 24. Known for the 'Lagidze waters', drinks which the Lagidze brothers made to a secret recipe, rather like Coca-Cola; however, on the street corner stairs lead down to a long narrow café which serves Adjaran *khachapuri* as good as any you'll find in Batumi, for GEL1.60. *Open 10.00–22.00.*

✗ **Pizza Palermo** Rustaveli 26. Serves fast food & German beer 24hrs a day; it also has branches at

Dadiani 9 & across the river at Tsereteli 67.

✗ **New Asia** A block south at Griboedov 11/3 (actually on Mitropani); ✎ 922107. A reliable Chinese restaurant.

✗ **Khinkhlis Sakhli** (the Khinkhali House) At the west end of Rustaveli, at the south entrance to the plaza under Republic Sq, at the rear of Rustaveli 37. This is the place for a huge meal of dumplings (inc vegetarian options) at low cost.

✗ **Paradise Lost** Rustaveli Sq (opposite McDonald's); ✎ 999207. Supremely kitschy décor (& as a rule a London taxi parked outside) but good food.

Near the flower market

✗ **Tamada** Orbeliani 37; ✎ 923280. A well-known tourist restaurant, with staff in Georgian costume serving pretty decent Georgian cuisine, with live Georgian music.

✗ **Mshrali Khidi** (Dry Bridge) Sanapiro 3; ✎ 921455. More or less behind the former US

embassy, this is a popular steak house of long standing.

✗ **Dzveli Sakhli** (or Old House) Sanapiro 6; ✎ 923497. One of the best Georgian restaurants, if a bit touristy, with music & a dance display on weekend evenings.

Perovskaya Akhvlediani Street (still best known as Perovskaya) leads west from Republic Square towards the Philharmonic, in what was the academic and literary quarter; along it are many of Tbilisi's most popular bars, most of which offer food of some type, although it tends to be a featureless blend of Georgian and international styles. There are some good restaurants too:

✕ **Picnic** Akhvlediani 13. Just 4 tables but it says there's no need to book; there's a good spread of Georgian dishes on the menu.
✕ **Matiane Restaurant** & **Nostalgia** Akhvlediani 14; ☎ 986925. An upmarket pub with food, & jazz on Sun nights.
✕ **Csaba's Jazz-Rock Café** Vashlovani 3; ☎ 923122. On a side street off Akhvlediani, this café offers Hungarian food as well as music. *Open 12.00–04.00.*
✕ **Emigrant** Vashlovani 6; ☎ 986164. Decorated with suitcases & foreign signs, this place serves excellent Georgian/European food (notably steaks) & does a good line in business lunches, with jazz after 19.00.
✕ **Stones** Akhvlediani 17; ☎ 923574. Serves food cooked on hot stones. *Open 12.00–midnight.*
✕ **Maharajah** Akhvlediani 24; ☎ 999799. A curry house serving fairly authentic dishes.
✕ **Ovatio** Akhvlediani 19; ☎ 931084. Serves Georgian/international cuisine.
✕ **Santa Fe** Akhvlediani 20; ☎ 935848. Offers Mexican food.
✕ **Caruso** Akhvlediani 20; ☎ 417146. Offers Italian food & cocktails.
✕ **Taverna Sancho** Akhvlediani 23; ☎ 995751. Serves tapas, supposedly 24hrs a day.
✕ **Profile** Kiacheli 8; ☎ 923007. Serves the same bland mix of cuisines as most Akhvlediani places; open 24hrs a day.
✕ **Picasso** Vashlovani 4; ☎ 989086. Chinese restaurant just off Akhvlediani by the Super Babylon department store.
✕ **Sakartvelo** Melikishvilis 12; ☎ 221334. In the closed hotel of the same name, this is a mafia haunt serving Georgian & European food. *Open 13.00–01.00.*
✕ **Le Cabernet** Tatishvili (formerly Kazbegi) 8; ☎ 225865. A fine French restaurant.
✕ **Rainer's** Barnov 39; ☎ 982982. Just up the hill from the Philharmonic, Rainer's serves a mix of German, Italian & French cuisine from noon till at least 23.00, & also delivers pizza.
✕ **European Bistro** (usually just known as Zandukeli 40) Zandukeli 40; ☎ 933633. Also owned by Rainer Kaufmann & serves good affordable Georgian & European food to a bluesy soundtrack.
✕ **Café Goethe** Zandukeli 16. Also run by Rainer Kaufmann. Serves good cheap food in a great garden.
✕ **Best Georgian Food Takeaway** Barnov (by the viaduct). This does what it says on the box.
✕ **Varazis Khevi** Kekelidze 13. Below the viaduct, this is a simple local-style eatery.
✕ **Nikala Café** Gamsakhurdias 12. Just one branch of the chain.
✕ **Café-Pizza Palermo** Gamsakhurdias 19. Specialises in fish.
✕ **Café Batumi** Gamsakhurdias 21. Also specialises in fish.
✕ **Gusto Pizza** Gamsakhurdias 35 (opposite Vazha-Pshavelas).
✕ **Xiangang** (ie: Hong Kong) Gamsakhurdias 41 (on Gagarin Square); ☎ 379688. A flashy Chinese place; in addition to Hong Kong specialities it also serves Beijing smoked duck.
✕ **Prego** Vazha-Pshavelas 2 & Paliashvilis 14 (near the UN Circle); ☎ 373610). Serves good-value pizza.
✕ **Pizza Uno** Abashidze 30; ☎ 913205. More good pizza.
✕ **La Gorda** Abashidze 5; ☎ 221015 Tbilisi's first Spanish restaurant, serving good paella & tapas.
✕ **Fantastico Pizza** Nafareuli 3A; ☎ 294675. Near the university, a great cheap Italian place (for pizza, pasta and desserts) - smokey, but they do takeaway.
✕ **Il Garage** Mtskheta 1 (on the UN Circle or Round Garden); m 877 78009. The most authentic Italian restaurant in Tbilisi; it's moved from the original garage & is still small but has a good-sized terrace. A free portion of bruschetta is followed by huge portions of pasta or pizza. *Closed Sun.*
✕ **Round Garden bar-restaurant** Barnov 83; ☎ 252052. A pleasant place to take a break.

If you need **food on the run**, Georgia's first branch of **McDonald's** opened in 1999 next to the Rustaveli metro station, and there's now a second branch on Marjanishvilis Square; they're smoke-free so make a popular meeting point for expats. There are also plenty of pastry shops, at some of which you can sit and take a break; there's a particularly good range at an unnamed café and pastry shop at Leonidze 11 (on the corner of Ingorokva). Near Freedom Square there's the **Market Café-Bar** (serving Adjaran khachapuri) at Rustaveli 2 and a snack bar at Rustaveli 1 (by the National Museum), as well as an unnamed café by the subway exit in Freedom Square, which is a pleasant place for an al-fresco drink or meal and often has live music in the evenings. The **Swiss Bakery Shop** at Melikishvili 14 sells expensive rye loaves and the like. **Donut and Coffee** at Abashidze 10 is a Starbucks-style café (with non-smoking section) that also serves salads, sandwiches and pasta.

THE LEFT BANK The **Sheraton Metechi Palace Hotel** has a variety of very fine restaurants (✆ 772020); if you are staying here with an expense account, you need look no further.

✘ **King Gorgasali** 10th floor (with great views). This is the best of the bunch & serves seafood & steaks, & has Georgian wines dating back to the 1930s. *Open Mon–Sat 19.00–23.00, closed Sun.*

✘ **Narikala** Specialises in Georgian cuisine & offers a buffet for US$15. *Open 07.00–23.00.*

✘ **Slammers bar** Offers burger, pizza & TexMex food – it's a casual spot popular with single business travellers. *Open 17.00–01.00.*

✘ **Metekhis Chrdilishi** Ketevan Tsamebuli 29 (opposite the Metechi Palace); ✆ 779383. In Metechi's Shadow, known to expats as 'In Sheraton's Shadow', this is an expensive place serving Georgian cuisine with programmes of music & dance, & great clifftop views across the city & a winter garden, linked by a bridge to the main restaurant.

Chugureti To the west of the Metekhi church and the Europe Square roundabout, in the Rike or Peski area used by the Tbilisoba festival, are several popular restaurants, including the **Deda Zoya**, **Erisioni**, **Odishi**, **Saradjishvili** and **David**. There are various small Turkish cafeterias between Davit Agmashenebelis 110 and 120, and the similar **Armazi** at No 76. The Guria at No 100 offers cheap local food but with an English menu, and the **Café-Bar Alba**, nearby at Marjanishvilis 7, also serves 'Georgian National Dishes'; it has basic café-style décor but the food is good and cheap. **Taverna Integrali**, at Marjanishvilis 4, offers country-style cooking and is good value with dishes costing about GEL4. **Shemoikhede Genatsvale** (Step In, Darling; tel: 910005), at Marjanishvilis 5 (on the ramp left down to the embankment) is a cheerful noisy Bierkeller-style place that specializes in khinkhali and mtsvadi. There's also a branch of **McDonald's** on Marjanishvilis Square. On Saarbrucken Square, **Tiflis** is a simple place that serves the best kebabs in town as well as mtsvadi, lobiani and salad.

BARS AND CAFÉS

Most bars simply serve their locals and don't bother with any sign beyond that supplied by Heineken, Guinness, Budvar or Grolsch; others make more of an effort and can really be quite stylish (and even pricey). Many bars serve food and may be listed in the previous section.

LEFT BANK On the left bank there are various bars and cafés, none of any great distinction.

⬚ **Muza** Davit Agmashenebelis 71. A chic new café-bar.

⬚ **Plekhanov** Davit Agmashenebelis 98. At the western exit from Marjanishvilis Square, this is a good local bar.

⬚ **Café Lux** Davit Agmashenebelis 86. A café with some fast food.

⬚ **Ludia** On the embankment just west of the Marjanishvilis bridge. This bar is actually part of the Kazbegi Brewery, & there are also drive-up windows

where commuters can buy takeaway beer or stand & drink from plastic glasses; old women sell plastic jugs & dried fish, the indispensable accompaniment to Georgian beer.

⬚ **World Sport Café** Mayakovksi 5/Tseretelis 2; ✆ 950236, 958062; e wsportcafe@hotmail.com. In the Mushtaid Garden near the Dinamo Stadium, this café has big-screen TVs, a Formula 1 car stuck to the high ceiling & the best ribs in Georgia.

Old Town There's more excitement in the old town, where Sharden is now the city's trendiest street. Nearby, as mentioned above, the pedestrianised Irakli II is lined with pleasant cafés.

Ð **Sharden Bar** Sharden 4, ☍ 752044. Poor food & service but a nice place to sit outside in summer.
Ð **Kala** Irakli II 8; ⌨ 899 799737. Western prices & beers; live jazz 21.00–23.30 nightly.
⊒Ð **Ars Longa Vita Brevis** Irakli II A French-style pavement café.
⊒Ð **Agora** Irakli II 11; ☍ 488082. A café with low tables & armchairs where all the cool hipster kids gather on a Sun afternoon; there's rock music in the basement on weekend nights.
Ð **Argo** Irakli II 17; ☍ 999723. This has a basement bar that is something like a single-deck trireme, with round portholes & a walkway over a fish pool. *Closed Mon.*

Ð **Kaiserbrau brewpub** Sioni 8; ☍ 920322; www.kaiser.ge. On the embankment just west of the Sioni cathedral, marked by two griffons. Beers are unfiltered & brewed to the traditional German recipe with no preservatives; you can also eat German food & watch European soccer on a big screen.
Ð **The Hangar** Shavteli 20; ☍ 931080, 911080. One of the main expat drinking holes, with free WiFi & major sporting events screened live.
Ð **Ar Idardo** or Don't Be Upset (also known as the Sans Souci or Gabriadze's) Shavteli 13; ☍ 986594. A great place for a drink, although it only has foreign beers as well as lots of teas; there's WiFi, & one of Georgia's best pianists plays here from 22.00 nightly.

South of Freedom Square In this area there are quite a few cellar bars, some rather trendy (and with English names), others less so. These include:

✗ **Sakhinkle** Dadiani 8. A good local basement restaurant.

Ð **Solo Cellar Bar** Dadiani 13

Along Rustaveli

⊒Ð **Sarangi** Rustaveli 37. Opposite the Academy of Sciences. A café/patisserie.
⊒Ð **Café Rustaveli** Rustaveli 30. Another café/patisserie.
Ð **Marco Polo Tavern** Rustaveli 44; ☍ 935383. A Western-style pub-bar with almost Western prices.
⊒Ð **The Fashion TV Café** Rustaveli 18; ☍ 922288, 300930. A café-bar (with WiFi) & a very trendy nightclub (from 22.00) aimed squarely at the wealthiest & shallowest; the staff are all wannabe models, of course. There may be an entry fee when international DJs perform. *Closed Aug.*
⊒Ð **Caliban's Coffee** Prospero's Books, Rustaveli 34.

A popular expat meeting place (the coffee's pricey but good, & there are free refills).
⊒Ð **Vincent** Rustaveli 19. A fashionable & pricey tea house.
Ð **Business Club** Tabukashvili 43. Despite its name, this is a cellar bar.
⊒Ð **Apollo Café** Lagidze 2 (by the Opera House). Pleasantly rough-&-ready.
♀ **Acid Bar** Lagidze 2 (by the Opera House). Trendier than the Apollo.
⊒Ð **Elada coffee bar** At the corner of Chavchavadze St & Griboedov.

Along Akhvlediani

Ð **Nali Pub** at the angle of Kiacheli. Near Republic Square, this is supposedly Irish.
Ð **Dublin** Akhvlediani 6 (on the corner of Ekaladze). Another 'Irish pub'.
⊒Ð **Chveni Ezo** Akhvlediani 14. A restaurant-café-bar.
Ð **Wheels** Akhvlediani 16. This also has an Irish tinge.

♀ **Metro** Akhvlediani 11. Painfully hip but popular with the late-night crowd.
⊒Ð **Ovatio & Bar Paradise** Akhvlediani 21. As much a restaurant as a bar; popular with expats.
♀ **DJ's Café** Akhvlediani 23. A disco-bar that's crowded with young Georgians.

Along Vashlovani, Kiacheli and nearby

⊒Ð **Csaba's Jazz-Rock Café** (see above) Vashlovani 3; ☍ 923122 offers good food & music.

Ð **Manhattan** Vashlovani 8; ☍ 986944
Ð **Toucan & Profile** pubs Kiacheli 8

Colibri Kiacheli 12. With draft Bitburger beer.
Kartuli restaurant Kiacheli 14. With Staropramen Bohemian beer. At the end on Nikoladze are a Krombacher bar & a café.
Rainer's Biergarten A block further uphill at

Along Chavchavadze Avenue

Bistro 2 Near the university. A really simple cafeteria-style place with decent pastries, tea, coffee, beer & juice at student prices (don't bother with the savouries).
Acid Bar Chavchavadze 16. (See above.)
Café Batonebi Chavchavadze 23; ℡ 250669. An expat-friendly place serving Georgian & Western food, inc salads, pizza, burgers, sandwiches & TexMex egg rolls; there's also WiFi.
Bar 24 Chavchavadze 40. So called because it's open non-stop.

Other coffee houses

Whittards of Chelsea There are several outlets, known as English Tea House, or Elite Tea House (www.teahouse.ltd.ge), at Marjanishvilis 5, Paliashvilis 32 & Vekua 3 (in the Georgian Trading Centre).
Literary Cafés (www.literaturuli.com) Kostavas 46, under the Philharmonic; ℡ 921649,

Barnov 32. Open 12.00–midnight.
Café Petozi Petriashvili 20. A nice but slightly smokey little café with Lavazza coffee, 3 types of khachapuri & salads.

Smuggler's Inn Chavchavadze 42; ℡ 253314. A British pub complete with dartboard, which is one of Tbilisi's main expat hangouts.
Café Albatros Chavchavadze 46; ℡ 225158. This trendy place offers Italian food & burgers.
Rio Arabica Coffee House Chavchavadze 22; ℡ 252252. Part of a chain that's rather pricey & annoying (those listed below are rather more attractive); there are other branches at Kostavas 44, Kazbegi 2 & elsewhere.

Gamsakhurdias 31; ℡ 313097 & Abashidze 22; ℡ 220276, which incorporate interesting bookshops & hold book launches & talks.
Café Canapé Abashidze 14. More of a café-bar, with alcohol, as well as WiFi.
Bar Capo Abashidze 10

ENTERTAINMENT

NIGHTCLUBS Tbilisi doesn't have a wild nightlife, with just a couple of clubs open to 04.00.

☆ **Adjara Casino** 26 May Sq 1. One of Georgia's best jazz quartets plays here for 5hrs every night; with leading Georgian DJs following on Fri nights & European DJs on Sat.
☆ **Beatles Club** Kostavas 25 (opposite the Philharmonic); ℡ 920950. A Tbilisi institution, with its Sergeant Pepper-style décor, this almost closed in 2006 – it was saved, but no longer has live music.
☆ **Blues Brothers Club** Rustaveli 38; ℡ 931226; e bluesbrothers@bluesbrothers.ge. A café (with Georgian & English dishes), with live music Thu–Sun from 22.00 – jazz, blues & rock, with local & foreign musicians, & also a 1980s' disco.
☆ **Club Neo** Kazbegi 12A; ℡ 382707. Dancing to house & trance music.
☆ **Metechi Night Club** Sheraton Hotel. There's also the Club Karavansarai on the 10th floor. Open daily 18.00–02.00, to 04.00 on Thu, Fri & Sat.

☆ **Night Office** under the Baratashvilis Bridge on the right bank; ℡ 923016. The gimmick here is that staff in one bar are all women, in the other all men; it's a modern high-tech club with laser show & 3 bars inc chill-out zone. Open only Fri & Sun 21.00–05.00, admission men GEL11, women GEL7.
☆ **Noa Noa** Rustaveli Av 12 (opposite the Marriott Hotel). Jazz, Latin jazz & pop.
☆ **The Tunnel** (Gvirabi) Asatiani 30; m 898 177715. In a nuclear shelter built during the Cuban Missile Crisis, this is one of the most popular youth venues at the moment.
☆ **TwoSide** 7 Bambis Rigi (Cotton Row); ℡ 439038. The Left Side is an American 1930s-style restaurant; The Right Side is a hang-out club, with jazz, then DJs from 22.00. Admission GEL20.

CASINOS These are decidedly unglamorous places dominated by slot-machines & businessmen offloading their ill-gotten gains.

☆ **Adjara** 26 May Sq 1; ☎ 334520. Open 24hrs for blackjack, poker & roulette.
☆ **Berikoni** Irakli II Sq 2 (on the embankment); ☎ 932877
☆ **Flamingo** Rustaveli 14
☆ **Grand Tbilisi** Rustaveli 40; ☎ 920026

☆ **Grand Casino Sakartvelo** Melikishvilis 12 (former Hotel Sakartvelo); ☎ 221478
☆ **Iveria** Inashvili 16; ☎ 982463
☆ **Nali** Melikishvilis 1 (at the Philharmonic); ☎ 987680

THEATRES These close at the end of June for the summer.

😃 **Shota Rustaveli State Theatre** Rustaveli 17; ☎ 981894, 936583. Newly refurbished, with 2 modern theatres seating 300 & 800 people plus a studio theatre. Tickets GEL5–25.

😃 **Zakaria Paliashvili State Opera House** Rustaveli 25; ☎ 206040; www.opera.ge, www.ballet.ge. Tickets GEL5–15 from the box office on the east side (open 11.00–14.00 & 15.00–18.00).

😃 **Basement Theatre** Rustaveli 42 (up the alley); ☎ 999500; e sardapi@sardapi.ge; www.sardapi.com; also Chavchavadze Av 32, Vake; ☎ 912795. The best avant-garde theatre in Georgia. Tickets GEL10.

😃 **Pantomine Theatre** Rustaveli 37; ☎ 982506

😃 **Griboedov Russian Theatre** Rustaveli 4; ☎ 931106; also the **Liberty Theatre** (☎ 985821) at the rear, with a ship's bow & portholes.

😃 **Nabadi Folk Theatre** Rustaveli 19; ☎ 989991; e nabaditheater@yahoo.com. A 90min show presenting the history & culture of Georgia, with wine. Starts at 20.00 daily except Tue.

😃 **Reso Gabriadze's Marionette Theatre** Shavteli 13; ☎ 996620. Puppet theatre for adults.

😃 **Fingers Theatre** Javakishvili 19 (just below Rustaveli); m 822 933272. The dancing fingers perform Georgian dance, the can-can & Michael Jackson routines, all in great costumes. Open Thu–Sun 19.00, children's performances Sat & Sun at 12.00. Tickets GEL7.

😃 **Tbilisi State Puppet Theatre** Davit Agmashenebelis 105; ☎ 957874

😃 **Mikheil Tumanishvili Movie Actors' Theatre** Davit Agmashenebelis 164; ☎ 959734, 340937

😃 **Abashidze Musical Comedy Theatre** Davit Agmashenebelis 182; ☎ 348193

😃 **Dumbadze Children's Theatre** Davit Agmashenebelis 60; ☎ 950309

😃 **Marjanishvilis Theatre** Marjanishvilis 8; ☎ 955500; f 957668. Built in 1928, with the usual Moderne ironwork & newly refurbished, this is the headquarters of the annual GIFT festival – see page 44.

😃 **Old House Theatre** Metekhi Hill 1; ☎ 770464

😃 **Armenian Theatre** Avlabari Sq, Ketevan Tsamebuli 8; ☎ 741656

😃 **Veriko Anjaparaidze Single Actor's Theatre** rear of Anjaparaidze 16; ☎ 221338

😃 **'Garek's theatre'** This is a new private (Soros-funded) puppet theatre off Tsulukidze kucha (behind Avlabari metro station), currently working only in the Armenian & French languages.

😃 The **Royal District Theatre** (Samepor Ubenese Teatri) Georgi Abesadze 10, Sololaki; ☎/f 996171; www.rd.theatre.ge. This theatre was built as a caravanserai in 1898, became a Cultural Centre under Beria, & was abandoned in 1987. In 1992 Isa Grigoshvili, leading lady of the Rustaveli Theatre for 30 years, was sacked for going on a tour of Germany without permission, although she claimed it was because of her Zviadist politics; she, her husband, actor/director Mairab Tavadze, & their son Nico Tavadze, decided to set up an independent company in the Royal District Theatre & were ready to reopen in 1995, when a Jewish group claimed it as a former synagogue. A furious legal battle erupted & all the city's unemployed actors joined an 'act-in', 24hr a day for 10 days, until they won the right to open as a theatre. It is now an important venue for the GIFT festival & scene of much of the city's liveliest drama.

CINEMAS There are plenty of cinemas in the suburbs, although they're suffering from TV and video competition; the main venue for art films (mostly dubbed into Russian) and home of the Tbilisi International Film Festival in October (www.tbilisifilmfestival.ge) is the **Amirani Cinema**, under the Philharmonic at Kostava 36 (☎ 329310; e amirani@amirani.ge; www.amirani.ge). There's also the **Kinos Sakhli** (or Dom Kino) in the west end of the Academy of Sciences on Rustaveli Square (the top door, above the restaurant), which has been well refurbished recently. The best commercial cinema is the **Rustaveli** (or Century

21) at Rustaveli 5 (✆ 997605). Phase 1 of the Cinema City project, on Davit Agmashenebelis diagonally opposite the Dinamo stadium, should open in late 2007, with six screens, a hall for live shows, a café, and ultimately a cinema museum.

MUSIC **Classical music** is performed at the **Philharmonic** (✆ 984523); the Tbilisi Symphony Orchestra (*www.tcmc.ge*) was founded in 1993 by Djansug Kakhikdze (1935–2002), splitting away from the Georgian State Symphony Orchestra, and is now conducted by his son Vakhtang. Other venues are the **opera house** and the **Rustaveli Theatre**, the **summer theatre** at Davit Agmashenebelis 123, and the **Conservatoire's concert halls** at Griboedov 8 (✆ 922446; e *classical@classical.ge*) (see page 114).

There's good **jazz** at the Adjara Casino (*26 May Sq 1*) and the Café Kala (*Irakli II 8*) and less good jazz at bars on Akhvlediani; rock venues include the Agora (*Irekli II St 11*) and Griboedov 14 (*at Griboedov 14, where else*). Tony O'Malley (once of Kokomo & 10cc) currently plays on Sat nights at Noa Noa (Rustaveli Av 12, opposite the Marriott Hotel) – recommended.

BATHS Traditionally Tbilisi's baths are for women only on Tuesdays and Wednesdays. The best-looking ones are the **Orbeliani** (or Chreli) baths at the top

---

EMBASSIES IN TBILISI

Armenia Tetelashvilis 4, 1 block west of Marjanishvilis Square; ✆ 951723, 959443; f 990126, 964286; e armemb@caucasus.net. Visas for 21 days can be obtained at the border for US$30; e-visas are valid only for arrivals by air.

Azerbaijan Kipshidze St block 2, building 1; ✆ 252639, 253526–8; f 250013; e secretariat@azembassy.ge; www.azembassy.ge. Take bus 61, 71 or 55 from Rustaveli & get off on Chavchavadze Av just before Victory Sq, walk down the street by a large statue & then take the first right & the first left. Visas cost US$40 & need 2 photographs; those for 7 days can usually be issued the same day (leave your passport between 10.00 & noon & collect it between 16.00 & 18.00), those for 1–3 months take 2–4 days.

China Barnov 52; ✆ 252175; f 252283; e gzj@access.sanet.ge

European Union Chkheidze 38; ✆ 943763; f 943768; www.delgeo.ec.europa.eu

France Gogebashvilis 15; ✆ 999976, 934210; f 953375; e ambafrance@access.sanet.ge. Schengen visas issued at Gogebashvilis 11 (✆ 922851; open Mon, Tue, Thu, Fri 09.30–13.00).

Germany Davit Agmashenebelis 166; ✆ 447399, 953326; f 911651; e deut.bot.tbilissi@access.sanet.ge; www.tiflis.diplo.de. Due to earthquake damage the consulate is at the address above but the rest of the embassy is semi-permanently on the fourth floor of the Sheraton Metechi Palace Hotel, Telavi 20 (✆ 447300, 910332; f 447364).

Iran Zovrety 16; ✆ 986990–2, 376829; f 986993, 381257; e iranemb@geonet.ge

Israel Davit Agmashenebelis 61; ✆ 951709; f 237133, 955209; e tbilisi@mfa.gov.il

Russian Federation Chavchavadze Av 51; ✆ 912406, 912645; f 912738; e russianembassy@Caucasus.net

Turkey Chavchavadze Av 35; ✆ 252072–4; f 220666; e tiflisbe@yahoo.com, tiflisbe@dsl.ge

Ukraine Oniashvilis 75; ✆ 311161, 989362; consul ✆/f 237145; e ukraina@access.sanet.ge

UK GMT Plaza, Freedom Sq 4; ✆ 274747; f 274792; e british.embassy.tbilisi@fco.gov.uk; www.britishembassy.gov.uk. Open Mon–Fri (except Georgian & British holidays) 09.00–17.00.

United Nations Kazbegi 2A (on the UN Circle); ✆ 998558, 375228; f +49 5151 12013 ext 182

USA Balanchine 11, Didi Digomi, 0131 Tbilisi; ✆ 277000; f 532304; e consulate-tbilis@state.gov; http://georgia.usembassy.gov. Consulate open Mon–Fri 14.00–17.00 & by phone 09.00–12.00 (take marskrutka 192).

of Abanos kucha (*open Sat–Thu 08.00–20.00, Fri to 22.00*), which cost GEL2, or GEL10 for a cubicle for an hour, but are not tourist-friendly. There are other older baths in the brick domes just below, including the **Sulphur Baths** and the **Royal Baths** (signed in English) which are more welcoming, although the scrubbers (it's not really massage) communicate only with signs; suites have a TV, and tub and massage table in a separate room. On the left bank are the **Gogilo** baths, below the Metechis Chrdilshi (Shadow of Metechi) restaurant; across the road, the Sheraton Metechi Palace Hotel has a health club with pool and sauna, costing GEL14 a day for non-residents. There's another sauna on Ghvinis Aghmarti, between Avlabari Square and the Metekhi church.

SPORTS The main spectator sport (other than watching other people work) is **soccer**: Lokomotiv play at Vake Park while Dinamo Tbilisi and the national team play at the Boris Paichadze Stadium (see page 122); this was refurbished in 2006, just before the World Cup finalists France and Italy visited. The Dinamo Tbilisi Fans' Union is at Gogebashvili 29 (✆ *233168 from 13.00 to 18.00*).

The Paichadze Stadium is also home to the Lelos, the national **rugby** team (*lelo* also means a try), who are doing well in the second tier of European competition and performed very creditably in the 2007 world cup (not totally surprising, as almost the whole team plays professionally in France).

The city's main **tennis** clubs are the newly renovated Jan Homer Tennis Complex (*Ljubljana 18*) and the Leila Meskhi Tennis Academy (✆ *953800*); courts (from GEL2 per hour) are also available at the Mtkvari embankment (✆ *995905*), and in the Vere and Vake parks.

The city's main **swimming** pool is the Laguna Vee, Kostavas Lane 34, between Heroes' Square and Vere Park. The outdoor Vake Pool at Chavchavadze Avenue 49B has natural warm water and is popular with expats before work, all year round; there's also a covered pool and fitness club here (✆ *252575; www.vakefitness.ge*).

At Kazbegi 14 is the **bowling** club (✆ *330350; open Mon–Fri 14.00–02.00, Sat–Sun 14.00–02.00*); next door at Kazbegi 12A the **pool** club (✆ *375693; open 12.00–06.00*).

OTHER PRACTICALITIES

MONEY AND BANKING There are now plenty of ATMs around town, especially on Rustaveli and Chavchavadze Avenues, as well as on Tamar Mepis below the Voksal, opposite the Samgori and Isani metro stations and at the airport.

$ **Bank of Georgia** Pushkin 3; ✆ 444444; f 985304; e customerservice@bog.ge; www.bog.ge. On the north side of Freedom Sq, with a beautiful hall (dating from 1902); Canadian & various European currencies (cash) exchanged next door.

$ **Bank Republic** G Abashidze 2; ✆ 294598/9; f 227566; e info@republic.com.ge; www.republic.ge. Now part of the French Société Générale Group.

$ **Basisbank** Ketevan Tsamebulis 1; ✆ 921921/2; f 986548; e info@basisbank.ge; www.basisbank.ge/en

$ **Cartu Bank** Chavchavadze Av 39A; ✆ 925592; f 221519; e cartubank@cartubank.ge. Formerly AbsoluteBank.

$ **Intellectbank** Davit Agmashenebelis 127;

✆ 237164–6; f 942290; e cbr@ intellectbank.com.ge. Taken over by Bank of Georgia.

$ **Post Bank** Tsinamdzgrishvilis 95; ✆ 964371, 966988; f 940110; e gpb@iberiapac.ge, info@postbank.ge

$ **ProCredit Bank** Davit Agmashenebelis 154; ✆ 202222; f 250580; e central@procreditbank.ge; www.procreditbank.ge

$ **TBC Bank** Marjanishvilis 7; ✆ 777000; f 772774; e info@tbcbank.com.ge; www.tbcbank.com.ge/en. Founded in 1992, now the largest bank in Georgia, & the second largest in the Caucasus.

$ **United Georgian Bank** Uznadze 37; ✆ 995736; f 999139; e admin@ugb.com.ge; www.ugb.ge. Now Russian-owned, to be VTBank Georgia.

COMMUNICATIONS

Telephone The main telephone office on Rustaveli has old coin phones, new 'Pelican' card phones, operator-connected phones, and fax and (slow) internet offices; next door (away from the Iveria Hotel) is the international phone office (open 24 hours), and then the post office, which is always heaving with people. Telecom Georgia also has an office on the southeast corner of Marjanishvilis Square. Digital exchanges are being introduced and numbers are changing slightly, for instance from 740000 to 770000. There are very few public phones as most people use mobile (cell) phones (see page 76).

Post office Technically the main post office is the one at Davit Agmashenebelis 44, which is where you should check for *poste restante*.

Couriers

DHL Tsereteli 105 & also at the Marriott Hotel; ✆ 696060, 699966; f 340393; e dhltbs@dhl.ge; www.dhl.com. *Open Mon–Fri 09.30–18.00.*

Federal Express Ketevan Tsamebulis 39 & also at Sky.ge, Rustaveli 19; ✆ 919140/53; f 273432; e fedexge@ti.net.ge; www.fedex.com/ge. *Open Mon–Fri 10.00–19.00, Sat 10.00–19.00.*

Georgian EMS Rustaveli 13/31; ✆ 956513, 942020; Chavchavadze Av 21; ✆ 943797

Georgian Express Post Davit Agmashenebelis 44; ✆ 956513, 953198

TNT Express Worldwide Melikishvili 41; ✆ 226461, 250328

United Parcel Service Kostavas 47; ✆/f 920344; f 920356

Internet Internet access is available at various hotels, at Prospero's Books (see page 109 – very pricey at GEL4 per hr), and at various cybercafés, mostly on Rustaveli Avenue. Perhaps the best are the non-smoking **CityNet**, opposite the No 1 Wine Factory on Melikishvili (*open 09.00–22.00; GEL1 per half-hr*); and **Java Cyber Café**, down an alley at Rustaveli 18 (✆ 995560; m 895 560674; *www.javacybercafe.com; open 24hrs*), charging GEL1 per hour, or GEL3 from 23.00–09.00, so you can hang out after a late arrival or before an early departure. You can burn CDs and DVDs, or make internet phone calls worldwide for GEL0.20 per minute. Others are at Gamsakhurdias 7, Kazbegi 1 (both open 24hrs), Chavchavadze 21, Rustaveli 40, Leselidze 6, and across the river at the rear of Marjanishvilis 31. At Tamar Mepis 9 there is a very cheap place with a sign only in Georgian, which is fast enough for GEL0.50 per half hour. There's free WiFi at Western-style cafés and bars such as The Hangar, Sans Souci and Café Batonebi. The main providers for home use are Sanet at Rustaveli 37 (*opposite the Academy of*

WORSHIP

Georgian Orthodox Sioni Cathedral; Sunday 09.00 (magnificent singing)
Russian Orthodox Church of St Alexander Nevsky, Ivan Javakhishvilis 69; daily 09.00
Roman Catholic Church of SS Peter and Paul, Ivan Javakhishvilis 55; daily 09.00, Sunday 10.00 (in English), 11.00 (in Georgian) and 17.00 (in Latin); also the Cathedral of the Assumption of the Virgin on Abesadze, in the Old Town; daily 10.00, Sunday 12.15, 18.00
Armenian Church of St George, Samgebro 5, Gorgasali Square; daily 09.00
Synagogue Leselidze 47; daily 09.00
Mosque Botanikuri 32; Friday 13.00
Baptist Kedia 4, Didube; Sunday 10.00 (Russian), 12.00 (Georgian), 14.00 (Armenian)
Lutheran Terenti Graneli 15; Sunday 11.00
Tbilisi International Christian Fellowship Eristavi 1, Didube; Sunday 17.00 (interdenominational, in English)

Sciences; ✆ 922949; e info@sanet.ge www.sanet.ge) and Geonet (Vazha-Pshavelas 41; ✆ 470000; e info@geonet.ge; www.geonet.ge).

MEDIA

Newspapers The English-language papers are available from Prospero's Books, at newstands on Rustaveli and Chavchavadze Avenues and Marjanishvilis Square, or by subscription or on the web (see page 75). The library of the **British Council** (*Rustaveli Av 34;* ✆ *250407;* f *250409;* e *office.bc@britishcouncil.org.ge; www.britishcouncil.org.ge; open Mon–Fri 12.00–18.00, Sat 12.00–17.00*) has three-week-old British papers; similarly the French have the Service Culturel library at Gogebashvilis 15, as well as cultural events at the Alliance Française, at Chavchavadze Avenue 60 (✆ 252427) and the Centre Culturel Français at Gudiashvili 7/10 (✆ *922855; www.ccf.caucasus.net*); Germany's Goethe Institut is at Zandukeli 16 (✆ *938945; www.goethe.de.tbilissi*).

SHOPPING

MARKETS Tbilisi's **central market** (*Bazroba*) is by the station, a bustling place, where you'll find better quality (at higher prices) upstairs; beware pickpockets in this area. There's an open-air flower market, between Baratashvilis and the Alexandrov Park, but the old food market here has closed and it now occupies stalls cutting keys, repairing watches and so on. The **Lilos bazroba** is a huge flea market 20km east beyond the airport on the Kakheti highway, where you can find anything you need; don't forget to bargain. This is really the wholesale market for the whole country, with direct buses from cities such as Kutaisi, and several marshrutka lines terminate here, as well as bus 76 from Samgori metro.

SUPERMARKETS There are some joint-venture 'supermarkets' with a selection of Western food and personal items, most of which accept credit cards (though at a poor rate). The best are Zemeli (*Rustaveli Av 37, opposite McDonald's;* ✆ *998393; open 24hrs*), Big Ben (*Chavchavadze Av 52;* ✆ *250405*), Eurocentre (*Chavchavadze Av 54;* ✆ *227208*) and Euromarket (*Gudiashvilis 2, opposite the Art Museum;* ✆ *933550–56; open 24hrs*). The excellent Populi chain of neighbourhood supermarkets (*open 24hrs*) started in 2001 and aims to have 25 branches in Tbilisi by the end of 2006, and perhaps 100 nationwide by 2008. There are smaller shops at Leselidze 2 and Kostavas 54, both with a good range of wines, and a couple on Marjanishvilis Square and Dutch Food on the UN Circle. Georgia's first hypermarket is Goodwill in Didi Digomi (✆ *595262*), by the main highway westwards. The *Georgian Trade Center* at Vekua 3 is a two-storey mall with boutiques selling designer clothes, shoes, jewellery, electronics and so on; there are ATMs and cafés.

WINE Shops selling Georgian wine (and carpets, and notaries, for some reason) tend to have a sign in English. Wine is available 24 hours a day at **Vazi** (*Pushkin 19;* ✆ *999985*); the wine shop of **Tibaani Village** (in Kakheti) is at Janashia 11/18, at Khorava, behind the ex-Hotel Sakartvelo (✆ *233692*); the **Vere** wine factory shop is at the bottom of Veres Dagmarti (aka Javakishvili Hill); and the **No 1 Wine Shop** (Melikishvili 45), which looks like a cemetery, has a fine Tsinandali. On Kostavas there's the **Wine House** at No 41 (✆ *936351*) and **Sachashniko** at No 60 (✆ *220735*). **Dzveli Megvine** (The Old Winemaker) is behind McDonald's at Brothers Kakabdze 16/2 (✆ *920414; www.khareba.ru; open 10.00–22.00*). Tamada Wines have a shop, **Sauketeso Gvinoebi** (Best Wines) at Chavchavadze Avenue 58 (✆ *253588; open 10.00–20.00*); **Taro Wine** has shops on Berdzhenishvilis around the corner from Chavchavadze Avenue 62; opposite the Voksal; and at

Davit Agmashenebelis 140. Also on the left bank, the **Syraji Wineshop** (of Anaga village) is at Davit Agmashenebelis 81 (✆ *963821*).

BOOKS **Prospero's Books**, down an alley at Rustaveli 34 (✆/f *923592*; e *prospero@access.sanet.ge; open 10.00–21.00*) is the best place for English-language guides and novels, as well as news magazines, maps and video rental; they buy and sell secondhand books, and there's Caliban's Coffee (see page 102); the noticeboard is a good place to look for rooms, drivers and so on. Other good bookshops are at Kostavas 6 (art books and maps), Sharden 17 (tourist books and maps), Rustaveli 28 (including tourist books in English), Rustaveli 42 (which sells a good map of Tbilisi) and Rustaveli 44 (secondhand English and Georgian books).

SOUVENIRS For souvenirs such as daggers, drinking horns and national costume (see page 75), look in the shop in the Opera underpass and the pavement in front of the Academy of Science. There are quite a few 'antique salons' in central Tbilisi; artworks and handicrafts can also be bought at the TMS Gallery (*Rustaveli 16;* ✆ *939124*), Ars Longa Vita Brevis (*Irakli II 21*), Carvasla (*upstairs in the History Museum at Sioni 8; closed Mon*), Hobby in the Literature Museum (*Chanturia 8;* ✆ *989899; www.hobby.com.ge; open Tue–Sat 12.00–18.00*), and the Art Salons at Baratashvili 12 (✆ *932590*), Rustaveli 19 and Davit Agmashenebelis 68. The galleries at Sharden 12 (*open daily 12.00–19.00*) and Irakli II 8 (*open Mon–Sat 11.00–18.00*) specialise in cloisonné enamel, continuing a great Georgian tradition; also at Sharden 12 you can watch looms at work in the window of the State Academy of Tapestry. Maison Bleue produces high-class textiles at Barnov 94 (*at the UN Circle;* ✆ *999374;* e *tbmaisonbleue@yahoo.co.uk; open daily 12.00–18.00*) and also has a shop at Irakli II 10, 2nd floor) (*open daily 12.00–21.00*). Artists also sell their work at weekends at the Vernissaj, the open-air market in Rikhe Park by the Dry Bridge; above, by the road between the bridges, crowds of people gather with placards around their necks, offering to sell their houses and just about anything else, although the city is threatening to close this down.

Carpets are, of course, a speciality throughout the Middle East; although they're common in the Islamic countries, they are made in Georgia too. The best places to buy carpets (including Georgian ones) are across the Caspian in the bazaars of Bokhara, Ashghabat and other cities. In Tbilisi the best shop is Antique Carpets & Kilims, on the south side of Gorgasali Square (*Samgebro 5;* ✆ *723546*), which has good pieces at very high prices which can be reduced with several days of bargaining. Firma Narikala, nearby at Abanos 1, also sells carpets, but is less good. Caucasian Carpets is at Irakli II 8 (✆ *877 405311;* e *carpetsgallery@posta.ge; open daily 10.00–20.00*), and Old Carpets is at Kostavas 5, opposite the Rustaveli metro station; others are at Irakli II 3, Leselidze 10, Rustaveli 34 (by Prospero's Books, and opposite the Mshrali Khali restaurant under the Dry Bridge; they tend to have English signs nowadays).

MISCELLANEOUS There are **sports shops** around the Dinamo stadium; SportTime at Davit Agmashenebelis 93 has hiking and skiing gear; there's an Adidas outlet at Chavchavadze Avenue 58; and the Competitive World of Sport shop at Vazha-Pshavelas 12.

Film can be found fairly easily, but don't expect slide film or any of the faster or more specialised varieties. Fuji is available at the central post office on Rustaveli and at Marjanishvilis 24; Kodak at Rustaveli 40 and 46 (Sakinformi); and Konica at Rustaveli 44 and Marjanishvilis 11. For developing, try Photoworld (*Kodak Express; www.photoworld.ge*) at Melikishvilis 6 and Gamsakhurdias 31A, or Photo Express, Davit Agmashenebelis 83 (at the northeastern corner of Marjanishvilis Square).

For **music**, Audio Video (*Rustaveli 44*) has a decent range of Georgian, Russian and Western pop, classical and Georgian folk music (cassettes cost about GEL6, CDs about GEL25); the shops at Rustaveli 26 and 32 just sell a bit of Georgian pop, also available from stalls in the subways under Rustaveli.

MEDICAL SERVICES

✚ **Cito** Arakishvili 2; ☎ 290671; f 290672; e cito2@access.sanet.ge; www.cito.ge. A Swiss-Georgian joint venture.

✚ **Curatio** Vazha-Pshavelas 27B; ☎ 901, 253625;

emergency, ☎ 938061; www.curatio.com/medical

✚ **Tbilisi State University Medical Diagnostic Centre** Chavchavadze Av 5; ☎ 822 25199, emergency doctor: m 899 581991

There are plenty of aptekas (**pharmacies**), most now part of the Aversi and PSP chains, and many open 24 hours (with a night window). Medicinal herbs are sold at Leselidze 55. The Stomatological (Dental) Clinic is at Davit Agmashenebelis 155.

A DAY'S TOUR OF TBILISI

This provides an outline of a tour of Tbilisi which should take about a day, although if you visit all the museums as you go around it'll take far longer; it can also be speeded up by taking minibuses along the main streets, and by omitting its western extremities.

THE OLD TOWN The Old Town of Tbilisi (the Maidan or Kala) lies higgledy-piggledy on the crowded slopes between the river and the citadel of Narikala. Here, in an area inhabited, at various times, by Persians, Tatars, Jews and Armenians, you can visit a mosque, a synagogue, and Armenian and Georgian churches, all still in use, and a Roman Catholic church, built in 1804 and reconsecrated by the Pope in 1999. The best starting point for a day walk is **Gorgasali Square**, across the river from the Metekhi church; this was the site of the city's bazaar, and it is still surrounded by Silversmiths' Street, Blacksmiths' Street and so on, marking where various trades were once concentrated. There were two bridges across the Mtkvari here, and a mosque, until the 1930s, when Beria replaced them with the present Metekhi Bridge; but when the river is low the foundations are still visible to the west. To the east and south of the square are various sights that would take all day to see if you were to do it properly; however, those willing to walk hard may wish to see those described in the following two paragraphs, before continuing with the day tour itself.

Just to the left of the south side of the square is the **Armenian Church of St George**, founded by the Armenian Prince Umek in 1251, although what you see now is largely 18th century and fairly standard in form, apart from the choir gallery. Continuing eastwards on Samgebro, the first turning to the right leads up to the **Narikala Citadel** (see page 119); you'll emerge on Botanikuri, which leads steeply up the hill to the right through the old Azeri quarter to (as you might expect) the **Botanical Gardens** (see page 127), passing the **Sunni mosque**, the only one left in the city (with Sunni and Shia now worshipping together), at No 32. Built in 1895, it's red brick with a relatively discreet minaret, opposite a memorial to the Turkish artist Ibrahim Isfahanli (1897–1967).

Immediately across Botanikuri, beyond the carpet shop, is Abanos kucha (Bannaya ulitsa in Russian), named after the **bath houses** found here. At the end of the road just to the right you'll see the most striking bath house, the late 17th-century Orbeliani (or Chreli) baths, with a façade of bright-blue tiles and two short minarets, recalling the design of a mosque. The other old bath houses are underground, their presence betrayed only by rows of brick domes. The oldest surviving is the Irakli, on the corner of Abanos and Akhundov; opposite this is the early 17th-century Simbatov baths, while the 18th-century Bebutov baths are on Akhundov. In 1817 Sir Robert Ker Porter, court painter to Alexander I, was able to bribe his way into the women's baths and was shocked to find that 'they seemed to have as little modest covering on their minds as on their bodies'.

Sionis kucha The tour proper begins by heading west from Gorgasali Square, with the river to your right. The busy main road is Leselidze, a 19th-century Russian construction which is lined with various shops, restaurants and banks, as well as the **synagogue** (1913) at No 47 which has a gloomy lower hall for daily services (at 09.00) and a brighter upper hall with large chandeliers for Sabbath and festivals. East of this are two churches, the first of which is the Georgian Jvaris-Mama church, built in the 16th century and modified in 1825; it's small and tall, with a gravel floor and interior walls now repainted, and a brick iconostasis. The other, larger, church is the Armenian Norashen church, built in 1793 and now disused.

However, the historic main street of the old town is Shavteli, parallel to the river; US$1.3 million has been allocated to beautify the pleasantly shabby area through which it runs. To reach it, take some steps down beside a patch of grass on the west side of Gorgasali Square, to the short pedestrianised Sharden Street, which curves past an art gallery in a former shoe factory to the traffic-calmed Sionis kucha. Almost immediately on your right, at No 8 is the **caravanserai** or Carvasla, built in 1650 as a trading centre for visiting merchants, rebuilt in 1912 with an Art Nouveau façade, and now housing the Museum of the History of Tbilisi (see page 126). The interior seems like classic 1980s' architecture, in fact very similar to the Metechi Palace Hotel, with a high atrium and three galleries overlooking a café by a fountain, which was once a drinking pool for pack animals. If you happen to pass its rear, on the Mtkvari embankment, you'll see two sculpted griffons, with three of their four wings missing. Opposite is an Orthodox seminary, and immediately west of the caravanserai is the **Sioni cathedral**, seat of the Catholicos of Georgia, who lives in the villa immediately to the west. The original Church of the Assumption was built between AD575 and 639, but little of that is left; the present church is a typical domed Georgian church built in the 13th century of tuff stone from Bolnisi, and nothing special architecturally. However, it is the centre of religious life in the city, partly due to the presence of St Nino's cross, which she made by binding two vine branches together with her own hair (hence the drooping arms of the Georgian cross); a replica is displayed to the left of the iconostasis, but it's hard to see much as even this is in an ornate early 14th-century reliquary. The frescoes and iconostasis (1850–60) are by the Russian Grigori Gagarin. Across the road is the handsome bell tower or *kolokolnaya*, the first example of Russian neoclassicism in Georgia but now in very poor repair; it was built in 1812 at the wish of the Russian Viceroy Prince Paul Tsitsiani, who had died in 1806 and been buried in the cathedral. This is also where the playwright Griboedov married Alexander Chavchavadze's daughter Nina. To the north of the cathedral (towards the river) is the original bell tower, built in the 13th century and 1425, and restored in 1939.

Shavtelis kucha Continuing westwards, Sionis kucha soon becomes Irakli II, a pedestrianised street with lots of tables and chairs on the street, and trendy art galleries and bars; it's very nice at weekends, especially Sundays, the only time you see expats walking in jeans instead of driving in 4x4s. This brings you to **Irakli II Square**, the historic centre of old Tbilisi, once the site of open-air courts and punishment with a cast-iron fountain from France. On its north side a balconied building is the palace of Giorgi XII (which housed the Museum of Drama, Music and Cinema but is now semi-permanently closed); underground and adjacent to this by the embankment are the remains of the 17th-century baths of King Rustum and Vakhtang VI's press (1709). To the east is the former governor's palace (built in 1802 and now a police building); to the west of the square is an attractive park and an old people's home and chapel. To the north of this is the narrow Shavtelis kucha, with, at No 7, the **Anchiskhati church**, the oldest and one of the most loved in Tbilisi, with the best choir, singing on Saturdays (16.00–19.00) and Sundays (09.00–12.00). Dating from the early 6th century, it's a basilica with two pairs of bare brick columns and stone walls flanking its narrow three-bay aisles. It has been rebuilt several times, most notably in 1675; the present frescoes (with wording in Old Church Slavonic script) probably date from the 18th century. Its name means 'the icon from Ancha', after a wonderful 6th-century icon in a golden frame (now in the National Museum), which was moved here in the 17th century from Ancha, in Turkish-occupied territory. The gate-tower, with a residence above the gate, was built in 1675 and is most unusual with its Islamic-influenced brickwork. Opposite the gateway is a small bar (now part of The Hanger), once a café renowned for its oriental sweetmeats and startling décor, with mirrors and plastic lions' heads, in the jaws of which a cigarette butt can conveniently be perched.

Beyond the next minor road junction is the marionette theatre; turning left at the junction and left again, immediately behind The Hangar at Chakhruhadze 17, is the house-museum (rarely open) where the poet Nikoloz Baratashvili lived from 1841 to 1845. At the west end of Shavteli is the Children's Art Gallery, easily identified by the statue of *Misrule* (seemingly children playing) outside and its jolly nursery paint scheme. The 'N' Gallery is on the third floor (*open 16.00–19.00 except Mon*); even if there's no specific exhibition on, it's worth looking through the front door to see the foyer.

This faces Baratashvilis, the main road from the Baratashvilis bridge (rebuilt in 1966 as the Stalin bridge, with a lower urine-stinking pedestrian level) up to **Freedom Square**, running along the outside of the old **city walls**; on its east side many houses were built into the wall in the 19th century, while the blocks on the western side date from the 1950s and 1960s. Beyond these lie the city's former central market, the former US embassy (in the splendid 1860s' Orbeliani Palace, now obscured by a security wall), the aptly named Titan shop with imposing caryatids, Alexandrov Park, and the Dry Bridge or Mshrale Khidi (1851); this crosses a former channel of the Mtkvari (now a busy highway) to Rikhe Park (formerly Madatov Island), where people with placards around their necks gather to exchange or sell pretty much anything, and artists display and sell their works *en plein air* at weekends. However, the city has decided to tidy it all up.

THE NEW TOWN

Pushkin and Freedom squares Walking up to the left/south up Baratashvilis, you'll pass various bars and restaurants in the city wall, as well as a wedding registry. The road swings up to the left as Pushkin Street; on the right is Pushkin Square, where old men gather to play backgammon under the trees and a bust of Pushkin; at some point a tourist information kiosk should appear here. Also here is the grave of Kamo, a Bolshevik activist who was killed by a car in 1922, in what was almost certainly a murder organised by Stalin. The **Art Museum** (see page 124) faces Pushkin Square, in a building which was built from 1827 to 1834 as an hotel, then served as a seminary until 1908, and became an art gallery in 1933. Noe Zhordania, the prime minister of independent Georgia from 1918 to 1921, studied here, as did Stalin.

Just beyond this you'll reach Tavisuplebis Moedani or **Freedom Square**, laid out by the Russians between the 1820s and 1870s. Originally Yerevan Square, it was then Lenin Square until 1990; the statue of Lenin in its centre has now been replaced by a grassy roundabout. An ugly fountain was added for the Tbilisoba Festival in 2001, on the site of the city's first opera house, built in 1846 (the south wall was unearthed 30 years ago when the Rustaveli Avenue/Pushkin Street underpass was built). A very tall column, the Monument of Freedom and Victory, has now been erected here with a bronze of St George and the Dragon donated by the sculptor Akaki Tsereteli. The square is dominated by the **City Hall**, built in 1880 by the German architect Peter Stern, with a third storey and clock tower added in 1910–12; this is an attractive building with stripes of sandy green and white and mauresque stucco. There's an antique pharmacy on the ground floor, with a free display of posters on the history of Georgian medicine. The west side of the square was gutted in the civil war, but new buildings such as the Courtyard by Marriott Hotel have now filled the gap. Just above the square at Leonidze 5, uphill from the main entry of the National Bank of Georgia, the **Museum of Money** (*open Mon–Fri 10.00–13.00 & 14.00–16.00; admission free*) is modern and expensively furnished, with lots of marble, and all captions are in Georgian, English and Russian. It exhibits Georgian coins dating as far back as the 6th century BC (from Vani), a stater issued by Alexander the Great in the 4th century BC, Roman denarii, Parthian coins, then 11th-century Bagratid coins from Georgia, irregularly shaped coins issued by Tamar, more from 13th- to 18th-century Georgia, 16th-century Venetian gold ducats, and Austrian and Polish thalers, then roubles issued by the Transcaucasian Federation and the USSR, coupons issued in 1993–94, and finally a colourful display of modern notes, from Europe, Iraq (Saddam), Iran (Khomeini), Israel, the central Asian 'stans, Asia, the Antipodes, the US and (very nice) Madagascar.

Rustaveli Avenue Rustaveli Avenue (Rustavelis Gamziri in Georgian or Rustaveli Prospekt in Russian) leads off to the northwest. Almost 1.5km long and lined with plane trees, it's a fine stately avenue that's spoilt by the amount of traffic roaring up and down it these days. There are pedestrian underpasses, but people also cross the road with great nonchalance, waiting on the centre line until there's a gap. On the right/north side at No 3 is the **State Museum** (see page 123), built in 1923–29; this houses the national collections of archaeology, history and ethnography, based on the collections of the Caucasian Museum, founded in 1852. A treasury houses a superb collection of pre-Christian gold; jewellery and icons from the Christian era are in the treasury of the Art Museum. In the same building is the Georgian Arts and Culture Centre, which houses temporary shows (*open 11.00–18.00, except Mon*); it's two flights up a staircase with a very funky three-storey chandelier in the well. Just beyond the museum is the Rustaveli Cinema, built in 1939 (by Nikolai Severov, who also designed the National Museum), with idealised statues of Soviet youth on the façade. Behind them is the National Library, housed in three imposing buildings along Gudiashvilis; the easternmost block is a fascinating neo-Romanesque creation with lovely murals on its ceiling (including an external arcade) – feel free to step inside. Below the library is the Trinity Church (1790, with more recent frescoes and a Baroque iconostasis), busy with weddings at weekends.

Immediately on the left at the start of Rustaveli is the Universal Shop (the city's main department store, built in 1975), with the Griboedov Russian Theatre behind it; originally a caravanserai, there's been a theatre here since 1845. At its far end is the Freedom Square metro station at Rustaveli 6, and steps up to the Chancellery, and beyond that the Young People's Palace, built in 1807 as the Russian **Viceroy's**

Palace, with an arcade in front added in 1865–68. Stalin installed his mother here at one time and it then served as the Pioneers' Palace, housing the Soviet youth organisation and a Museum of Children's Toys. It's still used for youth activities, and is the best place to find classes and displays of Georgian folk dance and the like.

Beyond this is easily the most dominating building on Rustaveli, the **Parliament Building**. This was built as a U-shaped block in 1938 (on the site of the Alexander Nevsky Church, built in the 19th century for the Russian army); a very solid portico of tuff was built by German prisoners of war and the building opened in 1953. It was on the steps before the Parliament that the massacre of 9 April 1989 took place, and you'll still see memorials to the dead here. This was also the focus of the civil war, with Gamsakhurdia and his supporters holed up inside; the side wings were gutted, but the portico resisted the National Guard's shellfire, giving rise to comments on the superiority of German building to Soviet efforts. It stands opposite the site of the Artists' House and the lovely Hotel Intourist (built in the 1870s), both sadly destroyed in the civil war.

Immediately beyond the parliament is the **High School No 1**, founded in 1802 as the first European-style high school in Transcaucasia; it educated many of the leading figures of recent Georgian history, including Kostava, Gamsakhurdia, Sigua and Kitovani. It's a good example of Russian neoclassicism, with statues of Ilia Chavchavadze and Akaki Tsereteli (1958) in front; you might want to look inside and enquire about the Museum of Education housed there, although it's unlikely to be open. A plaque commemorates those killed by the Soviet security forces on 9 March 1956.

At No 9 on the north side is the **Kashveti Church of St George**, built in 1904–14 on the site of a 6th-century church demolished as unsafe at the end of the 19th century. It was built by the German Leopold Bielfeld, and based on the 11th-century church of Samtavisi. The altar apse was decorated by Lado Gudiashvili (who lived just behind the church and for his pains was expelled from the Communist Party and lost his job at the Academy of Art) in 1946. There's a separate church in the crypt, used for Russian-language services. Henry Mowatt, a Scottish engineer who worked on the Surami rail tunnel and married a Georgian, is buried here.

The attractive Alexandrov Park is behind the church (with decent public toilets), and next to it, at Rustaveli 11, the **State Academy of Fine Art**, which houses temporary shows (*open 11.00–17.00 except Mon*) in a fine blue building known as the Khram Slavi (Temple of Glory), built in 1883–85 as a Museum of Military History, to commemorate Russia's conquests. In front are statues of painters Elena Akhvlediani and David Kakabdze. Beyond this, at No 15 (opposite the Ministry of Transport and Communications) is the Hotel Tbilisi, built in 1915 as the Hotel Majestic and gutted in the civil war. It reopened in 2002 as the luxurious Marriott Hotel. Behind it at Chanturia (formerly Georgiashvili) 8 is the **State Literature Museum**, a nice 19th-century building facing the park, which also has temporary art shows, but erratic opening times.

Beyond the hotel, at No 17, is the splendid French neoclassical façade of the famous **Rustaveli Theatre**, built in 1899–1901 and refurbished in 1920–21 for the new Rustaveli Theatre Company; it was refurbished again in 2002–05 and in 2006 a Hollywood-style 'walk of the stars' was begun in front. It boasts marble staircases, classical statues, and frescoes by Lado Gudiashvili, Moise Toidze and David Kakabadze in the Kimerioni (Chimera) café on the first floor.

At Rustaveli 24, on the south side of the avenue, is the Lagidze café, and behind it at Griboedov 8, the **Conservatoire** (music college), built in 1904; there's a museum (although you need to persuade a member of staff to show you around) with Rachmaninov's piano, autograph scores by him and Tchaikovsky and vintage photos; on the ground floor at the east end of the building are the newly refurbished Grand Hall and a lovely chamber recital hall where Horowitz played. The poet Titsian Tabidze lived from 1921 to 1937 at Griboedov 18, where his friend Boris Pasternak allegedly did many of his translations of Georgian poetry; the apartment is a museum supposedly open from 11.00 to 17.00 except on Saturdays.

The imposing Supreme Court stands on the next street uphill, Brothers Zubelashvili. You can continue to Republic Square along Griboedov, passing the **Academy of Arts** at No 22 – a very fine building erected in 1858, with a display of students' work upstairs; there are rather splendid murals in the hall and mosaics above the staircase. There is a sculpture park opposite, by a flight of steps back down to Rustaveli.

If you continue from the theatre along the north side of Rustaveli, you'll pass the permanent crowd of smoking students outside the Georgian State Institute of Theatrical Arts and come to the **Paliashvili Opera House** at No 25. Founded in 1851, it was burnt down in 1870, and replaced with the present Moorish building in 1880–96; it saw the start of Shalyapin's career before it too burnt down in 1973, and was rebuilt in 1977, On the first floor are a few cases of memorabilia of Paliashvili operas. Outside it is a statue (by Merab Berdzenishvili, 1973) of the composer Zacharia Paliashvili; this is next to his grave and that of Vano Saradzishvili, the first great Georgian singer. On the same side of Rustaveli, at No 29, is an imposing colonnaded building built as the Institute of Marxism–Leninism, which housed the obligatory Lenin Museum, with a copy of his Kremlin study; it was the seat of the State Council when Shevardnadze returned to take power and is to be a Kempinski hotel. There are four blank cartouches high on the façade where the heads of Marx, Engels, Lenin and Stalin were removed in 1991. Beyond this is a brutalist block built in the late 1970s, housing the main post and telephone offices and the PostBank. Opposite this, Rustaveli 42 was the first major Soviet public building in Tbilisi, constructed in 1926–28; it's also brutalist plain concrete but with a few neoclassical details, and very modern for the period, perhaps influenced by Czech functionalism.

Here the modern plaza of Republic Square opens up to the right while Rustaveli kinks to the left past the **Academy of Sciences**, a large pompous building (built in 1953) in which 7,000 research staff once laboured. In its courtyard is a flattened circular building housing the terminal of the disused cable car to Mtatsminda. The avenue ends at the small **Rustaveli Square**, on the site of the former Moscow Gates, where a statue of the poet (by Koté Merabishvili, 1937) now stands by the Rustaveli metro station, next to Tbilisi's first McDonald's.

Republic Square to the Philharmonic Republic Square was laid out in the

1980s, above a road underpass and a very dark shopping complex (with effective stained glass); in 1991 it was the rallying point for the opposition to Gamsakhurdia. To the north is the high-rise **Hotel Iveria**, built in 1967, which dominates most of the city; long inhabited by IDPs or refugees from Abkhazia, who were given US$7,000 per family to move, it's now being converted into a Radisson hotel. At the west end of the square most traffic swings left to Rustaveli Square; ahead are two minor streets, Kiacheli (to the right) and Akhvlediani. The latter (still better known as Perovskaya) is not particularly attractive, but it is lined with the city's most lively bars and restaurants. Confusingly, the Elena Akhvlediani house-museum, one of the most enjoyable in the city, is at Kiacheli 12; it's currently closed due to lack of funds. Traffic from Rustaveli Square passes under the Republic Square plaza and drops down Vere Hill to the Marjanishvilis Bridge, leading to the left/north bank of the Mtkvari.

The city's main traffic axis continues west as Merab Kostavas kuca (the former Lenin Street), and soon splits in front of the striking circular building of the **Philharmonic**, built in 1969–71, largely of glass; a bronze sculpture of *The Muse* (1971, by Merab Berdzenishvili) stands in front of it. To the right/north of the square in front of the Philharmonic is the Vere (formerly Kirov) Park; to the right in the park (ie: at the end of Kiacheli) you'll pass a flight of steps that climb from beside the petrol station on the embankment road, and come to the **Lurdzhi monastery**, and the very Russian **Church of St John the Theologian** (1901) next to it. The Lurdzhi church is smaller, and can be identified by the blue roof that gives it its name. Built in 1155 and rebuilt in the 16th and 17th centuries, it's high with virtually no nave and a plain iconostasis, and an unusual round cupola added in 1873; a modern belfry is going up now. In communist times it housed a Museum of Medicine, while the Russian church was quite clearly left untouched; now the tables are turned and it's the Russian church that looks abandoned. This is entered from the far side and is painted in eggshell blue and white, with a gold iconostasis that just manages not to be *too* over the top. From here you can go up to the Vere district (see below), or continue to the newer parts of the city.

Around 26 May Square Forking right in front of the Philharmonic (behind which is Phikris Gora or Dream Hill, an enclave of nice hotels), Kostavas soon drops down to the ugly roundabout and underpass of Heroes' Square (Gmirta Moedani), in a ravine filled in in the 1930s; there's an Eternal Flame with guards at the heroes' memorial. To its left is the **zoo** (see page 128) and the Mziuri (Sunshine) children's park (threatened by a plan for new apartment blocks), and to the right is the **circus** (built in 1940) and the bridge across the Mtkvari to Tamar Mepis Gamziri (Queen Tamar Avenue) and the Voksal (railway station). Carrying on straight ahead, Kostavas climbs again to 26 May Square, laid out from 1940, with the Sports Palace and Politekhnikuri metro station to its right and the high-rise **Hotel Adjara** ahead (also now cleared of refugees and being rebuilt by Kazakh investors); beyond here, the main road continues to the left of the hotel as Konstantin Gamsakhurdias Avenue, becoming the main road towards Mtskheta, while side roads turn left into the Saburtalo district. To the right of the hotel, Kostavas leads to the statue of Giorgi Saakadze and the main building of **Georgia Technical University**, a fine white-and-ochre neoclassical pile, beyond which the Vakhushti Bridge crosses to Didube on the left bank. To the southwest of the Hotel Adjara, at the end of Sairmes kucha, is **Sairmis Gora** or Sairme Hill, where government ministers and the like shamelessly built suspiciously expensive homes until Saakashvili clamped down; there's also a dozen German war graves here.

Vake Forking left in front of the Philharmonic, Melikishvilis kucha (widened in 1948) leads past the massive Hotel Sakartvelo, now closed apart from its restaurant and a few other businesses, and the Tbilisi wine cellars to the **Tbilisi State University**, the country's leading academic institution, housed in a fine domed building built as a lycée in 1900–16, as well as some rather less attractive blocks behind this and a large modern complex on the western edge of the city, beyond Saburtalo. There's always a crowd of students blocking the pavement here, a great social coming and going which is the nearest thing to a *passeggiata* that Tbilisi offers. The main road continues west as Ilia Chavchavadze Avenue, lined with the city's most fashionable shops. To the right at No 21, marked with a jokey statue, there's an entrance to the Mziuri Park (pleasant but with an unfinished feel, and surrounded by tatty high-rises), and nearby the statues of the poets Galaction Tabidze and David Guramishvili (1966, by the omnipresent Merab Berdzenishvili).

After 3.8km (with frequent buses) Chavchavadze finally reaches Victory Square (Gamarjvebis Moedani), overlooking **Vake Park** to the left/south. This is a spacious and well-tended area of 226ha, where the grave of the Unknown Soldier lies at the foot of a flight of steps up to the statue of Victory, erected in 1976. A cable car (*GEL0.20, weekends only*) rises over the park to Kus Tba (Turtle Lake), where there are cafés; swimming is free, and good if you can avoid being run down by a pedalo (*GEL20 per hour*) or row boat (*GEL8 per hour*); it's been sold to an entrepreneur who plans to provide beaches of real sand. The lake can also be reached by a 3km road, from just beyond the park, halfway along which is the open-air **Museum of Georgian Folk Architecture and Daily Life** (see page 126), which has a restaurant with a great view. There's also the Squirrels' Park, opened in 2006, with free children's games and wooden picnic huts. Just beyond the park, at the western end of Chavchavadze Avenue, is the Vake Cemetery, with its tall cypresses, grand tombstones and ivy-clad mausoleums, which featured as a setting for the film *Repentance*. The main road continues through the so-called 'mountain resort quarter' of Tskhneti (now swamped by tasteless *dachas* built with illegal money after 'accidentally' burning down an area of forest) to Manglisi and Akhalkalaki.

If your legs permit, it's interesting to return to the centre along Irakli Abashidze, a couple of blocks south of Chavchavadze; this passes through the **Vake** (Plain) district, which was once home to the communist bourgeoisie, and now, because it still has the city's best telephone and power supplies, is home to most of the city's expatriates and NGOs. The district was built by Beria on top of the mass graves of the victims of his purges; the Bolsheviks executed many of the Georgian aristocracy here in 1923, and a public toilet was built on the site, now replaced by a memorial. After the Round Park, more commonly known as the United Nations Circle, Abashidze becomes Barnov and passes through **Vere**, an older district that is also popular with expats and young professionals; you'll end up back at Rustaveli Square.

Mtatsminda If you turn right up Tamriko Tshovelidze (still better known as Belinskis) where Barnov begins to curve left, you can turn left after two short blocks on to Gogebashvilis, and at its end right on to Makashvilis, which runs along the slopes of Mtatsminda. If you wanted to leave Vake and the Museum of Folk Architecture for another day you could walk directly up from Rustaveli Square. With wide views over the city, Makashvilis then Chonkadze (marshrutkas 67 and 137) pass a Russian church (1910) and a few houses before reaching the crossroads just below the **Pantheon**, up a few tight cobbled hairpin bends. It's also known as Mamadaviti or the Monastery of Father David, after St David, one of the Syrian Fathers, who lived here in a cave in the 6th century before moving on to Davit-Gareja. The present church was built in 1859, in plain brick on an artificial terrace; however, what's of interest here is the graveyard, repository of the remains of the leading figures of Georgian culture. These include the poets Nikoloz Baratishvili, Galaction Tabidze, Akaki Tsereteli and Georgi Leonidze; painter Lado Gudiashvili, dissident Merab Kostava and educationalists, critics and philosophers such as Iacob Gogebashvili, Niko Nikoladze and Vazha-Pshavelas, as well as Zviad Gamsakhurdia and Stalin's mother. Set into the cliff face are grottoes housing the Russian playwright Griboedov and his widow Nina, daughter of Alexander Chavchavadze, and the secular saint Ilia Chavchavadze (no relation).

A little further along Chonkadze is the lower terminal of the Mtatsminda **funicular**, which was built in 1903–05 by Belgian engineers, an odd contribution from so flat a country; now out of action, it climbs at 55° for five minutes (with a path winding up and criss-crossing it) to reach its upper terminal, at an altitude of

727m on the edge of **Mtatsminda**, the Holy Mountain, so called because of St David's Cave. Above the terminal is the vast colonnaded Funicular restaurant built by Beria and now disused. Just to its north is the upper terminal of the cable car from behind the Academy of Sciences, which was built in 1958 with British cables and closed in the early 1990s after collapsing. Behind it is the massive TV tower, like a 300m oil rig visible from all over the city, and the funfair of the former Stalin Park, with a lonesome Ferris wheel still waiting for customers. There is a restaurant on the far side of the funicular terminal, but nothing much else to see up here. Nevertheless there can be a view as far as Kazbeg, weather permitting, and it's a pleasant 20-minute walk through pine woods to reach the Kojori road. If you happen to be coming up by car, it's a very sharp right turn into the park at a no-entry sign, virtually opposite a yard with a wire sculpture of an elephant with a mahout on its back. The Pantheon and Mtatsmida restaurant (and the Kartlis Deda statue, Parliament, Chancery, and Sameba, Sioni and Mtskheta churches) are now lit at night; the TV Tower had lurid flashing lights put up for Christmas 2005, and not turned off since. It seems that Mtatsminda is being restored by US investors and should be open in 2008.

It is of course possible to extend this brief tour of Tbilisi in various directions if you have the time and stamina.

East to Ortachala From Gorgasali Square, the main road to the east along the Mtkvari embankment is Gorgasalis kucha, built in 1851 as Vorontsov ulitsa. About 100m beyond the bath houses it passes the kneeling statue of the painter Pirosmani (1975, by Elgudja Amashukeli), the Tbilisi Balneologic Health Resort (founded in 1938 by Shevardnadze's father, and apparently run now by Saakashvili's father!), and then, in the grassy reservation between the carriageways, the '300 Aragveli' monument, a 23m-high stela (and eternal flame) raised in 1961 on the spot where in 1795 King Irakli II was rescued from Aga Mohammed Khan by 300 men from the Aragvi Valley (on the Georgian Military Highway), who were all killed in the process. This was also the scene of one of the closer assassination attempts on Shevardnadze. Note that the 300 Aragveli metro station is actually on the far side of the river.

Continuing eastwards, you'll pass the equestrian statue (1982) of Pyotr Bagration, who distinguished himself in the campaign against Napoleon in 1812. To the left is the Ortachala Dam, still bearing portraits of Stalin and Lenin in relief, and on the clifftop beyond this the wonderfully phallic former **Palace of Weddings** (see page 120). To the east the road now runs along the course of the channel that used to make a small island, past the Interior Ministry, the Public Prosecutor's Office and the city's main prison; the Krtsanisi palace, built by Beria and home to the president until Shevardnadze neglected to move out, is hidden away just to the south. In fact, Saakashvili refused to move in, preferring to build the new Avlabari Palace. The highway continues past the Ortachala bus station, built in 1973 to replace the cramped former terminal by the Marjanishvilis Bridge; however, most bus services use the chaotic yard at Didube, and Ortachala's echoing halls are used mainly by international services, to Azerbaijan, Armenia and Turkey. On the façade you can see *The Wheel*, a mosaic by Zurab Tsereteli; to the rear there's another fine mosaic on a fire station.

Beyond Ortachala the main road continues along the river and then splits, to Rustavi and Baku to the left, and Marneuli and Yerevan to the right.

South of Gorgasali Square and Narikala For the best sense of how Tbilisi's Old Town used to be, you should explore the back alleys of **Kala**, to the south of Gorgasali Square, core of a protected area of 90ha. It's crumbling, due to neglect and earthquakes, but some restoration work is underway and it has been taken off the list of the world's most endangered monuments and sites. This remains the best place to get a feel for how life used to be in the teeming multi-cultural city, with multi-storey houses surrounding courtyards, and *musharabi* balconies with stained-glass windows overlooking the narrow streets. The Betlemi area has been inhabited since the 5th century but the oldest houses now extant date from the 17th century, and most are 19th century, with far older churches hidden in between.

From Leselidze, take Asatianis kucha (formerly Bebutov) up to the left before the 6th-century Jvaris-Mama and Norashen churches; there are good Moderne (Art Nouveau) buildings at Asatiani 38, 44, 50 and 66. You'll pass the tiny Tumanian Square on the left and soon emerge into Puris (Bread) Square, which is not much bigger. To the left/east Betlemi runs below the Narikala Citadel, and steps lead up to the Ateshga or Fire Worshippers' Temple, a rock-cut altar built by the Persians.

Asatiani continues uphill between the Mognisi church to the west (built in the 18th century and now abandoned) and the Upper and Lower Betlem (Bethlehem) churches (founded in the 7th century but both now largely 18th century) up well-made steps to the east. The upper church (to the left) has a bare interior with lots of icons, and a bell tower to the east; the lower church (to the right) has recently been fully decorated with attractive frescoes. At Asatiani 28 is the former Girls' College (opposite the end of Dadiani, which leads to Freedom Square), now the Tbilisi Institute of Law and Economics; behind No 30, where Walter Siemens lived in 1860–68 as representative of his family firm, is The Tunnel (*Gvirabi*), built as a nuclear shelter during the Cuban Missile Crisis – it leads through to the Botanic Gardens, but is now used only as a nightclub.

Until recently it was possible to climb steps from here to the Sololaki Ridge, but now you should either go up from Gorgasalis Square to the Narikala Citadel or take Sololaki Lane, the road, lined with lime and cypress trees, that turns off the Kojori highway (marshrutkas 12 and 196) at the eyesore of a huge new hotel/business centre with a flying saucer helipad. It takes five minutes to reach the ruins of some medieval fortifications and a view to the right over the Botanic Gardens (there's a turnstile and a rough path down); and the 20m-high aluminium statue of **Kartlis-Deda** or Mother Georgia, visible all over the city. There's a great view down to the old town, marred by huge amounts of litter; there are lots of charms tied on a tree behind the statue. This was made in 1958–63 by Elgudja Amashukeli; sword in one hand and bowl in the other, it shows Georgia as hospitable but ready to defend herself. Also nearby are the ruins of the ancient Shakhtakhi Fort (from 'Sahis Tahti' or Throne of the Shah), which was used as an observatory in the 7th to 9th centuries. Heading east along the ridge (with views and a path down into the Botanical Gardens to the right), take the path to the left by the Folk Museum, moved to the Sioni caravanserai in 1984. This leads you to the left of the ridge, past trees covered in cloth charms. Don't follow the road to the ruined buildings, but fork left on to a rough path around to the gate of the **Narikala Citadel**, also reached by a road climbing steeply from near the Armenian church. The citadel (also known as Shuris-tsihke) was built in about AD360 by the Persians, and restored by Mustafa Pasha's Turks in the second half of the 16th century, before being ruined by an earthquake in the 19th century. It's always open and entry is free, although there's a minimal charge for parking. Locals often come up here for picnics and to enjoy the evening views of the city. Near the car park is the 12th-century Church of St Nicholas, largely refaced in new stone, and with a painted interior and a simple modern stone iconostasis. The fort walls are either over-restored or untouched; you can walk along the battlements, although there are some very steep steps. At the citadel's south end, the square Istanbul tower was a prison under Turkish rule.

THE LEFT BANK OF THE MTKVARI The left or north bank of the Mtkvari is, with the exception of the Metekhi church and the area immediately behind it, relatively recently developed; although it contains little of touristic interest, there is much of practical use here, and it's safer than the traditional affluent/expat areas. Its heart is the area to the south of the Voksal (railway station), along Davit Agmashenebelis Gamziri (David the Builder Avenue), which was built up in the 19th century.

To the east, the highway from the airport and Kakheti runs in alongside the railway and then dives under it to turn right on to Ketevan Tsamebulis Gamziri just east of the **Palace of Weddings**, reached by going straight across the road from the 300 Aragveli metro station. Intended by the communists to attract couples away from church weddings, it's very modernist, but with a classical statue (of a naked male) in front of the blatantly phallic carillion tower. However, it's been bought by the oligarch Badri Patarkatsishvili and you can no longer get inside.

Avlabari Not far to the west of the 300 Aragveli metro station, the Metechi Palace Hotel rises above the road to the right/north; this is the base of various airlines and the Dutch and German embassies. A little further west is the Avlabari Square and metro station, heart of Tbilisi's Armenian quarter. At its west end is the Echmiadzin church, named after the Armenian equivalent of Canterbury; built in 1804, it now has a crack in its east end and scaffolding inside, due to vibration from the metro trains passing underneath.

To the left, Meskhishvilis leads towards the massive new **Sameba** (Trinity) Cathedral on Mount Elia, begun in 1995 and finished in 2004. Regarded as an eyesore by many people, it is equally venerated by many others, who cross themselves whenever they glimpse it on the far side of the city. It was built on the Armenian Khojavank cemetery, which was treated with a scandalous lack of respect. It's the largest religious building in the southern Caucasus, with interior dimensions of 56m by 44m and an interior area of 2,380m². It's certainly way out of scale for a Georgian church, even though it's in an exaggerated traditional Georgian style; a long esplanade, with fountains, leads past a belfry to the cathedral with a sort of triple-decked west end. The apses are very high but the windows only reach two-fifths of the way up. The interior is still being decorated but is quite bare at the moment; there are five additional chapels in the crypt. The terminal of marshrutka 155 is outside the main entry.

Opposite the Armenian church, a flight of steps and an alleyway lead to the Chapel of the Transfiguration, set on the battlements of the **Sachino Palace**; although the Avlabari cliffs have long been fortified, all that remains is this chapel and a round pavilion both built in 1776 for Darejda, wife of Irakli II and then Queen Mother. They're set in an attractive garden, from which there are views stretching from the bath houses to Tbilisi State University. The chapel has a simple, vaulted nave and sanctuary with a very low dome at the west end under a belfry with external bell ropes. There are some early 20th-century frescoes, and plenty of whitewashed areas.

The Metekhi church There are two routes from here to the Metekhi church: firstly you can go back down the steps and turn left and left again down Ghvinis Aghmarti (Wine Hill), a steepish street lined with Pirosmani-styled restaurants that drops down below the walls of the Sachino Palace, mostly made of rows of riverbed stones alternating with double rows of brick. Alternatively you can head east along an alley to turn right on to Metekhi Street, and then right down Metekhi Rise, lined on the left with the fine merchants' homes (now occupied by hotels and restaurants) whose triple-decker balconies you may already have admired from the far side of the river. In either case you'll end up at the north end of the Metekhi church precincts, set on a crag over the Mtkvari; the view of this church, with the equestrian statue of Vakhtang Gorgasali below it, is one of the most widespread images of Tbilisi.

The earliest churches on this site were built in the 5th and 8th centuries, but the present church of the Virgin was built in 1278–89 by King Demetre II the Self-Sacrificer (so called because he answered a summons by the Mongols to near-certain death rather than cause an invasion). The ground plan is actually quite complex, with a cross filled out to a square, and lateral apses projecting at the eastern end. Four free-standing pillars support a central dome (rebuilt in the mid 18th century). The external stonework is very worn, and the interior is bare.

The present churchyard was long occupied by a castle which was ruined by Shah Aga Mohammed Khan in 1795 and rebuilt in 1819 as a prison, which housed Beria's offices and less willing guests such as Kalinin, Gorki and Kamo, the last of whom escaped down the cliff on half-a-dozen sheets tied together. This was demolished in 1937 when the present bridge and the Mtkvari embankment road were built. The church was used as a youth theatre until it was finally restored to worship in recent years. The statue of Vakhtang Gorgasali, overlooking the city he founded, was constructed in 1958–67. Below it, by the bridge, the tiny new chapel of St Abo Tbileli (a 7th-century Arab convert, killed here by Muslims) is being built by hand.

Looking upstream, beyond the roundabout at the north end of the Metekhi Bridge and the mouth of the tunnel under the Avlabari cliffs, you'll see an open area known as Peski with restaurants set against the cliffside. This is the site of the Tbilisoba Festival on the last weekend of October, when stages are set up for performers and the whole area is hidden by the smoke from *shashlik* stalls (also up on Republic Square). Baratashvilis Hill descends to the bridge of the same name from Avlabari Square; under construction to the north, looking down on the bridge, is Saakashvili's new presidential palace; the area is prone to earthquakes, and very run-down, but it'll presumably see some regeneration on the back of the palace and the Sameba Cathedral. You can get here from the north side of the Echmiadzin church along Meskhishvilis and to the left.

Just west, Akhvlediani Hill (formerly Uritskis Hill) leads down to the river beyond the Baratashvilis Bridge and a statue of the poet Nikoloz Baratashvili, by Boris Tsibadze (1975). Up some steps behind a closed hotel the All Saints Church was built in 1620–30 and is now being restored; it has new paintings in a nice light style and semi-naïve icons.

Chugureti
To the west is the Chugureti district, largely settled by Germans and Poles in the 19th century; one block inland at Chkheidze 38, the EU embassy is a surprisingly beautiful three-storey building (built in 1888) quite out of keeping with this tatty brick district. The main road swings away from the river, soon passing the Ilia Chavchavadze house-museum (*supposedly open 10.00–18.00 except Mon*) at Javakishvili 7, and continues to the Voksal and out towards the northwestern suburbs.

However, soon after a relatively uninteresting early 19th-century church on the embankment, Tolstoy kucha leads off to the left to Saarbrucken Moedani, at the north end of the Saarbrucken (formerly Vorontsov, then Marx) Bridge, and on as Davit Agmashenebelis Gamziri. This was built as Mikhailovskaya in the 1830s, and was then known as Plekhanov under communism. By and large it's really not an impressive thoroughfare. Despite appearances and a total lack of contraflow markings, it's not a one-way street – a few marshrutkas do go the 'wrong' way so be careful. At this eastern end there are a few local bars and a couple of antique shops, but it's hardly Knightsbridge; the first buildings of real interest are No 60, the University Hospital, a neogothic pile built in the 1860s, and opposite it at No 61 the former Soviet Propaganda Centre, now housing the NATO Information Center and various embassies. This is a brutalist block built in 1977 with on its façade a lurid high-relief mosaic (42m by 12m) by Zurab Tsereteli, celebrating the 60th anniversary of the Bolshevik Revolution. Don't spend too long admiring this, or you'll be accosted by Israeli security guards.

A little further along Agmashenebelis you'll come to Marjanishvilis Square, laid out in 1948–56, with a metro station in its northwestern corner; there are some decent cafés here, and just to the north some excellent vegetable stalls (as well as exchange counters and shops selling air tickets). Yevgenii Primakov, Russian Prime Minister in 1998–99, grew up just to the north on what was then Leningrad Street; appropriately this is close to the present Russian embassy.

Two blocks north, Marjanishvilis kucha (formerly Kirochnaya) crosses Ivan Javakhishvilis (formerly Kalinin); on the corner to the left (at No 69) is the city's main **Russian Orthodox church**, and just to the right at No 55 is the **Roman Catholic church**, a low-key neoclassical building, both now in great condition, thanks to foreign funds. Continuing to the north on Marjanishvilis you'll come to Tionti Chebinasvili Square (formerly Sovietskaya), on the road to the Voksal; on its far side, beyond the statue of Gorki on Terenti Graneli, is the new **Lutheran Church of the Reconciliation**. The Germans' first church was where Marjanishvilis Square now is; this was replaced in 1897 with a larger church (by Leopold Bielfeld, who also designed the Kashveti church on Rustaveli Avenue), which was closed and demolished in the 1940s.

Continuing westwards on Davit Agmashenebelis, there are some grander late 19th-century buildings, such as No 108 (with stucco pilasters) and No 101 (with caryatids supporting a balcony), and a nice park behind. Beyond some fast-food cafés, No 123 houses the Composers' Union and a casino, and the State Symphony Orchestra, with a garden in which they give summer concerts. Just beyond it at No 127 is the Cultural Centre of the Railwaymen of Georgia, a fine neoclassical pile built in 1934 and set back from the road in front of a park; here too is the Tumanishvili Movie Actors' Theatre and documentary film studios, in a pseudo-medieval castle and tower built in 1930. At Davit Agmashenebelis 150 is the Observatory in which Stalin worked in 1899–1901, just before the junction with Tamar Mepis, leading from the Voksal to the river.

Didube Beyond Tamar Mepis, Davit Agmashenebelis soon reaches the well-kept Mushtaid Park on the left (with dodgems, Ferris wheel and a miniature railway), and the Paichadze National Stadium, better known simply as the **Dinamo stadium**; this was built in 1937 and rebuilt in 1976 to accommodate 70,000 fans. Several marshrutka lines, recognisable by a soccer ball symbol, terminate here. Here you enter the Didube district; the main road is Tseretelis Gamziri, a block to the right/northeast, which passes first the Orthodox Church of the Nativity of the Virgin (1883) where there's another pantheon of lower-league celebrities such as football players (and poet Terenti Graneli), and then the **Baptist Church**, before reaching the huge modernist Exhibition Centre (Tseretelis 118, opposite the Electrodepo metro station), which now houses car showrooms and the like. It's quite a bit further to the Didube bus station, which is best reached by metro.

Rather than heading into the wilds of Didube, it's probably preferable to turn either left to the Tamar Mepis Bridge and Heroes' Square, or right to the Voksal, where you can catch the metro. The **Voksal** is a huge brutalist concrete block;

although relatively few people actually catch trains here, it's the main terminal for the city's marshrutkas and buses, and the **main market** is immediately to the southwest, so the whole area is always heaving with people. Buses and minibuses to cities such as Kutaisi, Batumi and Zugdidi mainly leave from a car park on the north side. Behind the Voksal roads lead up past the gypsy palaces of Lotkin to the Tbilisi Sea (Tbilis Tskalsatsavi), the natural Lake Djairan enlarged in 1951 to form a reservoir (fed by the Iori River); there are restaurants and beach resorts here, reached by marshrutka 130, but the holiday camps are full of refugees and the water is not really clean enough for swimming. However, it is good for windsurfing, though you have to bring your own board.

MUSEUMS

National Museum (*Rustaveli 3;* ⤵ *997176, 998022; admission GEL3, inc admission to the Treasury, but you'll also have to pay GEL10 for a guide, required for security but well worth having anyway as long as she (usually) speaks a language you can understand; open 11.00–16.00 except Mon*) This museum houses an amazing treasury of largely pre-Christian gold and silver, as well as ethnographic displays. Whereas the Greeks preferred filigree decorations and the Persians encrustation, the Georgians chose granulation (*tsvara*), with tiny lumps creating texture; they also set their jewellery with semi-precious stones, such as cornelian (found all over Georgia).

The treasury contains 25 display cases in three rooms; the first 16 now have captions in English, but details follow here anyway. A DVD (in English, French, German or Russian) is available for GEL30.

The first case displays very fine goldwork from Kakheti, made in the early Bronze Age; a tiny golden lion with an intricately worked mane, dating from 2600-2300BC, is one of the most remarkable pieces in the whole collection. In the second case is slightly more recent jewellery from Trialeti, including a king's sceptre, a silver cup with a frieze of religious ritual and hunting, and a gold bowl from about 1800BC encrusted with precious stones. The third case displays pieces from Vani, produced in the 5th century BC, including a superb diadem, earrings, and necklaces, including one with 31 tiny turtles (symbolising longevity) hanging from it, and others with swastikas. The fourth case is similar, with very finely granulated necklaces, bracelets and an enamelled pendant, the oldest in Georgia. The fifth case houses pieces of the same period from Racha and Vani: diadems, bracelets, signet rings, and coins imitating Greek and Roman originals. In the sixth case is jewellery from Iveria, also from the 5th century BC, including silver bowls and earrings and gold buckles and sheep's-head rings, and more of the same in the seventh case, including a lovely pair of gold pendants showing horses with a type of harness only used in Georgia, and a necklace of frogs (symbolising fertility).

The eighth case leaps forward to the 2nd century AD, and a tiny part of the Hellenistic-style Mtskheta treasure, such as the gold and cornelian signet of Asparuch, and a sheath for a gold sacrificial dagger. The ninth case houses jewellery from a queen's tomb at Mtskheta, from the same century, including a diadem of gold and garnet, a ring of gold and amethyst showing Actaeon's death, a necklace of gold, garnet and turquoise, and very sophisticated high-relief silver bowls from Greece. In the tenth case are some of the contents of the tomb of the same queen's daughter, who died aged 21 towards the end of the 2nd century; these include a necklace bearing an amethyst sheep's head containing two of her milk teeth, as well as agate scent bottles.

By the early 3rd century, granulation was giving way to encrustation, and gold served mainly as a support for precious stones. The eleventh case contains an assortment of silver bowls and gold jewellery from 3rd-century Baghineti, including two mystery items, perhaps metal covers for the feet of table- or chair-legs, made somehow from a single unseamed piece of silver. In the twelfth case oak leaves from a king's funeral crown symbolise royal power; in the thirteenth case, from early 4th-century Kartli, there are more gold oak leaves, as well as rings, bracelets, coins, and a nereid and dolphin carved in one piece of agate and set in gold. The fourteenth case houses more leaves, earrings and bowls, and bracelets of jet and garnet, from the first half of the 4th century.

In the next room, the fifteenth case displays a huge pin of agate and gold, buckles bearing big blocks of cornelian, and a golden house from Svaneti with two musicians, and birds on the roof. The sixteenth case holds silver pitchers and unusual inlaid gold necklaces, and the first crosses in Georgian jewellery. The seventeenth shows evidence of Georgia's history as a crossroads of trade, with Persian, Greek, Roman and Byzantine coins going back to the very earliest days of coinage; the eighteenth has 11th- and 12th-century pieces including St George and the St George cross. In the nineteenth case there's a 13th-century icon of the Archangel Gabriel, showing the use of classical Greek-style colouring; the twentieth case covers the 12th and 13th centuries, the heyday of Georgian national culture, with a silver jug and an imposing gold relief of God the Father, Mary and John the Baptist, both with inscriptions in Georgian.

In case 21 are the 15th-century silver bowl of Alexander I and a 12th-century silver jug with writing that modern Georgians can still read, telling how the jug was sacrificed as a token of esteem for their ruler. In case 22 are items such as silver bowls donated to clergy in hope of divine or practical favours; the late medieval items in case 23 show Persian influence (with hints of Arab and Mughal styles). Cases 24 and 25 contain coins, the first with Oriental and the second with Western influence, including French, German and Russian inscriptions, and from the Transcaucasian Republic of 1918–20.

On the ground floor are a room of carpets (Iranian, Azeri, Turkmen and Afghan) and a small room with a very modern display (sponsored by BP and including a film) of the earliest hominid relicts found outside Africa (at Dmanisi) including the skull of a toothless old man who survived for years after losing his teeth, suggesting care for the elderly and hence compassion and social structure.

Upstairs there's a display of history from 1801 to 1921, including swords that belonged to Irakli II and to Napoleon, as well as other weapons used in the wars with Persia and Turkey. There's also the Georgian copy of the Treaty of Gurgievsk (1783) in a case with a bullet hole from the civil war of 1991–92. The next room covers agriculture, crafts and industry, with displays ranging from wine vessels to an oil pump from the Rothschild refinery in Batumi. The new Museum of Soviet Occupation covers the period from 1921 to 1991, with film and newsreel (in Georgian only) in the first room, followed by a disturbing walk up a long carpet to a Stalin-era desk from where you might learn your fate. There are images, documents and items depicting the brutal Soviet rule that led to 80,000 Georgians being shot, 400,000 deported and another 400,000 killed in the Great Patriotic War, with examples of prominent musicians, artists and poets lost in Stalin's terror.

The ethnographic displays are another flight up, the first room housing weapons, household implements, jewellery, ceramics and musical instruments from the first half of the 19th century. The second room has a display of textiles, including the range of natural dyes used, as well as reconstructed peasants' and nobles' houses, and the third room houses a wine press in an oak trunk, a sort of harrow used for removing the outer husks of corn, and a huge mill for pressing sunflower seeds.

Art Museum (*Gudiashvili 1; ☏ 996635, 999909; admission GEL1.50, plus GEL3 for the Treasury, plus GEL10 for the indispensable guide (go to the room behind the kassa on the*

*right to find your guide); catalogues are available in English, French and German for GEL20;
open 11.00–16.00 except Mon)* Housing the Treasury of gold- and silverware and
cloisonné enamel from the Christian era, the Art Museum is if anything even more
amazing than the collection in the National Museum; the museum also has
western European, Russian and Georgian paintings from the Renaissance onwards.

After passing copies of frescoes from Betania and Kintsvisi, you'll start with the
Treasury. Naturally most of the exhibits are icons, in fine golden frames – many are
of St George, who is often shown lancing the Roman Emperor Diocletian rather
than a dragon or devil, as a symbol of the triumph of Christianity over paganism;
St George is also shown being tortured on the wheel. Three-dimensional
sculptures of the saints were forbidden by the Orthodox Church, but relief was
permitted. Encaustic enamels, in which the colours were mixed with wax, were
(from the 6th century) another speciality, reaching a peak in the 10th to 12th
centuries; the technique of firing them so that the colours were melted, but not the
gold frame, was lost in the 15th century.

The collection has many highlights, firstly the chalice from Bedia (in Abkhazia)
made in AD999, with a fine relief of Christ, the Virgin and Apostles; and the 11th-
century *tondo* from Gelati, a circular, silver plaque with a high relief of St Mamai
on a lion. Queen Tamar's pectoral cross has almost mystic significance for many
Georgians, as a tangible link with one of their greatest rulers; it was made at the end
of the 12th century, of gold set with emeralds, rubies and pearls, and has a 13th-
century *starotech* or holder. The icon from Ancha was enamelled in the 6th century
and brought to the Anchiskhati church in Tbilisi in the 17th century; its frame was
made for Tamar in the second half of the 12th century, with a grape motif that
never repeats itself. The wings of the frame were added in the 14th century, well
after the Georgian Renaissance but still proof of good craftsmanship, while the
cherubim on top are from the 19th century.

The Khakhuli triptych has a similarly tangled history: the head of Christ is a 6th-
century encaustic wax painting, to which the Virgin (the largest piece of cloisonné
enamel in the world) was added in the 10th century. These, with 115 cloisonné
enamel medallions dating from the 8th-11th centuries, were set in a gold frame
(with gilded silver wings) in the first half of the 12th century, after it was brought
to Gelati from Khakhuli, now in Turkey. The Russian Governor of Imeretia,
Levashev, tore out much of the gold and jewels in 1859; only the Virgin's face and
hands have been recovered. The Martvili Icon of the Virgin, dating from the first
half of the 12th century, is of gold with small enamels of the Evangelists in the
corners and in the middle of the right side a medallion of St Peter from the 9th
century, the oldest known Byzantine enamel. The 15th-century cross of Gori-jvari
is 2m tall and bears 16 silver plaques, with reliefs of St George.

After the 12th century, Georgian metalwork lost its way somewhat, although
good pieces were produced again from the 15th century; from the 16th century
icons from eastern Georgia show Persian influence, with floral motifs rather than
vines.

By the 18th century emphasis was on secular jewellery; there's a display of the
jewels of Katarina Dadiani, daughter of Alexander Chavchavadze, and the
possessions of other notable families, including a three-litre *khantsi* or drinking
horn, *karkara* wine jars with a spout twisted to make a glugging noise, silver fire
shovels, David IV's stirrups (11th century), Irakli II's spectacles (18th century), a
royal glass stamp, a travelling inkset, and an 18th-century Italian marble table.
Weapons include Vakhtang VI's shield (18th century), and the sabre of Tamar's
grandson (13th century).

From here you can go downstairs to the collection of Iranian art in the basement
(including 16th–19th-century miniatures, and carpets), or upstairs to Georgian and

Western painting. Although there's plenty of good stuff here, it's a bit of a jumble. Most of the 18th-century works are somewhat naïve in style, but in the later 19th century the influence of French art can clearly be seen, as well as a certain amount of Orientalism.

The earliest works are 16th-century icons from Moscow and Yaroslavl, followed by a 17th-century Italian portrait of a senator of the Contarini family, and 18th-century Flemish and German portraits. There's a Winterhalter portrait of a lady (1855), and two Kandinsky abstracts. Russian painters who are less well known in the West include S F Shchedrin (1791–1830), I E Repin (1844–1930), V A Serov (1865–1911) and Z Serebryakova (1884–1967).

There's some very interesting 20th-century Georgian art here: first some intense thickly painted Modernist works, then lighter Modernism including works by Kikodze, Djokidze and other rather decadent painters of the 1920s, and five by David Kakabadze, with a remarkable range of styles, notable the abstract *Decorative Landscape* which is a masterpiece. There are five paintings by Elena Akhvlediani (a curious mix of darkness and idealism), seven by Lado Gudiashvili, seven absorbing symbolic works by Shalva Kikodze, and seven more by Mose Toidze.

Then, famously, come two rooms of naïve Rousseau-esque paintings by Niko Pirosmani depicting Georgians feasting, dancing, singing and drinking. There's a couple more rooms of works by lesser Georgian artists, sadly suffering from heat and humidity, leaving them faded, dull and drained of impact.

Next door is the 'architectural gallery', ie: a barely labelled collection of capitols, mosaics and copies of frescoes from the 5th century onwards, and photos and models of churches.

The Museum of the History of Tbilisi (or Carvasla) (*Located in the caravansarai at Sionis 8;* ↘ *725126, 721706; admission GEL3; open 11.00–16.00 except Mon*) Here you can see a range of interesting exhibits, from 4,500-year-old ceramics from Avlabari, through 10th-century manuscripts, to photographs of 19th-century Tbilisi and dingy models of balconied houses and churches in old Tbilisi. The bulk of the text is only in Georgian, but captions are also in Russian and English. The upper floor (presumably once displaying the history of communist Tbilisi) now houses temporary exhibits, offices and empty rooms, much like the damp-smelling basement.

The Museum of Georgian Folk Architecture and Daily Life (also known as the Ethnographic Museum) (*Vake Park;* ↘ *230960; admission GEL3 (GEL0.50 for Georgians), plus GEL10 for an entirely optional guide; open 11.00–16.00 except Mon*) The lower houses, nearer the entrance, are furnished and open, while those further up can usually be safely viewed from a distance. You'll see three roof types: thatch in western Georgia, red channel tiles, and shingles.

Going around to the left (clockwise), you'll come first to a big open-plan house from Abacha in Mingrelia, with a sleeping platform; then a farmstead, also from Mingrelia, with attractive wooden panelling around a *bukhari* or chimney. An 18th-century house from Imereti is built of logs on a stone base, also open-plan with a central chimney; above a house from Lanckhuti (in Guria), which has an ingenious babywalker on the veranda, a smithy is still in use. The shorter route back passes another Imeretian house, with the traditional Georgian *marani* or winestore; the alternative is to climb up the hill to a restaurant by the road, near large and impressive houses from Adjara and a Svan defensive tower on the ridge. Returning down the hill you'll pass a house from Teliani (near Kaspi) just before the ruined 6th-century Church of Sionis Tianeti and a row of tombs (one, with an inscription in Old Georgian, under glass); beyond this a stone building half-set into the hillside is from Kakheti. Finally, hidden away right at the bottom is a 2m phallic stone from Abkhazia.

You may find Ivan Togonidze at work in the smithy, where he makes striking metal sculptures, or Gia Akhvlediani (great-nephew of the famous Elena Akhvlediani) selling his woodcuts and sketches in the house below. As you go around you'll also see odds and ends such as old muskets, wooden claws to protect the fingers while scything, and cots with a pipe leading to a gourd for urine below.

There's a good restaurant, Rachis Ubani, open seasonally in a restored house from Racha.

OTHER MUSEUMS The **State Academy of Fine Art** (*Khram Slavi; Rustaveli 11; open 11.00–15.00 except Mon*) houses temporary art shows from time to time. Just below it, the **State Literature Museum** (*Chanturia (formerly Georgiashvili) 8; open 10.00–17.00 except Mon*) reopened in 1999, but has only temporary displays upstairs, while downstairs is now a commercial art gallery.

HOUSE-MUSEUMS The best of Tbilisi's house-museums is the home of **Elena Akhvlediani** (1901–75) (*Kiacheli 12, one flight up and on the right, with posters on the door*); it's currently closed due to lack of funding. If you can get in you'll find a room with a huge wooden column in the middle, modelled on peasant architecture, as well as small wooden galleries, and hanging rugs. Akhvlediani's paintings are hung up to five high on the walls, and you'll also see examples of her theatre and film designs and book illustrations, as well as photos and mementoes. Although not the most challenging of artists she did have a very wide range of styles, and is loved for her warm depictions of daily life.

There are two other artists' house-museums in Tbilisi, but they are both occupied by decidedly eccentric ladies who are very reluctant to open up without prior booking. Your best bet is to ask the folk at either the Art Museum or the Akhvlediani house to phone for you. One is the home of **David Kakabadze** (✆ *934372; Kakabadze 11a, just above Rustaveli Sq*), whose studio has been described as 'a splendid room filled not only with paintings but with drinking horns, daggers, sheaths, ceramics, early Georgian jewellery and metalwork, and beautifully engraved Persian jugs'.

The other is that of the fantastical **Lado Gudiashvili** (Gudiashvilis 11, just below the Kashveti church). There is a couple of sketches by his friend Modigliani here, as well as his portrait of Modigliani. It has been refurbished and reopened in 2007; see also the dandyish statue of Gudiashvili in the adjacent (southeastern) corner of Alexandrov Park.

BOTANIC GARDENS

(€3 *for foreigners, although it's quite easy to get in for the local rate of GEL1; open 10.00–19.00 except Mon*) These gardens are one of Tbilisi's least-known treasures, a beautiful place to wander for an afternoon, with both cultivated beds and greenhouses and wilder quieter areas higher up the slopes. The main entry is at the top of Botanikuri, above Gorgasali Square, and it can also be reached by paths from the second hairpin of the Kojori highway, at the junction to the Sololaki Ridge, or near the Kartlis Deda statue; if you enter this way guards will send you down to the main gate to pay.

The gardens were established as a royal pleasure ground in 1636 on the right bank of the Tsavkistiskhevi (Fig Ravine), with a natural waterfall, and became a municipal garden in 1801, growing vines, vegetables and fruit. In 1845 it was taken over and expanded by the Russian Viceroy Mikhail Vorontsov (who also founded the lovely gardens in Yalta), using the steep valley, and a Muslim cemetery, and in the 1890s it became an academic body, publishing its proceedings and a seed exchange list from 1895, and the Bulletin of the Tbilisi Botanic Garden from 1905; from 1897 it was organised into bio-regional sections (such as pine grove, saline soils, and Turkestan). In the Soviet period it expanded on to the right bank of the stream and became more practical in outlook, as well as opening sections in Kutaisi and Zugdidi. Taken over by the city in 2000, it was desperately short of money and in a terrible state until being rescued by oligarch Bidzina Ivanishvili. There are still virtually no labels on plants and no signs or maps.

In its 128 hilly hectares (of which 85ha are cultivated) there are 4,900 species, including 2,300 species and forms of trees and shrubs, and over 900 species of tropical and subtropical plants in greenhouses. Local people see the gardens mainly as a venue for picnics and wedding photos; an EcoCentre, funded by the Worldwide Fund for Nature, is being set up here, as a key part of an environmental education programme.

There's a fine specimen of *Pinus pithyusa* (Pitsunda pine) inside the entry, from where a gravel path leads up the valley to bridges below the waterfall; the main building and greenhouses are across the valley to the left, with a winding asphalt road continuing up the valley, not very interesting at first with fields and scrubby shrubs, as well as some succulents and thorny shrubs, and some hidden gardens stumbled across at random.

Near the head of the valley you'll enter conifers (with bamboo) and then untended scrub of birch or alder, ending at a locked gate. Here you're above the roof of the Sololaki Conference Centre, and not far from Tbilisi Horizont (Horizon), a gated community that's visible all the way from the airport road. The gardens' saviour Bidzina Ivanishvili appears to be winning a lawsuit against it, and it may be demolished. It's possible to loop back to the left, below the cliffs, or to the right down a cypress alley (on a gravel path).

Tbilisi's **zoo** (at the Heroes' Square roundabout; admission GEL0.50) has been criticised for its small concrete-floored cages, and equally has no money and has lost many of its animals. Under new management since May 2006, it has moved the animals to more suitable housing and opened a veterinary centre. At the moment it has a few camels, elephants, zebras, gibbons, baboons, bears, hyenas and peacocks, and also a kids' funfair with dodgems and the like, which needs to be moved away from the animals. It was planned to move it to Lake Lisi, above Saburtalo, but a US$60 million resort is now to be built there by 2011 (at present the lake is full of weeds, and the cable car from Nutsubidze is inoperable, but it should be a pleasant outing in a few years).

4

Shida (Inner) Kartli

When you follow the main routes westwards from Tbilisi, you pass through the heartland of Georgia, beginning with Mtskheta, the country's spiritual capital. Most tourist agencies in Tbilisi run day trips to Mtskheta and Gori, with your car or theirs.

MTSKHETA

Named after Mtskhetos, son of Kartlos, and overlooked by Mount Kartli, supposedly still home to the soul of Kartlos, **Mtskheta** (pronounced 'Skayta', with the first two letters more or less silent) is at the absolute heart of Georgia's spiritual identity. Inhabited for over 3,000 years, the site at the confluence of the Mtkvari and Aragvi rivers was the centre of the pagan cult of Armazi (the Georgian version of the Zoroastrian fire god Ormazd of Persia), adopted in the 4th century BC by King Parnavaz I of Kartli, who established his capital 2km southwest of present-day Mtskheta. It was known to the ancient Greeks as Armosica and to Pliny as Armasicum, and is now Armazistsikhe (Armazi castle). There are traces of older Hittite and even Sumerian cults; the surrounding hilltops all housed pagan shrines which have now been replaced by churches. From the 4th century BC until the 5th century AD this was the capital of Iveria (present-day Kartli), the scene of the royal family's conversion to Christianity, and continued as seat of the Georgian Church until the 12th century. The town's churches are included on UNESCO's World Heritage List.

The main cathedral, though no longer seat of the Catholicos, is far more impressive than Tbilisi's Sioni Cathedral, and effortlessly dominates the town (now little more than a village), especially as seen from the main highway across the river. There's another fine ancient church in Mtskheta, and the Jvari church, high on a crag across the Aragvi, is one of the most architecturally important in Georgia, setting the pattern for virtually all those built in the following centuries.

GETTING THERE At the Didube bus terminal there's always a marshrutka (GEL1) loading for Mtskheta, as well as about 15 buses a day (GEL0.60). Buses also leave roughly every half hour for Gori and most hours for Kutaisi, passing below the Jvari church. There are 15 trains a day each way between Tbilisi and Gori, and all except the Batumi day trains halt at Mtskheta, although the station is hardly central; this is a far easier way to get here from the west than bus or marshrutka.

Buses cross the Didube Bridge heading for the statue of King David the Builder (and a spectacular statue of St Nino above) where they join the main highway. If you come directly from the city centre along Gamsakhurdias Avenue you'll first pass the most striking piece of modern architecture in Tbilisi, the Ministry of Transport, composed of towers and horizontal blocks of offices built into and out of the hillside in 1977, the modernist effect now spoilt by the new (traditional-style) church in front.

129

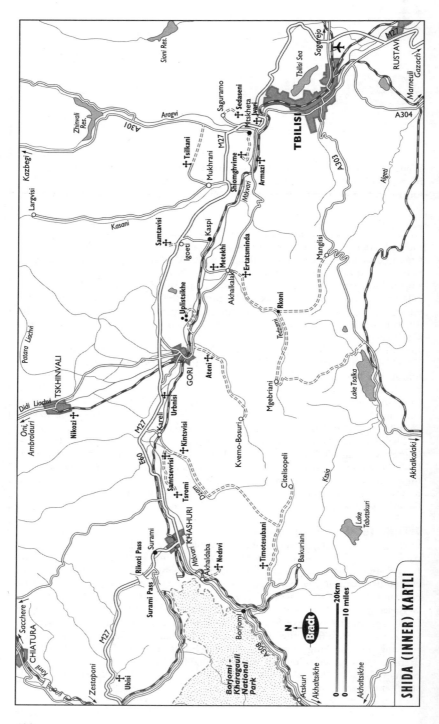

SHIDA (INNER) KARTLI

After the usual outskirts clutter of restaurants and petrol stations, together with a rash of development associated with the new US embassy (the ugly big white building away to the right), the dual-carriageway leaves the city limits at km16 and swings left along the right/south bank of the Mtkvari (passing the Zemo-Avchalskaya hydro-electric station, built in 1927 and now very small and old fashioned). After just 2km, the Jvari church is signed (in Latin script) to the right, but it's still 7km away and you shouldn't get off the bus here. It's just 1km more to the turning to Mtskheta, which takes off to the right and goes under the main highway just before it crosses the Mtkvari. Coming by road from the west you should get off here, immediately after the bridge, and go 200m west to a bus stop; marshrutkas from Tbilisi are often full, but there will eventually be a bus.

It's a deceptively long walk into town from here, following the river past the town, then after 40 minutes crossing a bridge (with what seems to be a statue of a skateboarding eagle at its south end) and doubling back. The main highway passes below the Jvari church, high on its rock, crosses the Aragvi at km25.5, and meets the local road from Mtskheta after a pedestrian underpass leading to bus stops on the highway; it's another couple of kilometres to the flyover at the start of the Georgian Military Highway, just before the km28 marker.

Mtskheta and the Jvari church are quite close as the crow flies, but they're separated by the Aragvi River; if you don't have a car the easiest option is certainly to take a taxi from Mtskheta to Jvari (GEL10–12, including waiting time), but you could also take a bus along the main highway from Tbilisi (for instance, to or from Gori or Kutaisi) and ask to be set down at the roadside immediately below the church, at about km21, from where you can hike up in about 15–20 minutes. The road takes a long looping route, ending at a large car park, with a tiny drinks stall and a toilet below it.

Once you've seen the church (see below), it's possible to descend, either by the road, or directly down the northern hillside by a clear 4x4 track that turns left off the tarmac road just off the top. Once on the flat cut straight across the meadow heading for the giant advertising bottle outside the Aragvi restaurant on the far side of the highway (you'll have to cross the dual carriageway on the level, but this shouldn't be too hard); it'll take 30–45 minutes each way. A path leads down immediately between the Aragvi and Khideshelis restaurants to a footbridge (where locals swim); there's also a cable ferry from the Aragvi restaurant just to the left.

Once you're across the river, turn right along the road and then cut through to the left to the road past the derelict campsite, or continue for five minutes along the road to the open-air theatre below the early-medieval castle of Bebris-tsikhe. This rises beside the road between the historic village and the modern town of typical communist blocks, set tactfully (for once) 1–2km to the north; from the castle it takes ten minutes to walk to the left/south to the Samtavro church. Going from the centre to Jvari, head north past Samtavro church, turn right around the north side of the derelict Univermag shop, right following the tarmac road past the former campsite, and right again at the junction to find the footbridge on your left.

IN MTSKHETA Entering by road from Tbilisi, you'll turn right by the railway station to cross the river (where the foundations of Pompey's Bridge, dating from 65BC, are visible when the water is low) and swing right to continue for 1km (past the former Motel Mtskheta, now full of refugees from Abkhazia) to the post office at the start of the one-way system. You'll see the cathedral on your right before reaching a plaza with the Armazi cinema (with a colourful fresco depicting Georgian history) on your left; it's built over the remains of the Old Town gates, visible through the glass façade. If you see the Samtavro church to the left it's time to get off.

Buses back to Tbilisi return past Samtavro and the cinema and along Davit Agmashenebelis, the next road up the hill, passing the United Georgia Bank at No 37. There's no ATM here, but there is one at People's Bank, opposite Samtavro. A tourist information centre is planned opposite the cathedral (where two 'presents and souvenirs' shops have appeared), and until then you can make enquiries at the Tourism Department of Mtskheta-Tianeti Region (*Davit Agmashenebelis 136;* ℡ 27 322530, 322170). The Mtskhetoba Festival, usually attended by the president and Catholicos as well as 100,000-plus others, is held in October; there's also a Festival of Performing Arts in early June.

⌂ WHERE TO STAY

⌂ **Hotel Mtskheta Palace** (8 rooms, 3 suites) 200m off Davit Agmashenebelis at the north end of the bridge; ℡ 910202; f 911717; e mtskhetapalas@ posta.ge; http://nacnobi.myweb.ge/mtskhetapalas. This modern hotel provides the only accommodation now available in Mtskheta. It has a covered pool & sauna, & 3 dbl rooms with AC, TV & a good bathroom with toiletries & hairdryer, 5 larger ones & 3 suites with massage shower, like a vertical jacuzzi, all inc b/fast. *Dbl GEL150, large dbl GEL200, suite GEL300.*

✗ WHERE TO EAT

There are next to no services in Mtskheta; once upon a time a restaurant opposite the cathedral gates supposedly served the best *shashlik* in Georgia, but if you go around to the left from the gates you'll find the rather run-down **Café Guga** at Ansuvidzis 23, opposite a fine but neglected garden. There's also the **Tamariani** restaurant by the river at the entry to Mtskheta and the **Armazi**, by the highway bridge and junction. The **Salobio** restaurant, about 4km towards Tbilisi by the riverside, has always been a favourite outing for the people of Tbilisi, offering a wide range of traditional dishes such as *lobio* (for which Mtskheta is famed), *chadi, pirozhki, khinkali, shashlik* and *khachapuri.*

WHAT TO SEE

Sveti Tskhoveli The cathedral of Sveti Tskhoveli rises on the site of the palace of the kings of Iveria, to which part of Christ's crucifixion robe was brought soon after his death by Elias, whose sister Sidonia died of joy clutching it so tightly that it had to be buried here with her. The cedar which grew out of her grave was felled to build St Nino's first church here, and one column supposedly hovered in the air until Nino brought it down by prayer; in addition miraculous sap is said to have flowed from it at her behest.

The church derives its name of Sveti Tskhoveli or 'Life-giving Column' from this; in any case it could also be said that the name is clearly pagan in origin. The first church here was built of wood in the 4th century AD; this was replaced in 575, and the present church was built by Patriarch Melchisidek in 1010–29, incorporating the tiny 6th-century building. It's now the largest-surviving church in Georgia. It was damaged by an earthquake in 1283 and by Tamerlane at the end of the 14th century before being restored in 1412–31 and 1656. Built just a few decades before the great Norman cathedrals of England, you may find some similarities in style.

Perfectly proportioned, with its great pepper-pot dome of greenish stone rising high above the village and the river, it sits in a large square of walls added by Irakli II in the 18th century, with the main entrance to the west. As you approach you'll see two carved bulls' heads, which are pagan fertility symbols. Externally, the stonework is well decorated but not excessively so; note particularly the beautifully carved trees on the western façade, and a hand holding a bevel-square over the central arch of the northern façade. This illustrates the story of the builder Arsukisdze's hand being chopped off by his jealous teacher (though there are various versions of this story).

The church has a three-bay nave that seems huge by Georgian standards; incorporated into the second bay to the right is a 14th-century copy of the chapel of the Holy Sepulchre in Jerusalem. In the next bay is a high-sided 17th-century pavilion built over the tomb of Sidonia, and to the east of this is the patriarch's stone throne, also 17th century. Immediately ahead you'll find the royal tombs, of which three can be identified: the last two kings, Irakli II (1720–98) and Georgi XII (1746–1800) lie on either side of the altar steps, and Vakhtang Gorgasali, founder of Tbilisi, is the second back from Irakli (and roped off).

The most notable frescoes are in the centre of the south wall of the south transept, although much is missing; what's left of this 17th-century Apocalypse is a wheel of the zodiac radiating out of a central Christ figure, with the Apostles to the right and a sea with monsters to the left. Intriguingly, the writer Daniel Farson states that there were undeniably two flying-saucers painted at eye level on the altar fresco of the crucifixion, and another over the arch; others felt they were just floating faces shining down. In any case they had been whitewashed over by 1991.

There is excellent singing here on Saturday and Sunday mornings; knees, shoulders and women's hair should be covered at all times.

Samtavro Just five minutes north, beyond the plaza with the Armazi cinema, the Samtavro nunnery stands on the site of Georgia's first church, which is now a royal residence and administrative centre, with a tiny 4th-century chapel (with poor frescoes) in the grounds marking the spot where Nino lived in a log hut. The main Church of the Redeemer dates from the first half of the 11th century (the dome was restored after damage by a 13th-century earthquake); the most notable feature is the tomb of King Mirian and Queen Nana, the 4th-century founders of the Chosroid dynasty, incongruously set under a 19th-century Italianate marble canopy in the church's southwest corner, just left of the entrance. Otherwise the church is big and spacious, with bare walls and some very battered frescoes in the dome and above the altar. Externally, there are good decorative carvings on the north and east walls and the dome; the belltower (obviously shaken by earthquakes) dates from the 13th century.

Jvari The Jvari (Cross) church stands on a spur of the Sagurami Hills 150m above Mtskheta, and now seems to grow out of the rock. It's one of the finest examples of old Georgian architecture, a marvellously simple but sophisticated edifice, in advance of most European ecclesiastical architecture of the period. Built between the AD580s and 604 by Staphanoz I, it was the first 'apse-buttressed' cruciform church, in which the gaps between the arms of the cross are filled by small chapels, producing a virtually perfect square ground plan; this allows a wonderfully lofty and spacious interior in which four pillars support an octagonal drum and a round dome covering the entire central space. It stands on the spot where Nino first set up her cross overlooking the pagan shrines of Mtskheta; the ruins of a late 6th-century church survive next to the present church. Closed in 1911, it was reconsecrated in 1988, and still appears partly ruined, the main columns seemingly hewn out of raw rock. Above the south door is an exceptionally fine bas-relief of a pair of winged angels bearing a cross. Inside it is big and bare, with a huge plinth in the centre bearing a cross, and a low wooden iconostasis.

AROUND MTSKHETA

To the northeast of Mtskheta, beyond the main road and the Jvari church, is the **Saguramo Nature Reserve**, which is to become the Tbilisi National Park in May 2007 and is to be expanded; it's mainly of recreational importance and not very species-rich, although there are wolves and bears, and a wildlife rescue centre.

At km24 on the main highway a road turns to the right/north to Saguramo, where there are some luxurious holiday homes and a modern winery; you can visit the house-museum of Ilia Chavchavadze, the reformer who became a secular saint after his murder nearby at Tsitsamouri in 1907 by agents either of the Tsarist regime or of the Bolsheviks (see page 171).

From here a track leads about 7km south to the monastery of **Zedazeni** (also known as Aktimo), set on a hilltop at 1,390m in the heart of the reserve. It was founded by Ioane of Zedazeni, one of the Syrian fathers, who lived here in a cave from AD501 to 531; the monastery was built over his tomb in the 7th–8th centuries and has a 7th-century fresco of St George and the Dragon. Ioane's disciple founded Kvemo (Lower) Zedazeni at the foot of the mountain, and a three-nave basilica was built in the AD860s and 870s; now reopened, it's sending out monks to repopulate other disused monasteries.

In the hills 12km west of Mtskheta, the monastery of **Shiom-ghvime** is built into the hillside in a spectacularly picturesque manner, though the buildings look more like a farm than a monastery; it was founded in the 6th century by the Assyrian monk Shio Mgvimeli, another of the Thirteen Syrian Fathers, who voluntarily spent 20 years in a cave. A church was built over his grave in the 11th century, as well as the monastery of the Virgin, built by Davit Agmashenebelis in 1103–23, a 12th-century refectory, and a 7km aqueduct at the end of the same century.

There are no buses, and it can only be reached by a robust car; the road is signed (12km) between the Armazi cinema and the Samtavro nunnery. This passes the Gvtismshobeli and Mgalobliant-Kari churches (both just to the north of the road and both 17th century), then the Tsminda Demetre and Kaloubiani churches (both to the south and both 12th century). The first three are within 2km of Mtskheta and make a pleasant walk.

WEST OF MTSKHETA

From its junction with the Georgian Military Highway, the main highway west to Kutaisi and western Georgia runs to the north of the hills along the north side of the Mtkvari; it's a fast road through fairly empty, featureless countryside, except for the spectacular 16th-century castle of Ksani visible to the south as the road crosses the river of the same name at km40.5. Natakhtari is the current end of the four-lane highway; another 16km to Aghiani are now being turned into dual carriageway, and the plan is for this to reach the Gori and the Tskhinvali junction by 2008, Khashuri in 2009, and (optimistically) Batumi in 2011. An alternative, if you want to meander along rough back roads, is to follow the south bank of the Mtkvari, visiting ruined castles and ancient churches in villages that see almost no visitors despite being just a few hours from Tbilisi.

ARMAZI The road from Mtskheta to Tbilisi crosses the Mtkvari and turns to the left; the road to the right/west is unsignposted but soon reaches the station and continues towards Armazi, Akhalkalaki and, ultimately, Gori.

The first station is Armazi, just 2.5km on; from here you should backtrack almost 1km to the 'Archaeologists' House', where the site of Parnavaz's capital is being excavated. On the hillside across the river is the Kaloubiani chapel, off the road to Shiom-ghvime, but sadly there's no way across the river here. Virtually opposite the archaeologists' gate you can take a tiny path diagonally up over the railway embankment to the km0.3 marker. A path, and for a while a water pipe, run along the true right side of a dry ravine into low forest of oaks and hornbeams, with lots of birds in residence. After about seven minutes you'll reach a pool with charms tied to the tree branches; the path continues briefly in the stream bed then beside it, curving to the right. After about ten minutes more the path crosses to the left bank and forks; if you stay on the right bank and follow the path uphill for a couple of minutes you'll reach **Armazi church**, a twin-naved brick construction now almost wholly ruined. It's a grassy spot visited mainly by cows, and makes a lovely campsite. If you cross the stream and fork left, following the stream and then climbing up to your right, you'll come in about 20 minutes to a saddle below the ruined tower of Armazistsikhe, spectacularly set amid cliffs of dramatic strata, with views to the chapels on the hilltops around Shiom-ghvime. It's possible to climb down on the far side of the saddle and loop back to the stream, but I wouldn't recommend doing it alone.

AKHALKALAKI AND AROUND

At the west end of Armazi village (all modern concrete blocks) a comical eagle sculpture points the way left under the railway; the road, fairly well served by buses, soon heads south away from the river through dry sandy hills, and eventually reaches **Akhalkalaki** (New Town – one of many), where there's an EU-funded home for disabled children at the road junction.

From here a road follows the Tedzami Valley southwest as far as Rkoni, where there's a 7th–8th century church (altered in the 11th century), a medieval bridge and an 18th-century fort.

From here it's possible to hike or mountain bike through the Algetis Nature Reserve, across the Trialeti Ridge, to Manglisi. A three-day hiking route follows the Tedzami Valley to Mgebriani and then follows an ancient trail south across the Trialeti Ridge by the Kldecari (Rocky) Pass to Lake Tsalka, by the main road from Akhalkalaki (the other, more important one) to Tbilisi.

By the graveyard at the south end of Akhalkalaki is a simple 10th-century basilica church, with traces of frescoes on its west wall; another 2km to the south (20km from Kaspi) the church of **Ertatsminda** was built in the 13th and 14th centuries. It's a cruciform church, with carved crosses on all four façades, and a blind Romanesque-style arcade above the aisle roof line. This is a settlement of stone houses which has something of the feel of a real mountain village. It's known for a priest who was martyred after leading invaders the wrong way to save the village.

Akhalkalaki is a long thin village with a defensive tower near its northern end; just beyond this the Gori road continues to the left (passing the Uplistsikhe cave-city), while straight on to the north it's 11km to Kaspi. It's just a couple of kilometres along this road to the village of **Metekhi**, where the 13th-century Metekhis Sioni Church has a unique tapering design of pepper-pot dome. Otherwise it's a simple cruciform shape within a square plan, with carved crosses on all four façades. The other feature of interest in the village is a golden statue of Stalin to the west of the road just north of the church.

KASPI AND SAMTAVISI

Kaspi is a small town with a chemical plant, and a relatively major stop on the railway 48km west of Tbilisi; however, there's nothing to see and no services for travellers. It's 9km south of Igoeti, at km56/496 (from Tbilisi/the Russian border) on the main Tbilisi–Kutaisi highway; minibuses follow the valley from the flyover east of the rail station; the road signposted from the station leads up to a simple and run-down basilica, and then down to join the main road after a couple of kilometres. The junction with the highway is marked by the Restaurant Igoeti (not much good), and about 200m east (right by the road) there's a small 9th-century basilica of brick on stone foundations; about 600m west (still within Igoeti) is the junction to the superbly decorated church of **Samtavisi**, definitely a worthwhile stop for anyone taking the road between Tbilisi and Kutaisi. By bus this is more easily done eastbound, as any bus is likely to stop and take you on to Mtskheta and Tbilisi, while westbound you'll have to struggle with reading destination boards.

The Samtavisi road continues straight ahead where the highway swings left at the so-called Curve of Death to the River Lekhura Bridge, and curves to the right/northwest. The church is soon visible, but is bigger than it seems; in fact it's about 1.5km away (and 11km from Kaspi). Stick to the main road through the village, then turn right where a bridge comes into view ahead, to reach a gate on the north side of the church complex. To the left as you enter are the remains of the bishop's palace; the belltower under which you enter dates from the 17th century, but the church itself is a unified structure dating from 1030–68. Outside, the north, west and south sides are relatively simply decorated, although the north side has what seems to be a fake clock; the east end is richer (perhaps the best stone-carving in Georgia), with the two deep recesses that are typical of Georgian architecture marking the shape of the altar apse within and the lateral apses on either side. They draw the eye upwards to the incised cross and the dome above, stressing the verticality of the building. Inside, the church is high and bare, with the central dome set on four free-standing pillars that are not quite parallel. There are some battered fragments of 17th-century frescoes in the altar apse, and in the cupola (you'll notice that the figure of Christ is always the right way up for the priest, not the congregation), and tombstones dating from the 11th century. If you want to spend more time in the area, there's a fine-looking **fort** which is easily reached by a track northeast from the next village to the north.

GORI გორი

The highway from Tbilisi to Kutaisi runs several kilometres to the north of Gori, a fairly unattractive city known above all as the birthplace of Georgia's most infamous son, Stalin. Even if you choose to boycott the Stalin Museum, Gori is nevertheless the base for visiting the cave-city of Uplistsikhe and several fine historic churches, notably Ateni Sioni.

There have been fortifications on the hill dominating Gori since the first half of the 1st millennium BC; the Roman General Pompey besieged it in 65BC, but there was no real civilian settlement here until 1123 when King David the Builder established a city, partly settled by Armenian refugees. In 1892, when Stalin was 13, Gorky described Gori: as 'quite small, no bigger than a fair-sized village… The whole place has a picturesque wildness all its own. The sultry sky over the town, the noisy, turbulent waters of the Kura, mountains in the near distance with their 'City of Caves' and further away the Caucasus range, with its sprinkling of snow that never melts.' The population at this time was 9,000 at most, but is now 64,000, with a relatively high proportion of Roman Catholics. It's a largely unattractive place, with dogs investigating piles of rotting rubbish, which seems largely to sum up the gory legacy of Stalinism.

GETTING THERE There are regular trains from Tbilisi, the fastest taking 1 hour 10 minutes. The town centre lies on the left/east bank of the river Liakvi at its confluence with the Mtkvari, and its railway station is on the far, south side of the Mtkvari. From here (having seen the statue of Stalin still dominating the waiting room), take trolleybus, minibus or new yellow bus route 2, or climb the steps at the west end of the platform to reach the bridges over the tracks and the river and carry on northwards along Stalin Prospekt for 15 minutes to reach Stalin Square. You'll know this instantly by the 17m-tall statue of Stalin, the only survivor of the thousands of similar edifices that once graced every city square throughout the Soviet Empire (although there are still many smaller busts). From the north side of the square Chavchavadze Street leads west past the theatre to the bus station and market within about 500m; some buses leave from a second terminal across the bridge to the west. Marshrutkas for Tbilisi (GEL4) wait by a ticket kiosk across the road to the west of the bus station.

The junction to Gori is at km472/80 (about 60km west of Mtskheta), and it's 4km more to the centre (GEL4 by marshrutka from Tbilisi); from the west turn off at km468.5/83.5 if you have your own wheels, or continue to the Tskhinvali junction, where taxis (GEL6) wait.

WHERE TO STAY AND EAT

Hotel Victoria Tamar Mepis 76; ↘ 370 75586; m 877 402372; f 70050. To reach the Victoria, continue south from Stalin Sq towards the rail station for 300m, then at the lights go 200m or so to the left, or else follow Chavchavadze east & then head south after the hospital (now taken over by the army). All rooms have TV, shower & fridge; this is a modern building with AC, satellite TV & a sauna. *Rooms GEL65–150 inc b/fast & tax.*

Hotel Intourist 26 Stalin Av; ↘ 72676. This is a large hotel built in 1959 to house pilgrims to the Stalin Museum; it's remarkably tasteful (the foyer is almost worth a look in itself) if now rather tatty upstairs. Some German is spoken by the manageress, & the restaurant next door is excellent. It may well be worth a stopover here just to minimise exposure

to the high-price hotels of Tbilisi. *Most rooms (costing GEL20) have cold water, with shared toilet & shower, although there are 3 rooms at GEL50 with water heaters, towels & better locks, & others at GEL70 (a bit less for Georgians).*

Hotel Gori 3km from town on the highway to Tbilisi; m 270 70818, 827 050266. You'll see this hotel, the best place to stay in Gori, on the left as the bus from Tbilisi begins to turn off into Gori; you can get off & cross the dual carriageway to reach it. It's a very nice 4-star place, about the standard of a European Best Western & much more affordable. The staff speak enough English, & there's a good restaurant, with Georgian dishes from GEL4–6 (or GEL30 for caviar). *Semiluxe (with bathroom & TV) dbl GEL80 & luxe (much the same but bigger) GEL150.*

OTHER PRACTICALITIES There's a Rio Arabica **coffee house** facing the Stalin statue and a Bank of Georgia **ATM** just south, symbolising the changes the city has seen in recent years. There's also a Bank Republic **ATM** at the post office (*Stalin Av 15*), a ProCredit **ATM** west of the centre (*Chavchavadze 10*) and half-a-dozen **internet** places around town, due partly to the presence of Peace Corps Volunteers for training; they also rave about the **swimming pool** behind the sports school south of the market.

WHAT TO SEE The **Stalin Museum** (*Admission GEL10, Georgians GEL3, photo permit GEL30, video GEL100, inc guide; open 10.30–16.00*). To the north of Stalin Square the large landscaped plaza of Stalin Avenue, lined with imposing buildings, has replaced the jumble of slummy shacks in which Josef Djugashvili grew up; the two-room house, then Sobornaya (or Cathedral Street) 10, in which he was born in 1879, remains beneath a glass-roofed Doric temple (thought by some to be more like a metro station) erected by Beria in 1939. Immediately behind this is the massive Italianate museum to his memory that was defiantly built in 1957, the year after Khrushchev's denunciation of Stalin and his crimes. This was officially closed in 1989, but school groups continued to be shown around; now the pretence of closure has ended and it's open to all again.

To the people of Gori there's little purely political significance to this: Stalin is simply the only important thing ever to come out of Gori, and is revered as the 'strong man' rather than for his views or deeds. There's no doubt that the locals are far too quick to overlook his immense crimes, but you would in any case be foolish to expect any mention of the gulag or the Ukrainian famine in a museum like this, and if you ask you'll be told they're waiting for proof, much like George W Bush on climate change.

Captions are in Georgian and Russian only, but detailed factual information is not likely to be your objective here. The displays are upstairs; the first floor deals with his youth and pre-revolutionary career – it's remarkable what a good-looking youth Stalin was (in a romantic revolutionary style), and how literary he was, writing quite passable poetry, working in secret presses and then being the first editor of *Pravda*. In the second room, bringing events up to World War II, he gradually becomes more Stalin-like, with the bristling moustache and bushy eyebrows and hair (which prevented his hats from fitting for many years). Kalinin and Gorky remain prominent, but Trotsky has been cut out of the photos, and there's no mention of the Molotov–Ribbentrop Pact or of Lenin's testament warning the Communist Party against Stalin ('a coarse, brutish bully acting on behalf of a great power'). It was once thought that Stalin might have been a double agent for the tsarist secret police in the pre-revolutionary period, but it's less clear which foreign power Lenin might have been thinking of – quite possibly Britain, which was vilified for its occupation of Transcaucasia.

The third room deals with the Great Patriotic War – even if we can't forgive Stalin's crimes, we should give him credit for saving us in the war. The next room is dominated by tributes from a motley collection of world figures such as Kirov, Ordjonikidze, Ibarruri, Barbusse, Roosevelt, Churchill and de Gaulle, and the museum culminates with a sort of symbolic lying in state by a bust of Stalin. After this there are more miscellaneous photos, and off the grand staircase a room of cabinets displaying gifts to Stalin. Naturally you can buy Stalin postcards and badges here. Beside the museum it's also worth glancing at Stalin's massive private rail carriage, on six axles to carry the weight of its armour-plating.

ELSEWHERE IN GORI Immediately to the east of the bus station and market a hill is dramatically crowned by the **Goris-Tsikhe Castle**; this is best reached from the east side, although a path does lead up from the road by the market to the entrance on the south side of the castle. The best view is from the west, where the walls form a series of defensive enclosures tumbling down the hillside. Although the fortifications (mostly from the 7th and 13th centuries) have been rather over restored, the castle is rather run-down and used mainly as a public toilet area. Nevertheless, it offers good views of the Mtkvari Valley, the solid snowy wall of the Caucasus to the north, and on a high spur across the river to the southwest the 6th-century **Church of Gori-Jvari** (*open May–Nov on Tue, with a festival on 6 May*), rebuilt in the 12th century and the 1980s; taxis charge GEL20, although it's a delightful walk. There's also a **Museum of Martial Glory** at Stalina 19 (by a ceramic relief memorial to the dead of 1941–44 and an eternal flame), which is an annexe of the Stalin Museum; ask there if you want to visit. There used to be a Museum of Local History and Ethnography in the Roman Catholic Church of the Dormition at Lomauri 7, northeast of the castle hill, which has now been taken over by the Orthodox parish.

AROUND GORI

UPLISTSIKHE About 10km east of Gori along the Mtkvari Valley, visible from trains along the main line, is the cave-city of Uplistsikhe. The Silk Road ran along the hills to the north (hence the positions of Gori, Kaspi and Mtskheta, all on the north side of the Mtkvari), and Uplistsikhe was a trading centre by at least the 5th century BC. Later it became more isolated and was inhabited by monks until it was destroyed in the 13th century by Chinghiz's son Khulagu.

Over the centuries the site has suffered greatly from the elements, although channels were built to carry off storm water and prevent flash floods (drinking water was brought 5–6km from a spring just 44m above, through a beautifully engineered system of ceramic pipes and a tunnel). Most of the caves have been at least partly eroded away, so that it takes a considerable feat of the imagination to really understand what the city was like.

The tour of the ruins is only for the able, starting by scrambling up rocks past grain pits to the remains of a theatre built in the 2nd or 3rd century AD, complete with orchestra pit; the auditorium side has now all collapsed into the river and been washed away, and the stage roof is held up by concrete pillars. There's even a bread oven in the middle of the stage. The largest hall in the city is known as Tamar's Hall, although Queen Tamar never lived here; its front wall has gone, but it's otherwise intact. The *marani* (wine-storage room) next to it, one of three in the city, dates from after her time. There's an underground prison, 8.5m deep, just below Tamar's Hall, and to the south is what must have been a pharmacy, with eight layers of storage spaces (about 15cm cubes), where traces of herbs and wrapping parchments have been found. To the north of Tamar's Hall is another hall, now roofless, which was once a church – there's very little left except for the stumps of four columns, and a basin for the blood of sacrificed animals. Further up there's a very obvious conventional church, a three-nave basilica built of red brick in the 9th–10th centuries, which survived the Mongol onslaught, although all 5,000 resident monks were killed. The church's frescoes were all whitewashed in the 19th century.

On the way back down you'll pass the market, with its stone stalls, and may finish by going down through a 41m tunnel (designed to be used by water carriers) to exit on the track beside the river. This leads to a village immediately to the west, whose inhabitants were removed in 1968 (though at least one house is clearly in use again). You might be tempted to set out to walk back to Gori along the north bank of the river, but you should be aware of the deep gullies blocking the way.

A World Bank cultural heritage project paid for an interpretation centre (usually locked), walking itinerary and better guides. At present there are reasonably well-informed guides, whose services cost GEL20 on top of the ticket price of GEL6 (students GEL1.80), but they speak only Georgian and Russian. There are plenty of people flogging postcards, but no real interpretative materials. In addition, cracks are developing in many of the caves, which may crumble away in the next ten to 30 years unless action is taken.

Getting there and away A local bus runs every couple of hours from Gori, passing the railway station (by an odd one-way system), forking left in the first village, Khidistavi, and then turning left at an English sign marking '5km to Uplistsikhe'. After a bridge across the railway the bus heads to the right through the village of Kvakhvreli (where local *electrotreny* call at the station) and follows the river for 1.5km; get off where the bus turns right (away from the river), carry on by the river and head left over the bridge after five minutes. Coming by train from Tbilisi (the Borjomski platforms west of the Voksal), it takes about 1 hour 45 minutes to Kvakhvreli; turn right off the platform and go about 1km down the road to the river, turn right and follow the bus route to the bridge; to return it's best to wait at the station and take a bus to Gori if one turns up before a train. There are usually no taxis waiting at the site. It takes another ten minutes to walk back westwards to where the road ends at the gate to the ruins (9.5ha in area). It runs below cliffs of weathered yellow sandstone which act as a heat trap, with bushes in bloom and bees and butterflies even in winter, as well as rare lizards and two species of hamster. The best time to visit is late afternoon or early evening, when the setting sun brings a special warmth to the rocks.

ATENI SIONI From the road junction at the west end of Khidistavi, an asphalt road, also served by regular local buses from Gori, leads south to Ateni, following the left/west bank of the Tana stream. The village of Patara (or Little) Ateni stretches from km2.5, with metal frames training Atenuri vines out over the road from almost every house. At km6.5 the tiny Ateni church hides to the left of the road; built of green tuff in the 7th century, with a dome added in the 9th or 10th century, it's just 5m by 6m in area and very sparsely decorated.

It's another 1.5km to the church of Ateni Sioni: this is one of the loveliest churches in Georgia, due above all to its setting at a bend of the narrow Tana Gorge, which is especially stunning in winter. Terraced fields by the river give a central Asian feel, while just to the south there's a great view down the valley to Mount Kazbeg. The writer Fitzroy Maclean said of it that it made:

> as great an impression on me as any [church] in Georgia; … architecturally Ateni
> Sioni impresses by its simplicity, but what struck me most of all was its magnificent
> position and the feeling it gave me of age, serenity and strength.

It was built by a certain Todos in the first half of the 7th century in the new style initiated at Jvari (Mtskheta) at the end of the 6th century; its decoration is finer than at Jvari, and it's in a better state of preservation. The lower parts are in red sandstone, with yellow-green tuff above. The ground plan is a tetraconch cross, its arms ending internally in four half circles, with corner rooms rather than aisles and transepts. The spacious interior effectively has eight columns, supporting four squinches and a relatively low dome. There's just a low minimalist iconostasis. The frescoes are famous, with the image of Gabriel, painted in 1080, a highpoint in Georgian art. Externally, the façade is a copy of Jvari in local stone, restored in the 16th century; note also the two stags (pagan symbols) in the tympanum of the north door.

In fact it's well worth taking a bus all the way to the end of the road, in the heart of the rugged Trialeti range, and then back to Ateni Sioni; then you can walk down to Sioni church and the village to catch a bus back down the valley. Taxis charge about US$10 return from Gori, including waiting time.

SOUTH OSSETIA Gori is also the base for visits to **Tskhinvali**, capital of Samachablo or South Ossetia. There are now no bans on travel there, with buses and marshrutkas from Gori and from Tbilisi, and trains from Gori to the station of Nikozi, in the southwestern suburbs of Tskhinvali, 3km from the centre. Driving from Tbilisi, the junction is at km84.5, on the highway to the north of Gori. However, there's little to see in the city, which is a drab place of typically communist concrete blocks. There are plenty of bullet holes in buildings, and in the main cemetery it's interesting to see the portraits of the civil war dead, looking like lithographs on their gravestones. In the Georgian village of Nikozi there's a 5th-century cruciform church, rebuilt in the 14th century, and the ruins of a royal palace built in the 9th and 10th centuries. The former Intourist Hotel, unimproved, is the only accommodation, at US$3 per head. However, there's fine walking in the hills to the north, which have largely escaped the erosion of the Kazbegi area. Roads continue northwards to Oni in Racha, and towards the Roka tunnel into North Ossetia, although both are closed to foreigners. The villages immediately north of Tskhinvali are Georgian-populated and ignore Ossetian rule; Java, the first major village on the Roka road, is Ossetian and was the epicentre of an earthquake in 1991.

WEST OF GORI

Continuing westwards from Gori, within a few kilometres of rejoining the main road, you'll pass another village church that is well worth a brief halt. The bus stop is at the western end of **Urbnisi**, at km94.2, from where you can follow an asphalt road south through the village until you see the church to your left. Passing through a stone gateway topped by an octagonal brick belltower, you'll enter a churchyard in which a surprising number of large wine jars are lying around. The church is a relatively long three-nave basilica, built in the 6th century; the lower part is of stone, with the upper part of thin Roman-style bricks, supported by two brick arch-buttresses on either side, an unusual sight in Georgia. There are also a few inscribed stones on the exterior and a high relief cross on the east end. Just to the west, at km96 (just west of a café in an old railway carriage), a sign shows the turning to **Ruisi church**, a typically Georgian cross-and-cupola church built in the 7th to 9th centuries.

SOUTH OF KARELI There's a group of interesting and attractive churches south of the Mtkvari between Gori and Khashuri, at Samtsevrisi, Tsromi and Kintsvisi; note that the ITM/ERKA map currently shows these in the wrong places. At km101.5 (km450.5 from the west) a bus shelter stands at the junction south to Kareli, a small town on the railway on the south side of the Mtkvari. Minibuses shuttle the 2km to the bridge and level crossing just beyond, and then left to the rail and bus stations. Buses run hourly to Gori until 16.00, six times a day to Khashuri (the last at 14.40), and to Tbilisi at 08.00 daily. Buses run at 12.00, 15.00 and 18.00 to Zguderi, to the south beyond Kintsvisi.

From the T-junction 100m south of the level crossing this road heads right/southwest to the modern town centre and left at a roundabout. At km2 a minor road leads right for 2km to **Samtsevrisi**, at the far end of which two old churches (visible from the Tbilisi–Kutaisi highway and railway to the north) stand on hillocks on either side of the road. The first, in a cemetery to the left/south, is a tiny dome church built in the first half of the 7th century, with a small bit of 16th-century stonework to the southwest; it's a 'free-cross' church, with a horseshoe apse in a cross plan, and is simply a perfect example of its type. The other, about 1.5km from the junction, is a small simple basilica beside the well-preserved ruins of a 16th-century castle, with a circular underground chamber which could have been a dungeon or water cistern. The road continues for another 8km to Akalsopeli (reached by a couple of buses a day), and perhaps 5km more to **Tsromi**. The Church of the Redeemer here, built in AD626–634, is the oldest of its kind in Georgia, with four free-standing columns to support the cupola; its roof has mostly been ruined by earthquakes, but it's important as the model for many churches in Georgia and far beyond. It can also apparently be reached from Gomi, at about km118 on the main road from Gori to Khashuri and Kutaisi.

Continuing south from the junction at km2, you'll see a couple of very odd towers on the hillside to the east, and after 6km more enter the village of **Kintsvisi**, where a sign by a bridge marks a road to the left leading to the Kintsvisi monastery in 3.5km. With the help of a few short cuts, it takes about 40 minutes to walk up, climbing from fields to oak and beech forest to the lower edge of the conifer belt. The monastery has reopened, with lots of restoration work under way, and you'll first pass the priest's modern house before curving right up to the church at the end of the road.

Built in 1207–13, of brick despite standing on limestone hills, the church has a single-bay nave and aisles, with a large porch to the west and others to the north and south. The three apses at the east end are the same length, the central one being distinguished only by being slightly wider and by its solid stone iconostasis. The church's frescoes are absolutely magnificent, if damaged by mould (now being treated), in particular the 13th-century Resurrection (a copy of which you can see in Tbilisi's Art Museum), and a Virgin and Child in the apse, as well as portraits of royalty and the 14th-century encyclopaedist Zasa Panaskerteli-Tsitsishvili; the painting of the cross inside the dome is typically Georgian. There's also a small stone chapel to the west of the main church, and the eastern half of a former church poised on the edge of the hill to the west, with a fantastic Virgin and Child, in Sutherland-esque swirling robes, rather exposed to the elements but still in good condition.

It's a long way on a very rough road, but theoretically it would be possible to continue south through the village to Zguderi and on to the churches of Tkemlovani and Timotesubani (see page 165); perhaps a route best suited to the hardier type of mountain bikers.

KHASHURI AND SURAMI Continuing westwards, the main road passes through an unattractive district of light industry (although there is the attractive modern Silk Road Hotel in Agara at km108/444), and then, from km118, a stretch of road with several Turkish truck stops, confusingly marked on signs as 'Camping' (or Tir-Park), as well as *Lokantasi* (Restaurant). There's also a Turkish 'Tir Hotel' at the east end of **Khashuri** (km126), just beyond a car-part market and a new EKO petrol station, offering the possibility of spending the night in the company of the Turkish truck drivers who thunder up and down this road.

Khashuri (pronounced 'Hashuri') boasts glass and textile factories, but its chief significance is as the junction of both road and rail routes to Kutaisi and southwest to Akhaltsikhe and the Turkish border. The road passes to the south of the centre, and at km129/423 (45km from Gori, 113km from Tbilisi, 32km from Borjomi) reaches the road junction (at a roundabout with a big cross), where the bus station is located, as well as a 24-hour fuel station and ATM. Fast trains take just under two hours from Tbilisi (GEL3.80); the station has been nicely renovated, and there's an ATM opposite. Marshrutka 1 runs from the railway station to the roundabout, about ten minutes' walk west. Marshrutkas to Kutaisi and Batumi wait just west of the roundabout, and those to Borjomi wait about 100m down the road to Borjomi and Akhaltsikhe. The town has no other services or features of interest.

The main road to Kutaisi and the west soon climbs to the **Rikoti Pass** and into Imereti; but first it passes through the climatic resort of **Surami**, which is a far better bet than Khashuri for food, drink and accommodation. The poet Terenti Graneli was detained in the TB/mental hospital here in 1930–34. First, as the main road climbs up on to the hillside to the north of the town, it passes a dramatic small castle, which served as residence of the Dukes of Kartli in early medieval times, to the south of the road at km133. This can be easily reached by a lane past a small brick church, built in the 18th and 19th centuries, with barrel domes – not the more recent church just west of the road on a rock in the pine forest. The film *The Surami Fortress*, by the Tbilisi-born Armenian director Sergei Paradjanov, tells the legend of a young man built into the castle's walls to preserve them. There are scores of wicker stalls baking and selling excellent bread by the roadside (and after the tunnel there are lots of beehives and stalls selling honey to go with the bread); you can also ask here for a room. In addition the Hotel Surami (*Mshvidobis 12; 32269*) claims to have non-stop light and hot water, and charges around US$30 per person per night.

After being reunited with the road through the town to the left, the road soon reaches the Rikoti Pass where, at km141 there's a choice of a tunnel, about 2.5km long (with a toll of GEL1 for cars eastbound only), or the old road over the 997m pass, 4km of tight, hairpin bends. Trains use a far longer tunnel to the south, leading to Kutaisi via Manglisi and Kharagauli, and there's also a back road from the town of Surami over the Surami Pass (949m) and on beside the railway, which is recommended only for those with mountain bikes.

5

The Georgian Military Highway

The Georgian Military Highway has existed as a route since before the 1st century BC, but had only evolved into a bridle track by the time the Russians finally converted it, by the Herculean efforts of 800 soldiers, into a carriage road in 1783. In 1829 Pushkin followed this route, as did many other great Russian writers, such as Lermontov, Gorky, Tolstoy and Mayakovsky, all inspired in various ways by the experience. In 1846 Shamyl attempted to close the highway in his rebellion against Russia, and it was his failure which persuaded the other tribes of the northern Caucasus not to join him, though his rebellion continued until 1864. The route finally lost much of its importance with the opening of the railway via the Caspian coast in 1883. Almost a century later, in 1981, the 2.5-mile-long Roka Tunnel opened between South and North Ossetia, although given the instability of these regions it has not become a major through route.

The Georgian Military Highway still serves as a link to the province of Khevi (The Valley), around Kazbegi, which lies on the northern slope of the Caucasus, and offers the easiest access from Tbilisi to the high mountains. Unfortunately the hillsides are heavily eroded in this area, due largely to over grazing but also to tourism, and the road is in an appalling state for much of its length. It suffers greatly from snow and ice and the pass is frequently closed in winter.

NORTH OF MTSKHETA

The highway starts with a flyover junction just before km28 on the highway from Tbilisi to Kutaisi, immediately to the northwest of Mtskheta. From here it's 58km to Pasanauri, 124km to Kazbegi, and 168km (just over 100 miles) to Vladikavkaz in Russia.

The highway runs along the right/west bank of the Aragvi, in a wide valley between sandy foothills; just before km3 a side road turns west to Tsilkani, where there's a church built as a basilica in the 5th and 6th centuries and remodelled as a dome church in medieval times. Originally founded by one of the Syrian Fathers in the 4th century, this was one of the first churches in Georgia, and was famous for its icon of the Virgin painted by St Luke on a board from Christ's cradle. This road continues to the Mukhrani Valley, where *champanska* is produced on what was the Bagration family estate.

At km15.5/123.5 another road leads 6km west to Lake Bazaleti, formed according to legend by the tears of the Georgians at the death of Tamar's child; it's too full of weeds for swimming, but fishing is popular. The Hotel Bazaleti (✆ *032 934173, 936412*) has three double rooms at US$30 each and is planning to build four-star 'cottages'. To the north of the lake is Bodorna Monastery, where the medieval dome church of St Mary (rebuilt in the 18th century) has a row of hooks outside for hanging sacrificed sheep, and caves in oddly-shaped yellow cliffs were used as refuges from the Tatars. Further north (10km from the lake) is Dusheti,

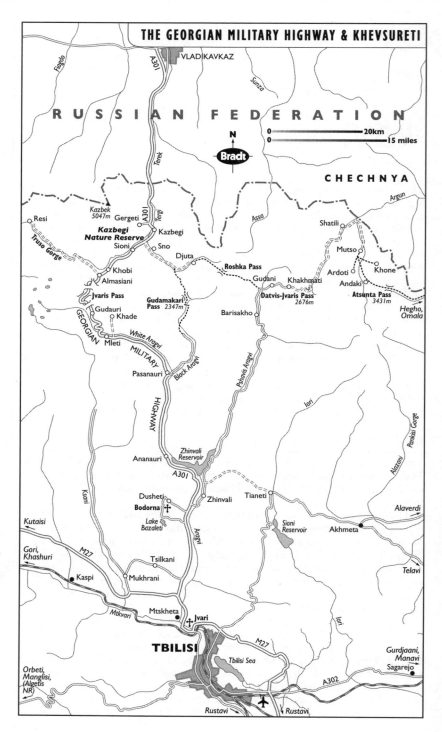

which was the capital of the Aragvi princes in the 17th century and received a municipal charter late in the 18th century; now it's just a small village with some Art Nouveau buildings. From here it's 5km back to the Georgian Military Highway, at km19.

At km26 a minor road turns right to follow the Pshavis Aragvi valley to Khevsureti (see page 154); the Georgian Military Highway rises above the right bank to pass the Zhinvali Dam at km28; this has flooded the area of the confluence of the Aragvi and the Pshavis Aragvi, where the forested mountainsides begin to press in on either side. Companies from Tbilisi are now organising rafting trips on the Pshavis Aragvi.

ANANAURI The highway climbs along the hillside, then drops from km35 to cross a modern viaduct and reach the amazing churches of Ananauri just before km37 (ie: after km102 from the north). These stand within a crenellated wall at the head of the reservoir; the village, which stood below, has largely been destroyed and relocated to the north and, amazingly, it was seriously proposed to build the dam higher and flood the churches too. However, the kind of popular protest movement that was almost unheard of in Soviet times managed to defeat this plan.

The entrance on the south side of the wall leads you to the **lower church**, the larger and more recent of the two crammed together here. Dedicated to the Assumption of the Mother of God, it was built in 1689 and is big and bare inside, with two pillars supporting the barrel dome, and frescoes of saints and the *Last Judgement* on the south wall. The interior was damaged by fire in the 18th century, and many fine frescoes were lost. However, its carved external decorations are superb, above all on the south wall where a huge cross stands on the backs of two dragons, flanked by two vines (being eaten by deer) above two odd moustachioed angels and two lions; there's another angel up at the top left corner. The pagan elements in the design clearly show Persian influence. There are also stones with carved rams' heads, an older pagan motif, now piled up inside the gateway.

Immediately above this church is a 12th-century **watchtower**; the wall of the church pressed up against this carries wonderful carvings, presumably for the eye of God alone. Above that is the smaller **Hvtaeba church**, built in the early 17th century. Although externally of stone, the interior is of brick and it too is bare, with the remaining frescoes largely ruined by graffiti, mainly Russian. It has a two-bay nave and aisles, with a barrel dome above the crossing, lit by deep-set lancet windows. At the top of the slope, set into the ring wall, is a solid **tower** known as 'The Intrepid'; this has five chambers, one above the other, all made safe with concrete and connected by wooden ladders. It's well worth climbing to the top for views of the church domes and the surrounding hills, and you can also walk most of the way around the battlements. At the lower end of the complex is a small 17th-century **bell-turret**, nowadays looking out over the lake as well as a ruined Armenian church. Down some steps by the bell-turret is a hiding place where soldiers could lurk before rushing out to attack intruders.

Ananauri was in the wars many times, most famously in 1717 when Prince Bardsig, the Eristav of Aragvi, seized the wife of Prince Chanche, Eristav of Ksani; Chanche allied himself with the Lesghians of the northern Caucasus, and captured Ananauri; he reclaimed his wife successfully, but the Muslim Lesghians burnt the churches and destroyed many of the frescoes.

PASANAURI The road continues between thickly wooded hillsides that Fitzroy Maclean found rather reminiscent of Perthshire. Small villages offer the occasional café, while footbridges give access to walks on the eastern side of the valley. At km53 you'll see the first of the remaining watchtowers, which once stood at every curve in the valley, providing a relay chain of signal stations for times of danger. The only town between Mtskheta and Kazbegi is Pasanauri, which consists of just two streets, Rustaveli (northbound) and Kostava (southbound) between km59 and km60.

This is a climatic resort at 1,014m, where the White (Tetri) Aragvi, the main river, is joined by the Black (Shavi) Aragvi from the northeast; the water of the Black Aragvi is often noticeably darker, with the two flowing side by side before merging. There's little to do here other than rest and walk to the **Chabarukh Gorge** (where there's a waterfall) and the **Gudamakari Gorge**, and to the **Church of St George of Lomisi**, at 3,000m on a ridge to the west; this is the centre of a pagan cult, where boys are taken at the age of 11 or 12 for initiation, a ceremony apparently described by the anthropologist Margaret Mead. There's accommodation at the old Hotel Intourist (*Kostava 60;* ☎ *032 444*), next to a restaurant in a solid stone building with an attractively carved wooden balcony.

GUDAURI Continuing northwards in the Mtiuleti district, the valley is still relatively wide, with a good new single carriageway alongside the old highway as far as Gudauri. Near km66 you'll see a watchtower high to the left; at km73 you'll see one to the right and another pair ahead, and near km74 there's a tower to the left and a chapel and then a tower to the right. The road passes through the village of Nagvarevi at km75–76 (followed by stalls selling comical sheepskin hats), then at km79 reaches the village of Mleti, at 1,410m. At about km80.5 there's another tower to the west, and after Zemo (Upper) Mleti (1,556m), where there's a spring and roadside stalls selling drinks, woolly socks and sheepskin hats, the road climbs 640m up the Mleti cliff, with the help of six hairpin bends. As you climb, the High Caucasus finally comes into sight, first the Red Mountains, and then the Seven Brothers, both massive ranges of red volcanic rock. Near the top (just after a roadside shrine at a hairpin) is a viewing platform with metal rails giving great views as you lean out over the abyss.

At the top is Gudauri, a scattered Ossetian village which is, at 2,196m, the highest settlement on the Georgian Military Highway, and Georgia's main ski resort.

Where to stay

Cross Pass Hotel (12 rooms, 3 suites) ☎ 032 943446; m 899 510904; e hotel@crosspass.ge. Up the hill at the entrance to Gudauri village (150m from the chair lift), this hotel has rooms with satellite TV & AC, as well as 3 suites & a cottage, a sauna, jacuzzi, & 2 restaurants; horses & mountain bikes are on offer in summer. *Winter rates sgl US$45–91, dbl US$84–124.*

Daisy Guest House (4 rooms) m 899 507606. Behind the Coca-Cola sign at the road junction, this guesthouse has 2 twins & 2 4-bed rooms. *US$35 pp FB.*

Hotel '7' (12 rooms) m 899 962894; www.gudauriresort.com. All rooms en suite with satellite TV. Internet, billiards, sauna & a shuttle to the lift. *Sgl/dbl US$100 in winter; US$45/50 in summer.*

Hotel Gudauri Alpine Hut m 899 272291, 899 398123; www.gudaurihut.com. *Dbl rooms US$35 en*

suite, US$25 sharing facilities in winter, US$25/20 in summer), plus dinner (US$5) & sauna (US$15).

Hotel Ozone (20 rooms) ☎ 543496/7; e ttugishi@caucasus.net; www.ozon.ge. Sauna. *En-suite rooms US$30-45 pp inc 2 meals, parking & free shuttle to the lift.*

Hotel Panorama (10 rooms) m 899 330003, 899 900075; e info@skihouse-panorama.com; www.skihouse-panorama.com. Run by a paraglider pilot, this hotel is 500m from the chair lift; all rooms have satellite TV. It also has a minibus, a small pool & sauna. *Rooms from US$100 FB.*

Hotel Shamo (10 rooms) m 899 500142, 899 192924; www.allgudauri.ge *Sgl/dbl US$60/85 HB.*

Hotel Shino (10 rooms) m 899 565913. At km92, just before the police post (with an English sign), an asphalt road turns right, leading in a couple of hundred metres to this biggish chalet-style building with a cosy lounge & en-suite twin rooms.

US$30 per room, plus meals at about US$5 each.

🏠 **Sno-Inn I & 2** 📱 899 575387, 557309. Immediately across the car park from the SportHotel, this inn is very friendly & considerably cheaper; it consists of 2 cottages each with its own dining room & fireplace. *US$25 pp FB*.

🏠 **SportHotel Club Gudauri** (78 rooms, 44 suites) 📞 32 202900; 📱 899 559222, 899 579222; 📠 32 202901; 📧 hotel@gudauri.ge; www.gudauri.ge. The hotel entrance is at about km89 (2hrs from Didube); 1,990m, by a Coca-Cola billboard. The only Western-style ski hotel/resort in the country, this 4-star establishment was built by an Austrian entrepreneur in 1988. It struggled to survive in the absence of direct flights from western Europe to Tbilisi but it may now have a brighter future. It offers all the comforts required of a hotel of this class, including an indoor swimming-pool & tennis courts, gym, sauna & jacuzzi; although primarily established for skiing (with the lifts starting immediately behind the hotel), it's also an ideal base for walking in summer. You can also book through Alpin Travel (PO Box 14, CH-8880 Walenstadt, Switzerland; 📞 +41 81 720 2121; 📠 +41 81 720 2120; 📧 at@alpintravel.ch; www.alpintravel.ch), who operate heli-skiing packages. Summer rates sgl US$80, twin US$130, dbl suite US$175, with FB & use of all facilities; winter rates are about 40% higher.

🏠 **Hotel Truso** (14 rooms) 📱 899 507606, 899 250044; 📧 hoteltruso@gmail.com. 100m from the lifts. FB, satellite TV & sauna. *Sgl/dbl US$80/120*.

Hostels Opposite the Hotel Shino (see above) is a very cheap ski hut where beds cost about US$8 each – ask for **Nikola**. From here you can hike onwards and follow the chairlifts up to reach the **Khade Hut** (📱 899 500105), at 2,650m by two radio masts, in about 40 minutes; also known as Kosta's Chalet, this is busy with skiers in the daytime and quiet and cosy in the evenings. There's communal accommodation here at US$50 with three meals, and you're guaranteed to be the first on the slopes in the morning.

What to do The Sukhia ski race, effectively the Georgian championship, is held here in odd years (in even years it's in Bakuriani). Good Doppelmayr chairlifts run northeast from the SportHotel to the Khade Hut (2,650m) and on to the col at 2,860m between the stony Mount Kudebi (3,006m) and Mount Sadzele (3,307m), from where skiers have a vertical drop of almost 1km. There are 19km of pistes, the longest 5km, with plenty of snow at least until the end of April. It's not much further north to Mount Sadzele, and heli-skiing is available from 4,200m. It's possible, on foot or horseback, to go in about three hours from the Khade Hut to the Khade Gorge (1,600m), which still has more than 50 defensive towers in seven villages; a 12km dirt road leads down to Kvesheti on the highway below the Mleti cliff.

INTO THE TERGI VALLEY From Gudauri the road (in awful condition) dips briefly down and passes through an avalanche gallery into the Devil's Valley, which as the poet Lermontov explains is really a mistranslation of Frontier Valley; above to the right is the original Russian road, which makes a pleasant short hike. To the left of the road a large viewing platform (and a small one without rails, to be avoided) looks over the 'Stone Chaos' of the Gudaur Abyss and the 'zebra-striped' summit of Gud-Gura. If the view is too much for you, there's a 70m-long Soviet mural on the inside of the platform, created in 1983 to celebrate the 200th anniversary of the Treaty of Gurgievsk; some of the colour has gone but the outlines are clear.

From here it's not far up to the **Jvaris Ughelt** or Cross Pass, better known in Russian as the Krestovy Pereval (2,379m, 127km from Tbilisi); open only from May to November, it's the highest point of the route and there are many fine descriptions, notably by Lermontov and Dumas, of the struggle to cross the pass in foul weather. To the east of the present road stands the cross erected by Yermolov in 1824, replacing the so-called Tamar's Cross, in fact erected by King David the Builder; this stands on the old road, rather higher than the present one, and is visible from the Devil's Valley at the top of a steep rise.

Descending the Bidara Valley into the watershed of the Tergi (Terek in Russian) River, you'll pass five avalanche galleries, which traffic uses only in winter. The fact that the road surface is in just as appalling a state inside the galleries as outside indicates a long history of neglect. The alpine meadows are interrupted by rocks stained red by the sweet mineral waters that are common here; the bearded vultures seem to dye their 'beards' red by drinking the iron-rich water.

Almasiani (1,960m), the first part of the village of **Khobi,** lies to the left of the road at a police barrier, by some caravan-cafés. This is the start of a superb hike (signed in English at the junction) to the west up the **Truso Gorge** (nicely described by Tony Anderson as 'a geological fantasy on the duel between water and rock'), which follows a dirt track alongside the Tergi through the villages of Nogkau, Shevardeni, Okrokana (Ukrakani in Ossetian), Ketrisi, Abano and Resi. You may get a ride for the first couple of kilometres, after which only 4x4 vehicles can continue through the gorge and into the lovely wide upper valley. This is wonderfully spectacular scenery, with the steep slopes of this glacial valley on the southwestern flank of Mount Kazbek rising high above the defensive towers of the villages; there are many more mineral springs at the foot of the cliffs to the south side, especially between Okrokana and Ketrisi, and at Abano (ie: Bath, about 25km up the valley), where there's a mineral lake. There's good camping here, unlike the Sno Valley where you allegedly need to keep a fire alight all night to keep wolves away.

The upper valley is inhabited in summer by Ossetians, and the borders of South and North Ossetia meet at the top of the valley; don't go beyond a Georgian flag. The main road on was almost miraculously smooth in 1998, thanks to a flying visit by Shevardnadze, then fell apart again but was rescued with US$20m from the World Bank; at about km106 it passes the centre of **Khobi** (1,932m), where there are greenhouses as well as a big bus shelter with a goat mosaic. There's a café where you can ask to rent the caravan for GEL5–10 a night.

It's possible to take a good hike up the valley to the east. You'll have your first view of the immense Mount Kazbek ahead (just as on the beer labels), before the road passes through the Baidari Gorge (named after Toti Baidarashvili, an Ossetian mountaineer posted here in the 18th century by King Irakli to rescue travellers from snow). The only villages are away to the west, perched on the cliff on the left bank of the Tergi, crossed by a cableway.

The next village by the road (148km from Tbilisi) is **Sioni**, where you'll see the church and watchtower on a crag overlooking the road more or less opposite the turning to a bridge to the villages across the river; to reach them you need to continue to a junction by a green caravan-café. From here, head right/east for 500m to a T-junction, then follow the road back southwards for 1km, all on asphalt except for the final zigzags up to the church. This is a three-naved basilica built in the late 9th and early 10th centuries; externally it is quite rectangular, although internally there is an apse behind the altar, as well as a five-arched stone iconostasis. The watchtower, beyond an abandoned modern building, is a late medieval construction; at ground level there's no door (a ladder having been used for access), but tasteless Russian graffiti instead.

Beyond Arsha, just to the north, where there's a 9th–10th-century fortress, another dirt track leads east through Atchkhoti, just off the highway, and to the villages of Sno and Djuta, another highly recommended hiking route. **Sno**, where the asphalt ends, is about 4km along the wide glaciated valley, beyond some sculptures of local writers; it's the birthplace of Ilia, the Catholicos of the Georgian Church. There's one watchtower here and not a lot else.

It's about 18km further to the end of the side road at **Djuta**, the highest village in the area at 2,200m and one of the highest in Europe. It is home to 20 Khevsur extended families, mostly named Arabuli due to having traded with 'Arab' caravans, living in solid houses with verandas. Immediately southeast of Djuta is the seven-peaked Mount Chaukhi (3,842m), the north face of which offers 800m-high cliffs for climbers (best in September/October); the base camp is at 2,600m, two hours' hike from Djuta.

From July on it's also possible for trekking groups to reach the village of Roshka (2,050m) in Khevsureti; the path has largely vanished, so a guide is needed, but this route is safe otherwise. In fact it's just a ten-hour hike by the direct route over the Chaukhi or Roshka Pass (3,056m), but it's more interesting to cross the Djuta pass (3,287m) north to the headwaters of the river Assa and Akhieli (just four houses and an abandoned tall tower); it's part of the three-hamlet community of Arkhoti, a beautiful valley that's very isolated, with fairly easy access to Ingushetia to the north but only two hard passes into Georgia to the south. It's a ten-hour hike across the Arkhotis Pass (2,935m) south to Roshka, where there are two huge erratic boulders, the smaller of which measures 19m by 5m by 7m. It's also possible to hike south along a pony track from between Sno and Djuta over the 2,347m Gudamakari Pass to the Black Aragvi Valley and Pasanauri.

STEPANTSMINDA (KAZBEGI)

Another 4.5km brings you to Kazbegi, at 1,797m and 153km from Tbilisi; this is the only town in Khevi province (or Mokhavia) and the only place with anything resembling shops and accommodation. However, with a population of just 4,000 and relatively little through traffic to Russia, commercial opportunities are inevitably limited, though it's worth looking for the local woollens, such as socks and hats.

It's a small, sleepy place, dominated by free-range highland cattle and pigs. Known in the 19th century as Stepan-Tsminda (St Stephen), the town was then named after Alexander Kazbegi (or Qazbegi; 1848–93), a local noble who became a much-loved pastoral poet, living as a shepherd for seven years; it has now reverted to Stepantsminda, but Kazbegi remains the more widely used name.

The square, dominated by a monument to Kazbegi, is lined with kiosks selling the usual mixture of booze and biscuits, as well as a bakery.

GETTING THERE AND AWAY There are one or two buses and half-a-dozen marshrutkas a day from the Didube terminal in Tbilisi to Kazbegi, as well as shared taxis from the same place; bus services back from Kazbegi leave at 10.00 and 13.00. Others run from Tbilisi as far as Pasanauri, and one goes as far as Gudauri, returning at about 16.00. Marshrutkas take around three hours and charge GEL10; shared taxis (which might even stop for you to take a photo) charge GEL15. There are local buses south from Kazbegi as far as Khobi, but none from Kazbegi northwards.

TOUR OPERATORS Trips can be organised through Extra Service, SAK-Tours (a day trip costs GEL140 including car or GEL50 with your own car), STC (two days for US$118–130, three days for US$158–175, or four days to climb Mount Kazbek for US$370), or Caucasus Travel (who offer an eight-day trip to climb Mount Kazbek).

WHERE TO STAY
Hotels

⌂ **Hotel Stepantsminda** (20 rooms) Behind the bakery; m 899 282819, 899 182296, 877 420210. This comfortable new hotel has large Western-quality en-suite rooms, with TV & stunning views. English is spoken (ask for Nata). *GEL30 pp.*

⌂ **Hotel Lomi** (Lion) (5 rooms) At the northern end of the square; m 899 403264. Basic (with shared toilets) but friendly, although no English is spoken. *GEL15 pp, plus GEL15 for HB.*

Homestays Next to the Hotel Lomi (to the right, with a green fence) **Stefan** has an excellent homestay, although only Georgian and Russian are spoken; decent rooms with shared WC and shower cost GEL10 per person.

One of the best homestays is **Vano's place** (↘ *52418*), across the river in Gergeti, about 15 minutes' walk from the square – head north across the bridge on the road to Russia, turn left and after crossing a stream either go diagonally left up a path between two walls and turn left, or keep going and take the road to the left; in either case Vano's place is on the right, opposite a cross, and above No 25. A bed costs GEL10 (only GEL5 if Mum is away) plus GEL5 for large meals, or you can camp in the garden, below a cliff·with fine vertical strata. Vano Sujashvili speaks several languages and is immensely helpful, but don't get him started on UFOs; his mother knows a lot about traditional cures and recipes.

There's also good accommodation (€20 for bed and food) with **Iago Kazalikashvili** (↘ *52401;* m *899 958993*) opposite the Kazalikashvili Museum of Alpinism (see below).

Alternatively, try the derelict shop-block up some steps opposite the Kazbegi monument. Additionally, the women running the kiosks on the square (open virtually until midnight) know which families offer accommodation.

WHAT TO SEE AND DO At the far end of the square the Georgian Military Highway forks left, while the road to the right leads past the church and the **Kazbegi Museum** (*open 10.00–17.00 except Mon*) to the town hall. The church is a very simple basilica with a few nice external carvings and a separate gate-tower. The museum is in Kazbegi's spacious home; downstairs are manuscripts, photos of Kazbegi and his three brothers, and stills from films of his stories, and upstairs is his furniture. Behind the museum is the post office, where it's possible to make international phone calls.

Immediately to the south of the church is Rustaveli kucha, just south of which, one block above the square (at Vazha-Pshavelas 24) is the **Kazalikashvili Museum of Alpinism** (ie: mountaineering), which is small and unpretentious and may be left open and untended, but gives a good insight into the allure of rock and ice.

Continuing south and left at Vazha-Pshavelas 48, it takes ten minutes to climb up to the three-storey glass-fronted building that houses the **WWF EcoCentre**; it should be possible to get information, maps and guides here, but unfortunately it is semi-permanently shut. A new information centre should open in 2007 in the old restaurant facing the monument on the main square. To the east of town it's a pleasant short walk up to the shrine of Elia, with views towards Kazbek.

THE KAZBEGI NATURE RESERVE The Kazbegi Nature Reserve was established in 1976, covering an area of 8,707ha. It lies at the divide between the Central and Eastern Caucasian ranges, with average precipitation in Kazbegi Town of 640mm per year and temperatures of –5.2°C in January and 14.4°C in August (an annual average of 4.9°C). At 3,652m (the Gergeti glacier weather station) it's far colder, with temperatures of –15°C in January, 3.4°C in August, and an annual average of –6.1°C.

There are 1,347 plant species in the reserve, of which 105 are trees. Around half the trees are birch, with pine, beech, and large areas of *Rhododendron caucasicum*, with smaller areas of barberry, buckthorn, aspen, willow, maple and juniper. There are many alpine flowers in the hay meadows, with campanulas and gentians above the tree line, and cushion alpines on the scree slopes. Mammals include the Caucasian goat or tur (*Capra caucasica*), chamois (*Rupicapra rupicapra*), hare (*Lepus europaeus*), fox (*Vulpes vulpes*), marten (*Martes martes*), weasel (*Mustela nivalis*), wild cat (*Felis silvestris*), squirrel (*Sciurus sp*), and birch mouse (*Sicista kazbegica*).

Bird species include lots of raptors, such as the bearded vulture or lammergeyer (*Gypaetus barbatus*), Egyptian vulture (*Neophron percnopterus*), Eurasian black vulture (*Aegypius monachus*), Eurasian griffon vulture (*Gyps fulvus fulvus*), golden eagle (*Aquila chrysaetus fulva*), imperial eagle (*A. heliaca*), lesser spotted eagle (*A. pomarina*), white-tailed eagle (*Haliaetus albicilla*), pallid harrier (*Circus macrourus*), long-legged buzzard (*Buteo rufinus*), lesser kestrel (*Falco naumanni*), peregrine (*Falco peregrinus*); also the jay (*Garrulus glandarius krynicki*), black francolin (*Francolinus francolinus*), chukar (*Alectoris chukar*), Caucasian snowcock (*Tetraogallus caucasicus*), Caucasian black grouse (*Tetrao mlokosiewicz*), great rosefinch (*Carpodacus rubicilla*), white-winged redstart (*Phoenicurus erythrogaster*), and red-fronted serin (*Serinus pusillus*).

The meadows are presently overgrazed and increasingly suffering from erosion; from Kazbegi southwards sheep flocks migrate along the verges of the Georgian Military Highway in spring and autumn as they move between their home villages and the high meadows, and the damage done can easily be seen. On the other hand, the provision of natural gas has reduced the damage done to forests by the cutting of fuel wood. The WWF (Worldwide Fund for Nature) is involved with projects here, including an ecotourism scheme. GCCW (the Georgian Centre for the Conservation of Wildlife) is also active, bringing groups of birders almost daily in May and June, and the economic impact has largely ended the poaching of Caucasian snowcock; June and July are also a good time to visit, with the rhododendron in bloom.

THE GERGETI HIKE The WWF presence in Kazbegi is still minimal, and is in any case confined to the high summer. In addition to the family accommodation scheme, they've produced a map of hiking routes up the Truso Valley and to the Gergeti and Devdoraki glaciers. The Gergeti route is an extension of the hike up to the Gergeti Trinity church, which sits high on a ridge west of the town of Kazbegi, silhouetted against the massive bulk of Mount Kazbek. This was reached by a cable car built in 1988 and very soon abandoned; no-one here ever wanted it, seeing it as an imposition from outside and an assault on the religious identity of the Gergeti church. The lower terminal behind the Kazbegi church is now derelict, while the upper one beside the Gergeti church has already virtually vanished.

The route starts by taking the Georgian Military Highway from the square in Kazbegi and across the Tergi and turning left up the road to the attractive mountain village of Gergeti. Following the asphalt up the left/south side of the village, heading straight for the Trinity church, you'll come to a point where a ruined defensive tower can be seen in a small side valley to the left; although it is possible to go up here to the rear/west of the Trinity church, it's far easier to turn right here (by a kiosk and a green gate to the left) to cross on the level through the village and then swing up to the left where a WWF sign is stencilled on a stone. From here a track leads up to the village cemetery, about 30 minutes from Kazbegi; *en route* you should ask for Genri Chiklauri's house, to ask for the key to the church; he or his wife may well come with you, in which case you should give them GEL3–5.

Above the cemetery (where there's an ancient chapel) the track crosses a jeep track and climbs past crooked birch (*Betula litwinowii*) trees then pines, with Caucasian chiffchaffs and green warblers, reaching the jeep track again in 20 minutes. From here the most direct route is to head left for five minutes and then take a steep path up through the forest for five more minutes (a minimum of an hour from Kazbegi); this emerges from scrubby birch and on to the ridge, where you'll see the church to the left, less than ten minutes away across the alpine grassland.

An easier route is to head to the right on the gravel track, which loops up to the left to reach the ridge in 15–20 minutes (with short-cuts possible).

The churchyard is entered through a gate-tower (with a chimney shaft) which opens directly onto a blind porch on the south side of the church; the main door is to the west. The Church of Tsminda Sameba or Holy Trinity was built in the 14th century, with the tower added a century later; it's a remarkably large construction for such an isolated location, at 2,170m. In fact the ruins of another church were found in 1913 at 3,962m on the slopes of Mount Kazbek. Paganism is alive and well in these remote areas, with crosses made of rams' horns; when I was first here a freshly decapitated sheep's head sat on the parapet of the churchyard; now monks are living here, and there are even reports of solar panels. The church's festival is held on 28 August, when sheep are sacrificed (attracting vultures for the next day or two).

It's a popular hike throughout the summer, and although there has been a report of a tourist being raped, it's usually busy enough to be safe.

Coming out of the church and turning left at a pile of stones, follow the gravel track which climbs to the ridge, turns sharply to the right, and continues westwards just above the tree line (with a steep drop to the north but pastures and alpine flowers to the south), to reach the Gergeti Glacier at about 2,950m, three hours (10.5km) from the village of Gergeti. Near the snout of the glacier it's easy to see Caucasian snowcock, wallcreepers, snowfinch, twite, Guldenstadt's redstart and great rosefinch, as well as lammergeyer soaring overhead. It's a straightforward hike as far as the glacier, which is about 7.3km long (and retreating fast), but only those experienced on ice, or with competent guides, should continue up the right/south side of the glacier and then across it to reach the former meteorological station, which was the highest in the Soviet Union at 3,675m. Now it's a climbers' hut, run since 1998 by Caucasus Travel, who have replaced the roof, and is known as Mtis Qokhi Betlemi or the Betlemi Hut; rooms cost up to US$20, although it's possible to sleep on a mattress on the floor for US$5; camping is also possible but it can be very windy. There's heat and light but no food available.

Nearby, at 4,100m, is the Betlemi (Bethlehem) Cave, the setting of Ilia Chavchavadze's poem *The Hermit*, where a new metal chapel has been deposited by helicopter. It's possible to climb from the hut to the summit and back in an eight-to 12-hour day, starting at 04.00.

Mount Kazbek, more properly known in Georgian as Mkinvartsveri ('Ice-Top'), is a long-extinct volcano 5,047m in altitude, and is by far the highest peak in this section of the Caucasus. It's laden with mythology, firstly of Amirani, the Georgian Prometheus, who was chained to the mountain as a punishment for his pride and whose shape can be made out in the rock from far away, and secondly of the tent of Abraham which was said to stand on the summit, protecting the Holy Manger, or the Tree of Life – or treasure. There are also legends of lost treasure connected with the Betlemi Cave.

Kazbek was first climbed in 1868 by Douglas Freshfield with colleagues from the Alpine Club of London and guides from Kazbegi; it's a UIAA grade II climb (PD, with just 100m of ice climbing in the final couloir) and is best tackled in September or October; the classic route on the icy south face is UIAA grade III+. Kazbek is far easier than peaks such as Uzhba in Svaneti; climbing it takes four days as a rule – one day to the hut, one day training and acclimatising, one day to the summit and back to the hut, and a day to return to town. It's a 1,855m climb from the town of Kazbegi to the Betlemi Hut – a good day's work if carrying food and climbing gear – and 1,381m more to the summit. It's also possible to turn left at the top of the glacier to climb Ortsveri (4,258m), another UIAA grade II peak, which makes a useful warm-up. A guide will cost about US$250, or about US$800 for four clients; if you need climbing gear, rent it in Tbilisi as there's none available here.

THE ARSHA HIKE This is actually a very pleasant and easy stroll up the west side of the Tergi Valley from Kazbegi, ending by crossing to the Georgian Military Highway. An obvious path starts from the road bridge at the north end of Kazbegi; it's also possible to start from Vano's homestay, simply turning right and following the track southwards, to reach the flood plain after five minutes. From here a gravel path leads in ten minutes to an obvious wellhead surrounded by boggy patches and pools full of frogs and tadpoles; it's another five minutes to a new pool (about 15m by 30m), full of fresh-tasting mineral water, by an unfinished concrete building. It's a good place to relax and watch the vultures soaring above.

Continuing, you'll join a gravel track below a ruined chapel and a defensive tower, passing a few houses, and reaching a junction after 20 minutes; turning left you'll cross a metal bridge to reach the highway roughly 4km south of Kazbegi and a few hundred metres north of the junction to Sno. Carrying on along the west side of the valley, you'll pass one-and-a-half towers (and the starts of some good paths up into the mountains), go through a hamlet, and then briefly go up to the right above a marsh, before following a gravel road straight to a bridge, 25 minutes from the junction. To the west there's a view directly up a valley with good waterfalls, which would be easy and fun to explore. Crossing the bridge, you'll reach the highway in a couple of minutes, opposite a pharmacy north of the centre of Arsha, a few kilometres north of Sioni.

NORTH OF KAZBEGI

The Georgian Military Highway continues north from Kazbegi on the left/west bank of the Tergi, passing through Tsdo (1,767m) and then Gveleti (1,850m), where griffon vultures nest on the cliff; just southwest of Gveleti you'll see a fine waterfall. The road crosses to the right bank here, but immediately before the bridge a track turns left to continue along the left bank, then follows the Amali Valley as a good hiking trail through subalpine birch forest to reach the Devdoraki Glacier. This is the lowest of all those in the Caucasus, its tongue reaching an altitude of just 2,300m; the trail is 9km each way, taking a minimum of four hours return.

Beyond the Zemo Larsi border checkpoint the highway enters the Daryal Gorge, its wildest section, where the road runs for a 12km on a narrow shelf below granite cliffs up to 1,500m high where lammergeyers nest. The gorge takes its name from Dar-i-Alan or 'Gates of the Alans', named after the forefathers of the Ossetians, who arrived here in the 5th century AD. Before that it was known as the Sarmatian gates or the Iverian gates, the point at which Pompey's advance into Asia was halted. At the southern entrance to the gorge, to the west of the road, are the ruins of the Daryal fortress, popularly known as Queen Tamar's castle, although it's far older than the 12th century. It was restored by the Russians and successfully held by General Gurko against Shamyl's forces in 1846.

Two or three people could take a taxi from Kazbegi most of the way to the border and back for about US$10; a taxi south to Almasiani costs about US$7. It's advisable not to go as far as the Zemo Larsi checkpoint at the entry to the Daryal Gorge, and without Russian papers you can't go on to the old border crossing at Chertov Most (Devil's Bridge), about 20km beyond Kazbegi. The highway ends after 168km at Vladikavkaz ('Rule the Caucasus'), founded in 1783 to be the base for the subjugation of the Caucasus. It was renamed Ordjonikidze after the Georgian revolutionary Sergo Ordjonikidze, Stalin's hatchetman, whose brutality horrified Lenin and who was in the end killed off by Stalin himself. Although there are still traces of the fashionable 19th-century climatic resort and garrison town, it has been surrounded by soulless communist tower blocks and was then knocked about during the first Chechen war.

Khevsureti is one of the most remote and unchanged areas of Georgia, a country where adherence to ancient traditions is of course very highly prized. The Khevsurebi are known for their unique textiles, with beautifully embroidered stars and crosses, probably a simplification of the pagan sun motif. The men are popularly supposed to have worn Crusader-style chain mail until the 1930s, and at the time of the protests after the 9 April 1989 massacre they certainly appeared in Tbilisi wearing 'knee-length, richly patterned tunics with half-metre silver daggers strapped to their waists'.

In the 1920s the population of Khevsureti was about 4,000, but nowadays many actually live in Tbilisi and only about 400 still live full time in the mountains. You may still be able to buy socks made from the wool of their aboriginal strain of sheep, and dyed only with natural products. The Khevsurebi are known for their brevity and straightforwardness, and for their unique poetry; they may actually speak in verse on day-to-day matters.

Their religion is still very pagan; icons are forbidden, and there are no real churches, only tiny sanctuaries for strange sacrificial rituals which may involve the *dekanozi* or priest drinking blood and 'sacred beer'. Beer is brewed to an ancient recipe (utterly unlike the Germanic lager found elsewhere in the region); the Khevsur firewater is *zhipitauri*, like vodka but more lethal. On the altar you're likely to find deer antlers and ram's horns instead of a cross. They are surrounded by spirits or *vohi* such as: Sakhlis Angelosi, guardian of the household; Mparveli Angelosi, guardian of wanderers; Goris Angelosi, guardian of the mountains; and Did Gori, the Father of the Great Mountain, responsible for storms and avalanches. Others are Otchopintre, a version of Pan, and Dali, the Georgian Artemis, while St George is identified as the God of War.

GETTING THERE Despite the Chechen war Khevsureti is far safer than, for instance, Svaneti, as there are plenty of Georgian frontier troops (who will check your papers) and OSCE observers (unarmed foreign military officers) based here. The OSCE's daily helicopter flights will occasionally remove people who manage to hike in from places like Djuta.

Khevsureti is reached by the road up the Pshavis Aragvi Valley from km26 on the Georgian Military Highway, south of the Zhinvali Dam; take the road at right angles which soon heads south down to a bridge, and then turns north through the village of Zhinvali. It turns right up a side valley, crosses the stream and soon swings left to a junction about 3km from the highway. The Khevsureti road heads left here, while another turns right to Tianeti, in Kakheti.

A daily bus from Didube in Tbilisi (at 10.30 or 13.00) runs as far as **Barisakho**, the administrative centre of both Pshava and Khevsureti; it stops at the bottom of the hill, from where you climb up to the village, busy with free-range pigs, dogs with clipped ears and a few bored soldiers. Only about 40 families live here, but it's a good base, giving access to three valleys.

WHERE TO STAY
Homestays

🏠 **Batria Arabuli** m 899 686510. He speaks Russian but not English.

🏠 **Shota Tsiklauri** m 899 399380. Also speaks Russian but not English.

🏠 **Shota Arabali** Just before the museum; m 895 503134. He's an artist & rents roms for up to 5 or 6 people. GEL10–20 pp.

WHAT TO SEE AND DO In Korsha, 2km beyond Barisakho, there's a **museum** in the former church (there's an English sign; GEL1). The museum houses rare Khevsur chain mail, remarkable traditional costumes with patterns unique to each clan (like tartans), fearsome spiky knuckledusters and agricultural implements.

Beyond here there's not even a kiosk and you have to find your own transport. You may wait days for a lift, but it's great country for walking, and there's no shortage of water. You can walk north up the Pshavis Aragvis to the hamlet of Biso and then west, to Roshka, 30–40 minutes from Barisakho on a terrible track; hikers can continue to Djuta (see page 148). There's also a lovely day hike to the Abudelauri lakes, one green, one blue and one white. In Roshka you can stay with Shota Tsiklauri's brother Badri. From Biso, you can go northeast up the Gudantistsqali Valley to Gudani and Khakhmati, the last village in Pshavi; there are defensive towers in both Gudani and Khakhmati.

From here a 4x4 track continues eastwards, climbing 1,000m or so with hairpin bends up to the Datvis-Jvaris (Bear Cross) Pass (2,676m, open only from May/June to October/November), and then swings north into Khevsureti to follow the Argun down the northern slope of the Caucasus through Kistani to a bridge where trucks stop below **Shatili** (1,395m), the main village of Khevsureti. It's an almost unspoilt complex of over 50 defensive towers and ancient houses with wickerwork balconies (some dating from the 6th century, though most are from the 10th–12th centuries) huddled together on a low cliff, facing another of Tamar's castles. They were largely abandoned in the 1950s then partially restored in the 1970s, when Shevardnadze also built a new village around the corner beyond a soccer pitch-cum-helipad; bizarrely, there's a row of villas with big balconies overlooking the Argun River. Now 15 towers have had urgent repairs, and one is to become a museum. The World Bank and UNESCO have a cultural heritage project here, with a new ecotourism hotel in two renovated towers, with a kitchen and real bathroom on the ground floor and a ten-bed room above (*GEL20 per person plus food*); you should book in advance, by calling Mindia Tsiklauri in Tbilisi (m *893 144644*). Mzi Chincharauli (*satellite phone: 882 1621 381001; m 877 729362; e vabula@posta.ge – GEL9 per min*) also provides accommodation, but speaks only Georgian and Russian. It's less than 100km from the Georgian Military Highway (under 50km from Barisakho), but it takes four to five hours to drive this distance.

The road continues north down the Argun Valley from Shatili through a border checkpoint and soon, below the necropolis of Anatori, swings southeast up the Andaki Valley. It's about 8km (with shrines marking excellent mineral springs) up the Andaki to **Mutso** (1,590m), the only other real settlement in Khevsureti, perhaps the finest (though most ruinous) of Khevsur villages. You'll climb up past massively built tombs (about 2m by 2m and 4m long), to a few towers on a narrow ridge, soon to be renovated, with luck.

The valley splits immediately south of Mutso, with Khone in a bowl to the southeast beyond Konischala and two plague huts still containing human bones; it's just 2km further to Chechnya, but the border is (officially) open only to incoming refugees – there's a road just 3km beyond the border, north of Mount Tebulos. Two hours south of Mutso is Ardoti, a few defensive towers with a church above, after which the valley splits again: to the southwest in the Chanchistsqali Valley is Khakhabo. The lower village is still inhabited, while Upper Khakhabo (2,150m) is a tiny cluster of ruined 11th-century towers. From the tiny hamlet of Andaki, to the southeast, hiking groups can make the tough crossing over the 3,431m Atsunta Pass into Tusheti, reaching Parsma in about 12 hours.

The track north from Shatili across the border into Chechnya is of course closed, and even in quieter times you should not attempt to cross the border here. You'll see abandoned helicopters and armoured cars in the area, and maybe some traces of a quixotic 1980s' railway project, and a half-built tunnel, used by Chechen fighters to store arms in the 1990s.

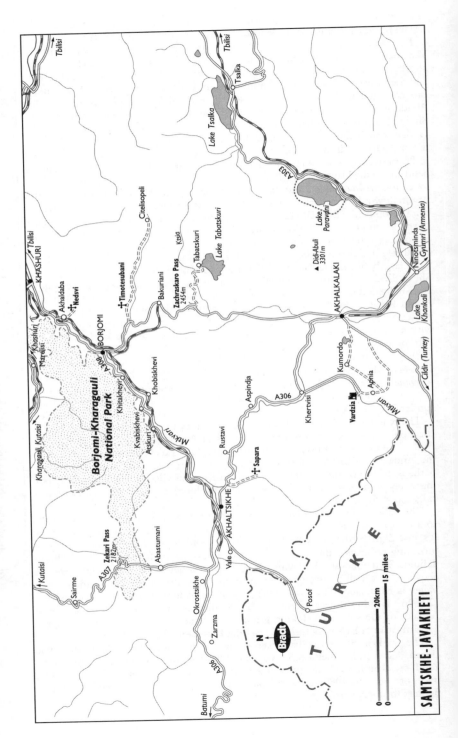

SAMTSKHE-JAVAKHETI

6

Samtskhe-Javakheti

This chapter covers three historic provinces: firstly the tiny and virtually forgotten **Tori**, around the spa of Borjomi; secondly **Samtskhe** or Meskheti, the high volcanic tableland around Akhaltsikhe; and then **Javakheti**, on the border with Armenia. Although part of Georgia's historical heartland, with the cave-city of Vardzia at its centre, the present region of Samtskhe-Javakheti has a population that is 90% Armenian and is in many ways autonomous. In 1624 the Georgian ruler of Samtskhe converted to Islam for political reasons; many Georgians left the area, but many of those who remained also converted. These so-called Meskhetian Turks lived here until their deportation to central Asia in 1944 and have not yet been allowed to return; their villages are now largely populated by people from Racha and Lechkhumi. In 1829 the Russians took control of the area, and Armenians came here from Turkey, taking the land of some Muslims who emigrated to Turkey. Thanks to its bleak climate and poor transport links, it remains a poor and isolated region, although the roads are being greatly improved.

NEDSVI

From the junction with the Tbilisi–Kutaisi highway at the west end of Khashuri, it's 32km southwest to Borjomi, following the Mtkvari into the Borjomi Gorge. Marshrutkas for Borjomi (GEL1.50) wait 100m down the Borjomi road from the roundabout. The road passes through the long thin village of Akhaldaba, from which you can hike into the Nedsvi Sanctuary to the east.

A bridge crosses to the right bank at km12.2, by the Akhaldaba Restaurant and (on the far side) a ruined tower; the road runs across a railway, continues to the right as Rustavelis kucha, and then swings right again to cross a stream and carry on up the valley as Kazbegis kucha. From here it's 3km to a *Turbaza,* something like a Soviet youth hostel but conceived for groups rather than solo travellers; it houses refugees from Abkhazia, but in high summer you should be able to find a bed here or in the Tbilisi State University field station opposite. Before this you should be able to find the path back up the ridge on your right/southwest side, to Tamar's Castle, a small group of dramatically located ruins. It's another kilometre to the end of the road at km4 (measured from the start of Kazbegis); a very muddy forestry track continues up the valley, reaching some fields and houses after an hour's hiking.

Just beyond these the track crosses to the right bank, and after about another 15 minutes you'll reach some summer-only houses at the meeting of two valleys; after crossing a stream you'll find some graves and a ruined church in a grove of trees on your left, as well as a table and shelter. This is all that remains of the monastery of Nedsvi and its three-naved basilica, built in the 9th century by Grigol Kandzdeli; forestry tracks continue up steep-sided conifer-lined valleys which offer very attractive hiking and camping. Nedsvi is within a new 9,000ha enclave of the Borjomi-Kharagauli National Park (see page 160) and wildlife should be recovering.

After km23 the main road up the left/west bank of the Mtkvari enters Borjomi, with the former Hotel Borjomi, now full of refugees from Abkhazia, on the right at km28; it's almost another kilometre to the centre of the town, with shops, market, and a bus station, which has departures more or less hourly to Tbilisi.

A tourist information centre is planned, but for now you'll have to ask at the national park headquarters (see page 161) or at BP's pipeline information centre at Rustaveli 129.

At an altitude of 800m the spa offers both health-giving waters and a bracing mountain atmosphere; in August the average temperature is 20°C, but it freezes from late October until March or later, and in January the average temperature is –2°C.

It's a town of 16,000, with a large plant bottling the water which used to be shipped all over the Soviet Union. In 1995 a French–Dutch joint venture, the Georgian Glass & Mineral Water Company, bought it with the Borjomi brand name, only to find that others had also been given licences to use the name; this was sorted out, but the company then lost US$7m when the Russian economy collapsed in August 1998. It merged with two Ukrainian companies in 2004 and had 8% of the Russian market until it was banned from Russia for political reasons in 2006.

BORJOMI SPA At about km28.5 a bridge crosses to the spa; this road, Kostava, crosses the railway by a small statue of Stalin and passes an attractive park on the left, with the beautifully refurbished Borjomi-Park station and a new church. Naturally there's no train information at the station (there's just a couple of slow trains to Tbilisi, and the overnight train to Vale) but there is a fine new restaurant.

Kostava soon reaches the Borjomka stream, lined by trees and late 19th-century villas; 9 April leads up to the right, ending (after about five minutes) at the gates of the former Ordjonikidze Park, now the **Ekaterina Park** (*admission GEL0.50 in summer*). The last villa (No 48), in the same style as the others but with glittery Arabesque decoration in the ceiling of the balcony, was that of Grand-Duke Mikhail Nikolayevich Romanov, brother of the tsar and Viceroy of the Transcaucasus; he renovated the spa in 1862, built a summer residence in 1871 and then the Likani Palace in 1892–96. The railway opened in 1894 and Chekhov, Tchaikovsky, other members of the tsar's family and Stalin were among those who came to take the waters here.

Inside the park a stately pile on the left now houses a library, and a pavilion houses taps spewing out the famous Borjomi water. Together with Narzan (from the northern Caucasus) this was the former Soviet Union's favourite mineral water, with 300 million bottles a year being filled when times were good. It's flavoured with sodium carbonate, tasting something like Vichy water – slightly warm and salty.

The park was refurbished in 2005, and will soon have a modern pool near the entry, as well as a roof over the springs, and restaurants, bars and a cinema. A bridge crosses the stream to new toilets and a hall with a 3-D panoramic model of Georgia, while the main promenade leads on up the right side of the valley past a café and play area; this gives access to the **Sadgeri Arboretum**, on the plateau immediately above the park, which covers 136ha and is laid out for invigorating walks for the spa patients in pine forests with splendid views. You'll also see the remains of a fortress, and the simple barn-like Church of St George, built in the 15th and 16th centuries. Outside the park gate a stylish little terminal houses a cable car to lift visitors the 100m to the arboretum and a Ferris wheel. Sadgeri can also be reached by a winding road which starts from 9 April and passes the

'Composers' House' where the next Tchaikovsky could seek inspiration on his summer holidays.

From km29, just south of the centre, a modern viaduct carries Gamsakhurdia kucha over the bus station and the river and railway to the spa. If you take the first turn to the right you'll see the army barracks, in a stone castle built in 1870, with crenellations added later.

Where to stay

Borjomis Khoeba (Borjomi Gorge) Rehabilitation Centre (21 rooms) Rustaveli 107A; ℡ 267 23072; m 899 323247, 899 323249; e info@borjomiskheoba.com; www.borjomiskheoba.com. This modern medical centre is probably the best place to stay. It has en-suite rooms available with satellite TV & a restaurant. *Sgl US$38, dbl US$60 (US$70 with a balcony) & trpl US$75.*

Hotel Borjomi (11 rooms) By the museum at Tsminda Nino 3; ℡ 267 22212, 267 21487; m 899 456463; e gentleman@caucasus.net. This old wood-sided house has satellite dishes plus a private mineral spring in the courtyard. The en-suite dbl rooms have good TVs, hairdrier & a fold-up child's bed. *Sgl GEL70, dbl GEL100 inc b/fast & tax.*

Hotel Likani (5 rooms) 1km south, immediately beyond the national park headquarters; ℡ 267 20637; m 899 51579. This hotel occupies the top 2 floors of a new chalet, with its entry at the rear; there are 2 *lux* rooms (with fireplace, kitchenette & a children's bedroom) & 3 others, 2 sharing a bathroom & a different pair sharing a TV. *Lux rooms GEL200 in summer, the others GEL50 pp, all FB (although there's a kitchen available too), with discounts in winter.*

Hotel Tbilisi Gorkova 2; m 899 180919. Take the first road, Ilia Chavchavadze, to the right off Kostava & turn left almost at once or go past the army barracks off Gamsakhurdia kucha (see above). This tower block was closed for some years but is now being restored room by room. It is now mainly occupied by schoolchildren. Guest rooms are on the fifth floor (without a lift), with jolly linen, a water heater in the bathroom, a balcony & no TV (or towel). *GEL15 pp without food.*

There are a few divey places on Kostava, mostly only open in the summer: the Joint-Stock Hotel at No 26 is very basic and may have no water, but only costs GEL10 per person. The Guesthouse Victoria at No 31 (℡ *267 22631; m 893 120283*) is open all year; at Kostava 2 (℡ *267 20780; m 899 575024*) there's a slightly better place with balconies looking over the river.

There's also accommodation from May to October in the Firuza sanatorium (℡ *267 23935; m 899 151898*) at Baratashvilis 3, to the right off 9 April; the Armed Forces Sanatorium (*Gamsakhurdias 17;* ℡ *267 23075, 267 22467*); and at Likani (see below).

Where to eat
At Kostava 29 the **Maka** is a decent café; around the corner on Robakidze near the Kostava Bridge, there's a small café serving *khachapuri* and then the better **Bistro Acuna**. By far the best place to eat is **Shemoikhede Genatsvale** (Step in, Darling!), opened in 2006 in the Borjomi-Park station by the leading restaurant group in Tbilisi.

Other practicalities
There are two **banks**, TBC Bank, at Rustaveli 121(℡ *267 21902; e borjomi@tbcbank.com.ge*); and Peoples Bank at Rustaveli 147 (℡ *267 23042*), which both have ATMs.

What to see and do
Museum of Study of Local Lore, History and Economy (*admission GEL0.50, GEL1 per photo; open 10.00–17.00 except Mon*) is at Tsminda Nino 5, signed to the west from the square north of the market; although dark, largely without captions, and with no English spoken, its exhibits do give interesting insights into the life of the Borjomi region. Starting at the top with tatty stuffed animals, there's then the Romanov porcelain collection on the floor below,

and Bronze-Age agricultural implements, photographs of ancient churches and 19th-century spa life, and by the entry, furniture made for the Romanovs from the antlers of deer they'd shot. You can also see a video made in 2002. Internet access is available at the rear of the museum.

Likani If you ignore the modern viaduct above the bus station and continue up Meskhitis, the main road southwards, and take the steps to the right at km29.2, just after the first bend (to the right), you'll find yourself in a cemetery with a brightly painted chapel and good views of Borjomi, including the ruined Gogiatsikhe (Castle of St George) on the ridge immediately behind the market; it's quite easy to scramble up to this. In medieval times this was the stronghold of the feudal lords of the Avalishvili family, looking across the valley to the 11th–12th-century Petristsikhe (castle of St Peter). Standing outside the museum in Borjomi, you might think you could climb up to the castle from that side, but the only paths are from the south.

The headquarters of the Borjomi-Kharagauli National Park (see opposite) is at km29.8/73.2, under 1km from the viaduct. You're already in Likani, and it's just another 500m to the gate of the former sanatorium (*Meskheti 16;* ☎ *267 23080, 267 21907;* f *267 23080*), at a large lay-by where local marshrutkas will drop you. Built for the Romanovs, this was later reserved for the élite of the Soviet Communist Party and was used for conferences and for Shevardnadze's meetings with Lyudvig Chibirov, then leader of South Ossetia. Agencies in Tbilisi were able to book accommodation here (even in 'Stalin's bed'), although the food was always poor. It was bought by Kazakh investors in 2006 and closed for up to a year for renovation; when it reopens as a luxury hotel, it should still be possible to walk through the lovely park and to the mansion, built in 1895 of grey painted stone and pink-painted brick. At the south end of the park (now separated) is a larger and grander quasi-Tuscan mansion with a tower that's still owned by the state and used by Saakashvili for his skiing weekends in Bakuriani.

BORJOMI-KHARAGAULI NATIONAL PARK

For a distance of 60km the Mtkvari River runs northeast from the Meskheti Plateau down to the central valley of Inner Kartli; this is the Borjomi Gorge, marking the division between the humid Colchic habitats of western Georgia and the drier landscapes of the east. There's also influence from the arid Anatolian plateaux to the south, so there's an intriguing mix of species here, as well as Tertiary relics and some endemic species (such as *Gladiolus dzavacheticus* and *Corydallis erdelii*). In 1880 Prince Mikhail Romanov established a royal hunting reserve, building rangers' huts and appointing a German chief forester; it became a nature reserve in 1935 and a National Park in 1995, opening to the public only in 2001. It covers 85,000ha with a buffer zone of 450,000ha – stretching much further north and west than shown on the ITM/ERKA map, and now including Abastumani and Sametskhavareo, the highest peak in the region at 2,642m.

What's more, it's the only protected area in Georgia to have a management plan, thanks to the help of the Worldwide Fund for Nature and the German government. These include ambitious plans for the development of ecotourism: hiking trails have been created and overnight shelters were built in 2001. In February 2007 Borjomi-Kharagauli National Park became a certified member of the PAN Parks network, in recognition of the high standard of its biodiversity and management. PAN Parks (www.panparks.org) is an innovative initiative to create a network of Europe's best wilderness areas from the Arctic to the Mediterranean. It combines nature conservation with sustainable tourism to promote a real future for these areas.

Trips can be booked through tour agencies in Tbilisi or through the national park – its headquarters are 1km south of Borjomi at Meskheti 23, Likani (↘ 267 22117; m 899 233449; f 267 23911; e welcome@borjomi-kharagauli-np.ge; www.nationalpark.ge; open Mon–Fri 09.00–18.00 & from Apr/May at weekends to 16.00). Rhododendrons bloom in April and May, and autumn colours are spectacular too.

GEOLOGY AND NATURAL HISTORY The area is composed mostly of Tertiary sediments (clay, marl, sandstone) and Quaternary volcanic bedrock (andesite, basalt, dolerite), with plateaux of petrified lava flows. There are 30 mineral springs, of which Zvare, Mitarbi and Nunisi are supposed to have medicinal properties, in addition to Borjomi water. The climate is moderately humid, with cold snowy winters and long cool summers, lasting three-and-a-half months below 1,100m and just two months above 1,500m, where snow lies for at least 150 days a year. Average precipitation is 687mm a year, although it's higher to the north with 1,842mm at the Rikoti Pass and 1,366mm at Kharagauli, and lower to the south with 576mm at Atskuri. Temperatures are also higher to the north, with an average in August of 23°C at Kharagauli, 19° at Borjomi and 16° at Bakuriani.

Forest covers 75% of the national park, mostly climax conifer forest. However, more than 60 species of Colchic trees and shrubs have been recorded here, including cherry-laurel, holly, chestnut, *Rhododendron ponticum*, yew and buckthorn. Forests dominated by oak (*Quercus iberica*), beech (*Fagus orientalis*) and hornbeam (*Carpinus caucasica*) can be found at up to altitudes of 1,800m, though mostly at lower altitudes, while spruce (*Picea orientalis*) and pine (*Pinus kochiana*) can be found from 1,000m to 1,800m, and Caucasian fir (*Abies nordmannia*) from 1,400m to 1,800m. From this altitude to 2,400m there's subalpine forest of crook-stem birch (*Betula litwinowii*), mountain ash (*Sorbus caucasigena*) and *Rhododendron caucasicum*, with alpine grasslands above 2,400m. To the south, the slopes of the Trialeti are dominated by the pine *Pinus sosnowskyi* with smaller species such as juniper, *Astragalus caucasicus*, meadow sweet, hawthorn, cornelian cherry and dog-rose. In addition the Nariani marshes, at 2,050m, are home to many wetland species. The Nedzvi and Ktsia-Tabatskuri reserves (9,000ha and 22,000ha respectively), described on pages 157 and 167, are detached from the main body of the national park, which lies to the west of the gorge.

The 55 species of mammal in the national park include red and roe deer, chamois, brown bear (*Ursus arctos*), wild cat, lynx, wolf, boar, badger, otter, pine marten, squirrel and some endemic species of bat (*Myotis emarginatus*, *Nyctalus lasiopterus*, *Barbastella barbastellus*). Nine bezoar goats (like small ibex) were reintroduced to the Atskuri section of the park in 2006.

Among the 95 species of bird are the golden and white-tailed eagle, black vulture, blackcock, crossbill and six types of woodpecker.

There are also snakes, three endemic lizards, newts and Caucasian salamander.

HIKING IN THE NATIONAL PARK Meadows are found as high as 2,500m on the flanks of Mount Sametskhavario, and are still used for seasonal grazing. Problems of overgrazing, leading to erosion, have been reduced by the new national park, and hunting and logging are also less of a problem than they were. There are nine four-man ranger stations around the edges of the park, notably (in a clockwise direction from Borjomi) at Kvabiskhevi, Atskuri, Abastumani, Marelisi, Nunisi, Kvishkheti and Zanavi. There should always be a ranger on duty, guarding against illegal logging more than poaching or anything else.

Atskuri lies at 950m on the road from Borjomi to Akhaltsikhe (see below); Kvishkheti (600m), at the northeastern corner of the national park, is 1km west of the Khashuri–Borjomi road at km7/96; and Zanavi (850m) is 1km west of the same road at km19.5/83.5, south of Akhaldaba.

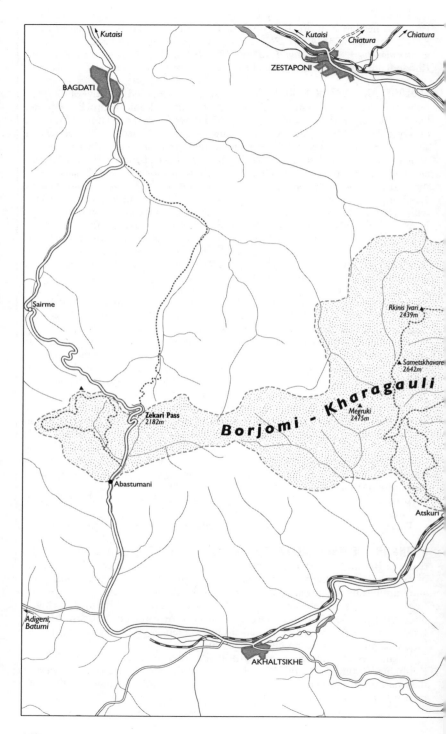

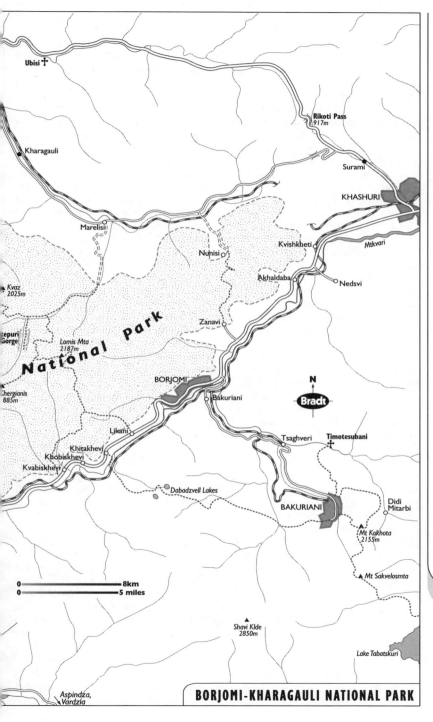

Ubisi †

Rikoti Pass
917m

Kharagauli

Surami

KHASHURI

Marelisi

Kvishkheti

Mtkvari

Nunisi

Kvaz
2025m

Akhaldaba

Nedsvi

National Park

Zanavi

epuri
Gorge

Lomis Mta
2187m

BORJOMI

N

Bradt

hergianis
885m

Bakuriani

Likani

Tsaghveri

Timotesubani
†

Khitakhevi

Khobiskhevi

Kvabiskhevi

Dabadzvell Lakes

BAKURIANI

Didi
Mitarbi

Mt Kokhota
2155m

0 ——— 8km
0 ——— 5 miles

Mt Sakvelosmta

Shavi Klde
2850m

Lake Tabatskuri

Aspindza,
Vardzia

BORJOMI-KHARAGAULI NATIONAL PARK

Specifically for tourists, there's a guesthouse in Marelisi (see page 175) and visitor centre in Kharagauli (also on page 175) as well as at the park headquarters in Likani. There's a pleasant 3km Interpretive Trail from the rear of the headquarters, with wooden sculptures by students of the Academy of Fine Art and labelled trees; it starts to the left of the building with poor switchbacks for a couple of minutes before taking a better path. It climbs up into pine forest, but the way down is unclear where logs have been slid down trails. There's a map at the start and nine educational boards.

There are also new **hiking trails**, marked with black/yellow/black stripes and mostly open to horses too, and also rangers' stations and tourist shelters (where you have to bring your own food and bedding). Hiking without a ranger was not initially allowed, but this has been relaxed; the park still prefers you to hire a freelance local guide. At the eastern end of the park, there's an isolated trail offering an easy day hike (12km, about 6hrs) from Zanavi north to the village of Nunisi (400m) with an old church and thermal springs which are supposed to heal eczema; it follows the Samotkhisgele stream which goes along a ridge to the Dedabera Pass (1,780m) and down past shepherds' summer huts (1,380m) to reach Nunisi. The Samta Nunisi Park Hotel is here (m *899 225580, or in Tbilisi* ☎ *913162*).

The Nikoloz Romanov Trail, from Likani to Marelisi (41km, about 14hrs) leads north from the headquarters through the Likani Gorge (you can take a taxi to the Ranger Station, 1.5km north of the highway) to a campsite, where you can get water. It then climbs and swings west to reach Lomis Mta (2,187m) in five to six hours; there's a tourist shelter here where you can stay the night (or you can camp; water is about 500m away). It's a short distance to St George's chapel.

The next day is mainly downhill, reaching the Shavtwala Valley in five to six hours; to the left it's half an hour to the Didi Sakhvlari tourist shelter, or you could go to the right and reach the Marelisi guesthouse in another couple of hours.

From here you could return south on the longer harder St Andrew's Trail (50km, about 15hrs) to Atskuri: this follows the Shavtwala through the Bjoliskhevi Gorge to the tiny settlement of Didi Sakhvlari (950m) and the Megruki tourist shelter (1,018m) at the mouth of the Stepuri Gorge, an exciting side-trip (especially if water levels are high after rain) of 5.5km each way. From here the St Andrew's Trail climbs to the northwest past the shepherds' summer settlements of Shertuli and Chishkara to a 1,920m pass west of Kvazvinevi (2,025m). It then follows a ridge past a ranger shelter (1,800m) to Rkinis Jvari (2,439m), the Iron Cross Peak on which St Andrew the First-Called placed a cross in the 1st century AD. It continues to the west side of Samteskhvareo (2,642m), the highest peak in the park, and over Megruki (2,475m). After a steep descent it reaches the Amarati tourist shelter (1,910m, with views to the Turkish mountains), from where you can either swing sharp left to follow the Ochora Ridge along the east side of the Barghebis Ghele Valley to Atskuri (6hrs), or take the more direct Panorama Trail (16km) along the ridge to the west of this valley.

The path northeast from the Amarati shelter also connects to the Shepherds' Trail (14km, 5hrs), which leads via Kiriles Klde (St Cyril's Rock; 1,992m) and Mount Khergianis (1,885m) to Lomis Mta and the Nikoloz Romanov Trail. From Lomis Mta you can also descend south through a dramatic gorge to Kvabiskhevi on the Following Wildlife Traces Trail, which also makes a good day hike from Likani (13km, 6hrs). There's also the Zekari Pass Trail (10km, 4–5hrs) well to the west to the north of Abastumani (see page 170).

TO BAKURIANI While here you should also make a side trip up to Bakuriani, once the most popular ski resort in the Soviet Union. Marshrutkas leave from Borjomi's bus station, with taxis waiting by the square just north. The road starts at about km26.3, 2km north of the centre of Borjomi; a bridge crosses the river to the Borjomi-Works railway station, where the Tbilisi–Khashuri–Akhaltsikhe railway connects with a rather amazing **narrow-gauge railway** on which tiny carriages are hauled by a large and ungainly electric locomotive at a very leisurely pace. Opened in 1902, the 920mm-gauge line was electrified (at 1.5kV dc) in 1972. The first 18km to Tsemi (where it crosses a 34m-high steel bridge designed by the Eiffel company) were upgraded in 2002 to allow the dizzy speed of 25km/h, but the next 19km are limited to 15km/h. Departures are at 07.00 and 13.15 from Borjomi, returning at 10.00 and 16.30. One of the steam locos that used to work this line is now set on a plinth by the Borjomi station.

The road passes through the sprawling water-bottling plant and then follows a valley to the southeast. At km9 it passes the minuscule hamlet of Daba, with the very simple basilica of St George, built in 1333, with some nice carvings, which can be seen from the railway, on the left/west side of the valley, or reached by road from km8.5. At km11 the road enters the village of **Tsaghveri**, where it swings right and climbs in hairpin bends out of the valley; the railway takes a far longer route, heading west to cross the Gujareti Gorge and wind slowly through dense pine forests.

Timotesubani A minor road (Toreli kucha) continues due east up the valley from Tsaghveri, through an impressive short gorge (with a ruined fort high above the left bank) and then past fields, reaching the village of Timotesubani (17km from Borjomi) in just over 3km; turning left at the junction in the centre, it's another 1km to the **Monastery of St Timothy**, just beyond the edge of the village at the end of the asphalt. Here the Church of the Virgin, built at the end of the 12th century, is famous for its frescoes, painted in 1205–15. The gate-tower, older than the church and now rather ruinous, is of red brick; the church is also red brick but with a band and crosses of turquoise mosaic on the barrel dome. Entering through the south porch, built later in limestone, you'll see plenty of bare brickwork, but also plenty of fine surviving frescoes, including a *Virgin and Child* above the altar, a *Crucifixion* to the south of the iconostasis, and *Paradise* at the west end; there are also plenty of saints and a flute-player in the north transept. The frescoes have recently had emergency work to treat mould. The monks have recently returned, living in an unattractive new house, and some speak a little English.

A rough road follows the main valley eastwards all the way to Citelisopeli, which was inhabited by Ossetians until the attempted secession of South Ossetia. Hardy mountain bikers could turn left/north at Sinubani to cross the ridge to Tkemlovani and ultimately Kintsvisi (page 141), a similar church to that of Timotesubani.

BAKURIANI

The road to Bakuriani passes above the Sanatorium-Pensionat Khetkhovi, just above Tsaghveri, where you'll find accommodation for about GEL5 and, climbing steadily, eventually reaches Bakuriani, 28km from the main road.

Established in 1932 at 1,700m, Bakuriani is still largely a traditional village, subsisting on grazing and logging, with large hotels built in the last two or three decades set at a respectful distance across the subalpine meadows. There's snow from November to March, or even May, with the heaviest falls in December; in January the average temperature is −7.2°C, but in August it's a pleasant 15°C, making it ideal for walking.

GETTING THERE Buses take under an hour, while the trains, covering 37km, take over 90 minutes up and 70 minutes down. Although very slow, they take a more interesting route, cost almost nothing (fares are collected on board) and more or less guarantee you a seat.

Buses usually turn right for 50m to the taxi rank (and police station) by the Hotel Santa, but some may continue straight along the main road, Svoboda. Arriving at the railway station, you should go uphill past the taxi rank to the main road; follow this up to the right and then loop left (where buses swing right on Davit Agmashenebelis, lined with new hotels) to reach the gear-hire shacks and the nursery slope, known as Otsdachutmetriani or the Twentyfive-metre-field, where there's a 40m drag and lifts up to 420m long.

WHERE TO STAY AND EAT

🏠 **Hotel Santa** (80 rooms) Right in the centre; ☎ 142783. No English is spoken. *En-suite rooms with TV US$20 pp.*

🏠 **Villa Fagus** (12 rooms) Close to the railway station; ☎ 70106; m 893 715855, 899 533683. A new chalet block. *US$50 for dbl with a good modern bathroom & radiators; US$70 for lux.*

The main road southwards, Kostava, is lined with traditional wooden cottages, in which rooms are available in the ski season; however, there are only the simplest restaurants and cafés here, so you'll have to arrange meals too.

🏠 **Hotel Saba** (9 rooms) Kostava 25; m 899 102463. French-owned, with satellite TV & swimming pool. *Dbl FB € 90.*

🏠 **Hotel Tbilisi** (75 rooms) Opposite the Saba; m 826 770141, 899 111644. A modern package-

style hotel with small rooms with balconies, TV & fridge-freezer. They're very friendly, although there's no English spoken. *Rooms GEL100 (plus GEL3 for a buffet b/fast, only from 09.00).*

To the left at the start of the road past the Twentyfive-metre Field are the **Pyramid Café** and the Villa Palace Hotel (not recommended); this road makes a 3km loop around the far side of the lovely meadow, finishing just above km26 on the Borjomi road (opposite house No 22) and is lined with disused communist hotels plus the smallish new **Hotel Alpina** (*Tsriuli 5;* m *877 999997*).

🏠 **Hotel Apollon** (15 rooms, 2 suites) Davit Agmashenebelis 21; ☎ 32 331446; m 899 571108, 877 730772; e ingula006@yahoo.de; www.welcome.ge/hotel_apollon. South past Kochta Gora, this hotel is open all year & rightly popular with expatriates in Tbilisi; it comprises 2 buildings (and 2 dining rooms), with a nice simple style & pine furniture, & rooms for 2 to 4 people plus families. There's TV in all rooms, plus video in the common area, sauna, billiards & table tennis as well as parking, a warm boot room, a garden & their own short ski-drag at the rear. They're very friendly & efficient & will do vegetarian food given notice, & Inga speaks good English. *From US$30 pp in summer or US$35 in winter including 3 meals (plus tea, cake & fruit).*

🏠 **Hotel Melisi** (17 rooms, 5 suites) Davit Agmashenebelis 55; ☎ 32 957403; m 899 231197; www.welcome.ge/hotel_melisi. *From US$25 in summer & US$40 in winter (dbl $100 in winter with full board).* A new spa hotel, with sauna, gym &

and tennis courts (in summer).

🏠 **Hotel Olimpo** (20 rooms) Davit Agmashenebelis No 76A; m 899 531100. Less glitzy than some, with billiards and cable TV.

🏠 **Hotel Lotus** (35 rooms) Tsriuli, near Kochta Gora; m 893 276039, 899 952595. *US$15–35 pp.*

🏠 **Guesthouse Rustaveli** Rustaveli 9; m 899 567637. *From GEL50 pp FB or GEL25 without food.*

🏠 **Vardisperi Sastumro** (Pink Hotel) Mtis 28; m 899 537716. A good family hotel.

🏠 **Villa Park** (20 rooms) Rustaveli 25; ☎ 267 40405; m 877 504747; www.mgroup.ge. Owned by the flashy Tbilisi M Group. Swimming pool, sauna & gym, & a Swedish buffet b/fast. *Rooms from US$100.*

🏠 **Varskvlavi** (Star; 9 rooms) Saakadze 6, near Kochta Gora; ☎ 267 40405; m 877 504747; www.mgroup.ge. Another M Group hotel. Smaller than the Villa Park with a skating rink in the yard & table tennis, as well as free access to the Villa Park's facilities. *Rooms from US$80.*

166

🏠 **Vere Palace** (36 rooms, 10 suites) Tsriuli 12; 📱 899 116045, 877 742931; www.verepalace.com.ge. Opened in 2002, this is an offshoot of the hotel of the same name in Tbilisi, with satellite TV, hairdryer & minibar. It has a swimming pool, sauna, gym, cinema, disco, business centre, nursery, laundry & ski rental. To get around, in addition to taxis, there are horse-drawn sleighs which cost about GEL1 per min, if you negotiate well. You can also rent a Buran snowmobile, which will do 80km/h, or slower ones for kids, plus quad bikes, toboggans, horses & horse sleighs; there's skating on a natural pond in Jan & Feb. *Sgl US$70, dbl US$90, both FB; US$20 less in summer).*

On the road parallel to Davit Agmashenebelis to the left are plenty of private houses, all of which rent rooms in winter; you'd be sure to find one in summer too, for about GEL10.

WHAT TO SEE AND DO There's a 1.3km run (very difficult at the top) on Kochta Gora (Pretty Hill; 2,255m) and also ski jumps; an old lift takes you to a restaurant and the radio masts on top. Behind, on the next peak south, is the 'Tatra-Poma' lift (owned and renovated by the Kazbegi brewery) by the Trialeti Palace Hotel, which has a good restaurant. You can also take a 3.5km run from the top of Mount Tskhra-Tskharo (2,711m), and from Mount Imerlebi (2,500m). The new Didveli slope is 3km to the southwest (GEL8 by taxi) at the end of Davit Agmashenebelis. It's owned by oligarch Bidzina Ivanishvili, who provided free skiing for the first season (when the lift was not yet open to the top). There's an eight-person Leitner gondola and a quad Doppelmayr chairlift here, and four interconnecting pistes, between 1,200 and 2,200m long.

President Saakashvili skis here most weekends (staying at the Likani Palace) and is promising two new lifts and snow-making equipment by 2007; he's backing a bid for the 2014 Winter Olympics, which is unrealistic but is great publicity for the resort. The big event until then is the Sukhia competition in early March of even years (in odd years it's in Gudauri).

Many of the hotels rent downhill skis for GEL5–10 per hour, but you'll have to bring your own cross-country skis, snowboard or snowshoes. If you have hired gear or an instructor (GEL20 per hour) you'll pay for the lifts when you finish; otherwise just pay GEL2 in cash each time (GEL0.50 for the nursery drags).

In summer there's good walking, of course, although chairlifts don't start until 11.00; the best access to the peaks is by a jeep track to the left from Davit Agmashenebelis by the Tatra-Poma lift; there's a pleasant hike to the right/south to the next two peaks. Unusually for a ski resort, Bakuriani also has a fine alpine botanical garden (📱 *899 573830; open 10.00–17.00 in theory*), founded in 1910 and reached through the green gates opposite house No 50 at km25.9 on the road to Borjomi; in an area of 17ha they have over 800 subalpine species of flowering plants, including around 100 trees and shrubs. This is also the site of the WWF Ecocentre, a centre for environmental education; incidentally, Bakuriani is known for a sort of 'chewing gum' made from pine resin.

AROUND BAKURIANI The village of Tsikhdvari, 9km west, is lovely, with a mineral bath built by Mikhail Romanov. Turning right off Davit Agmashenebelis, an unsurfaced road continues southwards through the Trialeti range and eventually down, through a Greek-populated area, to Akhalkalaki; immediately beyond the 2,454m Zachraskaro pass an even rougher road leads east to Lake Tabatskuri, at 1,990m. The lake (14.2km² in area) and the headwaters of the Ktsia River, to its north, are an important stopover for waterbirds such as grey heron, velvet scoter, Eurasian crane, black and white stork, great white egret, red-beaked swan, and also griffon-vulture; they're protected in a detached part of the Borjomi-Kharagauli National Park. It takes about two hours by 4x4 (not in winter) to get from Bakuriani to the east side of the lake, where the birds are most numerous.

Beyond Likani, the main road to Akhaltsikhe passes Khitakhevi, just north of which in the Khitakhevi Gorge is the lovely Mtsvane (Green) monastery, a simple 9th-century basilica with a deacon's nave to the south and porches to the south and west.

From km39/52 (10km south of Borjomi), a road is signed to Khobiskhevi, 3km to the southeast; here, by the Gogichant stream, are the most important secular buildings in the national park, lantern-vaulted houses (a style associated primarily with the historic Tori province) built in the 8th–10th centuries.

The A308 continues to the small village of **Kvabiskhevi**; beds and food are available behind a big pink house at km47. As mentioned above, a trail leads from here to Lomis Mta, starting near the rangers' shelter and campsite, behind which you can climb up to the Mariamtsminda (Holy Virgin) Church, a three-naved basilica built in the 9th and 14th centuries. It takes 90 minutes to the Kvabiskhevi fortress (1,150m), from where you can continue to Lomis Mta.

As the road emerges from the Borjomi Gorge, and gets rougher, there's a clear change to the dry bare landscape of the Anatolian highlands. At about km51 the railway (now on the left bank) passes through a tunnel under a castle, and at about km56 the road and railway reach **Atskuri** (950m), a small dusty village under the remains of a 10th–13th-century fortress high on a crag. Atskuri was an important trade centre from the 6th century BC, with Greek pottery coming via Vani; St Andrew is said to have brought an icon of the Virgin Mary here, and an important church was built later. The fortress was a Turkish stronghold until 1829, but then fell into ruin. Hiking routes lead north into the Borjomi-Kharagauli National Park from 2.5km east of the village, as described above.

AKHALTSIKHE Finally the Mtkvari swings away to the southeast, while the road and railway briefly head west to the small city of Akhaltsikhe, 70km from Khashuri and 200km from Tbilisi. Its name means New Castle, but the fortifications on the easily defensible hilltops actually date from the 12th century, long before Paskevich stormed the Turkish defences in 1828 and built a new fort. It's now a city of 20,000, about a third of whom are Armenian.

Getting there In 1995 it was agreed to open road and rail crossings to Turkey from Vale, just southwest of Akhaltsikhe; the road crossing to Posof is open, but the 124km railway from Vale to Kars is likely to take a while to build.

Aybaki buses from Tbilisi to Turkey can be caught at the Akhaltsikhe bus station, costing US$15 to Trabzon or US$50 to Ankara.

There are also daily buses to Batumi (via Borjomi; GEL18; 08.30, 11.30), Vardzia (GEL4; 10.30, 12.20, 16.00, 17.30), Kutaisi (via Borjomi; GEL8; 6 a day) and Akhalkalaki; almost all Tbilisi traffic (GEL7–10; up to a dozen buses and marshrutkas, between 06.20 and 13.00) take the faster route via Borjomi. To Vardzia you can also take a marshrutka for GEL10 or a taxi for GEL45–60 round trip including waiting time; the drive takes about two hours each way.

There are also buses to Yerevan (GEL25; 07.00 and 08.00) and marshrutkas to Gyumri in Armenia.

The railway station is behind the bus station, although it's served only by the overnight Tbilisi–Vale train. From Vale it's half an hour on a rough road to the border (GEL50 by taxi).

Where to stay There's a hotel upstairs in the bus station (m *899 108144*), charging GEL5 each for a very basic room and cold showers; the only TV is the one always blaring by the entrance, but they're friendly and speak some German. You may also be offered a homestay at the bus station.

There's also a new hotel at a former factory at the northern city limits, beyond a short stretch of dual carriageway on the road to Borjomi, and a couple of new guesthouses on the road leaving to Abastumani.

🏠 **Soldier's Hotel** (2 rooms) Kostava 6 (look for the English-language Kodak-Foto sign); 📱 899 983495. On the top (3rd) floor of a block of flats; hospital-style beds, a cold tap & a filthy toilet. *GEL10.*

🏠 **Meskheti** (formerly the Intourist) Kostava 10; ☎ 20420. The least bad hotel in the centre. Twin rooms have TV & shower. *GEL30 (there may still be cold-water rooms at GEL15).*

🏠 **The White House** Aspindzas Kucha 26 (actually beyond a block of flats on the right at the end of a side street to the left off Aspindzas, itself off the Vardzia road); ☎ 265 20410. This is a 15min walk south from the station or GEL2 by taxi, but it has lovely clean comfy en-suite rooms, with TV. Of the two managers, Manana speaks English (📱 893 248049) but Naira doesn't (📱 893 473558). *GEL50 pp inc b/fast.*

Other practicalities A **visitor centre** should open in 2007. The Bank of Georgia (*Kostava 25*) and People's Bank (*Naidze 6*) do not have **ATMs**, but there is one on the pedestrian link to the left off Kostava opposite the market, which continues north to the Central Stadium on Tamar (formerly Lenina), a popular evening viewpoint. The Vasilich Pub at Kostava 37 is a nice **cellar bar** serving good *khachapuri.*

What to see and do Turning right out of the stations and then right under the railway, you can make your way up to the left to the hilltop castle, still in relatively good shape; you'll find the **Museum of History and Art** (*admission GEL1; open Tue–Sun 10.00–17.00*) here, as well as a mosque, built in 1752. There's also a ruined two-dome Armenian church by the road just beyond the second entrance to the castle.

Turning right from the stations and then left at the same roundabout, you'll cross the river to the town centre; keep to the right up Kostava from the statue of Tamar (outside the House of Culture), and at the top of the hill you'll pass the market to your right. If you go on and turn left and left again to return on the other side of the one-way system, you'll have seen all there is to see here – not a lot, although the neatly built houses of volcanic tuff are very Armenian in style. Heading down Naidze (opposite the Hotel Meskheti) you'll reach the **Armenian church**, silhouetted on a small hilltop that's even more dramatic than the one occupied by the fort; built in 1868, its interior is bare and cold and not worth seeing. You can reach it by the rough steps up from the end of Naidze, or take a big loop left to reach it from the rear.

WEST FROM AKHALTSIKHE Heading west from the city, the road soon forks left to Vale (where there's a 10th-century cruciform church, remodelled in the 14th century) and the Turkish border. The main road continues westwards and then divides, with the A307 heading north to Kutaisi; this passes Amara, west of which you'll see the Amaravepe castle ruins on a hill, and enters **Abastumani**, a tiny spa which is the site of Georgia's main astronomical observatory (previously a Romanov villa and a TB sanatorium). At km9 (to the east from a statue on a rock) is the *banya* or spa, and at about km10 the hotel is on the east side of the road opposite No 56; about another 1km to the north, opposite No 7, a track leads 100m west to a footbridge and a tiny cable car which runs up to the observatory every few hours (the last, at 18.30, connecting with a bus from Akhaltsikhe). Alternatively you can take a path parallel to the cable car, which takes 20 minutes downhill and probably double that uphill, or a taxi, costing GEL5 – a 3km road turns left to the north of the village. There are four or five telescopes and typically Soviet apartment blocks in typically post-Soviet disrepair, plus a nunnery and a few nice new guesthouses, all strewn along a thin ridge which offers great views of the forested hills just north that are now incorporated in the Borjomi-Kharagauli National Park.

From a ranger shelter about 7km north of Abastumani a marked trail leads northwest and up, making a 10km loop on the south slopes of Mount Didimagala (2,588m) via the Didimagala tourist shelter, about 3km west of the road just south of the Zekari Pass. Mountain bikes are allowed here, but not in the main part of the park (and none are available to rent).

There's an unmarked three-day hike from Abastumani to Tsinubani, near Atskuri, starting with a 22km road up the Baratkhevi Gorge to shepherds' summer huts where you can camp, at 2,100m on the north side of Mount Tsikhisdziri. The next day takes you over the summit (2,252m), where you'll find the ruins of a fortress, to the south plateau, then eastwards to Mount Amagleba (2,277m), with a good site for camping on its north slope at about 2,050m; the next day you'll come down through the Kombekhi Gorge to the Tsinubanis Valley.

Organised groups also make a five-day hike west to Bakhmaro (see page 196), with great views to the High Caucasus and Ararat, via mounts Mamlismta (2,489m), Mepistskaro (2,850m) and Gomistsikhe (2,380m), then down along a ridge to the village of Grdzelgori (2,200m) and Bakhmaro resort (2,000m).

Two or three buses a day run from Akhalktsikhe as far as Abastumani, but none continue northwards to the 2,182m Zekari (Sun-gate) Pass over the Lesser Caucasus; this is often closed by snow between October and June, but if you can get here a short hike to the east soon gives superb views. There's accommodation in the national park's Zekari tourist shelters (2,080m), about 50m above some shepherds' huts south of the pass; from here it takes five hours (return) to climb Mount Didimagala (2,588m), the highest in the region, to the west of the road. The road descends through Sairme, known for its mineral waters, and Bagdati (see page 186), to Kutaisi.

The Batumi road, the A306, continues westwards up the Kvabliani Valley below Okrostsikhe (Golden Stronghold), the stronghold in early medieval times of the lords of Samtskhe-Javakheti province and an important obstacle to the Turkish invasions of the 15th and 16th centuries. Its huge towers and powerful walls are still visible. Crossing the river, you'll come to **Zarzma**, 29km from Akhaltsikhe, and see to the left the early 14th-century Church of the Transfiguration, with 16th-century frescoes, a fine large belltower and four smaller churches. Beyond here the road is very bad, and unsigned – there may be a few marshrutkas but no buses come this way. It climbs southwest out of the valley, entering Adjara just before the 2,025m Goderji Pass (92km from Borjomi, 115km from Batumi), which is often blocked by snow between October and May.

EAST FROM AKHALTSIKHE To the east of Akhaltsikhe, the Akhalkalaki road (the A306) soon rejoins the Mtkvari Valley, crossing it at the first village, Mikadze, and entering a gorge; on the north side of this you can see caves which prefigure those you're heading for at Vardzia. Before this you can turn off to **Sapara**, where there's an ancient monastery similar to that at Zarzma; turn right/south before Mikadze along a very rough road up a side valley, fork left after 3km and continue up the valley for another 8km. There's been a monastery here since the 10th century, but the present church of St Saba dates from the late 13th century, with fine early 14th-century frescoes in the Byzantine Paleologue style. Dramatically set on the edge of a gorge, with a fort above, it is a good example of the cruciform ground plan. It's possible to hike here from Akhaltsikhe in about three hours, or you can take a taxi (GEL15 return).

Soon after emerging from the gorge, at about km143, you'll see a statue of the national poet Shota Rustaveli, marking the entrance to the village of Rustavi, just to the left/north of the road. Here, not the post-war industrial city of Rustavi southeast of Tbilisi, is where he was born. Although the river is still fairly sizeable, the country becomes increasingly arid and unpopulated, although you'll see several ruined castles. In Aspindja, where the 'Eating House' has an English sign for some reason, the castle ruins on a hilltop to the north are easily reached from just west of the centre; there's also a rough, fairly old basilica at the eastern exit from the village. About an hour-and-a-half from Akhaltsikhe, the bus to Vardzia turns right off the A306 at **Khertvisi**, with the famous fortress directly ahead; it's immediately to the left after the bridge at the confluence of the Javakheti Mtkvari and the Artaani Mtkvari, and can easily be reached by a road on its far side. There were fortifications here by the 2nd century BC, long before a church was built in 985, when it was the administrative capital of the Meskheti region. The two main towers (one now being restored) were built by Tamar, and the present walls were added in 1354–56, according to the plaque over the entrance. Beyond it you'll see cave cells in the cliff above the houses to the left.

SOUTH TO VARDZIA Now running south along the right/east bank of the Mtkvari, after about 10km the road reaches a junction just before a relatively recent fortification; the bus turns off here to climb up to the village of Nakalakevi, where it turns round, returns to the road and continues southwards. It climbs steadily to pass through a dramatic defile known as Tamar's Gates, on the far side of which is the medieval castle of **Tmogvi**, wonderfully well placed to defend the approaches to Vardzia. It's best seen from a distance to the north, but from the road immediately opposite you'll see the curtain walls and the caves in the cliffs below, near the river. It's also possible to reach the castle in an hour or so following a track along the far bank of the Mtkvari from Vardzia; you could continue up to a track on the plateau above and eventually descend to a bridge just north of Nakalakevi – quite a hike, and you should be sure to carry plenty of water. The castle was built in the 10th and 11th centuries and destroyed by the Persians in the 16th century; subsequent earthquakes have more or less completed the job of reducing it to rubble.

From here the road descends for 3km to the turning to the cave-nunnery of Vanis-Kvabi (or Kvabebi), a smaller equivalent of Vardzia itself, built, or excavated, between the 8th and 13th centuries.

VARDZIA

It's another kilometre along the valley to the school at the entry to Vardzia, which is in any case not really a village at all. Before this you'll pass the turning to the Intourist Hotel, a huge concrete pile which is no longer functional but still dominates the view from the Vardzia caves. It's less than 1km south from the school to a ruined suspension bridge by a tin house with a small *Otel* sign on a telegraph pole (m *899 628114*); this is basically a hot-spring bath house with two very basic tatty dorms with trampoline mattresses and Turin shroud bedding. The manager is very friendly (and speaks some German) and charges just GEL5 for a bed, or GEL20 including dinner with lots of wine and an excellent mineral bath (a big concrete vat in something like a tractor shed). The next house (signed as *Bar*) has big modern three-bed en-suite rooms at GEL20 per person; there's a kitchen but no meals (there isn't even a drinks stall at the caves). It's certainly much easier to get here these days, with four buses a day in summer from Akhaltsikhe (GEL4), taking about two hours; they return at 08.30, 10.00, 13.00 and 15.00. You can also take a marshrutka for GEL10 or a taxi for GEL45–60 round trip including waiting time.

Vardzia is the site of the most famous cave-city in Georgia, which, largely because of its connections with Queen Tamar, is a place of almost mystic importance for most Georgians; having been in a closed border zone throughout the Soviet period, it's now receiving plenty of visitors, at least in summer. It's said that its name derives from 'Ak var, dzia' or 'Here I am, uncle' – Tamar's call when lost in the caves. First established by King George III in 1156 and consecrated in 1185, his daughter Tamar made it into a monastery, which became the chief seminary of southwestern Georgia (housing 2,000 monks) until an earthquake ruined it in 1283, slicing away a large portion of the rock face. Another quake in 1456 was followed by a Persian army in 1551 and the Turks at the end of that century, so that now around 600 chambers survive of a total 3,000, which included stables, barracks, bakeries, wine presses and stores. Likewise, only half-a-dozen levels remain of the 13 which once penetrated 50m into the cliffs. It's been protected since 1938; there was some heavy-handed restoration with concrete in the 1970s, but work now underway should be more sensitive. Heavy rain in 1998 caused a large section of cliff to collapse from 40–50m up; the Dutch government rapidly provided US$50,000 for emergency repairs, including to the stairs to the monastery belltower. Egyptian vultures are nesting in the caves, making their management yet more complex.

About 100m beyond the old bridge is a new road bridge; crossing this and turning right, you'll reach in a couple of minutes the car park for the cave-city of Vardzia, at about 1,400m altitude. There's a simple but relatively decent toilet block, and it's a nice spot, by the poplar-lined river, so it might make a decent campsite. The site is officially open from 10.00 to 17.00 except on Mondays, but they can be pretty tardy opening up out of season and can stay open till 19.00 in summer; nor are they likely to have change except in summer. Having paid your GEL6 or US$3 (GEL1 for Georgians), you and a guide (who only needs a small tip, especially as he'll speak nothing but Georgian or Russian) have to walk up a road for ten minutes. This ends at the Ananauri sector of Vardzia, which, dating from the 10th century, is older than Vardzia proper, but was swallowed up by it; immediately above the end of the road is a cave used as stabling for horses (note the holes in the rock used to attach head ropes), while a small path (from the top bend in the path leading north) leads to a church. This is usually locked but you can peer in and see its smoke-blackened 16th-century frescoes.

The path leads northwards below the cliffs to a belltower (built after the 1283 earthquake) and the refectory, and then (after a stretch where you're encouraged not to hang around, due to occasional rock falls) to a door, which is as far as you can get without a guide and a key. This leads into the Church of the Assumption (1184–86), the pivotal point of the complex; in front of you is a famous fresco of Tamar (one of just four painted in her lifetime) and her father, together with what seems to be an Annunciation but for the fact that the Virgin already has the child Jesus on her knee. If you don't have a torch (flashlight) with you, you'll have to buy some tapers here before being led down a dark tunnel to the pool known as 'Tamar's Tears'; the water is beautifully cool and sweet.

Returning outside, you can explore the rest of the city more or less at random; some of the chambers are interconnected, but thanks to the earthquakes most of them are now open to the outside world. Compared to the honeycombed hillsides of Cappadocia, in Turkey, this isn't really very exciting. There are a few frescoes, although most of the chambers are smoke-blackened; what's more interesting than the walls and ceilings are the floors, which are pitted with a surprising array of channels and receptacles for water and, of course, wine. At the far end you'll leave by a tunnel leading down to the river

SOUTH AND EAST OF VARDZIA The road crosses to the left bank of the river by a new bridge just upstream of the closed one; about 1km further south it reaches a hot spring, now feeding a swimming pool in a barn-like shed, where you can luxuriate in the warm sulphurous waters for next to nothing. Continuing, you'll eventually reach Zeda Vardzia (Upper Vardzia), where the writer Peter Nasmyth reported finding an old church surrounded by fields of marijuana.

The road to the former Intourist Hotel winds its way up to the top of the cliff on the east side of the Mtkvari Valley, and on to the village of Apnia. From here a very rough road leads to Kumordo, 12km southwest of Akhalkalaki, where there's a fairly large and complex church built in 964, with a large apse above the altar, two side apses at the east end and two more to the west; in the centre six pillars support the dome, which collapsed in the 16th century and was restored. At the west end an ambulatory was added in the second quarter of the 11th century.

The road on to Akhalkalaki is slightly better, but without a 4x4 you're best advised to travel from Vardzia to Akhalkalaki via Khertvisi. **Akhalkalaki** ('New Town'; 1,716m) is a small town of no importance now that Javakheti is governed from Akhaltsikhe, except as the terminus of a painfully slow railway from Tbilisi, a branch 160km long completed in 1986, and as the site of a Russian military base, which is vital to the local economy. This closed in 2007, although the locals were bitterly opposed, due both to the loss of jobs and to the perceived loss of security from Turkey, in an area that is 90% Armenian. It may gain slightly in significance if a new road crossing to Turkey opens at Cildir to the southwest and the railway is extended to Kars in Turkey.

NINOTSMINDA AND BEYOND

To the east, the railway and the A303 cross a high arid plateau dotted with a surprising number of lakes; the road is known for its terrible state but is being rebuilt thanks to the US$100m Millennium Challenge fund, also providing bilingual education in this poor and largely Armenian area. From Ninotsminda (or Bogdanovka, a town of 7,000 and, at 1,940m, the highest in Georgia) the A306 leads southeast to the Armenian border, passing through **Gorelovka**, the goal of Philip Marsden's quest in *The Spirit Wrestlers*. Here in June 1895, on what they called the Sacred Heights, the Dukhobors, a Tolstoyan Quaker-like sect of Russians, burnt their guns and refused to serve in the tsar's army, starting a long saga of persecution and eventual emigration to Canada (via Siberia, as a rule). Now some of their turf-roofed cabins remain, but few of the people. In 1990 nearly 7,000 Dukhobors lived in eight villages in this region, but today their community has shrunk to only a few hundred (still half of the population of Gorelovka). When collective farms were broken up in 1997 the Dukhobors chose to stick with the principle of co-operative work and established the Dukhoborets collective farm. Unfortunately they left no land for the local Armenians, and in 2006 the local council removed almost 5,000ha, leaving the Dukhobors with only 600ha, between 6ha and 15ha per family, They're now talking of moving back to Russia.

Just 1km southwest of Ninotsminda is Lake Khanchali, which also has a sad and complicated history. Until 1961 it covered 1,310ha and was home to lake trout, Caucasian herring, barbel and migrating ducks, but in that year it was drained to be adapted for fish farming. It remained dry until 1964, by which time the wildfowl had moved to Lake Cildir, in Turkey, on their migrations. As the lake was shallow and warm, the fish farming was successful, but even so it was abandoned in 1968, and the lake gradually reverted to its natural state. In 1985 a dam was built across the lake and two-thirds was drained again to grow hay, while the southeastern third was used for fish farming until 1990; in 1997 the dam began to collapse and the whole lake was drained for a year while it was patched together.

Amazingly, 40 bird species still stop here on their migrations, while another 24 (of which four are threatened with extinction) nest at the lake, including cranes and white storks. The Georgian Centre for the Conservation of Wildlife is campaigning for the restoration of the lake and buying 900ha of the lake bed, which will be first private reserve in the Caucasus; although the mainly Armenian population at first wanted the land for farming, 77% now want the lake restored.

The A303 and railway head northeast past Georgia's largest lake, Lake Paravani (2,047m), which is also threatened by a plan to farm non-native fish; at its northern end is the Dukhobor village of Tambovka. The road runs through Manglisi and near to Birtvisi and Betania (see page 247), and finally descends to Tbilisi, entering by Chavchavadze Avenue, while the railway takes a loop to the south.

Short-toed eagle

Imereti, Racha and Mingrelia

IMERETI

Imereti lies cradled between the High and Lesser Caucasus and the Surami range, inland from the coastal plains; it's a fertile, well-watered region that was one of the cradles of Georgian civilisation. The Imeretians are known as the most voluble and the most temperamental people in Georgia, and they also consider themselves the most hospitable. Its capital is Kutaisi, the second city of Georgia, an attractive friendly city which has a few creature comforts to offer the traveller.

The main road from Tbilisi crosses the Rikoti Pass from Khashuri and Surami and descends the lovely Rikotula and Dzirula valleys to Zestaponi, while the railway (and a back road) follow the next valley to the south. The main road has been improved, with lots of new bridges cutting off sections of road that take a much longer route along the curves of the river. Many of these still form village streets, and they can be used to make a far more enjoyable route for cycling; as most of these loops are to the north of the main road cyclists should head westwards (ie: downhill). With a good solid bike it would be possible to return by the Kharagauli road to the south, making a very pleasant loop; this is an awful road, but repairs are to be made.

HIKING TO THE NORTH OF BORJOMI-KHARAGAULI NATIONAL PARK On this route, the tiny village of **Marelisi** (450m; about 1hr by train from Khashuri or 3hrs from Tbilisi) is becoming a centre for hiking into the Borjomi-Kharagauli National Park (see page 160); there's a park guesthouse 4km south of the station and 3km north of the park gate (a taxi is available and can also shuttle your baggage). The guesthouse (*closed in winter*; m *899 233449, 893 907029*; e *welcome@borjomi-kharagauli-np.ge*) has four double rooms with food and hot water available, plus camping in the yard, and is becoming popular with Tbilisi expats at the weekends. Horses can be rented for easier forays into the park. The trails leads south up the Shavtwala Valley and then to either Lomis Mta and Likani, or Rkinis Jvari and Atskuri – see page 164 for details.

Kharagauli is the northern centre for the Borjomi-Kharagauli National Park, with special responsibility for the buffer zone. Rather more substantial than Marelisi, it consists of two main streets (across the river from the station and to the right) with some fine buildings of dressed stone built in 1933, one of which is now a park office and visitor centre. Kharagauli is served by local trains, and also by marshrutkas from Didube (the last at 15.30). Further west there's the large *Muza* sculpture by someone who'd obviously never seen a naked woman; the road heads into a gorge, passing a very odd sculpture, half-covered in ivy but seeming to represent grotesquified pagan myths. Thankfully the 10km road from Dzirula on the main highway to Kharagauli was rebuilt in 2005.

UBISI Emerging from the toll tunnel at km143.5 (or the old road over the pass), the main highway passes beehives and their keepers camping beside the road in

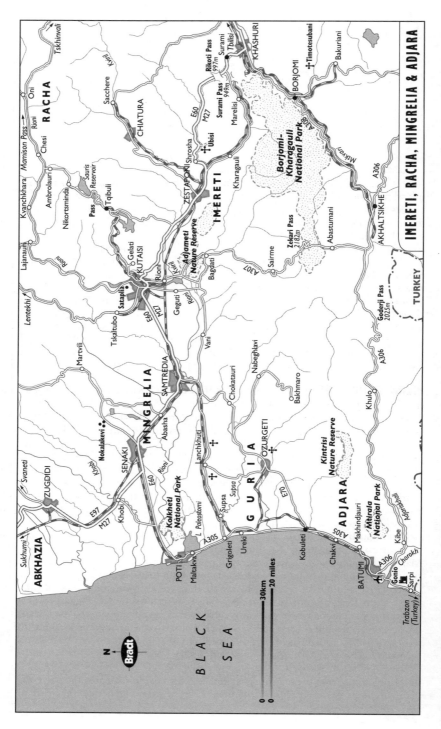

IMERETI, RACHA, MINGRELIA & ADJARA

summer and criss-crosses the Dzirula and then Rikotula streams many times, passing a new restaurant at about km149 and then attractive villages such as Khonevi (km155) and Boriti (km165).

Immediately after passing the piers for an unfinished concrete viaduct, to the left at km170/382, a road to Goresha turns left on a bend and drops to a bridge; it's well worth halting here to visit the charming little church of **Ubisi**, just before the bridge. Heading east, there's a good view of the church and the remains of fortifications above the unfinished viaduct. Built in AD826 by one Grigor Kansteli and painted in the next century by Damiane, it's a single-nave basilica, but with a double porch that more or less constitutes a southern aisle. The gate-tower, built of rounded river stones, has been doubled as well, and there are various other extensions tacked on to the main building. However, the belltower, a three-storey dwelling built by Demetre I in 1141 (when the church was also restored), with a ladder to reach the entrance, is separate. The 14th-century frescoes by Damiane, reaching almost to the floor, are lovely, with a supple grace that seems very Western, especially the *Last Supper* above the altar and the *Annunciation* (with the Virgin turning in surprise) to the north. The frescoes are turning slightly pink, but it is hoped to restore them.

In the long village of **Shrosha** huge quantities of red ceramics are for sale especially in a lay-by at km174 (km378 from the west), although the village itself is at km177; the good new Imereti restaurant is just west of km180. At km183 the Kharagauli road joins the highway, and the railway soon appears from the valley to the southeast and cuts across a bend in the river through a new tunnel; to the north the traces of the old single-track railway can still be seen and could also be used for a hiking or mountain-biking route from km184. At km189 a road bridge leads right into the village of **Shorapani**, while the highway (lined with stalls selling engine oil) loops to the left; to the right you'll see a ruined castle, then an old steam locomotive (an 0-6-0 tank engine) on a plinth above rail sidings.

ZESTAPONI Another kilometre to the west, at km192, the road enters Zestaponi, a grimy industrial town at the junction to Chiatura and Sacchere. This town sits on one of the world's richest manganese deposits, perhaps 222 million tonnes; Bidzina Ivanishvili, who's worth about US$4 billion, also comes from here, so the towns are not in the state of total post-communist decline you might expect. Zestaponi's museum is closed and the hotel is full of refugees from Abkhazia. The transit route turns right over the first bridge crossing the Kviril River, while buses pick up and set down here, continue on the south bank, then take the second bridge and turn left to pass the rail station and a park (through a colonnade to the south). At the western end of town they head under the railway to the bus station at km195.5 (the end of the transit route), then pass the metallurgical works (which supplies 6% of the world's demand for ferroalloy and was bought in 2006 by the British company Stemcor) and finally leave the town at km199 (km353 from the west). At km203 the road passes the Cholaburi 'wholesale base' (signposted thus in English), like a small shopping mall, just before the turning north to Tqibuli and Racha (see pages 188–9); the new Khareba winery is just another kilometre west.

KUTAISI ქუთაისი

HISTORY Kutaisi dates from perhaps the 17th century BC and was established as a Greek colony by the 7th century BC; by the 3rd century BC it was capital of Colchida, and from AD978 to 1122 it was the capital of the united Georgia, Tbilisi being occupied by the Turks. It was again capital of Imereti from the late 15th century to 1810. Kutaisi was spared by the Mongols, but was burnt by the Turks in

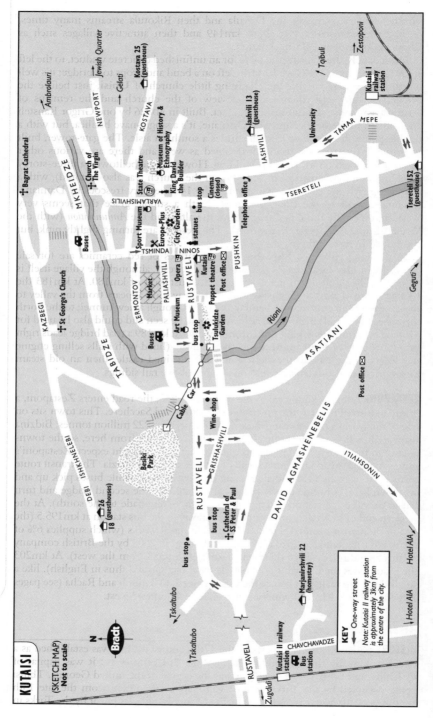

KUTAISI

(SKETCH MAP)
Not to scale

N

Bradt

KEY

➔ One-way street

Note: Kutaisi II railway station
is approximately 3km from
the centre of the city.

Besiki
Park

Rioni

Tskaltubo

Tskaltubo

Zugdidi

Debi Ishkhnelebi

26 (guesthouses)
18

Kutaisi II railway
station

Bus
station

CHAVCHAVADZE

RUSTAVELI

Marjanishvili 22
(homestay)

Cathedral of
SS Peter & Paul

bus stop

GRISHASHVILI

Wine shop

RUSTAVELI

DAVID AGMASHENEBELIS

NINOSHVILI

Hotel AIA

Hotel AIA

Cable Car

bus stop

Art Museum

Buses

St George's Church

KAZBEGI

TABIDZE

Market

LERMONTOV

PALIASHVILI

RUSTAVELI

Tsulukidze
Garden

bus stop

Opera

Kutaisi

NINOS

Puppet theatre

Post office

PUSHKIN

ASATIANI

Post office

Geguti

TSMINDA

Europe-Plus

City Garden

statues

Buses

MKHEIDZE

Bagrat Cathedral

VARLAMISHVILI

State Theatre

Church of
The Virgin

NEWPORT

Ambrolauri

Gelati

Jewish Quarter

KOSTAVA

Kostava 25
(guesthouse)

Museum of History &
Ethnography

King David
the Builder

Cinema
(closed)

Telephone office

bus stop

Sport Museum

TSERETELI

IASHVILI

University

TAMAR MEPE

Iashvili 13
(guesthouse)

Tereteli 152
(guesthouse)

Tqibuli

Zestaponi

Kutaisi I
railway
station

178

1510 and in 1666; they were driven out in 1770 by Solomon II, but he was in turn forced to abdicate by the Russians in 1810. Under communism it grew to be a city of 240,000, but its main employer, the Kamaz truck factory, has now closed.

GETTING THERE

By air Kopitnari airport is on the highway just west at km297, with the occasional flight to Moscow.

By bus At km223, after crossing a plateau covered with pine forest, long-distance buses turn left (on the E60, a road not clearly marked on the second edition of the ITM/ERKA map) to reach the Bagdati–Kutaisi road at km227.5 and turn right to cross the Rioni and directly reach the bus station of Kutaisi, 232km (142 miles) from Tbilisi. Local buses from Zestaponi (15 a day) carry straight on for 5km to enter the city to the north, terminating at the Kutaisi I railway station. There are also buses from here to Tqibuli (GEL2.50; 8 a day) and Terjola (GEL1.80; 6 a day); bus tickets are sold inside on the ground floor.

Other buses leave from the main bus station on Chavchavadze, 3km southwest of the centre. Buses for Tbilisi leave from bay 1 (at the west end, near the railway station), those for Zugdidi from bay 2, those for Poti from bays 2 and 3, those for Batumi from bay 4, and those for Samtredia from bay 5 (and, according to a sign, 'Transit busis' to Zugdidi, Poti, Batumi, Ozurgeti and Chiatura also stop nearby). Modern buses leave roughly hourly to Tbilisi (GEL10); there's a ticket kiosk on the platform.

From Kutaisi I railway station, turn right to walk 1km into the centre; from the bus station turn left then right up Rustaveli. Bus 1 links the two stations via the city centre, running every five minutes from 07.30 to 21.00 (GEL0.20); there are also slightly faster marshrutka minibuses (GEL0.30), but the regular buses are new and have more space and are particularly cheap here.

By train Kutaisi I is the main terminal for the daily trains to Tbilisi, as well as two trains a day to Sacchere. The Kutaisi II railway station is next to the main bus station, but only handles local trains to Tskaltubo (6 a day), Samtredia (2 a day), and a daily train to Batumi.

The only trains to Tbilisi consist of a couple of carriages trundled down to the main line at Rioni station and attached there to a through train; it's better to take a bus to Tbilisi, but if going to or from western Georgia you could use Rioni as a sort of parkway station. It's about 500m west of the road from Kutaisi to Bagdati, served by at least 25 buses a day.

➡ WHERE TO STAY

🏠 **Hotel Aia** Chavchavadze 10, just over 1km east of the bus station; ➍ 231 23676; ☎ 855 515770; e z_manduria@poola.ge. A comfortable new place that's handy for drivers in transit but is linked to the city centre by bus 1, trolley 8, & marshrutkas 5, 6, 18 & 22, which run up Asatiani to the centre & back on Ninoshvili. There's good Georgian food a 5min walk west at the Delikatessen restaurant, Chavchavadze 20. Dbl (with TV) GEL60, suite GEL150, plus GEL10 pp for b/fast.

🏠 **Hotel Europa** 10km west at a petrol station (at about km242/310). Also for drivers in transit.
🏠 **Hotel Kutaisi** (10 rooms) Rustaveli 5; ➍ 231 44277. Largely occupied by refugees from Abkhazia, 1 floor of this city-centre hotel is available for travellers. There's no food, no TV, & no English. It's a 1930s' block, in a fairly benign Stalinist style, with reception on the first landing; it's a bit tatty but friendly, & there's no hot water. Basic rooms sgl GEL15, twin GEL20, & 'luxe' rooms (ie: with cold shower) cost twice as much.

Private guesthouses This is the best option. Don't forget you can also ask taxi-drivers for cheap beds.

Gogelia guesthouse (3 rooms) Iashvili 13; ☎ 231 44842. Take the third left off Tamar Mepe (at No 38) & it's the first on the left after the junction above the oncology clinic. The door is a mess (to fool the taxman), but the interior is pleasantly bourgeois in style, with lovely guest & reception rooms. Only Georgian & Russian are spoken. GEL20 pp inc hot water.

Soso Bokhuchava (3 rooms) Tsereteli 152, near the Kutaisi I station (on the left at the end of a short alley; marshrutka 2, 3 or 12); ☎ 231 25550. 2 twin rooms & a trpl, with shared toilet & shower. The paint is peeling a bit, but the plasterwork is great. They're very friendly & Soso's grandchildren speak a little English. GEL25 pp, or GEL30 with food.

Zalimkhan's Guesthouse (12 rooms) Bagrationi 67 (near Soso Bokhuchava); ☎ 231 22441; m 899

554010. Clean compact light rooms with TV, shared bathrooms & excellent food. English spoken. GEL55 pp.

Lia's Guesthouse Kostava 25, near the Jewish quarter; ☎ 231 45012. Behind a grey gate & wall, this guesthouse has clean rooms with shared WC & shower, & huge luxe rooms with a poor bathroom. There does seem to be quite a bit of short-stay business here. GEL20 pp, luxe overpriced at GEL70–100.

Marjanishvili 22 This is the closest homestay to the bus station & is owned by Suselia Murtazi. From the right-hand end of the bus station, cross the main road with a moribund furniture shop on your right, go ahead & turn right following a line of poplars, & it's the second house on the left on the first real road to the left. GEL5 pp for a basic room with outside tap & toilet.

The nicest (but priciest) homestays are on Ukimerioni Hill just west of the Bagrat Cathedral, where large houses have secure parking & balconies with great views of the city.

Debi Ishkhnelebi 26 (5 rooms) ☎ 231 46923. They're very friendly & some English is spoken. 4 rooms are en suite. GEL30 pp inc dinner & b/fast.

Debi Ishkhnelebi 18 ☎ 231 48395. Lali

Jalaghiana has built a new wing here with nice big twin rooms with showers opposite (with solar water heating), but only Georgian & Russian are spoken. GEL30–40 pp inc 2 excellent meals.

✗ WHERE TO EAT The best restaurant in Kutaisi is the **Europe-Plus**, on Paliashvilis opposite the City Garden (it also offers a cocktail bar and beer bar). There's also Club **Al Mano** at Tsereteli 12 and the **Bistro** just around the corner on Davit Agmashenebelis Square, and a couple of pizza places between the university and Iashvili.

Otherwise the best nightlife in town, such as it is, is probably to be found across the river on Asatianis (formerly Tsulukidze); there are decent bars at the junctions with both Rustaveli and Grishashvili, and between them at Asatianis 16 is the '**Farm Store of the Kutaisi Wine Mill**', more a bar than a shop. Immediately south at No 18 is **El Dorado** bar, opposite the Farm Store is the **Dream** café/bar, and further south the boisterous owner of the **Argo** café-restaurant offers a limited choice of good home cooking and large carafes of homemade wine. Nearby at No 30 the **Sasauzme Khareba** is another acceptable bar, selling the produce of the Khareba winery. There are various good cafés on the east and south sides of the main square near the statue of King David the Builder, and another opposite the market steps on Paliashvilis serves good *khachapuri* and pastries in the daytime only. There are good pastries at **Nino's** on Tsminda Ninos near Paliashvilis, and the **Amberkasi I** bar is also nearby on Tsisperkantzela, at the rear of the opera; the nicer **Amberkasi 3** is below Europe Plus on Paliashvilis. There are also attractive cafés in the City Garden and at either end of the Tetri Khidi (White Bridge), by the Veriko Anjaparidze Garden. Nearby, just east of Tabakidze Park, the **Khakha** is a nice beer garden in a tranquil traffic-free location.

OTHER PRACTICALITIES The best place to **exchange money** is the bus station, where counters offer rates almost as good as in Tbilisi; there are **ATMs** at TBC

Bank (*behind the State Theatre at Davit Aghmashenebelis 2;* ☏ *231 30356–8*), United Georgia Bank (*well hidden at Paliashvilis 35*), Cartu Bank (*Paliashvilis 4*), Bank of Georgia (*Tseretelis 1*), Bank Republic (*Tamar Mepis 3*) and ProCredit Bank (*Tamar Mepis 85 and Chavchavadze 54*).

Internet access is available at Tseretelis 6 and Paliasihvilis 31. **DHL** have an office at Rustaveli 165.

Tbilavia is at Rustaveli 81 (☏ *231 43028*), a tiny Georgian Airways counter is nearby at Rustaveli 85, together with Georgian National Airlines and UM Air (for flights from Tbilisi and Batumi to Kiev, Ukraine). Flights can also be booked at the Air Agency on the stairs at the Hotel Kutaisi. At the moment the only flights to Kutaisi are from Moscow, but there's talk of flights to Syria too.

As for **entertainment**, the old cinema and the opera house are closed but the **Puppet Theatre** (*Sv Nino 11;* ☏ *45205*) is open and always popular with children, and there's a new cinema on Tsisperkantzela, south of Rustaveli in the centre. Kutaisoba, the annual city festival, is on or about 2 May.

A TOUR OF CENTRAL KUTAISI Rustaveli forms the main axis of the city, leading from the Zugdidi road to the city centre; there are plenty of buses, but if you walk from the junction by the bus station it'll take about 25 minutes to a square with a large block to the right. Behind this is the **Cathedral of Peter and Paul**, a Baroque pile built in 1901, with an outsized Baroque porch and a barrel dome; there are skulls and bones in a case in front of the iconostasis, and a big outdoor baptismal font.

The one-way system begins here, with inbound buses forking right, for no obvious reason, on to a rather over ambitious bus contraflow along Grishashvili; almost at once they rejoin Rustaveli Bridge to cross the river by a stone bridge built in the 1860s, which is flanked by two steel bridges dating from 1866 and 1872. Beneath the bridges, the limestone slabs from which the city derives its name are visible – '*kwata*' means stony.

To the left immediately before the river is a monument to Galaction Tabidze (the young poet being sent on his way by his muse) with the main marshrutka terminal opposite. To the right on the far bank of the river is the **Veriko Anjaparidze Garden**, laid out as a royal garden in the mid 17th century and now named after a famous actress; from its southern side a cable car ascends to the hilltop Besiki Park, where there's a small funfair and zoo. Next to it is the Tsulukidze Garden, a small sculpture park.

Continuing into the centre, the first building on the left is the **Art Museum** (*Rustaveli 8; open 10.00–18.00 except Sun*). Temporary shows are held downstairs, while the main collection is in one large room one flight up; this gives perhaps the best overview of Georgian art of any gallery in Georgia. Opposite the door are two large canvases by Elena Akhvlediani, with local hero David Kakabadze's *Imereti* in between. The seventh painting on this wall is by Lado Gudiashvili, of people in national dress celebrating the grape harvest. A painting of a man with a goat and firewood is by Robert Sturua, father of the famous theatre director. There are plenty of paintings of *My Imereti* and *The Seasons* as well as portraits of Vazha-Pshavelas, Ilia Chavchavadze, Rustaveli and Pirosmani, few if any done from life. See also the painting of a Svan village by the Svan Vladimir Margiani, and the last painting, to the right of the door, a portrait by Ketevan Maralashvili of the poet Titsian Tabidze, looking like Oscar Wilde with his red carnation and cigarette.

Just beyond the Art Museum on the right is the Classical Gymnasium (1902), the school attended by the poets Akaki Tsereteli (1840–1915) and Vladimir Mayakovsky (1893–1930), whose father, an impoverished Russian noble, worked as a forester in Bagdati, south of Kutaisi. Beyond this, at Rustaveli 5, is the Hotel

Kutaisi, and then a group of rather odd statues supposedly in praise of labour, although in fact one is also named *My Imereti*.

The centre of the city is the **City Garden**, a park full of trees where old men gather on benches and cafés serve the young. At its east end is Davit Agmashenebelis Square, dominated by a statue of **King David the Builder** (who was crowned and started his campaign of unification here) by Elgudja Amashukeli, Georgia's best-known monumental sculptor, which was unveiled by Shevardnadze during the 1995 election campaign.

North of this is the huge circular **Meskhishvili State Theatre** (*open for performances only*), and to the east the **Museum of History and Ethnography**, one of the best outside Tbilisi (*admission GEL2; open 10.00–17.00 except Mon; 11.00–16.00 in winter*). The Treasury (*admission GEL3 plus GEL10 for a guide*) contains some fantastic pieces of work, which unfortunately are not captioned; the guide is unlikely to speak anything other than Georgian and Russian. First come icons from Svaneti, including panels from a 10th-century altar cross, and 11th-century crosses from Racha and Motsameta. There's a small gold icon made at Motsameta during the reign of Queen Tamar, then a 13th-century icon of the Archangels from Kharagauli, another of Christ with Peter and Paul from the same period, and four pectoral crosses, set with pearls, turquoises and rubies, made in the 13th and 14th centuries. From the 15th or early 16th centuries there's an icon of an Archangel from Racha, another (very damaged) from northern Imereti, another of St George killing the pagan emperor Diocletian, and a gilded silver bible case. Items from the 16th century include a lovely gilded silver Madonna and Child produced in the Chedisi Desert Church in Racha, a pectoral icon owned by a Georgian ambassador to Russia, an icon of the Virgin and Child from Bichvinta (Pitsunda) in Abkhazia, a large icon of Christ teaching (produced in Gelati), panels from an altar cross from Barakoni in Racha, a bible cover from Nikortsminda, and a large icon of the Virgin and Child from Gelati produced in the 16th or 17th century. Next comes the large miraculous gold Paleostomi icon from Kutaisi's Bagrat Cathedral; some jewels were stolen by a Russian governor, and earrings were added as a replacement. Then there's a large winged icon from Gelati, the centre of which was made (of 3kg of gold) in the late 16th century, with the rest of gilded silver added in the 18th century (with portraits of Bagrat III and his wife). There are two 18th-century icons from Svaneti, and then 19th-century secular items such as travelling inkpots, buckles and daggers, as well as silverware belonging to the Dadiani family, rulers of Mingrelia.

The main exhibition begins by the front door with archaeology, with stone tools from the Lower Paleolithic and axeheads from the late Bronze Age onwards. There's a stone minotaur's head, found in Kutaisi, and a fertility god from Bagdati, with both breasts and phallus, produced some time between the 8th and 6th centuries BC, which is the museum's most famous exhibit. A seal bears a swastika, as a symbol of eternity. In the second room is jewellery from graves, ancient Greek ceramics, and *kvevri* or large urns used in Colchis for burying women – men were wrapped in leather and hung on trees. From early medieval times there are pieces of mosaic from the Bagrat Cathedral, dishes and weapons, with ceramics and frescoes from the churches at Vani on the staircase. Under the staircase is a good reproduction of an Imeretian peasant home.

Upstairs the displays include late medieval mail and weapons (showing a strong influence from the Islamic world), winemaking and hunting implements (including snowshoes), and a priest's punishment belt, bearing heavy crosses. There are more of Salome Dadiani's belongings, drawings by Castelli, a 17th-century Italian missionary who spent 27 years in Georgia, musical instruments, including bagpipes from Racha, a loom and national costumes, the first telephone used in Kutaisi, photos of 19th-century life, and a landau complete with a music box used for picnics.

Nearby, across the road to the west of the theatre, the **Kutaisi Sports Museum** seems to have shut up shop, which is a shame as it had surprisingly eclectic coverage, with insight into social context as well as the usual cases of medals. You might be lucky enough to find it open; a couple of doors down there's also a **Military Museum**, honouring the dead of World War II.

THE BAGRAT CATHEDRAL The city's great sight is the **Bagrat Cathedral**, which you'll see high on the Ukimerioni Hill across the river from the city centre; to reach it, head north on Tsminda Ninos (Saint Nino Street) from the west end of the City Garden. This leads past the market and across the river on a mock-suspension bridge to Mkheidze kucha; the terminal for buses to Racha is just to the right here, and steps from behind here (or a road further to the right) lead up to Kazbegi kucha and the cathedral site. There has been a fortress here since at least the 1st century AD; now there are remains from the 5th and 6th centuries, and late medieval fortifications. Occupied by the Turks, in 1769 it was bombarded by Solomon I and the Russian General Todleben from Mtsvane Kvavila. However, these are dwarfed by the Cathedral of the Assumption, commissioned by Bagrat III in 1003 (as recorded by the oldest Arabic numerals in Georgia), as a huge triconch cruciform church with a central dome. Later (although still in the first half of the 11th century) a portico was added to the west, with others to the north and south added in the 12th century. The cathedral was destroyed in 1691–92 by the Turks, since when it has been roofless and disused; however, UNESCO has placed it on its World Heritage List, and there has been talk of restoring it. The porches have been rebuilt, but the main church is untouched apart from hanging a few modern icons; there are traces of frescoes at the east end and over the north door. To the west on the same hill is **St George's Church**, built in the 19th century.

NORTHERN KUTAISI There are other interesting churches on the left bank of the Rioni, to the east of the centre; behind the State Theatre, Varlamishvilis (named after a local painter) leads to the **Church of the Annunciation of the Virgin**, rebuilt by French Roman Catholics around the start of the 20th century. It's a Georgian Orthodox church, with an interior that seems at odds with its Baroque exterior and Latin inscription. Further north (from the far side of the State Theatre) on Newport kucha (Mayakovsky kucha until it was named after Kutaisi's Welsh twin in 2000) is another attractive church, only a couple of centuries old; it's very compact, with single-bay aisles, lateral chapels and a high barrel dome. Finally, beyond the turning to Gelati, Newport kucha (formerly Jerusalem St) is the heart of what was the Jewish quarter, with three synagogues in the 19th century; in 1926 a tenth of the city's population was Jewish, and 5% of Georgia's Jews still live here. There are still two synagogues on Gaponov. On the hill above is the Mtsvane Kvavila (Green Flower) Monastery, with three churches including the 6th-century Church of the Archangels and a 17th-century church and belltower, as well as a pantheon that includes the grave of the composer Meliton Antonovich Balanchivadze (1862–1937), father of the choreographer George Balanchine. There's a good view back to the Bagrat Cathedral.

EXCURSIONS FROM KUTAISI

Gelati Wonderfully set in the hills just to the north of Kutaisi, the monastery of Gelati is one of the most beautiful spots in Georgia. Buses leave from the rear of the State Theatre in Kutaisi, although apart from summer weekends these are liable to leave you at the road junction 3km below the monastery, about 20 minutes from town.

Buses from Kutaisi I to Tqibuli also pass, although you're unlikely to get a seat if you board here heading north. A taxi will charge GEL15–25 for a combined trip to Gelati and Motsameta, including waiting time. You can stay in a very comfortable house in Gelati (*contact Maia;* m *899 926026*) with a lovely garden, for about GEL12 plus food.

The centrepiece is the great **Cathedral of the Virgin**, built by King David the Builder in 1106–25 (though in a style typical of the 11th century). The apses project to the east in a manner reminiscent of Abkhazian churches such as Bichvinta (Georgian churches usually have a flat east end). The narthex was added to the western end later in the 12th century, followed by chapels to the south in the 13th century and to the north in the late 13th or early 14th century. Burnt by the Turks in 1510, and by the Lesghians (from the north Caucasus) in 1579, it was restored, then closed under communism, and reopened in 1988.

The interior is full of light, and painted in fantastic colours (although a blue background is unusual in Georgian churches). The cupola, supported by the walls of the apse to the east and two free-standing columns to the west, bears a fresco of Christ Pantocrater, and on the spandrels the four evangelists were painted by Tevdore in the 17th century; the narthex was decorated with paintings in the first half of the 12th century. The south transept was painted in 1291–93 and in the 16th and 17th centuries, with portraits of King David the Builder (haloed and holding the church), Bagrat III and Giorgi II (both kings of western Georgia) and, across the corner from David, the Emperor Constantine and his wife Helena; above these is a fresco of Palm Sunday and above this, between the windows, the two saints Theodore. The north transept was painted in the 17th century – note in particular the *Death of the Virgin*, below saints George and Dmitri. Above the west door you'll see Pontius Pilate washing his hands, and Judas hanging himself.

However, the pride of the church (and one of Georgia's greatest works of art) is a remarkable mosaic (containing 2.5 million stones) in the apse, of the Virgin and Child with the Archangels Michael and Gabriel; created in the 1130s in a Byzantine style with specifically Georgian features, it was damaged by earthquakes later in the same century and subsequently; the lower half was restored by painting – although this is often denounced as communist vandalism, it seems that it was genuinely impossible to restore it as mosaic.

Outside, the belfry stands to the southwest, built over a spring in the second half of the 13th century. Next to this is the Church of St Nicholas, one of the oddest in design in Georgia; also built in the 13th century, it's a two-storeyed construction that looks rather like an English market cross, with the church above an arcade in which you can see a section of tree trunk once intended for use as a coffin. Beyond this, to the west looking out over the valley (in good weather it's possible to see to the Black Sea), are the remains of the buildings erected in 1106 by King David to house the academy of neo-Platonist metaphysical philosophy under Ioanne Petrisi; the portico, with four different types of column, was added in the 13th century. To the left is the south gate, built early in the 12th century; when King David died in 1125 he was buried as requested in the centre of the gateway, where churchgoers would walk over him and remember him for ever: an interesting way of combining self-abasement with a bit of egotism. The battered iron gate was made in 1063 in the Persian city of Ganja (now in Azerbaijan, on the main Tbilisi–Baku highway) and brought back by David's son Demetre I in 1129 from a campaign against the Persians. Finally, to the east between the cathedral and the present main gateway stands the Church of St George, built in the mid 13th century, burned in 1510, and restored and painted in the 16th and 17th centuries. It tends to be shut except at weekends, when weddings are often held here.

From the gateway the road continues steeply into the trees; turning right near the top you can walk to a viewpoint overlooking Gelati and the valley beyond; in the hills to the south are two further small churches, St Saba and St Elijah, a pleasant 20-minute walk.

Motsameta Slightly closer to Kutaisi (get off the Tqibuli bus at the police post 6km from the city, and go 3km to the right) is Motsameta monastery. It's smaller and quieter than Gelati, although its cliff-edge setting is more spectacular by far. It commemorates the brothers David and Constantine Mkheidze, killed by Arabs in the 720s for refusing to convert to Islam and thrown into the gorge here. They are now saints, with their skulls in a casket behind the red velvet curtain, and your wish will be granted if you crawl three times under their tomb, set on two lions on the south side of the church, without touching it. The monastery was founded in the 8th century, but the present church and belltower were built by Bagrat III in the 11th century; the frescoes were destroyed by the Bolsheviks. To the left of the gatehouse is a steep path down to the river, which makes this a very popular excursion in summer, when Kutaisi swelters.

Tskaltubo A dozen kilometres northwest.of Kutaisi, Tskaltubo is a spa where mildly radioactive water at an average 15°C is used to treat arthritis, rheumatism, polio, and fertility problems. In Soviet times none of the hotels in Kutaisi were open to Westerners, and they had to stay out here; the hotels and sanatoria were taken over by refugees from Abkhazia, so now you have to stay in Kutaisi and come here for a day trip. Marshrutka 22 runs from the junction of Chavchavadze and Rustaveli, near the bus station, passing through an area of low pines where wild camping would be possible. After 15 minutes you'll enter the spa, passing the station (served by a few trains a day from Kutaisi II) and a large park dotted with pines that's very attractive to the south but more unkempt as you get to the centre. The town is spacious and fairly modern with little to see; you can ask to try the waters at the big Stalinesque sanatorium. It's of more interest to cavers, the Kumistavi Cave, 7km from Tskaltubo, having been found only in 1983. It's 1.5km long and 145m deep, with 15 chambers, and a river (with waterfalls) runs through it; there are also ten–12 species of bats living here.

Geguti and Vartsikhe From Kutaisi's main bus station, buses leave from bay 12 at 10.00, 12.00, 14.00, 15.40 and 18.00 and marshrutkas (GEL1) from the northeast side of the bus station for **Geguti**, about 7km south in the plains of the Rioni, known in classical times as the Phasis. This gave its scientific name, *Phasianus colchicus*, to the pheasant, which was discovered here, perhaps by Jason. Geguti is the site of the great ruined palace of the Georgian kings, one of the few secular buildings left in Georgia from medieval times. Now it's a jumble of ruins covering 2,000m², set on a plinth 2.5m high housing heating conduits; you may be able to identify the large fireplace of the 8th-century hunting lodge, as well as one shattered arch of the 14m-wide dome of the 10th-century hall, and other ruins from the 12th and 13th centuries, including a church. The royal chambers are to the southwest, the treasury to the southeast, and the church and bath house to the northwest. In 1179 George III proclaimed his daughter Tamar his co-ruler here, and in 1360 David VII died here; later it fell into disuse and was destroyed in the 17th century. Arriving by bus, get off at the Restaurant Venezia (on the left) 1.5km from the village of Geguti, and walk up the paved road to the left for five minutes to the end where a series of unlocked gates on the right lead to the 'castle', which does look a bit like a tumble-down Tudor manor house.

Marshrutka 211 continues south to a dam across the Rioni, on the south side of which is **Vartsikhe**, once the Greek fortress of Rodopolis; from the lane leading to the Geguti 'castle' you can follow a farm track for 1.5km then turn left on the road about 3km short of the dam. It's a dull walk, although buses are barely faster due to the lunar road surface. From the dam it's another kilometre on to Vartsikhe, but the ruins are on the left immediately after the dam. There's not a lot to see, just 100m of ancient wall, some partially rebuilt, and another chunk of wall in a cemetery behind, by a small church. The fortress dates from the 4th–6th centuries, with a royal residence built here in the 9th–11th centuries. Vartsikhe is also known for its brandy. From the village it's 100m to the main road, where you can pick up buses between Kutaisi (to the left) and Vani (see below).

Vani On the far side of the Rioni, Vani is reached by 14 buses (GEL2) a day from bay 9, the last leaving at 19.00 from Kutaisi and 15.00 from Vani. It's also possible to go via Bagdati (10 buses a day from bay 9), on the main road to Akhaltsikhe (via Sairme, known for its mineral waters), although there's now little trace of one of the 20th century's greatest poets, Vladimir Mayakovsky (1893–1930), who grew up here.

Beyond the Technical University the road follows the left bank of the Rioni, through beautiful oak forest, which forms part of the Adjameti Nature Reserve, and passes 500m east of the Rioni railway station. After 15km Vani buses turn right off the Bagdati road at a police post on to one of the very worst roads in Georgia, and after 2km (30 minutes from Kutaisi) pass Vartsikhe (see above). It's 7km to the road from Bagdati, after which the surface is marginally better, but after 1 hour 20 minutes you'll be glad to reach Vani, where there's a big market opposite the bus station. There's a much better road to the west, with marshrutkas taking under an hour to reach Samtredia, which, however, is a town you don't really want to have to spend the night in (see page 190).

Cross the bridge over the river Sulori and the square beyond, and follow the sign (in English) to the 'Archeological Excavations'. You'll see the very obvious large **museum** (*admission GEL2; open 10.00–17.00 except Mon*) on the hillside ahead, although it takes about ten minutes to reach it, winding up Gorgasali; go under the footbridge and up the steps to the right to the entrance. Vani, known to the Greeks as Surium, was a major centre from the 8th to 1st centuries BC (at its peak from

600–400BC), and many of the finest artefacts from ancient Colchis were found here. The best are all in the Treasury of the National Museum in Tbilisi, but there are replicas here, as well as fine original pieces; what's more, captions are in English. By 1876 it was known that rain revealed gold objects on the hillsides here, and excavations began in the 1890s, with further work in the 1930s, from 1947 to 1963, and now under Otar Lordkipanidze, member of a well-known political family.

The ground-floor displays are mostly of weapons and tools, and the oldest and finest pieces are up in the gallery. In the 7th and 6th centuries BC gold jewellery by superb craftsmen was buried with nobles, together with fine ceramics from the 6th to 4th centuries BC. From the 4th century BC on burials were in *kvevri* (clay vessels or *pithoi*), making it easier to conserve the contents, which now included Greek imports from Sinope. By 100BC foundries were casting bronze statues; on the gallery there's a fine torso of a youth, in front of a small treasury of beautiful gold ornaments and lots of tiny silver coins from the 3rd century BC. Across the footbridge is a small area of ruins, including city walls and sanctuaries; a few are covered, but visitors can clamber over the rest. There's a fine view north to Kutaisi and the High Caucasus, with attractive wooded hills to the south.

It's also possible to visit the house of **Galaction Tabidze** (1892–1959), one of Georgia's finest and best-loved poets, near the Rioni in Ckhovishe, about 4km north of Shuamta, on the main road about 3km west of Vani. It's a simple cottage with little on view; what's more, the replica of Jason's ship, the *Argo*, which Tim Severin sailed here from Greece in 1984 and was on display, has been burnt! However, it's worth coming here on Galaction's birthday, 17 November, when there's always a celebration (followed on 23 November by Giorgoba – a good time to visit Georgia!).

Sataplia

Just 6km northwest of Kutaisi in the 2,000-year-old Kolkhuri Forest is Mount Sataplia (Honey Mountain), a forested area in which a cave 300m in length (up to 10m high and 12m wide) and full of stalagmites was discovered in 1925 by Peter Chabukiani, a Kutaisi teacher. There are in all five karst caves here, although only the largest is open to visitors; in addition about 200 footprints of dinosaurs have been preserved in Cretaceous limestone (120 million years old). This is said to be the only place where prints of both carnivorous and herbivorous dinosaurs are preserved together, although they are separated in time by several thousand years. They have suffered from tourism, and although Sataplia has been protected as a reserve since 1935, it's mainly seen as an excursion for the people of Kutaisi rather than as being of any great scientific value. However, the Regional Union of Scientists has established an EcoSchool here, to teach environmental awareness to the pupils of the city's elementary schools. The reserve covers 354ha, on the slopes of Mount Sataplia (494m) and Mount Tsinara (520m), with a humid subtropical climate (with an annual average of 1,380mm precipitation). Nevertheless, the average temperature in January is as low as −5°C, and 24°C in August, with an annual average of 14.5°C.

However, the reserve is of interest, as 95% of its area is covered with Colchic forest, where 544 species of flora have been recorded (66 of them trees and bushes). These include hornbeam, alder, box, chestnut, beech, ilex, medlar, ivy, rhododendron, bilberry and blackberry. There are small mammals such as moles, hedgehogs, hares, foxes, jackals and badgers, and birds such as larks, goldfinches, tits, jays, woodpeckers, hawks, sparrowhawks, cuckoos and hoopoes; the bees that produced the plentiful honey that gave the mountain its name are now few in number.

To reach Sataplia, take a bus towards Gumbra from the Paliashvili Bridge by Kutaisi Market; entry costs GEL4.

RACHA

Immediately to the north of Kutaisi is the small province of Racha (or Racha-Lekhumi), along the upper reaches of the Rioni river. Hemmed in by mountains up to 3,600m, it's a beautiful area which is mild enough in summer to produce both wine and tea, but so harsh in winter that most of the population move temporarily to the lowlands. The people are known for their strong traditional culture, with superb icons and honey and a unique genre of bagpipe music. Racha is also becoming known as a great venue for adventure tourism. The main road runs from Kutaisi along the Rioni past Ambrolauri, the chief town of Racha, to Oni, and then over a pass (open all year) to Tskhinvali, capital of South Ossetia, and Gori. From Oni the Ossetian Military Highway climbs to the summer-only Mamison Pass (2,820m), which you should not use to enter the Russian Federation.

Buses from Kutaisi to Ambrolauri leave from the minor bus terminal on Mkheidze, below the Bagrat Cathedral, at 10.00 and 14.00 daily, returning at 13.00 and 17.00.

Heading north along the right/west bank of the Rioni, you'll soon pass the **Kutaisi Botanical Garden**, now very run-down, and the **Gumat Dam**, a typical Soviet hydro-electric scheme of the 1930s; 25km from Kutaisi the road enters a fine limestone gorge, emerging before the village of **Mekvena** (km36) where a side road crosses to the left bank. The next village, **Tvisi**, known for its white wine, lies below high cliffs on which you can see vertical lines caused by logged trees being slid down the slopes.

At km54.5 (two hours from Kutaisi, on a pretty rough road), a road turns left to **Lajanauri**, known for its hydro-electric dam; this continues over a pass and joins the Tskaltubo–Lentekhi road. **Lentekhi**, at 800m, is nothing but a village, with the late-medieval ruins of a Dadiani palace, but it is the capital of Kvemo (Lower) Svaneti; this is far lower than Svaneti proper and has far less of interest to visitors. The only old churches are a couple dating from the 10th century just north of Zachunderi, from where a very rough track continues over the 2,623m Zagar Pass (open only June–October) into Upper Svaneti. Buses to Lentekhi leave three times a day from bay 14 of Kutaisi's main bus station, and take four hours.

Continuing up the Rioni from this junction, you enter Racha; the first village, across a bridge to the right, is **Zeda-Gvardia**, known for its large caves. In fact the whole of Racha is a caver's paradise, and two caves 5km long were discovered in 2001. At km74 the road enters the district of Kvanchkhara, known for its wine, which everyone will proudly tell you was Stalin's favourite. Now the valley opens up and the road improves, and it's not long before you see the modern sprawl of **Ambrolauri** on the far side of the river, 14km from Kvanchkara (and three hours from Kutaisi).

You can also get here by taking a bus to Tqibuli then marshrutkas via Nikortsminda (see opposite). It's still little more than a village, with a small daily market opposite the bus station and few other services. If you continue up the right bank of the side stream you'll pass a defensive tower, similar to those of Svaneti. You'll reach a T-junction in five minutes: to the left is the main square with the council building, a bank (without ATM), and (on the left) the largely derelict schools. To the right a bridge crosses cascades by a former watermill; there's a café in a former metro carriage, of all things, but nothing else other than houses on this side of the river. On the south bank of the Rioni 12km west of Ambrolauri is the 14th–15th-century hall church of Bugeuli.

Continuing eastwards up the Rioni, the next village (15km from Ambrolauri) is **Chesi**, where you'll see the Mindatsikhe castle and the Barakoni church, a cruciform dome church built in 1753. Beyond this lies **Oni**, at the junction of the routes to North and South Ossetia. There are no buses, but taxis charge just GEL4 from Ambrolauri. Oni is famed as a stronghold of the mountain Jews, living in isolation here for 2,000 years or more; the community has largely vanished to Israel, but there is still a synagogue on Vakhtang VI. The museum is closed due to earthquake damage, and its treasures are in the Kutaisi Museum. There's a homestay at Davit Agmashenebelis 29, run by Eka Beridze (m *899 157638*); she doesn't speak much English but is here all year.

A very lovely road, lined with mineral springs, leads northeast into the Caucasus for 25km past **Utsera** (where there are beds at the Fazisi sanatorium) to **Glola**, site of another of Tamar's castles. **Shovi**, a few kilometres east of Glola, was a popular resort in Soviet times, but now there are only a few fine villas and some moribund blocks set about a lovely meadow. The Pansionat Rachi and Turbasa Shovi offer basic rooms, and better accommodation should soon be available. Just beyond is the Mamison Pass into North Ossetia, which is closed to foreigners. A rough track leads northwest up the Rioni Valley from west of Glola to **Chiora** and **Ghebi**, a large lively village surrounded by glaciers, from where you can hike to the turquoise Sasvano tarns.

There's also a very bad road east from Oni to Tskhinvali in South Ossetia, which is presently closed; when it reopens, there'll still be no public transport, but it's easiest to travel on Sunday and Thursday with people returning from Oni market.

NIKORTSMINDA By far the greatest attraction of Racha is 15km to the south of Ambrolauri, at Nikortsminda, where there's a beautifully decorated little church set on a hillock on the edge of the village. Buses run several times a day from Ambrolauri, crossing the bridge south from the bus station and labouring up a modernised road to reach the village on a high limestone plateau; it's also possible to come directly from Kutaisi, taking a bus past Gelati to the logging town of Tqibuli and continuing by marshrutka on the Ambrolauri road up a winding road to a pass (a great spot for advanced paragliders) and past the Sauris Reservoir to Nikortsminda, 40km and 50 minutes from Tqibuli.

Just down a lane to the east of the bus stop, the Church of St Nicholas is built of mellow golden stone reminiscent of Somerset or the Cotswolds. It was built by Bagrat III in 1010–14 on a tight and tidy hexagonal internal ground plan; this was slightly spoiled in the mid 11th century by the addition of porches to the west and south, and a chapel to the south, which has a curved west end and Romanesque-style round arches. There was a porch to the north, but this has gone (there's a wooden pole in the way instead). None of this has interfered with the external carvings on all four façades. The finest is a figure of Christ on the north wall, above three perfectly proportioned blind arches. Inside, the hexagonal plan produces six apses radiating from the centre (instead of the usual four in the shape of a cross) which are all identical except that the eastern one (above the very simple blue-painted iconostasis) is marginally longer, and the western one leads into the porch. The dome is set on a splendid drum without squinches, pierced by 12 slim windows with finely carved architraves. The interior was fully painted in the 16th and 17th centuries, with the life of Christ (starting with the Nativity to the right of the entrance, together with a modern icon of the church's patron, St Nicholas) and portraits of local notables. The Annunciation is over the arch of the eastern apse, with Christ in Majesty beyond that; see also the wooden model church incorporated into the altar. The detached belltower, with its fireplace and spiral staircase, was added in the second half of the 19th century. Ask for the church key at the house with the two-storey glass front through the blue gate to the north of the church. It's half an hour downhill to Ambrolauri past the Khotevi Castle and Church of the Archangels at about km37/67. There are also great mountain views to the west and northeast.

The main highway westward leaves Kutaisi by the bridge over the railway next to the bus station and Kutaisi II railway station; at km254.5 it passes the turning to the left to Kopitnari Airport, and rejoins the Rioni at **Samtredia**, an industrial town where the bus station is a few hundred metres west of the railway station.

Going straight ahead from the station to the end of the pedestrianised street and turning right, the Hotel Samtredia is the obvious semi-highrise on the left; it's really pretty rough, inhabited by refugees from Abkhazia but with a few rooms available for GEL15, with water available only in a jug. Still, a towel and toilet paper are provided, and the staff are trying hard. It's better to try to reach one of the Turkish truck stops on the main highway, a couple of kilometres east at km 291/261, or the TirPark Hotel at a petrol station a little further west. There is a simple restaurant to the left/west at the end of the pedestrianised street, and an ATM at Rustaveli 28, at the railway offices.

Virtually all traffic into town uses the bridge about 500m east of the station, with vehicles heading west performing hazardous U-turns at the bottom; not an ideal spot to flag down marshrutkas but still feasible. This is a major road and rail junction; traffic to Batumi turns left/south here to cross the Rioni, while traffic to Poti and Zugdidi continues west and then northwest. This road is lined with long thin villages, each merging into the next, and each house has a garden full of citrus trees and a water tank on a tower (spot the polyhedral one painted like a football).

From Abasha (km280) a road leads 34km north to **Martvili**, where there's an interesting late-10th-century cruciform church and another from the first half of the 7th century; the railway and bus stations are 200m west of the junction, by a huge ugly monument.

Senaki is another industrial town and the rail junction for Poti. Entering from the east, the highway crosses the Tekhura River (at km292/260) and the railway, then bypasses the town to the south; buses turn off to cross back over the railway on a level crossing, then head down the old main road past the barracks where the 1998 mutiny began. In the centre they turn left to reach the rail and bus stations, then loop back over the railway by another level crossing, and stop again immediately across the tracks from the bus station; so if your bus appears to have left early, dash across the tracks and enquire at the ticket kiosk here; through buses and minibuses also stop here. The road junction to Poti is at about km301.5/250.5, 6km west of Senaki; from here it's 30km to Poti or 35km to Zugdidi.

About 18km northeast of Senaki (half an hour by bus towards Martvili) are the ruins of **Nokalakevi**, capital of Egrisi (Lazica) from the 4th to 8th centuries. In AD542–555 Shah Khusro I (and his famous general Mermeroes and his elephants) failed to capture the city; but in 737 it was destroyed by the Arabs and remained in ruins until the first excavations in the 1930s by the German Alfons Maria Schneider, continued since 1973 by the National Museum, with the help of Cambridge University since 2001. Known to the Greeks as Archaeopolis (Old City), it's also been known as Tsikhegoji and Dzicha (Tsikhe and Dzicha meaning 'castle' in Georgian and Mingrelian respectively).

On a hill to the left a few kilometres north of Senaki you'll see the ruins of Shkhepi (part of a chain of signal posts from the Black Sea, and a pleasant jaunt) and continue on a reasonable road through two villages, before reaching a museum and the gates of the ancient city to the left immediately after the bridge over the Tekhuri River. The archaeological site has now been fenced and there will probably be a fee of a couple of lari from 2007. In the museum (*open 10.00–16.00 except Mon*), the first room on the left upstairs displays relics from the 8th to 1st centuries BC, including ritual clay animals, silver and bronze bracelets (there were gold ones too, now in Tbilisi) and Greek ceramics, attesting to trade links across the Black Sea; to the right are *pithoi* (funerary urns) from the 4th to 1st centuries BC, and replica coins, agricultural implements, weapons (sling and catapult stones, and arrow- and spearheads), and pipes from a 'calorifer' (underfloor steam heating), as well as a few ceramic pieces from the 6th to 18th centuries AD.

The ruins are entered by a right-angled trap area and a gateway through a massive triple wall; the outer wall, of big blocks, was built in the 6th century AD, and the next two, of smaller stones, date from the 5th and 4th centuries. The walls enclose an area of 20ha including a 4th/5th-century citadel and two churches on the mountain behind. There is also a couple of modern houses, with beehives, inside the walls; you'll also see a gatehouse with external stairs and the church of the 40 Martyrs of Cappadocia (with tatty remains of frescoes, mostly hidden by a new iconostasis), both from the 6th century. Next to the church are the ruins of a tiny palace and the foundations of an older basilica, with those of a third church just to the west.

Beyond a house a tiny path leads up to a fort on a hill (as opposed to the citadel, higher up and reached by a jeep track to the north, a pleasant walk of an hour or so each way); at the northern end of a very solid 19th-century girder bridge (for pedestrians and bikes only) across the river are the remains of a 5th-century bath house (with three rooms for three different temperatures, and red ceramic heating elements). As in most Georgian forts, there's a tunnel down to the river, to get water during a siege. On the far side of the river is a popular, if stony, beach, and a road leading up into a dramatic gorge with popular hot springs a kilometre or two along. It's possible to stay at the archaeological base if it's not full, or Aleko Janjgava has a homestay.

At km311 the Zugdidi road crosses the river Khobi, and soon reaches the bus station of **Khobi**, opposite a massive sculpture of the sun, moon and stars, just east of a theatre with a matching sculpted frieze along its front and fly-tower. Buses from Batumi and Poti to Zugdidi join the road from Senaki here; a couple of kilometres north across the railway are the ruins of Khobi monastery, founded in AD554, and a church which dates from the 12th and 13th centuries, as well as medieval walls and a belltower.

ZUGDIDI

ZUGDIDI It's just over 100km from Kutaisi to Zugdidi (322km from Tbilisi), a city of 51,000 plus, at present, about 72,000 refugees from the neighbouring Gali district of Abkhazia. It's full of men standing around with nothing to do, as well as plenty of soldiers, police and aid workers; not exactly threatening, but nevertheless at present there's no reason to linger overnight. It's the capital of Mingrelia or Samegrelo, a province which has always gone its own way; it was ruled by the Dadiani family from 1046 at the latest until 1857 (paying tribute to the Turks from the 1460s until 1774, and nominally under Georgian rule at other times), and is now the stronghold of the Zviadists (supporters of the ousted president Gamsakhurdia) and of the nationalists who want a military assault on Abkhazia.

The main square, Zviad Gamsakhurdias Gamziri, is not unattractive; long and thin it has trees in the centre and a few cafés and bars. Buses go three-quarters of the way around the square to continue on Rustaveli, the bad main road westwards, past a market and so-called trade centre, bustling with traders heading for the de facto border with Abkhazia, just a few kilometres further west. To the northwest of the bridge you'll see a Svan defensive tower, built in the communist period to mark a Svan restaurant.

The main bus terminal is 400m west, at the railway station (reached by bus 1); tickets are sold in the hall opposite the railway ticket office. There are regular minibuses to Kutaisi, Poti and Batumi, and some to Tbilisi (as well as buses to

Moscow). There may be a bus or minibus for Mestia here but there's more likely to be something in the area by the Svan tower, where jeeps heading up to Svaneti wait for passengers (and your passport details will be noted).

Heading northwards along the length of the main square, past the Diadema Restaurant, a school to the left and a stadium to the right, you'll come in a couple of minutes to a park (with steps down towards the Svan tower to the left) on the far side of which is the neogothic palace of the Dadiani family, rulers of Mingrelia, until the Russians finally took over in 1857; it's now a museum (*admission GEL5; GEL1 for Georgians*).

Alexander Chavchavadze's daughter Katarina (sister-in-law of the playwright Griboedov) married David Dadiani, the last prince of Mingrelia (although the poet Nikoloz Baratashvili was in love with her); their daughter Salome was the god-daughter of Catherine the Great and married Achille Murat, grandson of Marshal Murat and Napoleon's sister Caroline. Thus one of Napoleon's three death masks has ended up here, together with other bits and pieces of Bonapartiana. The palace was built in the 17th century and extended in the 19th century; it became a museum in 1921. Together with the relics of Napoleon and the Dadianis, it also houses a notable collection of Colchian gold and silver coins. To the side are the small Church of the Icon of the Mother of God (built in 1838), with a bare interior and unusual semi-circular sides to the porch so that its ground plan is a circle in a cross plan. The chasuble of the Mother of God, brought from Jerusalem to Khobi's Monastery of the Dormition, and now in the museum, is taken in procession to the church on 7 July.

Just beyond are the Botanical Gardens established in 1840 by Katarina Dadiani, complete with picturesque ruin, which are free and make a nice spot for a stroll, especially in spring.

Where to stay

🏠 **Hotel Zugdidi** (14 rooms, 1 suite) Kostava 5A (the first left off Rustaveli, ie: just a block from the square); ☎ 215 54242; f 215 50001. All rooms have clean en-suite facilities with TV (not cable), hot water & towels, & there's a good little café-bar. Still, it's pretty over-priced. *GEL50 for a dbl inc b/fast, or GEL70 for the 2-room AC suite.*

🏠 **Sasha Toloraia** Pushkin 60; tel 215 52646; m 893 993679. This is a homestay in a huge mansion with sky-high ceilings. Amazingly, the owners seem to have a notion of privacy. *GEL20 pp (up to 10 guests) inc b/fast.*

Other practicalities The Bank of Georgia has an **ATM** opposite the Hotel Kugdidi at Kostava 6, and there are others on the square at Tabukashishvilis 1 and Zviad Gamsakhurdias 34. There's an **internet** café at Rustaveli 88 (GEL1 per hr), and the good new Atrium **cinema** is at Rustaveli 28.

It's not wise at present to continue along the main road towards Abkhazia, but when the situation is normalised again, it may be worth stopping in the village of Rukhi, where a fortress dominating the Inguri crossing dates from 1636.

POTI

From the road junction 6km west of Senaki, it's 30km to Poti and another 82km to Batumi. Poti was founded by the Greeks (as Phasis) and was re-established as a Turkish fort, which was the hub of the trade in Circassian slave-girls, the most highly prized in the Ottoman Empire. Development of the modern port began in 1858 and was boosted by the arrival of the Transcaucasian Railway in 1872. Nowadays it is Georgia's largest port, with a capacity of 5–6 million tonnes a year, largely containerised; a train-ferry terminal opened in 1999, to link Poti with Ilyichevsk (near Odessa, Ukraine) and Varna (Bulgaria). The Korean Hyundai Group took a 99% share of the shipbuilding yard, and the port itself has also been privatised.

It's a city of 50,000 people; unattractive and without much to see, it does offer a couple of comfortable places to stay. It's the base for the Kolkheti National Park (see below) whose headquarters and visitor centre are at Guria 222, south of town.

Crossing the bridge just south of the station to the big equestrian statue of Tsotne Dadiani (who led an uprising against the Mongols and was killed by being coated with honey and left to be eaten by insects), you'll find the market (and exchange stalls) immediately on your right, beyond a decent café-bar.

Turn right (westwards) past the market, and you'll reach the **cathedral**. Built in 1906–07 and based on Haghia Sophia in Istanbul, it was a theatre under communism and is now being restored as a church.

Heading north from the cathedral, you'll cross the river and pass the new building of the National Bank of Georgia (there's no ATM) and the grotesque new courthouse; Davit Agmashenebelis leads north past fine buildings built around the turn of the 20th century, of which a surprising number are now being refurbished and repainted; a stadium and lighthouse are visible to the left.

Eventually the road crosses a smelly channel to a roundabout. On the north side of the roundabout are statues of Alexandre Dumas the elder (the French writer, who arrived here) and Niko Nikoladze (the five-term Mayor of Poti from 1894 to 1912 who rebuilt the port and city). The road swings left to reach the port in around 200m; there's a big modern grey ferry terminal, and a small chapel. Immediately north of the terminal is the yacht club, with electricity, water and fuel available for yachts, and shower, sauna and café terrace for their crews; it also organises races and other events.

GETTING THERE There are day trains from Tbilisi and Kutaisi plus an overnight train from Tbilisi. Buses and marshrutkas for Tbilisi (09.00, 11.00 and 15.00), Batumi (hourly), Kutaisi, Senaki and Zugdidi wait at the market (the bus station, west of the train station, is closed).

⌂ WHERE TO STAY

⌂ **Hotel Kolkheti** (no tel) Kostava 2, turn right from the station to follow the river for about 800m to the bridge facing the cathedral. It's a typically run-down, turn-of-the-20th-century pile, housing refugees from Abkhazia but with some spare rooms. Administration is one flight upstairs & to the right in room 218. There's only cold water in jugs. *Sgl GEL30, or GEL10 if you allow someone to share the connecting room.*

⌂ **Hotel Anchor** (24 rooms) Gegidze 90, just to the right from the roundabout; ☎ 293 26000, 293 25305–7; f 293 24600. A good, modern hotel with AC, cable TV with good Grundig sets & a nice restaurant. English is spoken at reception, & they'll exchange US dollars. *Sgl GEL100, twin GEL120, suites GEL200.*

✕ WHERE TO EAT

✕ **Café Argo** Across a grassy square (now being built on) from Hotel Kolkheti. Offers dishes such as 'Veal Prepared by Reception of Sofie Loran'.

✕ **Café Bon Appetit** Just to the east of Hotel Anchor.

There are a few half-decent restaurants on Davit Agmashenebelis (the Bistro, really just a bar, the Asteroid, Aristokrat Café and Fazisi).

OTHER PRACTICALITIES There are **banks** with ATMs on Davit Agmashebelis, including TBC at No 22, IntellectBank at No 30, Peoples Bank at No 49 and ProCredit Bank at No 50

The city is clearly increasingly used to foreign visitors, with groceries for instance now signed in English and street names translated. There's an **internet** café at Kostava 5, which is slow and full of noisy kids; there's also internet access next door in the DHL office (*open Mon–Fri 09.30–18.00*), both charging GEL3 per hour.

MALTAKVA On the far side of the Hotel Kolkhida, Rustaveli leads past a park with various statues, fountains, dodgems and an unserviceable Ferris wheel, and continues (as Mshvidoba) to the sea; it's possible to walk south along the dirty grey beach for 3km to the Maltakva resort area, an impressively Modernist complex, built to hold water-skiing championships on the so-called Golden Lake. It's easier to follow the Batumi road, either from the statue or by taking Akaki, the fourth turning to the left from the Hotel Kolkhida, and then after about 1km turning right past a cemetery. Behind it is Lake Paleostomi, where you can see plenty of birds in season. In the migration seasons and in winter this is black with waterfowl, although there's little to see at other times. Under communism it was linked to the sea by an artificial channel, the Kapartcha River, and the changes in water level are causing major environmental problems; expansion of Poti port and the new Khulevi port to the north may cause further damage. From here it's 2.5km south to the national park headquarters and another 1km to the Maltakva turning.

Marshrutka 5 runs this way, mostly terminating 500m north of the Maltakva turning. You can walk through a turnstile to the right just south of this terminal, or take a road from km82/39 (opposite a large ugly monument of Jason holding the Golden Fleece, and an English sign to Maltakva). This leads through a pine wood and then after 200m right to the complex; from the beach you should turn inland at a half-built hotel isolated by the sea and cross a long, modern rusty-coloured footbridge. The water-skiing ramp is still there in the lake, but the spectator facilities are all derelict.

Where to stay

🏠 **Casino Golden Lake Hotel** Just before the footbridge; ✆ 293 21422. *Sgl/twin GEL50, luxe GEL60, both with b/fast.*

🏠 **Hotel Okrostbar** On the far/north side of the footbridge, under the grandstand for viewing the water skiing; ✆ 293 22772. A small place with tiny, cunningly designed, split-level rooms. Washing facilities are shared, & there's no b/fast. You can eat at a basic café across the bridge. You can also use the swimming pool & gym. *GEL20 pp.*

🏠 **Hotel Paleostomi** ✆ 293 20929. A further 1km to the south along the main road (or the old railway track bed about 100m west), at the Restaurant Iasoni (ie: Jason; km81/40), where the longer marshrutka 5 route terminates, a road leads 50m east to the Hotel Paleostomi. Ask at the house behind the 4 large bungalows in which you can stay. There's currently no b/fast & no TV, & no English is spoken. They're building an extension with 4 *luxe* rooms, with private bathroom & TV. This is an ideal location for birdwatchers, as Lake Paleostomi lies immediately beyond the hotel. *GEL20 pp with shared facilities; luxe rooms (when completed) GEL30–50.*

The **campsite** at the north end of the complex has closed, as has the Pioneer Railway in the park behind it, but you could camp wild near the Hotel Okrostbar.

KOLKHETI NATIONAL PARK Immediately beyond the lake, on three sides, is the Kolkheti (Colchis) National Park, now recognised as globally important wetlands and listed as a Ramsar site; the reserve is in four parts totalling 44,849ha (including 15,742ha of water). The best birdwatching is to the east of the lake, reachable only by boat. The coast both north and south of Poti and the wetlands inland, along rivers such as the Rioni, are very young, having formed only in the last 6,200 years. In other words, when Jason and the *Argo* came here from Greece in the 13th century BC, there was only open sea here. Then around 5500BC the connection from the Mediterranean to the Black Sea burst open, causing the biblical Great Flood, which in fact lasted for about 35 years, and raising the sea level by up to 100m. Now there is a coastal sandbank with peat bogs, up to 12m deep (ie: well below sea level) behind, with a system of lagoons. The largest is Lake Paleostomi, 18.2km² in area and up to 3.2m deep; it's a stopover for 21 threatened bird species, and there are 173 other bird species resident here. Despite heavy human impact, there are still important communities of endemic and relict plant species in the wetlands. Among the most interesting is the wingnut tree, whose only relations are in China and Japan, as well as an endemic oak; it's also one of the only two remaining spawning grounds of the Atlantic sturgeon. You may also see three species of dolphin offshore. Many international and Georgian NGOs are now involved in the conservation of the Colchic wetlands, notably the Worldwide Fund for Nature, the Poseidon Marine Association and the Georgian Centre for the Conservation of Wildlife. The park headquarters, where they're building a modern visitor centre, is at Guria 222, 4km south of the centre of Poti, and a long way from Guria 212 (✆ *293 23055;* e *knp@knp.ge; www.knp.ge*).

GURIA

Immediately south of the checkpoint at km40 you'll cross a bridge over the Kapartcha River from Lake Paleostomi to the sea, and at another 3km further south you'll finally leave Poti municipality and the province of Mingrelia, and enter Guria. This is a small province, known both for its immensely complex polyphonic singing, and for its people who are both very political and very forthright, which many of us would see as a contradiction in terms; nevertheless, it's the home of Shevardnadze.

The first village in Guria on the coast road is **Grigoleti**, populated by the descendants of Protestants exiled from Russia; here it meets the direct road (and, just south, the railway) from Samtredia to Batumi, via Lanchkhuti (31km from Senaki, with a fine Stakhanovite statue) and Supsa.

Just inland of Grigoleti (north of the junction with the coast road at km57), where four big storage tanks are visible, **Supsa** is the terminal of the refurbished oil pipeline from Baku, opened in 1999. This carries just 80,000 barrels a day or four million tonnes a year, which could be increased to ten or 12 million tonnes a year. The **Hotel Andamati** (m *899 446097; www.hotelandamati.com*) caters to the oil industry, with 24 doubles at US$80, six half-suites (US$150) and three suites with DVD, jacuzzi (US$240), with tennis court and seawater pool.

When the land was privatised, the élite took the best farming land, and the rest got the marshy land across the Supsa River to the south, which was then required for the terminal; however, the compensation offered was derisory, leading to a lawsuit and the detention of their lawyer on thoroughly dubious grounds. Meanwhile, the Khulevi port and refinery are being built on some 96ha of wetland north of Poti, home to migratory waterbirds and supposedly protected by the Ramsar Convention.

There are fish restaurants by the coast road south to Kobuleti, notably opposite the station of **Ureki**; this attractive little resort, on the coast 1.5km west, is famous for the healing properties of its iron-rich black sand. Soviet doctors sent patients for rest, relaxation and treatment at the resort's three sanatoria. Before his untimely death Badri Patatkatshishvili started redevelopment aimed at creating a Western-standard resort. Crossing the tracks and following the road ahead (with a good pavement), there are three good guesthouses on the last road to the right – the middle one is the Tetri Sakhli (White House), with a sign (in Georgian only, in white on blue with a red arrow) on the main road. Beds here cost GEL5–20 per person depending on season and which meals you take; you'll generally need to bring your own bed linen or a sleeping bag to the guesthouses. It's another 200m to the small park (refurbished by Patarkatshishvili) with modern toilets and lots of benches; on the far side of the roads lead down to the beach. A road follows the coast southwards only (the ITM map is wrong here); the first hotel on the left, the **Edemi** (m *899 101393*) is a new four-storey block with three rooms at GEL30–50 per room (June–August only); just beyond on the right is the **Kolkhida** (*Takaishvill 77;* m *899 205445, 899 118682;* e *info@kolkhida.ge*), once the main sanatorium and now a large hotel complex, open all year, with 76 double rooms, three apartments and 12 suites, with three soccer pitches. Further south are the **Riviera Guesthouse** (much like the Edemi), the **Hotel Elite** (m *899 540712*) and the **Hotel Premium** (✆ *647470;* e *hotelpremium@premium.ge*). The small restaurants near the park are adequate, pleasantly rustic but a bit samey, all serving fish *kefali* and *kambula*.

The capital of Guria is **Ozurgeti**, south of Lanchkhuti; it's a drab, uninteresting town, but the starting point for visits to some attractive old churches in the hills just to the southeast. The closest is the medieval Monastery of Shemokmedi, 7km south. The others are to the north near Lanchkhuti (on the main road from Samtredia to Batumi); from Chkonagora, 9km east of Lanchkhuti, a road is signposted south to the nunnery of Sameba-Jikhetis – the road is steep and passable only in good weather, but the views over the Kolkhetis National Park are great. It's best to take a guide with a 4x4 vehicle, and you may still have to walk the last bit; the Festival of the Virgin on 21 September is a good time to visit. The Maral monastery of Jumatis is to the south from km38, 7km west of Lachkhuti.

There's a better road southeast from Buknari, on the Samtredia-Ozuregti road, via the Nabeglavi mineral spring (famous for its sodium bicarbonate water, available in bottles all over Georgia) to **Bakhmaro**, in the mountains a mile above sea level just north of the Adjaran border. Once a Soviet children's health resort, it's only accessible from mid June to mid October; in July and August it's full of Georgians who come to hike, watch the sunset, drink wine and chat by a bonfire. Rooms are cheap and you can buy some food, but you may want to bring extra food and camping gear because there are no amenities.

Ozurgeti is now reached by a railway from the coast, with day and night trains from Tbilisi and a local from Batumi, but it's a very roundabout route and you're best off taking a bus from Samtredia or Batumi. Lanchkhuti is on the main road and railway between Samtredia and Batumi, and thus a very easy stopping-off point.

ABKHAZIA

Abkhazia, the westernmost district of Georgia, has effectively seceded, and is closed to Western visitors despite having been the Soviet Union's most popular area for beach holidays. Nevertheless, bodies such as the United Nations and the Red Cross are working there, and it may be possible to enter from Russia or by boat from Trabzon, so for the benefit of the few presently going there and in case the situation suddenly changes, here is a brief summary of the highlights.

Entering in the far west from Sochi or the Adler airport, both in Russia, you'll immediately reach **Leselidze**, site of a huge children's holiday camp and a training centre for the Soviet team before the Moscow Olympics, and then Gantiadi, where the Tsandripsh basilica, built in the 8th century, has perfect acoustics due to resonating hollows built into its walls. From here the road runs below cliffs to the town of **Gagra**, which claims to be the warmest place on the Black Sea, with bathing from February to November; you can see the ruins of a 5th-century castle, a 6th–7th-century basilica and a park stocked with subtropical plants. It is then 14km to the road south to **Bichvinta** (better known by its Russian name of Pitsunda), where a modern resort abuts the only forest of the relict long-needled Pitsunda pine *Pinus pithyusa*, stretching east for 7km along the beach. By the 14-

storey hotels is the late 10th-century Church of the Mother of God, large and externally very rounded. Large numbers of Russian tourists are once again visiting this area and there are now plenty of beach hotels; the season runs from May to October and hotel rooms can be had for just 200 Russian roubles (about US$7), with better rooms in guesthouses costing from about US$20 in April, May or October to double that in August.

Once back on the main road, this swings inland to run parallel with the railway, and in 7km reaches Bzyb (or Bzipi), where there's an attractive 10th-century church and the junction to **Lake Ritsa**. This road follows a valley into the hills inland for 41km to the lake, in a stunning location at 950m, below the 3,256m peak of Mount Agapsta on the border to the northwest. In normal circumstances there's a motel open here, as well as boat hire; in the Ritsa Nature Reserve you may see boar, roe and red deer, plus mountain goats and trout. Some of the world's deepest caves are in the Bzipi Ridge, including the Kruger Abyss, only found in 2005, and the Voronya Cave, now explored to a depth of 2,140m, currently the world record.

The main road returns to the coast at Musera (site of Gorbachev's *dacha*) and continues to Gudauta, a resort which is also the site of the 10th–11th-century Abaata basilica and a Russian army base; 5km north is Lykhny, site of the 14th-century palace of the Abkhazian kings and a 10th-century Byzantine church. It's another 20km along the coast to **Novy Afon** (known in Greek as Anakopia and in Georgian as Akhali Atoni), where the 9th–10th-century Church of St Simon the Canaanite (who came to this area with St Andrew in AD55 and is buried in Komani near Sukhumi) was the seat of the Bishop of Abkhazia. There's also a tower built in the 13th century by the Genoese. In 1875–86 the Monastery of New Athos was built by monks from Athos in Greece; it's been described as 'a delirious fantasy of a building with silver domes bubbling up out of the mountainside, its walls painted in rich yellows and red, crowned by spires'. Under the Soviet regime it was converted into a holiday camp, and suffered badly from 'official' vandalism. Just inland is the Psyrtskha holiday camp, and beyond it the Anacopia Cave in the holy Mount Iveri, which was discovered in 1961 and opened to visitors (except on Sundays and Mondays) in 1975, with an electric-train tour of its beautiful rock formations. There are nine chambers over 100m in length and 40–60m in height, and the longest is 140m long.

SUKHUMI The coast road soon crosses the Gumista River and enters Sukhumi, the capital of Abkhazia, which was founded in the 5th century BC as the Greek port of Dioscurias. The ruins of Dioscurias have been underwater for 2,500 years, and are still sinking slowly; the remains of the Roman fort of Sebastopolis, built in the 2nd century AD, survive by the quayside, and the 10th-century castle of King Bagrat stands on a 600m hill by the remains of an 11th–12th-century church. Also here is the 15th-century Turkish fort of Sukhum-Kale (Turkish for 'Water Sand'), rebuilt by the Russians in 1810. The Botanical Gardens were created in 1840, and the 32ha Forest Park, on a low hill to the northeast, was laid out in 1941–51. The Botanical Gardens were very fine before the war of secession; in an area of 25ha they had 5,000 species and varieties of plants, including 1,300 trees and shrubs and 2,800 herbaceous plants, as well as 500 species in greenhouses and 20,000 specimens in the herbarium. Abkhazia is known for the great ages its inhabitants can live to, and Sukhumi's Centenarians' Choir (*Nartaa*) had members up to 130 years in age. Also here is the Abkhazian State Museum, with Greek statues and local history.

Intourist used to provide accommodation at the **Hotel Abkhazia** (*2 Frunze St; ☎ 23311*) and the **Campsite Sukhumi** (☎ *29568*), just north at Gumista. For some years the only place to stay was the Hotel Aitar in a 1960s' sanatorium in what is now the UN compound, charging US$5 per person; now there are new guesthouses, charging from around US$30 for a room.

Georgia has some very rich people indeed, who made their money in Russia during Boris Yeltsin's 'gangster capitalism' period, and cashed out under Putin. Having returned home, they are now doing some interesting things with their money.

Badri Patarkatsishvili came home in 2001 and bought a new white mansion overlooking Tbilisi from Okrokana as well as the former Wedding Palace. Unable to travel to Russia due to fraud charges; he clashed with the Saakashvili government due to his Imedi TV station's pursuit of the Girgvliani murder scandal and was pressured with tax audits of Imedi and his other companies. In 2006 he sold 30% of Imedi to Rupert Murdoch, and in January 2008 ran in the presidential election, taking 7% of the vote. He was accused of plotting a coup but died in his English mansion in February 2008 of what does seem to have been a heart attack.

According to Forbes magazine, Bidzina Ivanishvili is the world's 173rd richest person, worth US$4.5 billion. He's now sold Impexbank and his minerals business in Russia (where he was known as Boris), and in Georgia his TV station, known for its balance, closed after the Rose Revolution. He returned to live in his birthplace of Chorvila, near Sacchere, and is busy making new friends by paying to restore Tbilisi's Rustaveli Theatre and Botanic Garden and Batumi's 26 May Park, among other projects, as well as building a new ski-lift in Bakuriani and a Disney-style park on the Black Sea coast.

Georgia's minister for economic reform is Kakha Bendukidze, who turned a small Russian biotech company into a huge conglomerate called United Machinery. He was a supporter of Yeltsin and a member of various government committees, but after the Rose Revolution sold up and returned to Tbilisi to join the new government. He is a strong advocate of liberal reform, deregulation and privatisation, although nationalists accuse him of being ready to sell the entire state to Russia.

Finally, Mamuka Khazaradze began his career buying and selling paintings, raising the capital to open two shops and then the TBC Bank, now Georgia's largest; he's also president of Georgian Glass and Mineral Water, and of the Georgian Reconstruction and Development Company, which has plans for a resort at Lisi Lake, on the edge of Tbilisi. TBC Bank has also put a great deal of money into civic projects, notably the US$6 million restoration of the bank's headquarters (the former Tbilisi Central Department Store, built in 1913) on Marjanishvili St, to launch the revitalisation of the city's less fashionable left bank.

FROM SUKHUMI TO ZUGDIDI Continuing east along the coast, 6km from Sukhumi a rough road leads another 6km up the west/right bank of the Kelasuri River to Kelasuri, where you can see the Great Wall of Abkhazia, built by the 6th century AD as a defensive line along the river. You'll also pass the 11th–12th-century arched bridge of Besleti, 13km from Sukhumi. It's another 13km along the main road (passing Gulripshi, where there are dolmens dating from the 3rd and 2nd centuries BC) to Dranda, near Sukhumi's airport, where there's a 9th-century church by the river Kodori. About 30km further east a road leads inland to Mokvi, site of a cave-church built in the AD960s, with five aisles, and a cupola on four pillars. Beyond the town of Ochamchire (54km from Sukhumi) the road heads inland through rich subtropical farmland and hazel trees, soon passing the turning north to Bedia, where a 10th-century church was home of the Bedia Chalice, now in the Art Museum in Tbilisi. The church's frescoes include the only portrait of Bagrat III (975–1014), the first king of a unified Georgia, to be made during his lifetime; unfortunately it was damaged after the fall of Sukhumi. Beyond Gali the road reaches the border at the bridge over the Inguri, not far short of Zugdidi; Unomig, the United Nations mission in Georgia, operates a free shuttle bus across the bridge several times a day.

8

Svaneti

Svaneti, the land of the Svans or *Svanebi*, hidden in obscure recesses of the High Caucasus, is an area to which much mystery attaches itself. It's seen as more Georgian than Georgia proper, the repository of the country's soul, due to having been the last refuge from the Mongols – the holiest icons and richest treasures were carried up beyond the Inguri gorges for safe keeping in times of crisis, and artistic and religious traditions are felt to have been better preserved here than elsewhere. At the same time the Svans are seen as strong but simple, speaking a 6th-century dialect of Georgian which is largely incomprehensible to the people of Kartli and Kakheti, and often disregarding the norms of law and order. Tourists may be held up and robbed (there are lots of Kalashnikovs around, and no police outside Mestia), so you'd be well advised not to go to Svaneti alone or without knowing where you'll be staying. More and more independent backpackers are arriving and people can see the economic benefits of tourism, but the total was still only 1,200 in 2005, and there are still robberies from time to time. During the civil war in Abkhazia, when refugees were fleeing from the Svan-populated upper reaches of the Kodori and Sakeni rivers, some were greeted by soup kitchens at the passes, but others were robbed by their fellow Svans. The typical Svan name 'Kurdiani' actually means 'thief', although the family has in fact produced many well-known Tbilisi architects and artists.

However, the Svans are for the most part very hospitable and friendly, and the amazing beauty of the surrounding peaks, the clusters of defensive towers that dominate the villages, and the frescoes and icons of the churches, entice ever-increasing numbers of visitors.

CULTURE AND HISTORY

The Svan culture shows clear ties with ancient Sumeria and Mesopotamia, though many of them are blonde with green eyes. They've lived here since the 2nd millennium BC, and the foundations of the oldest defensive towers can be dated to the 1st century BC. These towers are Svaneti's most distinctive feature, more elaborate than those in Khevsureti and elsewhere to the east, with fortified tops and roofs. There are now about 175 towers, dating from the 6th to 16th centuries (most being from the 9th to 13th centuries), and a couple of dozen have been restored. In Roman times the Greek geographer Strabo called the Svans 'a mighty people ... foremost in courage and power'; they were formally Christian by AD523 but even today their religion retains strong elements of paganism, such as sacrificing rams on religious festivals and placing their horns on the altar. The Svan sun god Lile may well be the same as the Sumerian Enlil, and the village of Lakhamu may be named after the Sumerian water god. Now, St Barbara is seen as an equivalent of the sun god, while St George (Dzgrag) is revered as an equivalent to the moon god. Nominally under the control of Colchis, then Lazika (Egrisi), Svaneti became part of Abkhazia then of a unified Georgia from the early 11th century; it shared in

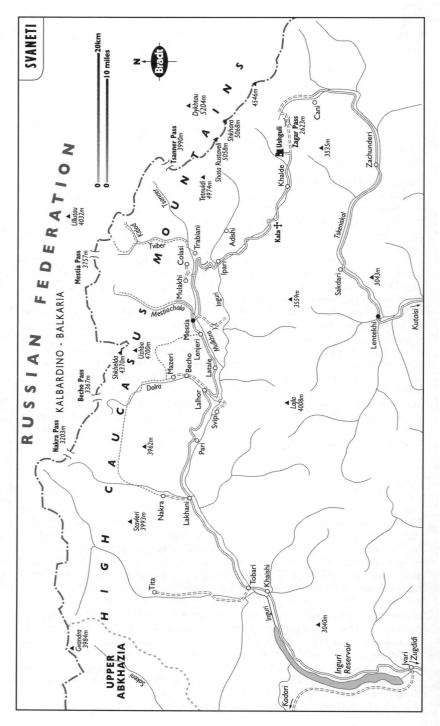

Death has always been nasty and premature for many Svans, even before the arrival of the motor car, so it's not surprising that many traditions have evolved to cope with it. Men don't shave for 14 days after a death, while widows wear black with a lapel badge bearing a photo of the deceased. In the home there is a shrine with more photos, and visitors will be given a drink, to pour a few drops on the floor, and toast the deceased with the rest. Forty days and three months after the death, family and friends go to the cemetery; a table is set up on the grave with food and drink (and perhaps other household items such as a radio). The women wail and cry, then the men line up, hats off, to say prayers and, of course, toast the deceased with chacha; then the table is removed from the grave, and the food is eaten.

As in every Orthodox church, tapers are lit by everyone who comes into a church; those at the front left are for prayers for women, those at the front right are for prayers for men, and those at the back are for the dead.

The dead are commemorated on Mariamoba (St Mariam's Day, 28 August), and also in Khaishi on Jvedi Ham, the second Sunday in January, when the souls of dead relatives stay overnight with their families, and in Ushguli on Lipanali, the Monday after 19 January. Singing at funerals combines pre-Christian wailing traditions with Christian singing, by both men and women but not together.

Georgia's golden age under Queen Tamar (who ruled from 1184 to 1213), who visited Svaneti several times and is still revered there. The Svans were largely undisturbed by the Mongols (although Tamerlane's horde passed through in 1397), and came under a Russian 'protectorate' in 1833, local autonomy being abolished in 1857; the last Tsarist governor was driven out in 1905, leaving Svaneti effectively independent until 1924. The wheel and the aeroplane both appeared in Svaneti in 1935; given their eight-month winter and the permanently ruinous state of the roads, most Svans are still happy to use heavy ox-sledges as their main means of transporting goods. However increasing numbers now live for most or all of the year in Tbilisi or other cities, as the disadvantages of the harsh mountain lifestyle become ever clearer. In Rustavi, built after World War II as a new industrial city, there are now Svan villages. In the winter of 1987 a terrible avalanche killed around 70 people at once, mostly children in a school in Ushguli, and the following year around 4,000 of the 16,000 residents of Zemo (Upper) Svaneti left. In all there are 45,000 Svans in Georgia, of whom 12,000 remain in Zemo Svaneti, about 2,500 of them in Mestia. Logging (probably about double the official level of 60,000m³ per annum) is leading to more avalanches and landslides, and 75–80 families are still leaving each year.

However, it has to be said that the bulk of the death toll is entirely self-inflicted, as young men keep on killing themselves in road accidents; when I was in Mestia three families were mourning three young men killed in entirely separate incidents. The 117km road from Zugdidi to Mestia is notorious as the most dangerous in Georgia, and is lined with shrines at accident sites. Under the shrine is a shelf laden with bottles and glasses, and friends will stop and drink a toast of *chacha* in memory of the deceased; the absurdity of drinking firewater in memory of someone who was probably drunk when he went off the road is lost on the Svans. It's also reckoned that between 1917 and 1925, 5% of the population (600 people) were killed in feuds, so now politeness is ingrained, and 'fool' is the strongest insult the Svans allow themselves.

A typical Svan village is actually composed of perhaps half-a-dozen separate clusters of around 30 households huddled around their defensive towers. These are normally about 28m tall (perhaps following a formula by which the height of the tower should equal the sum of the four sides), and unlike those of Ossetia and elsewhere they are crenellated and roofed. They were probably built by spiral scaffolding, with rocks hoisted up by oxen. In some villages the oldest and largest will be the 'war tower', standing separately on a hilltop. The traditional home or *machubi* consists of one spacious room with living space in the centre separated by carved wooden partitions from the livestock stalls around the walls. Churches are generally tiny, just 5–6m², and they're single-nave basilicas, mostly built between the 8th and 14th centuries, with frescoes painted between the 10th and 12th centuries, both on the inside and the outside of the churches. They tend to be opened perhaps twice a year for festivals, but the key holder may let you in. Svan icons are remarkable for the standard of their chased metalwork, and the finest examples, made at the end of the 10th century and start of the 11th century, are kept safe in the homes of the leading families.

The national dish of Svaneti is *kubdari*, bread stuffed with meat. They also make particularly fine *khachapuri*, known as *teeshdvar*. The local firewater is a particularly horrible form of *chacha*, made from bread due to the lack of grain.

Svaneti has kept alive a primeval and ethereal style of three-part singing, with pentatonic harmonies (unlike the rest of Georgia). This is often accompanied by the *changi*, the Svan harp, which looks as if it's come straight off a Greek vase, or the lute-like *chianuri*. Svaneti is also rich in round-dances, which gradually accelerate.

SVANETI FESTIVALS There are around 50 festivals throughout the year in Svaneti, not to mention the various inescapable ceremonies remembering the dead (see page 201).

- Jvedi Ham – in Khaishi on the second Sunday of January, a 'Long Night' when the souls of the dead stay overnight with their families
- Lipanali – in Ushguli on the Monday after 19 January, commemorating dead family members
- Lagami – in Latale and Lenjeri at the end of February, with a 'battle' of snow towers
- Lamproba – in all the Svan villages ten weeks before Easter, commemorating St George and the spiritual unity of the village with candles (lampari) for each male in the family plus one for St George
- Kashvetoba – in Lenjeri and Kala the third week after Easter, when women married in other villages return to their roots
- Kaishoba – in Nakra, Pari and Becho eight weeks after Easter, the Festival of the Archangels
- Hulishoba – in Nakra, Becho and Ushguli ten weeks after Easter, the adoration of God the Father, with animal sacrifices and sports such as horse racing, arm wrestling and rock lifting
- Giorgoba – in all the Svan villages on 6 May, the birthday of St George
- Petre-Pavloba – in all the Svan villages on 12 July, the festival of Saints Peter and Paul
- Kvirikoba – in Kala on 28 July, the main religious festival of Svaneti, commemorating Saints Kvirike and Ivlitta;

- Eliaoba – in Lenjeri and Tzvirmi on 2 August, the feast of the Prophet Elia
- Livskhvari – in Ushguli on the first Sunday of August, marking the start of the grass-cutting season
- Mariamoba – in all the Svan villages on 28 August, the Festival of the Virgin Mary
- Lalkhori – in Etseri on the first Sunday of October, a celebration of village solidarity
- Giorgoba – in all the Svan villages on 23 November, commemorating St George's martyrdom

For Kvirikoba, on 28 July, almost everyone in Svaneti descends on the mountaintop site of Kala for a real 'gathering of the clans'. As you'd expect, there's a lot of alcohol-fuelled singing and some religious observance involving the sacrifice of bulls or goats. Dating from Roman times or before, it's linked to the pagan deity Kviria, protector of the fertility of soil, man and animals. In addition you can buy hand-carved wooden drinking vessels, traditional Svan felt hats and other craftwork direct from the artisan, as well as traditional Svan food. Outsiders are welcome, and a trip is likely to be organised by GeoTrek (m *877 730489, 899 548292*; e *gmf@gol.ge*), at US$270–350 (depending on numbers) for five days/four nights (including two nights on trains to and from Tbilisi).

GETTING THERE

Global Georgian Airways (\ *988026*; m *899 440409*; f *939136*; e *mratiani@ yahoo.com*) fly from Mestia to Tbilisi at 09.00 on Wednesdays and Fridays, taking just 45 minutes and costing GEL60; these are subsidised flights (Svans pay half fare), routinely overbooked and weather dependent, and so are definitely not to be relied on. However the plane (a 17-seat Antonov) is available for charter the other five days of the week; there are also flights from Kutaisi. There's a marshrutka from Tbilisi at 07.00 daily (11hrs; GEL25), but this is for masochists only. It's far more comfortable to take the train to Zugdidi, from where marshrutkas leave from 08.00 for the drive up the Inguri Valley to Mestia (4.5hrs; GEL15–20), and in summer there may even be a proper bus. If you miss the marshrutkas you'll probably be able to get a ride in a jeep until early afternoon – see pages 191–2. On the return journey, you'll be stuck in Zugdidi for about eight hours if you plan to take the night train to Tbilisi; far better to get a marshrutka to Kutaisi and break your journey there.

By road, Svaneti is best reached from Zugdidi, although there is also a very poor (probably impassable) road from the less interesting region of Kvemo (Lower) Svaneti. From Zugdidi the road heads north across the plains straight towards Elbruz (across the border in Russia, and the highest peak in Europe at 5,642m), between two near-continuous rows of houses, then climbs up a side valley before cutting across to the west to reach the Inguri Valley upstream of Georgia's largest hydro-electric station; even so vehicles have to stop at a checkpoint manned by Russian peacekeeping troops. They'll want cigarettes, but should be no problem otherwise. The road, strewn with rock falls, follows the side of the valley high above the reservoir, passing through half-a-dozen tunnels. Above the head of the reservoir (where you can see how quickly it's filling with silt) the road relatively soon reaches Khaishi, the first of the Svan villages (comprising 20 separate little settlements), 76km and two hours from Zugdidi. The road crosses to the right/west bank after five minutes and gets much rougher as the valley closes in; after Lakhani and the turning north up the Nakra Valley, the valley opens out as it turns east into the upper Inguri Valley, with fantastic views of Elbruz, Uzhba, Tetnuldi and Shkara. The road passes above the village of Pari, once inhabited by notorious robbers who were eventually driven out by Cossacks. At km96 it passes Lakhamula (centre of a group of 11 hamlets), then Khveda Luka, before climbing steadily and then coasting down to Lalhor, almost four hours from Zugdidi. From here the Dolra Valley leads north to Becho, a village of 11 settlements right below Uzhba. It's not much further to Ienashi, a biggish settlement with defensive towers; this is the central part of the village of Latale, which means 'guard' and is the first of the truly Svan villages, having always been free from the feudal system. Latale, spread across the tongue between the Mulkhura and Inguri rivers, is perhaps the loveliest part of Upper Svaneti. The Matsqvari Church of the Saviour, a small one-nave basilica built in 1140 on the hilltop above the settlement of Matsqvarish (9km from Mestia), has fine 12th-century frescoes, including one of the coronation of Demetre I by the Svan painter Mikhail Maglakeli (1142), the only medieval painting on a secular theme in Svaneti. This shouldn't be confused with the Matsqvari church nearby in Nesgun, which has 9th–10th-century frescoes by a master called Giorgi. Just 2km further on, the road passes above Lenjeri, the first of the 'villages of Mestia' (and itself centre of a village of six settlements) with half-a-dozen fairly scattered towers; here the Lashtkhveri Church of Taringzel (the Archangels) has a very famous fresco of Amirani (the Georgian Prometheus) killing the devil Devi, painted on the northern façade in the 14th and 15th centuries, and a contemporary fresco of St George killing the pagan Roman Emperor Diocletian (in place of the dragon) inside.

MESTIA

It's another 2km to the town of Mestia itself, at 1,470m, with the Old Town on the right bank and a New Town, with apartment blocks, new museum and airstrip on the far, left bank. There's no bar, no café, no restaurant and no internet café. There's a spacious main square in the old town, but behind it the back streets are pure Svan, with steep stony alleys, hairy free-range pigs, rough stone houses and defensive towers – in 1887 the climber Douglas Freshfield counted 80 towers in Mestia alone, but now there are far fewer, with just 175 in all Svaneti. Buses will drop you in the square, where in summer you're likely to be met with offers of accommodation. It's best to arrange accommodation before you leave Tbilisi (with Caucasus Travel or GeorgiCa Travel, for instance) and to be met off the bus, but if not, you should seek out a homestay.

 WHERE TO STAY AND EAT

Nino Japaridze (4 rooms) m 899 572850; e mestia@yahoo.com. The former mayor & her sister Eka (m 899 380300) have a house on the left/west side of the square (look for a garage with grey metal doors) with private dbl rooms & 2 bathrooms with hot showers, & they can also organise hikes & excursions. US$20–25 FB.

Nino Ratiani Tamar 1, Akhalsheni; \ 224 21182; m 899 183555, or Buba Jafarli; m 899 541155. Nino is also very well connected, & speaks some English, while her daughter Tamuna is fluent; they're located at a mini-market only 2mins from the square back along the Zugdidi road, with clean white light airy rooms including large quantities of delicious Svan food. GEL30.

Boris Khordiani m 899 157091, 899 775670. The family also have a nice house with large rooms & hot water, but they speak only Georgian & Russian.

David Zhorzholiani Tetnuldi 4, right next to St George's Church; m 899 344948. Rooms for up to 4 are available inc all food & hot showers; they have a car available & can organise treks & trips, & make their own chacha! US$20 pp.

Tsiuri Gabliani (4 rooms) Rustaveli 16; m 899 569358. Tsiuri is an English teacher who also speaks German, with a good library. The street, formerly Rustaveli, was renamed after her father, a fine mountaineer; it's next to the 'hospital', 2mins from the square, down the lane by the run-down shop. US$25 pp FB.

🏠 **Nana Nizharadze** 🗲 932555. Nana organises accommodation for Caucasus Travel & CUNA for US$10–12 pp.

There's just one bad **restaurant**, but it doesn't matter as all guesthouses and homestays provide large quantities of food. It might be worth trying *khevi*, a sort of chewing gum made of fir-tree resin chewing gum, which sells for GEL1 and takes a lot of work to get it chewy.

WHAT TO SEE AND DO

Museum of History and Ethnography (admission GEL10 for foreigners, plus GEL10 for a guide, who doesn't speak English; open 11.00–16.00 except Sun). This museum is now in its impressive new home across the river, built several years ago across the river but not opened for a long time due to the political problems of persuading villages such as Ushguli to release their treasured icons. The exhibits now have English and Georgian captions; the ethnographic collection consists of bits and pieces such as a loom, a sled, Svan furniture and musical instruments, *chacha* stills, guns, wickerwork, and a jug that belonged to Tamar, as well as lots of copies of frescoes. You can also see Bronze-Age metalwork from Colchis, coins with Macedonian, Turkish, Russian or Georgian inscriptions from various eras, 10th-century church doors, an 11–12th-century Arab shield, jewellery made of alexandrite, Caucasian metal pots, and Svan mail armour. There are also fascinating photos of Mestia in 1890, showing very little sign of change since. However what is unmissable is the treasury, with the first room housing astounding Gospels from the 9th–13th centuries – perhaps only the Labskaldi one quite matches the *Book of Kells* for artistic richness, but to have half-a-dozen ancient books of such grace and finesse in one place is amazing. The second room contains wonderful icons and crosses all showing a remarkable quality of metalworking. The oldest, of Saints Mary and Barbara, was made in the 9th century, but most are from the 11th to early 13th centuries, the so-called Georgian Renaissance or golden age. One of the finest, though not made in Svaneti, is of the Forty Martyrs, from the 11th or early 12th century. There's one lovely icon in gilded silver made in the 14th century, and pictures of the Adishi gospel (dating from AD897), some rather tatty Byzantine tapestry, and a 6–7th-century incense burner.

In an alley off the square is the Church of St George, built in the 19th century to replace an 11th-century ruin; this is where the museum's icons were housed until the Church reclaimed its building. Now it has a plain interior and a minimalist iconostasis; there's a good metal icon of St George killing Diocletian and old painted icons of Christ and the Virgin and Child. Outside, the grandest grave is that of the climber Mikhail Khergiani (1932–69), who died in the Italian Dolomites when he got fed up with climbing on a rope; there's now a museum in his home (see below).

Continuing north beyond the museum, the main road leaves the main part of Mestia and passes the high school, where you can pop over a stile to a Narzan (mineral water) spring in the yard (there's another 500m along the Ushguli road, to the right), and then reaches a cluster of nine towers, the Lakhrami area of Mestia. Here you can visit the Khergiani Museum, beyond the 13th-century church of Matshovris, which has a fresco of Adam and Eve visible on the façade. The museum is both a memorial to Mikhail Khergiani, one of the world's leading climbers when he died, and a traditional Svan house; however, opening hours are erratic.

Architectural Museum (admission GEL1; you'll have to pay at the main museum). This museum, where you can visit both a defensive tower and a *machubi* house, is at the

top northeastern corner of central Mestia, above the road to Lakhrami; it's the house with a silver gate, just beyond a cemetery chapel and the defensive tower, which is left open, with fixed external steps then five flights leading up to the roof. The *machubi* house, which dates from the 12th century, has a central fireplace (with a chimney of fireproof *mukhra* wood, and a metal plate for cooking bread, by a wooden basin for mixing dough). The fire would have been virtually the only source of light, although there is now a sole electric bulb. Around the room, clockwise from the chest between the windows in which dishes are kept, there's a store for food and *chacha*, then stalls for sheep along one wall, and larger stalls for cows along two walls. Between 12 and 20 people would have lived in this room, sleeping above the animal stalls for warmth; yet there's only one chair, reserved for the oldest man of the family. Carved on the wooden stalls is a repeated sun or eternity motif, like an orange or apple flan seen from above, which also appears on Georgian coins.

Mount Mestia (2,300m). A wooden cross was erected on this hill high above this corner of Mestia, in around 1994, and it's an excellent, if exhausting, walk up. There's no single clear path so it's best to go with a local guide, the 800m ascent taking about two hours. At the top you have a birds-eye view of Mestia, an astounding panorama of the High Caucasus, and lush alpine meadows full of cows and brightly coloured plants, as well as a surprising number of cowherds' huts.

TOWARDS USHGULI The square in Mestia is the place to look for a jeep to Ushguli, if your guesthouse has not arranged one for you. It's best to find someone to share with, as drivers will charge as much as they can get away with. With luck you might be able to arrange a day trip, with just two hours in Ushguli, for US$40, but it's better to stay overnight.

A road leads down from the square to a bridge over the narrow gorge of the Mulkhra River to the left bank, and up to the right to the modern museum. To the south, the chairlift of the former Zuruldi ski resort has been out of action since around 1993, though keen skiers can still get to the top of the hill by taking the road to the TV tower. Swinging to the left, the road to Ushguli passes the closed Hotel Tetnuldi on the left. Leaving the town eastwards, you'll see the abandoned *Turbaza,* or mountaineering base, and mountain rescue (KCM in Cyrillic) centre, above the airstrip to the left of the river.

The road, far rougher than the one below Mestia, runs above a gorge, passing Rebra to the left (with no bridge), then Artsheli, and Murshkheli above it; these are all parts of the village of Mulakhi, which consists of 11 small groups of houses. There are mineral springs (marked by red stains on the rocks), on the near bank of the river, by a washed-out bridge; then a good bridge crosses to the left to Jamushi (also hit by a lethal avalanche in 1987) and Lakheri above it, before the towers of Trabiani come into sight ahead, in front of the giant peaks of Tetnuldi (4,974m) and, to the right, Shkhara (5,068m, the highest peak in Georgia). The road to Ushguli turns off to the right to climb over a pass (open only from April to December) to return to the Inguri Valley; to the left the road leads to **Trabiani** (sometimes called Zhabeshi, 15km from Mestia), the last part of Mulakhi, with a further left turn leading to a log bridge and the seven towers of Chulashi on the right bank. At the top end of Trabiani the Makhtsovari church is the oldest in Svaneti, dating back to the 4th century; it's a simple basilica with a three-sided apse, although it once had aisles to the south and north, and a porch to the south. Now it has a modern metal roof, to protect the frescoes and icons inside; ask for the key at the last house in the village. There's also a tower, built in the 10th century, and you may also notice the tiny St George's Church, isolated in the fields to the left as you enter Trabiani.

The Ushguli road returns over a 1,700m pass (with good views of Uzhba) to the Inguri Valley, where a side valley turns east to Adishi (see below), 27km from Mestia, and enters the village of Ipari (39km from Mestia). The Nakipari Church of St George was built in 1130 and decorated in the same year with frescoes by Tevdor, supposedly the court painter of King David the Builder (although there's no real evidence), which have survived untouched since then. The next village, as the road follows the increasingly precipitous Inguri valley, is Kala, where the hilltop **Lagurka** Church of St Kvirike, built in 1112, is the host of the most important pilgrimage and festival in Svaneti, Kvirikoba, on 28 July (see page 203). The last part of Kala, 10km below Ushguli, is Khalde, a rebel stronghold finally burnt down by the Russians in 1876; the Lalhor church is worth a visit.

USHGULI

Finally, 55km and at least two hours from Mestia, the road reaches Ushguli, the highest permanently inhabited settlement in Europe at an altitude of 2,200m. It's also a stunningly beautiful spot, with small clusters of towers huddled together amidst alpine pastures and beneath the highest peak in the country; fittingly, it's a UNESCO World Heritage Site. It is divided into three settlements, with a total of seven churches built and painted between the 9th and 12th centuries. The first settlement is Murkmeli, followed by Chazkhashi, which was terribly damaged by the avalanche of 1987, but still has over 200 medieval buildings. From here the road (now more or less unusable) continues to the Zagar Pass (2,623m) and Lower Svaneti; hidden out of sight over a ridge to the north is Zhvibiani, the last and most spectacular part of Ushguli, where domestic artefacts and a magnificent 11th-century carved door are displayed in a barn-like **Ethnographic Museum** (*admission GEL10*). There's also a superb collection of 11th-century icons here, but the curator is very protective of them and may refuse to allow visitors in; not surprisingly, he's also very reluctant to allow the museum's contents to be moved to the new museum in Mestia. On the ridge above Zhvibiani are some isolated towers that are supposed to have been Queen Tamar's summer home; her burial place is unknown, but the Svans naturally hope that it's here. When television arrived in Svaneti in 1975, the communists took great pleasure in installing the relay on Tamar's Towers. Also isolated high on a ridge is the Lamaria church, set against the backdrop of Shkhara in the finest setting of any Svan church. It's a small basilica built in the 9th century, with a defensive tower and 10–12th-century frescoes, somewhat deteriorated, including a portrait of Queen Tamar, plus scenes from the Amirani legend on the exterior. Pridon or Vladimir Nizharadze and Nanuli Chelidze are the people to ask for to open the museum and church.

WHERE TO STAY

Temraz Nizharadze (3 twin rooms) Just below the small chapel of Zhvibiani. A relative of Nana, Temraz offers rooms in his house with hot water & lots of excellent food. There's no phone, but a message can be transmitted from Nana's in Mestia. *GEL20–30 pp per day FB.*

Dato Ratiani m 899 912256). A superb homestay. *US$25 FB.*

HIKING IN SVANETI

This is the prime area for hiking in Georgia, and the possibilities are described in a couple of guidebooks. These were published before independence, and assume that hikers can freely cross the watershed into the Russian Federation. Nowadays most hikes will have to be adapted as there-and-back trips; however it's possible to hike from the Dolra Valley west to Nakra or east to Mestia. Hiking alone in Svaneti is not safe.

From west to east, the easiest crossing of the Caucasus is by the Nakra Pass (3,203m, practicable from July to October), starting from Lakhani on the Zugdidi road. Finishing at Terskol, in the valley immediately south of Elbruz, this gives fantastic views of Europe's highest peak (5,642m). This route was taken by British climber Douglas Freshfield in 1868, and was the scene of fierce fighting in 1942. It's also possible to hike from the Nakra Valley east to the Dolra Valley Pass via the Ledesht Valley, glacier and pass. The Nakra *turbasa* (a sort of climbers' basecamp hostel) is in fair condition and may be privatised.

It was Freshfield who explored this area and made the first ascents of most of the peaks, in wool and tweed and with alpine guides from Chamonix, as was the norm. In 1868 he climbed Kazbek and the east peak of Elbruz, then in 1887 Tetnuldi, Gulba, Shoda, and a reconnaisance of Shkhara, and in 1889 Laila, while searching for fellow climbers Donkin and Fox, lost on Koshtantau.

The Dolra Valley, meeting the Inguri below Lalhor, gives superb views under the distinctive twin peaks of Uzhba (4,710m), a beautiful mountain with the reputation of being a 'killer queen', which was only climbed in 1903 by a Swiss–German expedition (the lower north peak was climbed in 1888). Now, the south summit (the higher and easier one) is rated as French TD, UIAA IV–V, and can be climbed in a trip of four days (six days from Tbilisi), such as those run by Caucasus Travel in Tbilisi; Shkhelda (4,370m), just to the north of Uzhba, is rather easier (UIAA II–IV). Between these two peaks is the Uzhba Pass (4,100m), a very hard and high route. Easier routes involve hiking to the Uzhba Glacier (2,500m), and the 200m-high Uzhba Waterfalls, or to the Guli Glacier (2,900m); it's possible to go on over the Guli Pass (3,100m), south of Uzhba, and then down to Mestia. Occasional jeeps may run from Mestia to the tower settlement of Becho (1,500m), and maybe on to Mazeri (15km from Mestia), the highest settlement of Becho, from where the Guli route runs eastwards. From here the hiking route heads north along the left/east bank of the Dolra, passes through a gorge and then swings west to the confluence of the Dolra with the Becho, from the north, a couple of hours from Mazeri. From here routes lead west to the Nakra Valley, north to the Becho Pass (3,367m; open June–September) and the Baksan Valley, northeast to the Akhsu Pass (3,830m; crossed by Freshfield in 1889), and east to Uzhba and Mestia. It's another two or three hours via wild strawberries and the Uzhba Waterfalls up to the Uzhba Glacier, and the same again to the Gul Glacier and bivouac, start of the climbing routes on the south side of Uzhba; it's not much further to the Guli Pass, from where it's about four hours down to Lenjeri or Mestia.

From Mestia itself the easiest option is to follow the Mestiachala valley to the northeast towards the Lekzyr Glacier and ultimately the Mestia Pass (3,757m), which would be open from June to October if one could freely cross the border. A jeep track follows the left/south bank for about 6km, ending at a suspension bridge; from here the track leads through a gorge and climbs to a vast snow plateau leading to the pass.

There are two possibilities from Trabiani, both starting by following the right/north bank of the Tviber through a gorge known as the Gates of Georgia, where the trail follows a 1m-wide shelf for about 50m, to the confluence of the Tviber with the Kitlod at 2,400m, five or six hours from Trabiani. You should cross the Tviber using the ruins of a bridge, unless there's a snow bridge upstream, then continue up the left/east bank of the Tviber, reaching the Tviber Glacier in about six hours. Again, it would be possible to continue to the pass (3,580m) and down to Chegem if politics permitted; it's an easy pass, with safe glaciers and no need for anything more than a rope.

Having made the crossing of the Tviber, a path follows the right/north bank of the Kitlod to the Kitlod Glacier; with a short climb on snow, it takes about six hours to reach the Semi Pass (3,850m). From here there's a stunning view of the sheer white Bezengi Wall, 12km long, and the lovely pyramids of Tetnuldi (4,974m) and Gestola (4,860m), as well as Elbruz and Uzhba to the west. It's possible to continue northeast and then east along the watershed for four or five hours to the Upper Tsanner Pass (3,990m), from where there's a view of the other side of the Bezengi Wall, and the 5,204m peak of Dykhtau to the north. This is the most spectacular of the hikes currently possible in this region.

Finally, from Ushguli it's possible to hike northwest over the Khalde Pass (over 3,000m), from where there are great views to Elbruz, past the huge Adishi Icefall to the village of Adishi (1,900m, with a 10th/11th-century hall-church), below the peak of Tetnuldi, and over another ridge to Trabiani.

9

Adjara

In the far southwest of the country, Adjara (or Achara; see map on page 176) is the warmest and wettest of Georgia's provinces, with 2.4m to 2.8m of rain per year. Average temperatures on the coast range between 4°C and 6°C in January and 20°C and 23°C in July, and it's horribly humid in summer. It's cloudier than Abkhazia, which claims 100 more sunny days per year.

Christianity arrived here in the 1st century AD; the region has been under Turkish domination for much of its history and now many of the population, especially in the mountains, are Sunni Muslim in faith although ethnically and linguistically Georgian. People are fairly religious in the mountains, but less so in Batumi, where there's only one mosque. The Adjaran men's traditional costume (as seen in dance troupes) is particularly camp with its tight trousers. Russia took over in 1878, and after the convulsions of the war and revolution (including a brief British Protectorate), created an autonomous republic within Georgia in 1921 as a condition of peace with Turkey. Nevertheless 340,000km² of historically Georgian territory still lie within Turkey, including many of the finest Georgian churches (see the ITM/ERKA map of Georgia), and the Georgian population of Turkey has not always been well treated.

After the break-up of the Soviet Union Adjara was ruled as the personal fiefdom of Aslan Abashidze, whose family had been in charge here since the 15th century, and never tolerated much opposition (Tbilisi streets are named not after Aslan but other Abashidzes who were fine poets). Abashidze was appointed chair of the Adjaran Soviet by Gamsakhurdia in 1991, and always had strong support from the generals commanding the Russian (nominally CIS) base outside Batumi. He ruled firmly, keeping the Mkhedrioni out of Adjara, and handed over very little tax to Tbilisi; nor did he go to Tbilisi himself – although elected as a deputy, he never attended parliament and should technically have been dismissed. Meanwhile the Adjaran opposition lived in Tbilisi, due to threats against them in Batumi. It was unclear why Shevardnadze didn't stand up to him, given all Abashidze's insults and his talk of challenging for the presidency; as he had plenty of funds due to his take of the trade passing through Batumi from Turkey, he easily persuaded opposition parties outside Adjara to throw in their lot with him. Abashidze claimed to have been the target of frequent assassination attempts, which he blamed on the Shevardnadze government. No-one outside Adjara took this very seriously, but the streets of Batumi were full of young toughs in plain black clothes wielding Kalashnikovs.

All this changed after the Rose Revolution – in May 2004 Abashidze staged a confrontation with Saakashvili and had three bridges linking Adjara to the rest of Georgia destroyed. Saakashvili gave him ten days to disarm and return to constitutional rule, sending the army to conduct a major exercise just across the border, while activists were smuggled in to lead protests and seduce Abashidze's guard away from him. Fortunately he was also persuaded to go peacefully and was flown to Russia, and Adjara returned to being a normal part of Georgia.

On the coastal road from Poti or Samtredia, you'll enter Adjara (see map on page 176) at the bridge over the Choloki River, with a tourist information kiosk on the south side at km65/56. This is also the terminal of the yellow minibus that runs the length of Kobuleti from the station. The dunes just south cover the Pichvnari archeological site (see page 221). The road skirts the Ispani Marshes (also known as the Kobuleti Reserve), ecologically valuable wetlands similar to those near Poti (see page 194), and soon enters the long thin coastal sprawl of **Kobuleti**. A settlement has existed here since the 5th century BC; now it's chiefly a beach resort, although there is also a small port. With the closure of Abkhazia, this is currently Georgia's prime resort on the Black Sea, although the beach is black sand and everyone is aware of the polluted state of the Black Sea. The residents insist on cladding their buildings, even blocks of flats, with corrugated galvanised iron, which is perhaps not to all tastes.

The town centre lies just north of km75/46, 500m north of the modern rail station (where a 24-hour tourist information centre is planned), but this is a fairly dull area. Heading north on the main road along the coast, Davit Agmashenebelis (formerly Lenina), is where the accommodation begins.

WHERE TO STAY

Astoria Hotel Rear of Davit Agmashenebelis 213; ☎ 236 67177. At about km72.7, the Astoria is the first hotel you come to, a slightly tatty small hotel in a large house on Tamar Mepis, the beachfront promenade. *US$12.50 pp HB.*

Sanatorium Sakartvelo Davit Agmashenebelis 275; ☎ 236 67366. Just south of km71, currently closed for refurbishment, but with rooms available for tourists, with bath, 3 meals & 'heart profile' or cardiological assessment.

For the next kilometre northwards there's a lovely park to the west of the road, and restaurants and cafés in private houses to the east, making this by far the liveliest part of town in summer; private rooms are also available in almost every house in this area for US$10 per person, while cheaper rooms can be had in less fashionable areas, though still by the beach. In order of preference you could look for rooms at the following places:

Hotel Armazi Davit Agmashenebelis 356; m 899 150825. Offering basic but comfy en-suite rooms with lots of white tiles. *GEL20 pp.*

Natella's Davit Agmashenebelis 390; ☎ 236 66656; m 893 315273. Offering simple, clean & comfortable rooms, some with 3 or 4 beds making it ideal for families or groups. *GEL50 per room.*

Hotel Zauri Davit Agmashenebelis 382; ☎ 236 67744. Offering clean, bright *luxe* rooms with TV &

phone (now being refurbished). *GEL30 pp.*

Johnnie's Guesthouse Davit Agmashenebelis 408; ☎ 888 236 67134. Some English spoken here.

Davit Agmashenebilis 454 m 899 616168. With large basic clean rooms with TV, some with outside bathroom & balcony. *GEL10–20 (double that in Aug).*

Nani's Guesthouse Davit Agmashenebelis 338 (no phone). With basic rooms only. *GEL20 pp.*

This lively strip ends at km70 (just north of a pier and café) with two high-rise hotels, the Iveria & Kolkheti:

Iveria Now being rebuilt, in lovely gardens.

Intourist Kolkheti (300 rooms) Davit Agmashenebelis 285; ☎ 236 67820. Rooms cater for between 2 & 6 people, with a shower in each room but TV only in *luxe* rooms. *Open May–Sep; twin room GEL40 (sgl GEL25), without b/fast.*

Hotel Edem Davit Agmashenebelis 288; ☎ 236 66763. Down an alley across the road. *GEL30–75 per room.*

Beach Club Kobuleti Davit Agmashenebelis 373A; ☎ 236 66867; m 899 569677, 877 502932; e kbchotel@gol.ge; http://kbchotel.gol.ge. Near km66.5 & the last of a number of other isolated hotels to the north, this British-owned place is the best in town, with a Moroccan restaurant & a swimming pool. *Large dbl room US$140 (with king-size bed) HB, or sgl US$100 (there's also a smaller sgl room at US$80).*

✗ WHERE TO EAT/OTHER PRACTICALITIES You can eat at **Pizzeria Nikola** at km72 or at **Café-bar** Napoli and the **Green Café** (all signed in English) just south at Chavchavadze 12. There's a ProCredit ATM at Davit Agmashenebelis 104.

TOWARDS BATUMI From Kobuleti the road soon starts to climb away from the coast into the fringes of the Lesser Caucasus in a steep series of hairpins, while the railway follows an equally lovely route along the coast. Due to the influence of the mountains it's cooler in summer and warmer in winter than in Batumi; there's thick subtropical vegetation, with groves of bamboo as well as plantations of tea and citrus fruits. Thanks to this mild climate the road is in far better condition than similar roads elsewhere in Georgia. The road climbs past the ruins of the 6th-century Byzantine fort of Petra or Tsikhisjiri at km80, then drops from about km83 to Chakvi, a small coastal resort with a station at km 86/35 and the **Hotel Oasis** (*90 rooms; Batumi 16;* ✆ *222 70740;* f *70135;* e *hotel_oasis@gol.ge; GEL56–340*), to the west from the main bus stop at km87.5/33.5, 1.5km south of the railway station. Also here is the oriental Tea House, currently disused but a reminder that this is where Lan Chun-Chao introduced tea growing to Georgia. In 2005 a 657m-long road tunnel was opened through the ridge south of Chakvi; a second one to the north of Chakvi is due to open in about 2010. If you stay on the old road, it climbs again, then begins to drop towards the gate of the Agricultural Institute of the Academy of Science, which houses one of the best Botanic Gardens in Georgia (see below), at km93. The road is reunited with the railway at Makhindjauri (km97), a pleasant small resort of 15,000 residents; the most striking building is a restaurant opposite the station, built in 1917 by a Japanese architect, with a wrap-around verandah and nicely carved wooden lattices. A new two-star hotel and the Egrisi Restaurant are under construction by the park, east of the road. Finally the road and railway swing west along the shore of a bay to Batumi (km102/19), one of the most attractive and relaxed cities in Georgia. Most people will arrive by the route described above, but it's also possible to arrive from the Turkish border crossing at Sarpi, 19km south, and served by plentiful taxis and minibuses, or by the rough highway from Akhaltsikhe, to the southwest of Borjomi, untouched by pubic transport. This enters Adjara at the Goderji Pass (2,025m), which can be closed by snow any time between October and May, forcing a lengthy detour via Kutaisi. It soon enters the valley of the Adjariskhali River, which it follows to Kibe, where it meets the Chorokh River, flowing north from Turkey. This is a luxuriantly fertile region, with a profusion of vines, tangerines and watermelons, as well as magnolia, oleander, eucalyptus and cypress trees. Along the Adjariskhali there are also ten well-preserved Turkish bridges, built in the 10th to 12th centuries, spanning side-streams with surprisingly slender stone spans. The best known are at Makhuntseti and Dandalo. The mountain villages are home to the bulk of Adjara's Muslims; in addition the Tsiskara and Kintrishi reserves in the mountains to the north of the Adjariskhali, protect, in theory, Tertiary relict forests with some of the highest levels of endemicity in Georgia. Rare species include lynx, golden eagle, black vulture, falcon, Caspian snowcock, great rosefinch and Caucasian salamander, and many raptors migrate along the coastal flyway in September and October. The Tsiskara Reserve (now officially the 15,806ha Mtirala National Park) is just inland of Batumi; to reach Kintrishi, head north from Tskhmorisi (on the Adjariskhali) to Khino, where there's a ruined cathedral. It also lies on a new east–west horseback itinerary through the mountains.

Batumi, with its sheltered natural harbour, existed as a Greek trading colony by the start of the 2nd century BC at the latest; its name is probably derived from the Greek words *bathys limen* (deep harbour). Under Turkish rule it was never anything more than a tiny fishing village, but once the Russians arrived in 1878 it began a very rapid development. It was a free port from 1878 to 1886 and became the terminal of an oil pipeline from Baku, and in 1883 of the railway. In 1902 the man later to be known as Stalin organised a strike after the sacking of 400 workers from the Rothschild refinery; 15 lives were lost, and Stalin was sent to Siberia for three years. A week after the Armistice of November 1918, 15,000 British troops landed in Batumi to help protect Georgia and the Caspian oilfields from Germany and Bolshevik Russia; the last troops left on 9 July 1920, leaving the way open for the Bolshevik invasion and the takeover of Georgia. The democratic prime minister Noe Zhordania and his government fled from Batumi early in 1921. Now it's a city of around 130,000 people, and handles a great deal of trade with Turkey, both by land and sea.

GETTING THERE AND AROUND Until 2006 the daily slow trains from Kutaisi and Ozurgeti terminated at a halt almost lost in the sidings full of oil tankers just east of the bus station (take the footbridge by a preserved steam engine), but the trains from Tbilisi were too long to use this platform and used the station at Makhindjauri, 5km to the north. A **new train station** has been built in the northern outskirts of Batumi, south of the Chess Palace and beautiful House of Culture. This has a tourist information office and computerised ticketing; but it remains to be seen if the local trains will continue to the terminus near the market. Bus 100 and marshrutkas 101, 120, 150 and 201 run from the new station to the city centre. In addition to the day and night trains to Tbilisi, a new service has been introduced running on alternate days from 15 June to 15 September to Yerevan in Armenia (20hrs; US$25–47). You'll need to book several days ahead in summer for all these trains.

The **bus station** (✆ 222 30162/3) lies just off Tseretelis, not far east of the centre; the ticket hall is closed and you'll have to buy tickets from kiosks at the relevant bay. Grup Georgia buses, with air conditioning and reserved seats leave for Tbilisi at 07.00, 09.00, 15.00 and midnight; they take eight hours rather than six by marshrutka, but the buses are far more comfortable and restful. The fare is currently GEL18, for bus or marshrutka. Marshrutkas leave to Kutaisi and Poti almost hourly until 18.30; marshrutkas to Akhaltsikhe run via Kutaisi, leaving at 08.30 (6hrs; GEL18 to Borjomi or Akhaltsikhe). Buses run up the Adjariskhali Valley as far as Khulo, but only until 11.30; in the afternoons you should look for a marshrutka at the Hopa market, south of town.

The newly rebuilt **airport**, 3km south at Khelachauri (*marshrutka 110A/B;* ✆ 222 76649) at present only has flights from Odessa with Aeromost and from Kiev with UM Air (Ukrainsko-Sredizemnomorskiye Avialinii or Ukrainian-Mediterranean Airlines) and Georgian Airways, as well as one or two flights a day from Turkey. Aeromost's office is at ERA 86 (✆ 222 31422) and UM Air's is at Abuseridze 1 (✆f 222 76299).

It's also possible to arrive by sea, at the stylish **ferry terminal** at the north end of Zhordania – see page 57 for details of services (or ask at the 'Inquiring Office' in the terminal). Some cruises call here too.

There's no shortage of **taxis**, but for more comfortable and reliable Mercedes taxis try Taxi 2, waiting on the north side of the post office (✆ 222 31588); Taxi 777 (✆ 222 31070; m 877 511070); or Taxi 929 (m 899 929929).

Map of Batumi (Adjara, Georgia). Key labels include:

- BLACK SEA
- Jetty
- Promenade
- Beaches
- Lighthouse
- Riviera Yacht Club
- Ferry terminal
- Adjaran Assembly
- Stadium
- Old Ship Restaurant
- Intourist Palace
- Tennis club
- Park
- University
- Botanic Gardens
- Boji
- Market
- Batumi 2000
- New railway station, Kobuleti
- A305
- Footbridge
- Church
- Level crossing
- Bus station
- Hotel Tamamgzavri (Sputnik)
- Pedestrian crossing
- Bakuli
- Lavro
- Beso
- Market
- Sangsiro Restaurant
- Mosque
- Golden Keys
- Oscar
- Lotos
- Mercury
- Iliko
- Minibuses
- Former Roman Catholic church
- Bebo Guesthouse
- Polyclinic
- Piramida
- Church
- Armenian church
- Porto Franko
- David
- Tiko
- Metropol
- Montpellier
- Ritza
- Circus (closed)
- 'Producti' shop
- Post office
- City Hall
- Art Gallery
- Synagogue
- State Museum
- Esenin House
- Church
- Park
- Alik
- Theatre
- Oriental Sweets
- Turing
- New Cinema
- Puppet Theatre
- Old railway station
- Archaeological Museum, Sarpi, Turkey
- Bike shops

Streets: GOGEBASHVILI, MAYAKOVSKY, PUSHKIN, TSERETELI, KOMAKIDZE, CHAVCHAVADZE, GAMSAKHURDIA, ZHORDANIA, KUTAISI, KOSTAVA, MELASHVILI, GENERAL MAZNIASHVILI, GORGASALIS, K GAMSAKHURDIA, BARATASHVILI, PARNAVAZ MEPE, ZUBELASHVILI, TAVDEDUBLIS, ERA, ASATIANI, VAZHA - PSHAVELAS, CHINCHARADZE, NINOSHVILI, RUSTAVELI, SHIDZE, AB, MEMET, 26 MAY, MELIKISHVILIS

KEY
→ One-way street

N
Bradt
(SKETCH MAP)
Not to scale

BATUMI

TOURIST INFORMATION Adjara is the only part of Georgia that has a **tourist information** system (e *info@tourismadjara.com; www.batumi.ge/_en*), with five offices opened in 2006, and excellent new maps and leaflets. There's a tourist information kiosk (*open daily 10.00–20.00*) at the west end of Gamsakhurdias, at the seaside park; the staff speak English and are very helpful. There are others on Europe Square, the Sarpi border crossing, the Batumi and Kobuleti rail stations, and at the Cholokhi River, the entry to Adjara from Guria.

Note that in its wisdom the city has named two streets Gamsakhurdia (one for Konstantin, one for Zviad) and two for Khimshiashvili (Selim and Sherif).

WHERE TO STAY Unusually for Georgia, Batumi has a good choice of hotels, due more to the flow of businessmen across the border from Turkey than to tourism. Some of the flashier ones not only offer prostitutes, but are said to take serious offence if guests fail to avail themselves of their services. Currently Armenian, Kazakh and Tbilisi investors are putting US$100m into new hotels, in southern Batumi and all along the coast south to the border. Around 25,000 tourists from landlocked Armenia came to Batumi in 2005, a number which is expected to double within a couple of years, as they clearly don't mind the chain smoking and stony beaches. Refugees from Abkhazia have been paid US$7,000 per family to move out of communist blocks such as the Hotel Medea, which are being gutted or demolished and rebuilt.

Hotels are listed below from north to south.

Kaisa (12 rooms) Tamar Mepis 43; ☎ 222 70636; f 222 70638. In the Chess Palace, at the northern edge of town, are 9 dbls & 3 *luxe* suites, decent-sized rooms, but a tad plain & functional. There's no reason to stay out here except chess & the new rail station, although there is a new chapel in ancient fortifications on a hill across the road; marshrutkas 101, 120, 127, 150, 200 & 201 pass (& 102 terminates 500m south). *Dbl GEL40, suite GEL100.*

Tanamgzavri (still better known as the Sputnik) ☎ 222 76066/63; f 222 76396; e info@hotelsputnik; www.hotelsputnik.com. Set on a hill overlooking the city & the bay, this is a large-ish hotel, pretty disorganised in a likeable way. It's 2km from the bus station – follow the English signs inland & fork right, or take marshrutka 126. All rooms have a balcony, & some have large fridges. You may not want to stay this far from town, but it may be worth coming up here for dinner, & there's a swimming pool, table tennis & billiards. *Twin-bedded rooms GEL50, dbl GEL80, luxe GEL150, all inc b/fast.*

Boni (34 rooms) Mayakovsky 4; ☎ 222 71939, 222 74820; f 222 31171. Surprisingly good for its location just beyond the market, this is a modern block with a sauna (with cold pool), café-bar-restaurant & billiards, & good English is spoken. *Sgl GEL30 (which in fact is a slightly smaller dbl), dbl GEL40, plus 3 suites at GEL100, not inc b/fast.*

Batumi 2000 Mayakovsky 15; ☎ 222 72568, 222 54132; f 222 75500; e batumi2000@yahoo.com. Signed as the *Hotel-restaurant-poker club-disco club Batumi*, this is less good than the Boni but pricier, & virtually no English is spoken. *Sgl GEL40, dbl GEL60, luxe GEL80.*

Bakuri (11 twin rooms) Tsereteli 38; ☎ 222 76463; f 222 74788; e bakuriltd@yahoo.com. A decent modern block, with a bar but no other facilities; rooms are with shower, TV, & phone. *GEL30–90, not inc b/fast.*

Lavro (8 rooms) Pushkin 29; ☎ 222 32837; m 877 465167. A grotty guesthouse with rooms for 2 or 3 people. *GEL15 with shared bathroom & no TV, or GEL20/25 for an en-suite room with 30 channels of TV.*

Beso Zurab Beridze Seshakhveri (formerly Pereulok Kalieva) 15; ☎ 222 76669. A new building with restaurant-bar, pretty decent but no English spoken; rather post-Soviet single rooms. *GEL30–35, twins GEL30–40, & an apt at GEL80; all with bathroom & TV.*

Mercury (33 rooms) Chavchavadze 10; ☎ 222 31401–3; f 31405; e hotelmercuryBM@mail.ge; www.hotelmercuryBM.ge. A good new city-centre hotel that satisfies both businessfolk & Peace Corps Volunteers, this has a bar, bistro, sauna (GEL12 per hour), rooftop swimming pool & PCs with internet access. AC rooms with cable TV cost from GEL40 for 1 or GEL70 for 2 to GEL120 for a suite; they also have 3 'student' rooms without AC at GEL50 for 2, all inc b/fast.

🏠 **Lotos** Kutaisi 433; ✆ 222 76970. A small family hotel at the end of Gorgasali, opposite a local police station, it has rooms with up to 3 beds, all with shower, phone & TV. A bit of French is spoken. *Sgl GEL22, dbl GEL30, not inc b/fast.*

🏠 **Golden Key** (3 rooms) Gorgasali 3; ✆ 222 70789. Another small hotel. All rooms with shower & TV; some English spoken. *GEL25 for 1 or 2 people. Not inc b/fast.*

🏠 **Oscar** (9 rooms) Gorgasali 6; ✆ 222 76267. Similarly, a small place with rooms with shower & TV. There's AC, & everything's basic but clean. *GEL40 for 1 or 2 people, or GEL70 for a bigger luxe room with fridge, without b/fast, though with a small bar.*

🏠 **Venera Davitadze's homestay** Akhmeteli 9, Flat 32 (8th floor, to the left from the lift); ✆ 222 74232. Centrally located near the theatre & very friendly & well run, although they speak only Georgian & Russian. There's a big bedroom with a good bathroom & balcony, & a sea view from the sitting room.

🏠 **Ritza** Gamsakhurdia 14. Opening in 2007, a new city-centre hotel with rooms as well as *luxe* rooms (with balconies). *US$50–60.*

🏠 **Iliko** (7 rooms) Gamsakhurdia 42; ✆ 222 73892. A small, slightly grubby place in a courtyard, with twin rooms. There's a reasonable shared shower, & a café where you can get breakfast, & TV only at reception. *GEL15 pp (GEL20 ensuite).*

🏠 **Bebo** (5 rooms) Zubalashvili 31 (behind the former Catholic church); ▭ 899 584415. An ironclad house with washing facilities (occasional hot water) reached through the yard; 1 room with an external door & its own key, 4 others reached through the lounge. It's pretty rough, with trampoline beds, but fair for the price. *GEL10 pp, not inc b/fast.*

🏠 **Metropol** Nodar Imenadze 7 at Baratashvili; ✆/f 222 73794. A good modern building with twin rooms; also a huge AC apt with a remarkably small TV & 3 balconies. Snacks are available in the top-floor bar; limited English is spoken. *GEL50 for 1, GEL100 for 2, 4-bed rooms GEL120, apt GEL200, inc b/fast.*

🏠 **Montpellier** (6 rooms) General Mazniashvili 18; ✆ 222 76952; f 222 76950. Stylish, with TV, phone, minibar, hairdryer & Picasso prints; friendly, with a bit of English spoken, but still a bit mafia in style. Sited at what used to be the junction of Luxemburg & Liebknecht Streets. There are 3 twin rooms, & 3 'luxe' suites, all with TV, AC & b/fast. *Twin US$80, suite US$120.*

🏠 **David** (12 rooms) Baratashvili 33; ✆ 222 71718, 222 76530; f 222 76532; e hoteldavid@batumi.net; www.hoteldavid.ge. The best in town until the Intourist Palace opened, with big stylish rooms & a good restaurant, sauna, & tennis facilities; a café is being built next door. Good English is spoken, & there's internet & cable in all rooms. With standard twin rooms (good Sony TVs, full bath, minibar, hairdryer), & deluxe rooms (with jacuzzi), inc b/fast (no credit cards). *Twin US$120, deluxe US$220.*

🏠 **Alik** (40 rooms) Mehmet Abashidze 14; ✆ 222 75802; f 222 75803; e alik@gol.ge; http://hotelalik.gol.ge. A flash place with modern design, but bad art. All rooms inc b/fast & access to pool, gym & sauna (GEL20 per hr after noon). Also café & bar; English spoken. *US$70–80 for 1, US$100–120 for 2.*

🏠 **Zubelashvilis 4** (4 rooms) A small new pension, in an orange-painted house on a square near the mosque There are 2 bathrooms, a living room & kitchen, with fans but no AC. *GEL20 pp.*

🏠 **Tiko** (4 rooms) Zubelashvilis 40; ✆ 222 72715. To the south of Konstantin Gamsakhurdia, a slightly tatty guesthouse with 2 small sgls & 2 larger ones, all with TV & bathroom. There's no English spoken & no b/fast, but there's tea & coffee, & it's a friendly place. *Small sgl US$25, larger sgl US$30.*

🏠 **Intourist Palace** (146 rooms) Ninoshvili 11; ✆ 222 74600, 222 32123; f 222 33950; e info@intouristpalace.com; www.intouristpalace.com. A Stalinist block of 1939 totally remodelled & reopened in 2006 as a Turkish-run 5-star hotel. There are 4 swimming pools, 2 indoor, 1 outdoor & 1 for children. It's come a long way from the days when staff refused even to tell me the phone number for reservations. *Rooms from US$100 for 1 or US$115 for 2, to regular suites at US$225 & the presidential suite at US$955, all with b/fast & tax, plasma-screen TV & power showers.*

🏠 **Turing** (4 rooms) Dumbadze 5; ✆/f 222 73443. The Turing (as in Touring, not the pioneer of computing) is a large house with the usual men lazing around but few clients. Twin rooms (with dated bathroom, fan, cable TV & phone) & no restaurant. *GEL40 (for 1 or 2 people, inc b/fast).*

🏠 **Tennis Club** ✆ 74708; f 74700. Set in the park off Ninoshvili, these are lovely motel-style apts, each with a small garden; There are 8 artificial grass courts, costing US$10 per hr, & a bar above reception in the centre of the courts. Apt with 2 beds & a sofa cost US$120 (US$80 sgl), luxe apts for up to 5 people cost US$140–170, inc b/fast & an hour's tennis daily.

🏠 **Piramida** Vazha-Pshavelas 39 at Gorgasalis; ☎ 222 32204; 📱 893 732923; fax 222 72715. A small, newish hotel over a café-bar, with only Georgian & Russian spoken. Basic twin rooms with shower & TV, or larger rooms are available; b/fast is available in the café next door. *Basic room GEL20, larger room GEL30.*

🏠 **L-Bakuri** (33 rooms) Chavchavadze 121; ☎ 22276923/30; f 222 31310; e bakuri@ batumi.net. A block south of Melikishvili, a friendly well-run place with rooms ranging from sgls, dbls to 4 suites, all with bathroom, AC, fridge, TV; there's an adequate bar-restaurant too. *Sgl GEL40, dbl GEL70,* suite GEL120, inc b/fast.

🏠 **Tsereteli** (9 rooms) ERA 33; ☎ 222 76684; f 222 75873. A small place with dbl rooms (each with 2 beds), & 3 suites. All have AC, with satellite TV, minibar & balcony. There's a restaurant & bar & parking & laundry are available. *Dbl GEL70, suite GEL140, inc b/fast.*

🏠 **Astoria** (10 rooms) Selim Khimshiashvili 41; ☎ 222 32066; e hotel_astoria@mail.ru. All rooms have AC, 8 dbls, a 4-bed room, & a *luxe* room, with cable TV & fridge; internet access is available. *Dbl GEL60, luxe room GEL100.*

✖ WHERE TO EAT AND DRINK

There are relatively few good **restaurants** in Batumi, although you'll see signs with pictures of *khachapuri* outside cafés serving the cholesterol-laden Adjaran version of this snack. Other local snacks include *borano* (a fried cheese), *sinori* (a dough coil filled with curd and garlic), and honey-soaked *baklava* as a dessert.

✖ **Nazar Kabab** Kutaisi 27. One of the better *lokantas* (Turkish restaurants) by the mosque.

✖ **The Captain** Kutaisi 36; ☎ 222 70688. Facing the mosque's south side, this is a decent little fish restaurant.

Next to the Café Frontieri (Gogebashvili 26) are a few less smooth cafés serving grilled sardines.

✖ **Sanapiro (Coast) fish restaurant** Gogebashvili 7; ☎ 222 71549, 222 31271. A nice, pavilion-style restaurant, opposite the basic cafés on the promenade by the entrance to the harbour, very popular & being doubled in size despite its poor service.

✖ **Porto Franko** Gamasakhurdia 40, west of Zubelashvilis; ☎ 222 76222. Perhaps the best restaurant in town, serving Georgian food in a very slick setting.

✖ **The Dzveli Gemi (Old Ship)**. In a (new) wooden galleon between the stadium & the sea, serving Georgian food.

✖ **Salkhino** A good restaurant in the park between Ninoshvili & the sea (with *patzkha* wattle huts for private parties).

✖ **Princess Café** Mehmet Abashidze 45; ☎ 222 73733.

✖ **National Restaurant** 26 May 48, Gorgasalis; ☎ 222 76283.

There are plenty of cheap **cafés** around the market, some serving the Turkish version of pizza & strong coffee made the Turkish way in a bed of hot sand. Those worth checking out:

☕ **Café Batumi** Mehmet Abashidze 39, Tavdedubis; ☎ 222 146184. A good, relatively pricey café with nice historic photos of the city.

☕ **Café Saamo** Abashidze 37. Opposite the Batumi, brightly lit & less interesting.

☕ **Dzveli (Old) Batumi café-bar** In a stylish circular glasshouse north of the Roman Catholic church.

☕ **Mon Café** Marjanishvili 10, behind the Art Gallery.

Bars include the Český Pivní (Czech Beer) Bar (*Mehmet Abashidze 6*), serving Staropramen; the Racha and Temelas Dukani wine cellars (*Baratashvili 43*); and the Bar Senator in another cellar (*26 May 27 at ERA*).

In addition to the market by Tbilisi Moedani in the centre (being redeveloped), there's a good food market to the east on Mayakovsky. The House of Wine is a shop at Zviad Gamsakhurdia 43; decent souvenirs can be bought opposite the theatre.

ENTERTAINMENT Occasionally there's something worthwhile on at the **State Theatre** at Rustaveli 1 (✆ 222 74281), and the **Puppet Theatre** at Mehmet Abashidze 49 (✆ 222 70593) is still active; otherwise there are betting shops everywhere. There are two cinemas, the new **Cinema Tbilisi** (*Baratashvilis 6 at Bakuridze;* ✆ *222 73798*), by a huge interactive dancing fountain that's triggered by kids' movements, and the **Cinema International** (*Mehmet Abashidze 17*).

OTHER PRACTICALITIES

Currency exchange It's easy to exchange money in Batumi; there are exchange counters everywhere, even folding tables on the pavement around the market and Tbilisis Moedani, and also at the Hopa bazaar. In addition to the standard dollars, euro and roubles, some of them will also exchange pounds sterling, though at an awful rate. There are **ATMs** at Gamsakhurdia 19 and 34, Griboedov 2, Chavchavadze 10, 39 (opposite the old station), 78 and 131, Asatiani 18 (at Abashidze), Baratashvilis 25, Rustaveli 6, Ninoshvilis 35, on Asatiani at the rear of the Art Gallery, and also in Hopa at Davit Agmashenebelis 20.

Communications The **post office** is at Abashidze 33; there are a few new cardphones, and local calls can be made at kiosks with obvious telephone (PTT) signs, which also have faxes and photocopiers. There are just a few internet places, at Asatiani 58, Melikishvili 4, Inmadze 2, and upstairs at Zubelashvilis 14 (north of Gamsakhurdia, with a Cyrillic sign; closed Sunday and Monday). UPS is near the sea at Chavchavadze 99 (✆ *222 584375, 222 31452*) and DHL at Baratashvili 1.

There are bike sales/repair shops at Pushkin 59 and Pushkin 61.

A TOUR OF BATUMI If you leave the bus station and cross Tsereteli and the railway, you'll reach Gogebashvili, the main road along the harbour front. Confusingly, you head due north from the bus station to the sea, and the town lies to the west on a headland projecting into the Black Sea. Turning to the left/west, you'll cross Chavchavadze, where you'll find the best supermarket, and pass the port headquarters on your left and the ferry terminal on the right, always crowded with anglers. This is the start of the seafront promenade to the west and then south. Beyond it the **Riviera Yacht Club** is being constructed, to cater to the snobbiest of Batumi's new rich, who now laze about at the Tennis Club. Beyond this is the **Adjaran Assembly** or Council of Ministers and the **Ilia Chavchavadze Theatre**, and then a lighthouse at the end of Gogebashvili, by an area of wasteland with cars parked in lonely spots. Turning west here onto Ninoshvili, you'll pass the stadium and come to one of the city's finest features, the **Seaside Park** that stretches for a couple of kilometres along the shore; laid out by German and French gardeners (plus a Georgian who'd worked at Kew), it's now dotted with funfairs, cafés and restaurants; the beach, unfortunately, is stony, but still popular.

On the other side of the road are the Medea, Batumi and Meskheti hotels, all gradually being refurbished; heading inland just before the Intourist, on Konstantin Gamsakhurdia (formerly Lenina), you'll cross Rustaveli to the square behind the theatre, with a large statue of Ilya Chavchavadze to the left (where there was previously a statue of Lenin) and then government buildings and a plaza on the right. On the corner of Gamsakhurdia and Rustaveli it's worth looking inside the closed but intact **Oriental Sweets** shop for its glorious interior of gilt and stucco; similarly, you should pop into the **'Producti' shop** on Gamsakhurdia just east of Memet Abashidze (named after Aslan's grandfather; formerly Stalina). The tree-lined Gamsakhurdia is lined with some of the city's more snobby shops, and the **Armenian church** at No 25; it continues southeastwards through the Old Town to Tbilisis Moedani, the square which serves as terminal for most of the city's marshrutkas. beyond this is the central **market**, heaving with people and more like a Turkish bazaar than anything Soviet. If you take Chavchavadze, to the left of the market, you'll see the city's **mosque** to the left at Chkalov 6, just before reaching the harbour front again. Built in 1866, it's not particularly ancient and much like any small-town Turkish mosque, but it's more unusual in Georgia. Beyond this is the (relatively) Old Town, a tightly packed area of neoclassical houses, with balconies, columns and pediments, built about a century ago.

To the south of Tbilisis Moedani is the former **Roman Catholic church**. Built at the start of the 20th century in a sort of Baltic-Gothic style, with Arts and Crafts-like murals and stained glass, it's now an Orthodox church, although it remains largely unchanged. Just beyond it is the former railway station, a sadly abandoned pile (although there are proposals to convert it to a trade centre). Turning right here you'll come in three blocks to the **synagogue** at Vazha-Pshavelas 33, which reopened in 1998 after a thorough refurbishment; on the right-hand side of the street opposite, Chincharadze, at No 4, is the **State Museum of Adjara** (*open 10.00–17.00 daily*). This is a very old-fashioned (and easily missable) collection of stuffed wildlife (without scientific names), archaeological relics, tools, Arab metalwork and other odds and ends. Upstairs are some weapons, a display on the tea industry (including relics of the Chinese merchant Lan Chun-Chao who established the first plantations in Adjara), and photographs of Batumi's development in the 19th and 20th centuries; there are also some Byron-esque paintings of battling Turks, and a display on the Association of European Regions, the only international body to treat Adjara as a real entity, earning Abashidze's eternal gratitude. In the yard there's a whale's skeleton and a few medical monstrosities, as well as the toilet. You could ask here to see the two-room **Stalin Museum**, in the little white wooden house at Pushkin 19 where he stayed for a couple of months in 1901–02; it takes a reverential viewpoint now out of fashion in the rest of the world, with paintings and photos depicting him as the idealistic youthful union organiser, rather than the paranoid dictator he later became.

Immediately to the west, Vazha-Pshavelas crosses ERA kucha (Association of European Regions Street; formerly Gorki); across it to the right is the **Art Museum** at ERA 8 (*admission GEL5 for foreigners, GEL1 for Georgians; open 10.00–17.30, closed Mon*), which opened only in 1998, in a lovely building built in the 1930s to house a Museum of Communism. The upstairs gallery displays the older paintings, including pieces by Akhvlediani, Gudiashvili, Kakabadze and Pirosmani (a cow being milked, instantly recognisable); downstairs are pieces by more contemporary painters, a remarkable number of whom seem to have somehow been influenced by the Australian Sidney Nolan. Diagonally opposite it, facing Roses Square, is the **City Hall**, built around the start of the 20th century.

ERA continues south to Khimshiashvili and the new promenade (see below), but a block to the right, by a statue of a female aviator flying a one-winged toy plane with a child, is the main entrance to 26 May Park, surrounding a large lake; the oligarch Bidzina Ivanishvili is paying for its refurbishment, and also for a high-tech rebuild of the dolphinarium at its far end. The Russian poet Sergei Esenin lived at Melikishvilis 11 (formerly Engelska), on the northern side of the park, in 1924–25 between his fourth and fifth marriages (not to speak of his homosexual affairs); born in 1895, he was one of the most radical young poets at the time of the Revolution and an ardent supporter of the Bolsheviks, although he was refused party membership as he considered himself too much of an individualist. In 1922 he married the American dancer Isadora Duncan and set off to travel in Europe and

America, but he suffered a nervous breakdown and declined into alcoholism, with hallucinations. He then married Galina Benislavskaya, travelled to Batumi and Baku, then in 1925 married Sofia Tolstoya, Leo Tolstoy's granddaughter, and on 28 December 1925, hung himself in Leningrad, leaving a suicide poem written in his own blood. In Nice, in September 1927, Isadora was strangled instantly when her scarf caught in the wheel of her sports car.

Beyond the park, at Rustaveli 51, the **Aquarium** (*admission GEL1; open 11.00–18.00 except Mon*) stands on the campus of the State Maritime Academy and the Marine Ecology and Fisheries Research Institute; it's worth a visit, although many of the fish are in fact from the tropics. Bus 1 and marshrutkas 116, 120 and 155 come this way. South of the Maritime Academy the road turns 90° left and right, at the start of a new seaside boulevard, Sherif Khimshaishvili (not to be confused with Selim Khimshiashvili, running east from 26 May Park), where the city has built the fabulous 'Splashdance' animated fountain and lightshow, installed at great expense by a French company to be the centrepiece of the new tourist zone, with cafés, discos, bowling, tennis courts, a casino and so on. There's a Dutch-themed restaurant, marked with a windmill; other cafés along the promenade, such as the Fish Café, Dragon Café and Green Bar are to be rebuilt. There are also proposals to move the regional government offices to the end of Lermontov in the southern outskirts, to open up space in the city centre for development. North of Batumi (and unconnected with the development to the south) a Disney-style Aquapark is being built by Bidzina Ivanishvili.

Returning to the centre up Chavchavadze, a new **Archeological Museum**, behind Soviet arches at Chavchavadze 77 (*donations welcomed; open daily 10.00–17.00*) displays finds from Pichvnari, on the coast between Kobuleti and the Choloki River, where a joint Oxford University/Georgian team has been working since 1988 (see the Pichvnari homepage: http://home.jesus.ox.ac.uk/~mvickers). Meaning 'Place of the Pine Trees' in Georgian, Pichvnari is the site of a Greek trading settlement from the mid 5th century BC, on the site of an earlier Colchian settlement; there are Late Bronze Age, Early Iron Age, Classical and Hellenistic levels over an area of 100ha. Visitors would be made welcome at the site but there's not a lot to see, as the digs are in sandy soil and quickly filled in.

Here there are photos of the dig, Stone-Age pottery, Greek- and Roman-era articles including drinking bowls and medieval Arabic coins, including finds from graves at Gonio (see below); upstairs a large gallery is used for temporary shows.

One of Batumi's most interesting attractions is in fact 9km to the north: the **Botanic Gardens** at Green Cape (Mtsvane Kontskhi or Zheloni Meese), reached by minibus 150 (GEL2) which leaves from the corner of Gogebashvili and Chavchavadze and turns off along the old road above the tunnel. Get off at the hairpin at km28/93, go through the main gate and then right (the green gate to the left leads to the Agricultural Institute, which has beautifully labelled plants but they're mainly standard herbs and palms, bamboos and so on). Fork left to the gate and *kassa* (ticket office) (*admission GEL2; open 10.00–21.00*), and go below the administration building halfway down the hill. From here you'll gradually go down to the south, not far above sea, through some big mature eucalyptus trees as well as citrus plantations, to leave by the other gate at the Mtsvane Kontskhi train halt. This is served by just two trains each way per day, but marshrutka 101 (GEL0.70) leaves frequently, reaching the old road in 500m, just before its junction with the new highway from the tunnel.

Founded in 1912 and now run by the Academy of Science, the gardens cover 113ha with over 5,000 species of plants (and 1,200 varieties of rose) from around the world, as well as 40,000 specimens in a herbarium. As well as Caucasian flora, there are species from moist subtropical climes around the world, including Japan and the Himalayas. It's a great spot for a picnic in wonderfully lush surroundings, and the presence of the sea just below the trees always adds an extra frisson.

TO GONIO AND THE TURKISH BORDER Businessmen in black Mercedes race up and down the main road south from Batumi to the Turkish border; this starts by turning right off the road east to Akhaltsikhe at km107/14, at the entry to the village of Angisa. At km109 there's a turning to Batumi's airport, 200m to the west, before the road crosses the Chorokh River at about km110. At exactly km115/6 you'll find the gate to the fortress of **Gonio** on the left, with a mini-fort aptly placed in a playground across the road. Founded in the 3rd century BC, what is seen now is the outer wall of the Byzantine and Ottoman fort of Asparunt; it's a square of about 200m, with oranges, plums, strawberries and palms being grown inside, and mature eucalyptus trees outside, against a backdrop that's reminiscent of the gentler parts of the Nepalese foothills, with its luxuriant vegetation. Local people come in and out to tend their trees, but you'll have to pay the watchman GEL2 (if he's not around, ask at a kiosk, or the police are happy to find him); a paved path leads to the centre, where there's a relatively good WC with a tap outside, and excavations where lots of ancient pipework is being revealed. Outside the south wall a 5th-century burial site has been found, as well as a theatre and hippodrome from the 1st–3rd centuries. The grave of St Matthew the Apostle (Matthew Levi) is said to be by the cross to the left of the toilet block. It's possible to climb up onto the 5m-high walls at various points and walk around the square.

Getting there Minibuses charge GEL0.90 to Gonio or GEL1.50 to the Turkish border, 19km south of Batumi; a taxi to the border shouldn't charge more than GEL10, and coming from the border you may be able to share. It's a very busy route, and you'll be accosted by drivers yelling *'Sarpi Sarpi Sarpi'* as you arrive at Batumi's bus or train station. Minibus 142 (often with *Sarpi* on a sign in Latin script) runs from Tbilisis Moedani, in the centre of town; alternatively take a bus or minibus (14, 101 or 120) marked 'Khopa' (ХОПА in Cyrillic) to the Hopa Bazaar, on the edge of town, from where other minibuses and taxis run to Sarpi; you should be across the border in Hopa proper within a couple of hours, and in Trabzon in another three hours.

 Where to stay

🏠 **Guesthouse Gonio** m 899 577360. *Rooms GEL60.*

🏠 **Hotel Kakhidze** (11 rooms). *Rooms GEL80–100.*

To the south of Gonio (14km from Batumi) is Kvariati, also being developed for mass tourism, with a big spiral five-star hotel planned; at the moment you can stay in a couple of spacious modern beachfront hotels.

✗ **Where to eat**

✗ **Hotel Kvariati** (20 rooms) m 899 154500. *GEL120 in summer (GEL100 otherwise).*
✗ **Hotel Martini** (10 rooms) m 899 556464, 877 556464; www.martini.ge. *With 4 sgls and 6 dbls, & a cottage with 2 trpl bedrooms. All rooms are en suite with satellite TV fridge and balcony, & they also have a swimming pool, billiards, restaurant & bar. Sgl US$60 (from mid July to mid Sep; US$35 otherwise), dbl US$70 (or US$40), cottage bedrooms US$85 (or US$45) each.*

Other practicalities There is a **beach** at **Sarpi**, where the water is cleaner than in Batumi, but the air is thick with fumes from waiting trucks. Right behind the gate of the customs area is a **tourist information** kiosk, with helpful English-speaking staff who can book beds in Sarpi, Kvariati or Gonio, as well as Batumi.

A bed in a private house in Sarpi will cost about US$10 in August or about US$5 at other times; most of the houses on the road up to the right from the border crossing rent rooms.

Sarpi holds the Kolkhoba Festival on 20 August (in theory – check the date), a Laz festival based on the legend of the Golden Fleece that was revived in 1978.

There's a Turkish consulate at Mehmet Abashidze 8 (❧ 74790, 33909) in Batumi and a Ukrainian one at Melikishvili 71 (❧ 31478); there should also be an Armenian consulate by now. If you arrive in Georgia with a visa needing attention, the Ministry of Foreign Affairs has an outpost at Memet Abashidze 40 (❧ 70800–02; f 74111).

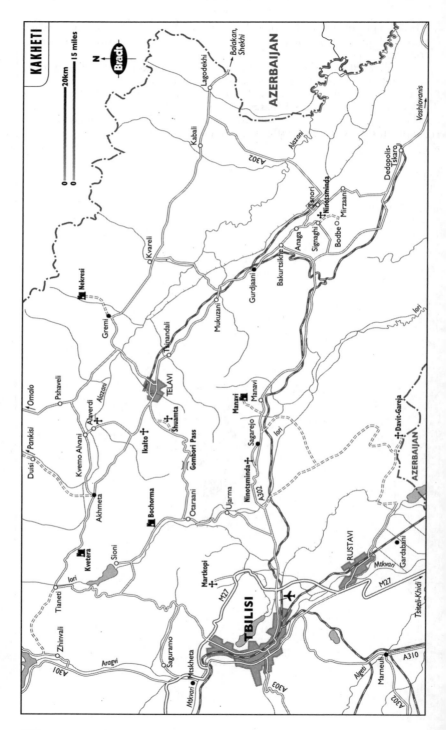

10

Kakheti

The easy-going, wine-growing province of Kakheti, to the east of Tbilisi, is justifiably popular for easy excursions of a couple of days (or even day trips from the capital), but it also gives access to Davit-Gareja and Tusheti, much harder trips along very rugged roads, but well worthwhile if you have the time. The *rtveli* or grape harvest in September and October is a fine excuse for a visit. The main road from Tbilisi runs to the south side of the Gombori Mountains, around their eastern end and then back to the northwest to reach Telavi, the capital of Kakheti; most buses and tour groups take this route, but it is also possible to cut directly across the 1,650m Gombori Pass by a rough road made worse by lunatic drivers.

In either case you'll head out of Tbilisi on the airport road, past the Isani and Samgori metro stations (terminals respectively for marshrutkas and buses to Kakheti – see page 86) with the white tower blocks of Varketili along the ridge to the left. After the flyover junction to the airport, with its needle-like monument, the six-lane dual carriageway becomes a four-lane highway, passing the huge Lilos Bazroba or open-air flea-market, and the Castell brewery, before leaving the city at about km21/139, by the intersection with the city's eastern bypass; from here it's single carriageway, with overtaking lanes up some hills. Heading north on the bypass and then going a few kilometres to the right on an unmade road would bring you to Martkopi, 5km northwest of which, on Mount Ialno, is the Monastery of St Anton, who spent his last 15 years as a hermit in a tower that still stands to the east; the church, founded in the 6th century, was rebuilt at the end of the 17th century (the belfry was built in 1629). At the top of a hill at km27 on the main A302, the direct route to Telavi turns left/north, passing through Ujarma, on the Iori River 45km from Tbilisi, where you can see an old stone church, the remains of a two-storey palace and fortifications with nine square towers. This was the residence of King Vakhtang Gorgasali, who died here in AD502; destroyed in the 10th century by the Arabs, the fortifications were restored in the 12th century. The road to the Gombori Pass, Shuamta and Telavi turns right in Otaraani, but if you continue up the left/east bank of the Iori to km56 it's possible to hike up to the 10th-century castle of Bochorma, with its six-apse domed church built in the 7th century.

NINOTSMINDA AND TSINANDALI

The main road soon descends from the Samgori steppe to cross the Iori and enter Kakheti at km35; you'll see the ruins of the 6th/7th-century fort of Khashmi to the north from a viaduct, and a few oil wells, and pass south of the village of Patarjeuli (km39), before, at km45.3, the old road turns left to run through Ninotsminda and Sagarejo, now bypassed. Buses to Telavi use the bypass (unsigned to the right), stopping for passengers only at the roundabout at its far end; if you want to visit Ninotsminda you'll have to take one of the local buses to Sagarejo, leaving from immediately outside the Samgori station.

There are no house numbers or street signs, so you should look out for the solid tower of Ninotsminda to the left of the old road around 2km from the junction, and 3km west of the centre of Sagarejo. You should get off the bus just west of a bridge over a dry stream bed and an unmarked petrol station, just before the road drops down to a bridge over a (usually) dry river and the town of Sagarejo. The site of Ninotsminda church has been used for Christian worship since the 5th century, and the present cathedral was built in AD575. It was largely ruined by earthquakes in 1824 and 1848, but is nevertheless profoundly impressive, the earliest large cruciform church to survive (anticipating the Jvari Church of Mtskheta). It has a tetraconch ground plan with corner niches, and in fact because the church is half ruined this is a good place to study the detailed arrangements. In the eastern apse are the remains of a 16th-century fresco of the Virgin and Child, and the western end of the church has recently been converted into a chapel. The belltower was built in the mid 16th century by Levan I; it shows strong Safavid-Persian influence, although it seems oddly primitive and almost African in feel. Around these are well-preserved defensive walls built in the 16th and 17th centuries.

Continuing across the Tvaltkhevi Bridge into Sagarejo (home of Chalice Wines, a Georgian-Californian joint venture), a roundabout marks the town centre, with a market just north; following the main road east, you'll fork right after five minutes and go downhill for almost 20 minutes to reach the roundabout at the end of the bypass (km50), where you can catch a bus onwards towards Telavi (marshrutkas for Tbilisi via Ninotsminda wait here too). Halfway down the hill you'll pass a small and very attractive old basilica.

EASTWARDS FROM SAGAREJO Continuing eastwards, at km59 you'll see the medieval Manavi Fortress, once the summer residence of the kings of Kakheti (known as 'Come and See Castle', as enemies always failed to take it) high on a hill to the left/north, with the church of Giorgi-tsminda (Saint George) below it. These can be reached by a road to the west at km51.5, which also gives access to the Mariamjvris Nature Reserve, one of the country's older reserves, protecting endemic pines in 1,040ha of the Gombori Mountains. At km64 a restored fort is visible just to the right. The main road climbs out of the Iori Valley and then from km94/66 drops steeply through woods into the Alazani Valley, past the junction to Signaghi (see page 238) at km 94.5, the Nakeduli restaurant (km99.5), and Vardiskheli (Cool Water) at km101.5, where there's a fountain and stalls, before reaching a roundabout at Bakurtsikhe (km103/57, an hour-and-a-half from Tbilisi), whose name implies that there is a castle here. In theory the main road is the one to the right, towards Azerbaijan, but most traffic turns left towards Telavi, 45km northwest.

GURDJAANI This road passes through Bakurtsikhe and reaches the centre of Gurdjaani at about km8/64. This is a large town known as a spa and a centre of winemaking; there is not a lot to see, but it's a pleasant place with lots of trees lining the streets. The second roundabout (with bus stand) marks the centre of town, and immediately to the right is the Aktala *kurort* or health resort, with mini-volcanoes belching forth healing mud, past which the pedestrianised Rustaveli leads downhill to the rail station. You can have treatment at the Aktala resort for an hour, or any period up to two weeks, except on Sundays; the mud is at its best in the mornings. Heading back towards Tbilisi, the market is to the left of the main road, more or less opposite the terminal of a disused cable car that once led up to a cool hilltop park; the road signposted to Arashenda also leads into the foothills to the west, where there's plenty of space for wild camping. About 2km southeast down the Tbilisi highway, at km6.5, a road (signed in English) leads up to the right for under

1km, to the house-museum of the great actress Nato Vachnadze, opened in 1989 due to the efforts of her sons, the film directors Eldar and Giorgi Shengelaia.

Continuing towards Telavi, the road passes below a war memorial in a large park, with a huge statue by Merab Berdzenishvili; about 250m beyond the town limits a road leads up to the east, rising above the left bank of the Kakhtubnis (or Gurdjaani) Gorge. Turning right after 1.5km you'll come to the Kvelatsminda church, the only ancient double-domed church in Georgia and perhaps Gurdjaani's main claim to fame. Built in the 8th century, it's a three-aisled stone basilica rather than a cruciform church, with two octagonal brick domes over the nave which are too small to dominate it. The church also has external galleries and lateral chapels, one of which projects to the northeast.

At km12 on the road to Telavi, in Chumlaki, a tiny old chapel stands on the right; there's no lock on the door, and inside it's very dark, totally blackened by smoke. There are no specific features of interest, but the place has an intriguingly pagan feel to it. At km18, just beyond the turning into the village of Velistsikhe, a road turns right to Kvareli (see pages 236–7), 17km to the northeast. The Telavi road crosses the railway and enters Mukuzani, where there's a simple basilica to the left of the road.

TSINANDALI There's a near-continuous string of villages, with vineyards behind them (and elaborate war memorials with busts of Stalin), until km36.5, at the far end of Tsinandali, where you reach the entrance to the Alexander Chavchavadze house-museum. Entering by a pedestrian gate beside the Tsinandali wine shop and restaurant, you'll cross a typically communist irrigation channel, huge and out of place, before following a cypress-lined avenue to the handsome pair of wrought-iron gates in front of the house. This is set in an ornamental garden of 12ha which you can enter without paying and is well worth a stroll. There are many fine, mature examples of rare trees, including umbrella pines, cedars, magnolia and lime trees, as well as bamboos and palms. To the right as you enter, the garden is relatively formal, leading to a big villa with large satellite dishes which is used as a holiday home by government officials, and is open to other visitors at other times. Behind it is a ruined chapel, all but the apse of which has now collapsed into the river bed. To the left the garden is slightly less formal, with a box maze; however it's too densely planted with trees to be an 'English park', as claimed. Beyond this section is a small zoo, now closed and empty. Behind the main house to the northeast are industrial buildings which house the famous Tsinandali winery, founded in 1884 by Alexander Chavchavadze's father. It can be visited by tour groups, who can taste the dry white wine, although not the 1814 vintage, which is the oldest in the collection. To the left/south of the winery is another hotel (✆ 2502 567499), once very stylish but now run-down, with erratic power and water supply.

The Alexander Chavchavadze Museum (admission GEL6 foreigners, GEL1 Georgians; open 10.00–18.00, closed Mon). The house itself is a relatively small and unpretentious two-storey manor house of local sandstone, which now houses a museum dedicated to the poet Alexander Chavchavadze, leading spirit of the Romantic movement in Georgia. Born in St Petersburg (where his father was Georgian ambassador) in 1786, he joined the Russian army and served against Napoleon and the Turks before settling in Georgia, marrying Salome Orbeliani, a member of one of Georgia's grandest families. The house at Tsinandali was built in the early 19th century as a summer house, and his main residence was in Tbilisi; although he wrote poetry, Chavchavadze's main importance was as translator of the poetry of the French Romantics and as chief animator of the circle of writers and critics who created Georgian Romanticism. Many of the

leading Russian Romantic writers also came to Tbilisi, usually with the army or government; these included Alexander Griboedov (1795–1829), who married Chavchavadze's daughter Nina when she was just 16. He was a notorious philanderer and is generally supposed (although the museum staff might disagree) to have seduced her and then been forced to marry her; almost at once he was sent on a diplomatic mission to Tehran which went tragically wrong when a mob stormed the Russian legation and killed all the Russians, brutally hacking Griboedov's head off. The teenage widow became a symbol of grief, and is portrayed as such on their shared tomb in Tbilisi's pantheon.

Chavchavadze himself died in 1846 in a bizarre accident in Tbilisi, when his cloak caught in the wheel of his carriage and he was thrown out, hitting his head on the ground. In 1854 the house was burnt by Chechen rebels, who kidnapped the Chavchavadze princesses and their children and servants and rode off into the Caucasus with them lashed across their saddles. Their leader Shamyl demanded the return of his son Djemmal-Eddin (or Jamal Al-Din), who had been handed over to the Russians as a hostage 15 years before, at the age of eight, and given a Russian education and then a commission in the army. Negotiations took nine months, but eventually the hostages were exchanged (together with 14,000 silver roubles for the rebels); alas, the last thing Djemmal-Eddin wanted or was suited to was a life in a rebel village in the Caucasus, and deprived of the glittering social life of the court he faded away and died within six months. Just one of the Chavchavadze children avoided capture by hiding in a hollow tree, which can still be seen beyond the maze.

In addition to the museum, which is captioned in Russian and Georgian only (although there is a German-speaking guide), you can visit nine rooms of the house, still with original furniture, including the French piano (with a folding keyboard) given by Griboedov to Nina. There's also a reproduction of the Winterhalter portrait of Chavchavadze's wife Salome.

TELAVI თელავი

To the west of Tsinandali is Kisiskhevi, where one of the churches has a circular tower built of river stones (and the BBC's former Moscow correspondent Rob Parsons has a share in a vineyard and a holiday home). From Tsinandali it's 5.5km to the city limits of Telavi, and about 3km more to the centre. The city sits at 568m on a hilltop above the Alazani Valley. In the 2nd century it was mentioned by the Greek geographer Ptolemy as 'Telada', and was the capital of Kakheti in the 11th century and again from 1615 (when Gremi was destroyed by the Persians) to 1762 (when Tbilisi took over); with a population of just 28,000 it's still the largest town in Kakheti.

GETTING THERE There are two bus stations on either side of the road immediately below the market; to the left is a small yard packed with buses to most destinations, including the frequent private minibuses to Tbilisi (there's a *kassa* and toilets at the bottom end), while a little further down and to the right is a large yard used only by buses and minibuses to Akhmeta, Alaverdi, Gremi and Kvareli, and buses to Tbilisi (every hour or so until early afternoon). Heading up the hill from the market (which has stalls selling good hot snacks) is a broad boulevard (Ketevan Tsamebuli) with a stream and trees in the middle; at the first crossroads you can turn right into a run-down residential quarter.

WHERE TO STAY AND EAT The city's two **hotels** are now both closed, the tower-block Hotel Intourist Kakheti, set in the ruins of the Vakhvakhishvili fortifications but now housing refugees from Abkhazia, and across the road to the right (to the right of the statue of Irakli) the Hotel Telavi at Kostava 2. However there are good **homestays**, especially along Nadakvardi, the road above the Hotel Telavi (turn right off Freedom Square past the theatre).

⌂ **Svetlana and Spiridon Tushishvili** Nadakvardi 15; ☎ 250 71909; m 877 756625; e sspiridon@rambler.ru; www.globalsalsa.com/telavi. They have beds in a lovely AC apt with b/fast, cable TV (including BBC World!) & swimming pool. English spoken. 1–2-day trips can be arranged with a

neighbour from GEL30. Beds GEL30 pp plus GEL5 for a big b/fast, or GEL45 HB (inc wine).
⌂ **Nana Shaverdashvili** Nadakvardi 9; ☎ 250 32185. Also with pleasant, clean rooms. English also spoken. GEL25 plus food.

There's another homestay on offer at No 9, and also No 1 and Chonkadze 11.

⌂ **Merab Milorava** Akhvlediani 67, just uphill from Nadakvardi. Merab works in the regional government building at the start of Kostava (up 2 flights & to the right) & offers rooms in a cottage in a lovely garden with room for 4 or 5 people, with safe parking, or a car is available. US$20 pp (US$60 for

4), or US$25 each FB.
⌂ **Lali Hosroshvili's Guesthouse** No 4 on the second lane off 26 May, which runs uphill from Kostava east of the theatre; ☎ 250 71824. There are 5 dbl rooms and a wine marani.

Others (not as a rule speaking English, but recommended otherwise):

⌂ **Mrs Asmati** 9 April 83; ☎ 250 73137
⌂ **Dodo Kalandadze** Chabua Amiregibi 10; ☎ 250 71829
⌂ **Nana Gurashvili** 26 May; ☎ 250 73238
⌂ **Teliani Valley** (8 rooms) Tbilisi Highway 3; m 899 363600; e nana-teliani@mgroup.com;

www.mgroup.ge. One of the more modern & dynamic Georgian wine companies, Teliani Valley (www.telianivalley.com) has a modern hotel at its winery on the eastern edge of town. There are 6 dbls & 2 suites, inc 2 meals & a tour of the winery with a tasting. Dbl US$50, suite US$80.

The best **restaurant** is the **Pakhas Dukani**, on the west (uphill) side of Ketevan Tsamebuli (signed in Georgian only); there's also a good café on Freedom Square and two pizza-cafés facing each other on Kostava.

OTHER PRACTICALITIES Teliani Group subsidiary **Via Travel** (☎ 250 303030) can arrange tours. In Telavi you can buy wine at **Shumi Wine Co** (Leonidze 33; ☎ 250 923692; f 250 922900; e shumi@shumi.ge; www.shumi.ge).

Internet access is available at Telavi Internet Club at Kostava 1 and Internet Café and Games uphill of Kostava at the corner of Ketevan Tsamebulis. **ATMs** are at Kostava 7, Ketevan Tsamebulis 11 and Irakli II 5.

WHAT TO SEE AND DO It's now hard to find the quaint old streets lined with elms (tela) and wooden-balconied houses which used to characterise Telavi, but there are traces here, as well as the zigzag patterns of river stones that are still typical of the region.

Turning left at the same crossroads, you're on the city's main street, Kostava, lined with relatively tasteful post-war blocks, housing the post office and so on, which leads to the large **Freedom Square**, with the **Batonistsikhe citadel** to the left. This contains various churches and palaces, now housing a school and museum. If you turn left (past a statue symbolising the wine harvest and towards a striking neoclassical hall) to enter on the near side, you'll pass the school on your left and a sculpture park on the right, and find the **Ketevana Iashvili Art Gallery** (GEL3) in front of you; opening hours are erratic, but it's worth a visit. In addition to the works of local painters (there are lots of views of Gremi and Alaverdi) and five paintings by Elena Akhvlediani (born in Telavi in 1901), it houses lots of 17th- to 19th-century German and French paintings, a few Dutch ones, and Russian landscapes. Continuing to its left side and past various other buildings, you'll find the **palace** of King Irakli II, a relatively small and low two-storey building built in the 1750s in the Persian style, one of the least expected buildings in Georgia. The correct procedure is to go on around the outside of the citadel to enter at the east end and buy a ticket (*GEL6 foreigners, GEL1 Georgians*) for a tour of the palace and the small museum of history and ethnography it houses. Beyond the palace are two churches, a tiny and very simple basilica, built of stone in the 17th and 18th centuries, which is always open although there's little to see, and a larger brick church, built by Irakli in 1758, which is abandoned and shut up. There's also a pantheon, bringing together the graves of sundry Kakhetian notables, and the ruins of the 11th-century royal baths.

Leaving the citadel by the east gate beyond the palace, you emerge by the large equestrian statue of King Irakli II, by Merab Merabishvili (facing a huge plane tree said to be over 800 years old). There's an attractive fountain below, now almost underground due to road improvement.

WEST OF TELAVI

Shuamta Heading west from Telavi, it's about 2km to the city limits and another 1km to the junction (at about km48/24) of the road south to Tbilisi and Gombori. Taking this road for about 8km to km57 and turning left onto the old road (not served by buses), you'll come to the monastery of Akhali (New) Shuamta, where you can see a cruciform brick church built in the second quarter of the 16th century and decorated with frescoes of the founders King Levan of Kakheti, Queen Tinatin and their son Alexander. Tinatin became a nun and was buried here; her tomb was found in 1899, and she is remembered on 3 September. Alexander Chavchavadze is also buried here, by the north wall. However the nuns who have returned here are somewhat fierce and unwelcoming. The real attraction is another 3km up the road, the nunnery of Dzveli (Old) Shuamta, beautifully set on an isolated hilltop in the forest. There are three churches here; the southernmost is a triple-church basilica dating from the 6th century, with a barrel vault and its original alabaster iconostasis. Immediately to its north is a tetraconch cruciform church with an octagonal dome, dating from the early 7th century (and modelled on the Jvari church), and to the east is a smaller 17th-century version of the same. There is supposedly a tunnel from here to Ikalto.

Families from Telavi often come to the lovely Tetris Khlebi Waterfall above Shuamta on the side of Mount Tsivgombori: a lovely spot for a picnic and a stroll.

Ikalto and beyond There's no shortage of local buses heading west from Telavi, to Akhmeta and Alaverdi, all of which pass through the village of Ikalto, famed as the site of the academy at which the national poet Shota Rustaveli studied; students kept a jug of wine under their desks, to renew their inspiration as required. At km53.5/18.5 (8km west of Telavi) there's a large signpost to the academy, 1.7km south up a good road along a valley. Halfway up you'll see a tiny chapel on the far left bank which, although open, is of no real interest. At the end of the road you'll find the three churches and the ruins of the academy crammed together in a relatively small compound, beautifully set among cypress trees. It was founded in the third quarter of the 6th century by St Zenon, one of the Syrian Fathers who established Christianity in Georgia, but the main church is the 8–9th-century Church of the Transfiguration (Gvtaeba), which is the oldest in Kakheti to have a central dome supported by four free-standing pillars. The belfry over the porch at the west end was added in the 19th century; its interior was whitewashed by the Russians, also in the 19th century, so there's little to see, although Zenon is buried here. To the east is the original 6th-century Church of the Trinity (Sameba), a small basilica with an odd groundplan, with apses off the side of the sanctuary, and steps to a chamber over the porch. Just to the south of the main church is the 7th-century Kvelatsminda church, another bare, undecorated basilica, and behind it the ruins of the academy's refectory, built at the start of the 12th century and destroyed by Shah Abbas in 1616. It lost its roof a long time ago, but the stone walls and window arches remain; Georgians find the ruins very moving because of the association with Rustaveli, but although they are doubtless 'romantic in the extreme' foreigners may find them of less interest. In Ikalto the Hotel Tamarioni (✆ 250 *50109*; m *899 567515*; e *thamarioni@yahoo.com*) has eight nice double rooms, with weekend breaks costing US$100; you can also camp here.

From the junction at km56/16, another 2.5km west, the main road continues for 16km to Akhmeta, a winemaking town of no particular importance (except for its 8–9th-century basilica and as the birthplace of the film director Sandro Akhmetili) near the point where the Alazani River emerges from the hills. A road follows it north to Zemo-Omalo, easily confused with Omalo in Tusheti (see below), but you should not go here – this is the Pankisi Gorge, notorious for kidnappings and other outrages. In any case you'll be stopped at the Dousi checkpoint, about 20km north of Akhmeta. There are seven villages in the Pankisi, populated by Kists, ethnic Chechens who settled here from the late 17th century to the early 19th century.

Kvetera, a ruined town-fortress, lies hidden in the hills to the west of Akhmeta; 9km along the road to Tianeti, you should fork left onto the upper road, and left again after 2km. In another kilometre you'll find the fortress and its tiny jewel of an 11th-century church. Built of white tuff, with blue tiles, it has a most unusual semi-diamond-shaped groundplan, with four equal transepts and four smaller niches between them. Tianeti itself, on the upper Iori River, is a tranquil village set in the foothills of the Caucasus; it's surprisingly close to Tbilisi, which can be reached by a poor road to Gldani, in the northwestern suburbs.

Alaverdi
Turning right at the junction 2.5km west of Ikalto, it's 9km north through the vineyards to the great Cathedral of St George at Alaverdi, 20km from Telavi. Founded by Joseph, another of the Syrian Fathers (whose festival is on 28 September), the present church was built in the early 11th century, one of the largest medieval churches built in Georgia. Built of *shirmi*, the tuff (or travertine) stone ubiquitous in Kakheti and Armenia, it was damaged by the Mongols (with repairs in brick in the 15th century), by Shah Abbas in 1616, and by an earthquake in 1742, after which it was restored by Irakli II. It was surrounded with defensive walls in the early 18th century, with the massive gate tower added in the following century. It is now, since the destruction of the Bagratid church in Kutaisi, the highest church in Georgia, its dome rising 50m from the ground. It's a triconch church, but with an ambulatory to the west as well, the north and south apses being incorporated into a rectangular plan.

The frescoes date from the 11th to 13th centuries and the 15th century; they were whitewashed by the Russians in the 19th century, and gradually uncovered and restored from 1967. They include St George over the west door, the Virgin and Child over the altar, and others in the south transept. See also the single hand, carved in relief on a flagstone to the left inside the entrance; the story goes that a local prince was captured by the Turks, and before being killed cut off his hand, so that it could be taken home and buried in holy ground. This is also the burial place of Queen Ketevan the Martyr, who was tortured to death by Shah Abbas in 1624.

To the northwest of the church are the ruins of the Persian governor's summer palace, built in 1615, including a low octagonal brick pavilion. The Alaverdovo pilgrimage and folk festival lasts for two weeks, climaxing on 14 September, the feast of the Exaltation of the Life-Giving Cross (relics of which were given by the Patriarch of Jeruslalem to King Levan in the 16th century). Buses continue to the village of Alaverdi, just north, and return after half an hour, making this feasible as a quick excursion from Telavi.

TUSHETI

Just beyond Alaverdi, on the far bank of the Alazani, is **Kvemo (Lower) Alvani**, a village which in summer is very quiet but in winter acts as home to the bulk of the population of Tusheti, on the far side of the Caucasus watershed. It's the starting point for travel to this wonderfully remote and scenic area. It's also the administrative centre for the Tusheti National Park (*www.tushetipa.ge – currently only in Georgian*), which comprises a total of 16,297ha in the Tushetis, Batcharis and Babaneuris reserves. In the Batchara Gorge, north of Akhmeta, there's a unique forest of yew trees, up to 25m high, 1.2m in diameter, and 2,000 years old; this is currently inaccessible due to the problems in the Pankisi Gorge, immediately adjacent (see pages 26 and 231). The Babaneuris Reserve, just north of Kvemo Alvani, has yews about 1,000 years old, from 950m to 1,350m altitude. The Tushetis Reserve protects possibly unique virgin forests of pine (2,000–2,200m) and birch (2,300–2,600m). The national park is new and not yet visible on the ground; it will be giving grants for guesthouses and for horse-trekking outfits to buy equipment.

The region of Tusheti was effectively autonomous as a tribal democracy until the end of the 17th century, and a road was not built here until 1978–82; power lines were also installed then, but these are now derelict and there is, simply, no electric power in Tusheti, and no telephones either. GSM mobile phones do work in places but have to be charged by generators. It's similar in many ways to Svaneti, with similar traditions of hospitality coupled with building spectacular defensive towers; but, unlike Svaneti, there have been no reports of robberies here. The scenery is almost as spectacular as in Svaneti, with peaks up to 4,500m, deep gorges and high waterfalls, and well-preserved pine forests of *Pinus kochiana*. Tusheti delicacies include *kotori*, a bread with a cheese and potato filling and very salty *gudiskweli* cheese, made of sheep's milk in a bag (*guda*) of sheepskin, with the wool on the inside. There's also homemade beer and *zhipitauri* firewater (as in Khevsureti).

A poor road runs north from Kvemo Alvani to the 2,927m Koja (or Abanos, meaning hot baths) Pass, which is only passable between mid June and mid October. You'll pay US$60–70 for a Niva jeep to Omalo (plus US$40–50 per day there), or GEL20 to ride on an old green ex-military truck which leaves Kvemo Alvani most days at about 08.00; you may also have to pay the same again for a rucksack, making a total of GEL80 for a return trip. It's also possible to take a small plane but it's not subsidised, unlike flights to Svaneti; contact Tusheti Air at Davitashvilis 7, Tbilisi (✆ *947765, 947046, 947765*). The road runs through Pshaveli, the main settlement in Pshaveti or land of the Pshavs, relatives of the Tushetians and Khevsurs living on the south side of the Caucasus watershed. The poet Vazha Pshavela ('son of Pshaveti') was born here and returned in the 1880s to live as a peasant.

It takes four to five hours to cover the 71km from Alvani to Omalo in a Niva, perhaps twice as long in the truck, passing through Khiso and then Khakhabo, marked by abandoned towers. In fact Georgian hiking trips may use horses for almost the entire journey from Alvani, taking two days to reach Omalo, with a decent wild campsite halfway. In Shtrola, south of Omalo, the Lukhumaidze family provides guesthouse accommodation for Caucasus Travel and anyone else passing through. Sergo Sulakuri can provide accommodation, transport and guides in **Omalo**, the village (at 2,050m) where Tusheti's airstrip, boarding school and hospital are located, as well as a small museum and a hotel (US$30). Omalo is also the base of the monitors of the OSCE (Organisation for Security and Co-operation in Europe), who are ensuring that no Chechen fighters cross the border; Georgian frontier troops may check your passports. The new town of Omalo, seemingly half-built Soviet houses, is by the track in the valley of the Pirikiti Alazani (known as the Andikoysu in Russia); old Omalo, a cluster of fortified tower-houses, is set high on the slope above. You can visit the 12th/13th-century fortress of Kesalo.

HIKING IN TUSHETI An attractive walk of about two hours back along the road south from Omalo leads to the village of Khiso, where there's a 12th-century fortress, and a similar distance to the southeast (crossing the Pirikiti Alazani by a suspension bridge) is Shenako (2,050m), where there's a spectacular 16th-century church, as well as a guesthouse. From Shenako it's a 15-minute walk to the abandoned village of Agiurta, dominated by a seven-storey tower. The people of Agiurta now live in Tbilisi but want to return home, and there are plans to help them find a sustainable livelihood here. A mountain path leads east from Shenako across the border into Daghestan, and another leads north, further into the heart of Tusheti. It's an hour or so to Diklo, overshadowed by the 4,285m peak of Diklos, to the north. This can be reached directly from Omalo, going northeast past the cemetery and the church of Tamar and her son Giorgi Lash, and hiking on for four to five hours. You can walk up to the hilltop village of Dano or make side trips to the Gometsri and Tsovati gorges, where there are 18th-century tombs in which plague victims are said to have voluntarily shut themselves up. There's also a path into Daghestan, in the Russian Federation. There are festivals here on 20 July and 10 August, and Lamzira Gotaidze organises accommodation. WWF is funding an ecotourism project in this area, providing alternative energy sources to boost tourism, and other sustainable sources of income, such as making honey and carpets, using natural dyes and the wool of the aboriginal Tusheti mountain sheep.

From Diklo a path continues westwards, at times only 50cm wide and hugging the edge of a vertiginous cliff, and then crosses the **Diklo** or **Sonekhi Pass** (2,560m) after three hours and drops slightly to Chigho (2,400m), known for its pagan festival of Lasharoba, when a ram is sacrificed 100 days after Easter, honouring the spirit of war. South of Chigho the trail meets a direct path (over a 3,000m pass) from Omalo, then heads up the Pirikiti Alazani Gorge to a bridge in the valley further west where you'll climb up past a ruined church to **Dartlo** (1,900m). Here there are about 30 towers and new guesthouses, run by Besik Elanidze (m 899 118993), Tsinari Bigoidze (m 893 120811) and Rezo Petriashvili (m 893 444229). Above Dartlo is Kvavlo, with a beautiful tower with a tetrahedronal roof. There are more towers, and shrines to those drowned in the river, as the trail continues west up the Pirikiti Alazani into the mountains (passing Jesho, just up a side-valley to the north, **Parsma** (1,960m, with fine medieval towers and houses linked as a virtual fort) and Chontio to reach the village of Girevi, just 11km south of the Chechen border, where the OSCE has a post. Most hikers will return to Omalo, but it is possible (when politics permit) to continue from Girevi by a long, tough trail to Khevsureti – allow a week from Omalo to Shatili. This follows the upper Pirikiti Alazani and then the Kvakhidistqali through largely abandoned settlements such as Baso and Hegho, before the tough climb on

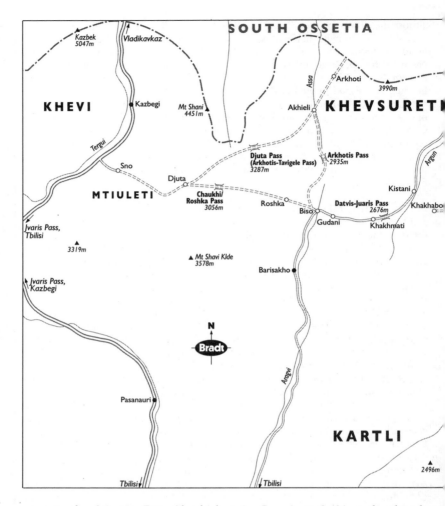

scree to the **Atsunta Pass** (the highest in Georgia at 3,431m; closed early October–March), between **Tebulos** (4,493m) to the north and a peak of 3,839m to the south. This is an unpopulated region, but as you camp in alpine meadows you may come across the occasional shepherd. Descending into the Andaki Gorge and heading northwest through Ardoti, you'll eventually reach **Mutso**, the first Khevsur village, from where a rough track leads virtually to the border and then south to **Shatili** (see page 155). Explore and the Georgian operators GeorgiCa, Caucasus Travel and the Sustainable Tourism Centre organise hiking trips along this route, when allowed. You can also hike west from Omalo up the Tushetis Alazani Valley to villages such as Beghela, Dochu and Jvar-Boseli, from where a pass crosses north into the Pirikiti Alazani east of Girevi.

EAST OF TELAVI – FROM GREMI TO LAGODEKHI Alvani lies on the road along the left/north bank of the Alazani, from Akhmeta to the Azerbaijani border. Heading east, it passes through Napareuli, a village known for its grapes, to reach **Gremi**, 19km northwest of Telavi by the road to the Lagodekhi border crossing.

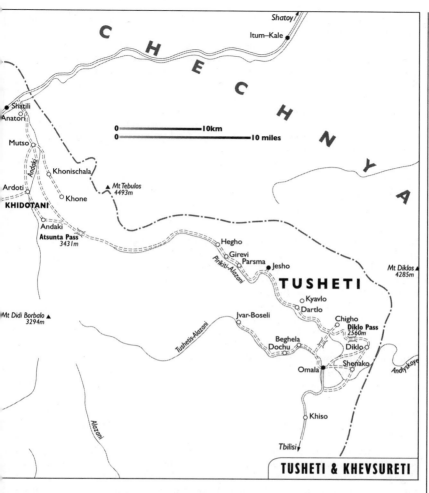

Marshrutkas run from Telavi to Eniseli, immediately beyond Gremi; from Telavi take the Tbilis road then then turn left at the edge of town, following an avenue of trees to the Alazani River, turning right at the junction west to Akhmeta, and going around a ridge with ruined fortifications. Gremi is now little more than a pleasant village (known for its brandy), but there was a city here by the 6th century AD, and it was the capital of Kakheti from 1466 until 1616, when it was utterly destroyed by Shah Abbas. High on a rocky ledge at the west end of the village (with good steps leading up from the main road), a few crumbling ruins remain of the fort, built in 1565, and the palace and three-storey dwelling-tower, built of red brick on stone blocks. The dome church is in great condition; it was built in 1575, with paintings completed in 1577, and reconsecrated in 1989. Along with the tower at Ninotsminda, the citadel of Gremi is the best example of Georgian adaptation of Persian styles of architecture, such as patterned brickwork (ie: arches in relief). There's a museum by the church displaying ceramics, spear- and arrowheads and various implements; there's a shop and they'll lay on a tour to Nekresi for US$3 – it's worth paying the GEL3 for the museum if only as a way to get the church opened and go up the tower, which gives great views to the Caucasus.

About 9km east of Gremi, a rough road is signed to the left, leading up into the hills to **Nekresi**, site of one of the oldest churches in Georgia, a little basilica dating from the third quarter of the 4th century. Inscriptions found here recently are claimed to date from the 1st to the 3rd centuries AD, making them the earliest examples of the Georgian alphabet. In the 6th century this monastery was the base of the Syrian Father Abibos, who was martyred by the Persians after pouring water on a Zoroastrian sacred fire; in the next century a three-church basilica, perhaps the finest example of the genre, was added (and painted in the 16th century), followed in the 8th and 9th centuries by a bishop's palace (with a tower added in the 16th century), and a cruciform church, by the present entrance. Frequently raided by the Lesghians, it was finally destroyed in the 18th century. From the end of the road you'll have to walk for 45 minutes to reach the monastery, a vertical kilometre above the valley. This is the only place in Georgia where pigs are still sacrificed, because a Persian army was driven away by rolling pigs' heads down the hill at them. Continuing eastwards from Gremi for half an hour, you'll come to **Kvareli**, home of the Kindzmarauli winery. From the highway junction the tree-lined Chavchavadze Avenue leads north for 2km, through the town to the marshrutka terminal; returning south for about 200m you'll see the Church of St John the Baptist to the right, opposite a white building like a Corbusier chapel. Built in 1978, this is the **house-museum of Ilia Chavchavadze** (1837–1907) (*admission GEL0.50; open 10.00–17.00 except Mon*), the editor of the popular newspaper *Iveria*, founder of critical realism in Georgian literature, and creator of Georgian theatre, translating Molière and Gogol and introducing the plays of Shakespeare. He also reformed the alphabet, and became a deputy in the Russian Duma or parliament. As leader of the moderate reformist and nationalist tendency, he was officially declared a secular saint after his murder by either tsarist or Bolshevik agents – just who is disputed, and both seem to have had an interest in removing him. The Iliaoba Festival is held on 8 November on Ilias Gora, a hill with the with country's largest statue of him, which is a popular picnic spot.

In the garden behind the museum is the defensive tower in which he was born in 1837 while the family hid from an attack by Lesghian tribesmen – this is seen as deeply symbolic, as he spent his life defending Georgian culture. Beyond the tower is the 17th-century house in which he lived until the age of 11; most striking is the huge *marani* wine-store with 40 *kvevris*, and two limewood wine presses, one for Saperavi grapes and one for Rkatsiteli. Across the road to the right is the house-museum of the theatre director Koté Marjanishvili (1872–1933), which unfortunately is usually closed, although it has a fine garden with sculptures.

About 500m to the south on Chavchavadze, you'll see the walls of a 18th-century fort to the right across a wide asphalt parade ground; the square of walls, with seven towers, is intact, but inside there's only a football pitch, visible through a gate on the north side. The **Kindzmarauli Wine House** (signed in English) is on a bend on Chavchavadze south of the fort, 1km from the highway roundabout (m *899 583972*; f *252 50062; open daily 09.00–18.00*); you can buy wine, and visit the 8km tunnel (at a constant 14°C), 3km of which is now in use for wine storage.

In the mountains to the north of Kvareli the Duruji Gorge is known for its healthy populations of raptors. There's camping near Kvareli Lake 6km north, and accommodation is available for GEL20 at Ioseba's Dukani (a restaurant) in Sadzmakaco, on the way to the lake.

From here you have the choice of returning by a direct road to km18, just west of Gurdjaani, or continuing for 41km to **Lagodekhi**, on the border with Azerbaijan; the junction is a few hundred metres to the east of the Kvareli junction (beyond the bridge). There's very little public transport between Akhalsopeli and Kabali on the Lagodekhi road, so it may be better to head 26km south to Gurdjaani and looping back via Tsnori from there. It's 41km from Tsnori up to Lagodekhi, crossing the Alazani Wetlands, mainly marshy, seasonally flooded woods with good birdwatching. There are marshrutkas (GEL8) and buses (GEL5) from Tbilisi, as well as from Telavi and Tsnori. These arrive on the main square; turn right/north at the end of the square and right again to find the one very basic **hotel**, the **Hereti** (↘ *22637*), which charges GEL5 per person with cold water – check in at the shop to the left on the ground floor. The new national park will be co-ordinating new homestays which are bound to be better than this, as well as a tourist information centre. Very strong tobacco is grown in the Lagodekhi area (as well as kiwifruit and peanuts), but immediately to the north the mountains rise very steeply to the Caucasus watershed, and it's just a few kilometres to the very wild and almost unknown **Lagodekhi National Park** (*www.lagodekhipa.ge*), the first in the Caucasus, founded in 1912 by a Polish general in the Tsarist army, on the basis of Prince Demidov's hunting reserve), with forests of chestnut, and red and roe deer, wolves, bear, lynx, chamois and tur. Red deer numbers have dropped from 750 in the 1980s to 150 in 2003, due to poaching. Bearded vultures live here all year, and griffon and cinereous vultures are here from May to September, plus Egyptian vultures passing through on migration. It covers 17,932ha, but borders the Zakatala Nature Reserve (in Azerbaijan) and the Tliarata Federal Sanctuary (in Daghestan), so the total protected area is considerable; entry is allowed only to the lowest part, but even a short walk from town soon takes you into fantastically unspoilt forest. One of the best day hikes leads through Ninoskhevi, St Nino's Gorge, to the Gurgeniani Waterfall.

SOUTHEAST OF TELAVI

SIGNAGHI The main road from the Lagodekhi border, the A302, heads south across the Alazani to the junction with the Telavi road 103km from Tbilisi, and 50km from Lagodekhi. The main attraction along this road is the walled city of Signaghi, which as a rule is most easily reached from the Telavi/Tbilisi direction, as the road surface is far better. About 4km from the roundabout at km103, the road crosses a stream, with the large barrel dome of the Anaga church visible about 1km upstream. The junction to Signaghi is on a hairpin bend at the east end of Anaga, at km110.5 (49.5km from the border). There are plenty of local buses along the main road to Tsnori, and you won't have to wait too long for a connecting bus up the hill to Signaghi, although it's a slow crawl, with plenty of time to study the fortifications ahead. If you're in a hurry it's better to go to Tsnori (km117.5/42.5, where the famous gold lion, made in 2300–2000BC and now in the State Museum, was found in a *kurgan* or burial mound) and take a taxi (GEL5/6) or a shared taxi (GEL2), waiting at the junction about 300m west.

The direct road from km94.5 on the Tbilisi highway (by a LUK petrol station and police checkpoint) passes a junction with a wrecked tractor on a pillar, another weird monument at km12/9, and beyond Nukriani a big monument of an ogre or a ninja turtle with sword and torch, after which you soon have a view of Bodbe church and sanatorium. Marshrutkas (GEL5) run from the Samgori metro station in Tbilisi (calling at Isani too), taking 90 minutes; the last return to Tbilisi is at 18.00 so a day trip from the capital is possible.

High on the ridge looking out across the Alazani Valley towards the Caucasus, Signaghi was ringed by a 4.5km wall and 28 towers by Irakli II in 1772. They surround a remarkably large area with a small town at its centre. With its cypress trees, it's reminiscent of an Italian hill town, featuring a sloping piazza with two large statues and also a bust of Stalin hidden away at its top end.

Tourist information and getting around There's a new **tourist information centre** (✆ 981107, 133541; m 899 554371, 899 133541; e sighnaghi2002@ yahoo.com, gia_ina@yahoo.com; www.sighnaghi.org.ge/english.html; open daily 09.30–13.00 & 14.00–18.30) in the left-hand door of the former wedding palace (an attractive 19th-century building) at Kostava 10, on the east side of Graz Square, at the bottom of town. They have good maps of the town and can book you a bed for about GEL15 without food, GEL30 with half board. The **Zedashe Cultural Center** (✆ 355 31511; e ivane@access.sanet.ge, jonathanwurdeman@yahoo.com) is not a building but an organisation running a fine choir and putting on concerts.

Taxis wait below the hotel, at the top of the piazza, while buses wait opposite the tourist information centre; there's little transport along the direct road to Tbilisi, so it may be best to go via Tsnori.

🏠 Where to stay

🏠 **Hotel Nugo** (20 rooms) m 899 413539. A friendly but basic hotel, with good views from the balconies. GEL10–15.

Homestays include **Todo's** at Ketevan Tsamebuli 3 (or ask at the Elite Bar; GEL 10); **Nana Kokiashvili** at Sarajishvili 2 (GEL15); and **Gia Rkreushvili** (✆ 31264, or at the Market shop on Bebribis Baghi, ✆ 31156), who speaks excellent English.

What to see To the right/east (facing the Hotel Nugo) the **Ethnographic and Archeological Museum** (open Tue–Sun 10.00–16.00; admission free), with a Stone-Age jumble including bits of mastodons on the ground floor and on the first floor (being refurbished) the ethnography display, including chain mail, musical instruments and so on, as well as a great view to the northwest over the plain. There's no English spoken or on the captions. Carrying on beyond this you can fork right by the mosaic-faced terminal of the abandoned cable-car from Tsnori, and head down the Tsnori road to the small **basilica of St George**, built in the 17–18th centuries, with a bare interior and a separate, 12-sided, brick belltower set on the base of a defensive tower. There are three house-museums in Signaghi, commemorating obscure musicians. There's not a lot else to see, but it's a nice place in which to stroll through the back streets; the most photogenic balconies are on Sarajishvili and Tsotne Dadiani to the west of Bebrebis Baghi (the Old People's Garden, the triangular plaza southwest of the upper one). At the bottom of Bebrebis Baghi is the **Center for Teaching Old Hand-Weaving Methodology of Georgian Carpets and Kilims** (open 08.00–18.00), where you may be able to watch weavers at work. At Bavatashvilis 18 Old Town, studios show the work of a local artists' cooperative. The best views of the Caucasus are from the very end of Tamar Mepis, to the northeast, and along Chavchavadze.

BODBE It's just 3km from here to the nunnery of Bodbe (also known as Ninotsminda), where St Nino, who converted Georgia to Christianity, is buried. Heading south beyond the bottom square, you'll soon fork left, and again after about 1km; a taxi will charge about GEL5 return including a wait. You can take a bus for Bodbe village, but you'll be getting off after about five minutes, about 200m beyond a closed petrol station, where an asphalt road leads down to the left. It's about 1km more through oak and pine woods to a junction on a hairpin bend; the nunnery is 300m to the right in a grove of cypress trees. The rather tatty, 19th-century buildings were used as a hospital in the communist period and have only recently reopened as a nunnery. Below it stand the older three-storey belltower and the church, largely red brick in the western European style with a nave, aisles and chancel, though its core probably dates from the 9th–11th centuries. A church was first built in the 4th century, over the grave of St Nino, the illuminator of Georgia.

Most of the kings of Kakheti were crowned here; it has attractive, slightly naïve frescoes, including Adam and Eve on the ceiling of the nave and a Last Judgement at the west end, and an elaborate golden iconostasis.

If you turn to the left at the hairpin bend, and then right below a sanatorium, a good unmade track will take you down the escarpment to the main road, about an hour's pleasant walk (less pleasant uphill). Turning right on to the Signaghi–Tsnori road, you'll reach the main highway at km117/43, 0.5km west of the centre of Tsnori; alternatively you can make your way through some residential lanes to reach the main highway further west at about km116/44. There's a new supermarket facing the taxi rank and Tbilisi marshrutkas, and a busy market uphill from the highway at about km117.5, while the bus yard is below, in front of the rail station.

From Tsnori a rough road continues east into the desert (dominated by wormwood, *Artemisia fragrans*) towards Azerbaijan, to the small town of Dedopolis-Tskaro (terminal of a freight-only rail branch). This passes through Mirzaani, the painter Pirosmani's home village, where you can visit the house-museum in his home; Pirosmani Memorial Day is on the third Saturday of October, when celebrations include a concert of Georgian folk music and dance, and a recreation of Pirosmani's painting of a supra, at the round table in the centre of the museum. An even rougher track continues a long way eastwards to the **Vashlovani National Park** (*www.vashlovanipa.ge*), the driest part of Georgia (with just 300–500mm of rain per year) and where temperatures may be over 40°C in summer. There's very dry steppe and savanna flora (*Tulipa eichleri* is endemic to the banks of the Iori), with light forests of pistachio trees and Paliurus thorns and three species of juniper, including the rare black juniper *Juniperus foetidissima*, and the endemic pear tree *Pirus sakhokiana*, with grassland dominated by *Bothriochloa ischaemum*. Cinereous vultures nest in low junipers, and Egyptian and griffon vultures and great imperial and steppe eagles are also seen here. Animals include wolves, bears, boars, lizards, tortoises, and the very rare striped hyenas and goitred gazelles; there are too many snakes for it to be safe in summer, although they concentrate on hunting hamsters; there are also fossils.

Northwards from Dedopolis-Tskaro, a yet rougher track leads past the Artsvisi Canyon to Khornabuji, a limestone pinnacle above the Alazani Valley, topped by the ruins of a fortress built by Queen Tamar but soon abandoned.

DAVIT-GAREJA

Also in Kakheti, though usually visited separately as a day trip from Tbilisi, is the Davit-Gareja complex of monasteries. In what is now virtual desert on the Azerbaijani border at 400–878m is a group of cave monasteries founded in the mid 6th century by St David (one of the 13 Holy Syrian Fathers), and his disciple Lukian, after his stay on Tbilisi's Holy Mountain. Over 20 monasteries have been identified, but only a few are widely known or visited; the roads are still appalling, and although cars can get here, it's best to have a 4x4. There's no way to get here other than by mountain bike, car, or a trip organised by a tourist agency; it's about 70km, or under two hours, each way from Tbilisi. A day trip costs around US$100 for two people, or about half that if you have your own car; if not you'll usually be accompanied by both a driver and a pretty knowledgeable guide. Tariel Tabashidze (✆ 648928; m 899 648928; e tariel_tabashidze@yahoo.com), who speaks good German and some English, is a good driver, and charges US$50 (including fuel) to take three or possibly four passengers in a 4x4 Subaru, with about three hours at the monasteries.

HISTORY The area has been populated for at least four millennia, as shown by Bronze-Age tombs and pottery; it was then a forested area, but iron smelting eventually led to deforestation in the first half of the 1st millennium BC, and thus climate change and desertification. When the monks arrived in the 6th century they had to construct channels and reservoirs for water, and their 9th-century frescoes show their close relationship with nature. The monasteries were constructed from natural sandstone caves which were expanded by heating the rock with fire then pouring on water to split it; all have a church with a main nave and a lesser deacon's nave to the north, as well as cells, stores and other chambers. Above, a dozen of the monasteries built towers to send signals between them. The high point of the monastic community was from the 10th century to the coming of the Mongols in the 13th century, although most survived until the early 17th century, when Shah Abbas massacred 6,000 monks (all subsequently canonised) during the Easter Night procession. The monasteries were re-established, but declined and were abandoned in the 19th century, although one has now been re-established.

Their greatest crisis has come in the last 50 years, during which the Soviet army used the area as an artillery range, often aiming directly at the monasteries. From the late 1980s nationalists demanded an end to military training in the area, and it was finally halted in 1991. The military were keen to train here because of its resemblance to Afghanistan, but once that war had finished in 1989 they lost interest. In 1994 the first cultural and biological survey of the area was undertaken, and some water channels were reopened. Another monastery, abandoned in the 12th century, was rediscovered in 1995, with domes of a type otherwise unknown in Eastern Christendom, as were 10–12th-century frescoes and graffiti, which have given interesting information on the development of the Georgian alphabet. In mid 1995 the Georgian army resumed training in the area, and in 1996 artillery firing; this was suspended in 1997 after protests and legal action, which was seen as proof of the development of 'civil society' in Georgia. The army appealed to the Supreme Court, but the Church finally joined the battle against it, and the cultural (and touristic) value of the area was eventually preserved.

It's pretty much a lunar landscape in many places, but it's transformed from April to early June when the steppe flowers bloom; the dominant species is the bearded grass *Botriochloa ischaenum*, with other grasses such as *Festuca sulcata*, *Stipa capillata*, *S. lessingiana* and *S. pulcherrima*. There's a healthy population of snakes, lizards and rabbits, and a remarkable range of raptors, such as eagles, vultures, buzzards and owls, that prey on them. In addition there are wolves, bats in many of the caves, and there were goitred gazelles until relatively recently. May and June are the best time for flowers and birds, notably nesting vultures and displaying chukar, as well as huge tadpoles.

GETTING THERE The best way in is via Rustavi, leaving Tbilisi on the main highway towards Baku; it's also possible to approach from the main road to Kakheti proper, although this involves far more driving on rough tracks. In this case, you can turn off the A302 either at km34, on the road to Krasnogorski, or at km51, just east of the roundabout at the east end of Sagarejo. From here a taxi will charge GEL50 including three hours at the monasteries. Don't be tempted by the bus to Udabno, a very remote village where you won't find a taxi to get to the actual monasteries.

Taking the Rustavi road, you'll see a military site on top of a hill to the right/west of the road, which is proposed to open as a military museum. Turning left soon after the end of the Tbilisi bypass, you'll pass through standard Soviet apartment-block suburbs before crossing the Mtkvari into the centre of **Rustavi** (also reached by frequent trains from the Samgori station in Tbilisi, and buses from the Dinamo Stadium). Established on virgin land immediately after World War II, it became Georgia's leading industrial centre, and its metallurgical plant was the republic's largest employer, closely followed by chemical and pharmaceutical works; these are mostly closed, with Georgia's first 'European-standard' prison (with closed cells) built instead. People moved here from all over the country, especially from mountain areas such as Svaneti, and its population is now in the region of 150,000, but the work conditions were so bad that workers retired at 45 or 50. It's worth noting that the town has no connection with the poet Rustaveli, who came from Meskheti (see page 171). There's an ATM at Meskhishvilis It's also possible to take a marshrutka from Didube to Gardabani, the last town before the Azerbaijani border (GEL2), from where a taxi will charge GEL40–50 to the monasteries and back. The road to Davit-Gareja starts by turning left in front of the immense administration block of the metallurgical plant (far grander than the city hall, to show exactly where the true power used to lie), crossing the railway and turning right to pass through a post-industrial wasteland for a considerable distance. To the right you'll see a modern Svan tower, marking one of several Svan villages here (there was a fresh influx in 1988 after a terrible avalanche in Ushguli), and a statue of a Svan fighting a bull. On a hill to the left there's another military building, which was used for a while as a terrarium (producing antivenom from snakes), and is now abandoned. Turn left (on an unsigned asphalt road) just after a barrier gate when the biggish white village of Jandara comes into view ahead, and then turn right at the top of the rise (with the white wall of a collective farm on the left), onto a very rough track (also unsigned), which climbs past wrecked armoured personnel carriers on to the very scrubby dry steppe. The Monastery of John the Baptist is visible to the left once on the plateau, where the road becomes slightly smoother; to reach it fork left and soon left again to go down a valley, forking right (with an abandoned collective farm to the left) to park just below the monastery, set into the cliff face.

THE MAIN MONASTERIES

The **Monastery of John the Baptist** was founded in the 6th century, but the main church was completed and painted only in the 13th century (there's a portrait of Queen Tamar in the rear right-hand corner). The refectory, with its Persian-style vaulting, was added in the 17th century, and there's a 19th-century tomb. Above is a tower decorated with blue tiles; it clearly used to be taller, as the foot of a tile cross survives.

Returning to the top of the valley, continue to the left (on the road to Sagarejo) and over a ridge, and fork right; to the right on the ridge is the tower of the Chichrituri monastery (founded in the 12th century), and then near the road a seismological station (which records around 100 tremors each year, and offers rather poor accommodation with food), just before Lavra monastery, about 1.5km from the junction. Park at the houses (there's a fairly horrid toilet in the field), and walk up to the **Lavra** (or Davitis Lavra) monastery just above. This was founded by St David in the 6th century and is now occupied by nine notoriously fundamentalist monks who take great exception to noise and especially to inappropriate clothing. There's a little kiosk that sells icons and candles but no water or snacks. Tourists are not allowed in the inner court or, of course, the monks' cells. David and Lukian are buried here in the Church of the Transfiguration (Peristvaleba) or Rock church, near a spring in the lower court known as the Tears of David. The diagonal lines of the rocks above the outer court and the cells are striking, and very photogenic; keep up to the right here, go through a metal door and to the right above the inner court to an 18th-century watchtower (home to a colony of horseshoe bats), and then follow a guide rail. This is the path to the **Udabno** (literally 'Desert') Monastery, constructed between the 8th and 10th centuries, on the far side of the ridge; this is in both religious and artistic terms the most important of the monasteries. The trail climbs to the left for about ten minutes and then from a hairpin to the right for another ten minutes to reach the ridge, with vast views of the desert in all directions. Heading down to the left you'll pass cave-churches with trees growing in their entrances, then the chapel of Demetre II (the Self-Sacrificer), decorated with the life of Christ, and a small church, before reaching the refectory. The monks knelt at the stone table down the middle, with their food hidden from each other in hollows; the frescoes of bible scenes were painted in the 13th and 14th centuries. Just a bit further on, the main church has superb frescoes from the late 10th and early 11th centuries, including the life of St David on the north wall (with a deer feeding on milk), the Virgin and Child in the apse, a Last Judgement on the east wall, and a Deesis in the east apse. The path continues for five minutes along the cliff edge, pocked with cave chambers, then climbs back to the ridge just before a triangulation point, from which you can return to the left past the ruins of a 6th-century chapel, reaching the hairpin bend on the path in about 15 minutes. From the ridge you have superb views across the desert, deep into Azerbaijan, and there are amazing sunsets here. The monastery with the best frescoes (painted 1212–13, including portraits of Tamar and her son Giorgi IV Lash) is Bertubani, which has been 2km inside Azerbaijan since the dying Soviet Union moved the border in 1991 to run across the Udabno ridge (813m; known in Azerbaijan as Keshishdag). Georgia is offering a land swap to regain control of Bertubani and Chichkhituri, but Azerbaijan is being bolshy.

From Lavra it's also possible to walk to the Dodos Rqa and Natlismcemli monasteries, both dating from the 6th century.

Pine marten

Kvemo (Lower) Kartli

Kvemo Kartli or Lower Kartli is the area to the southwest of Tbilisi, far smaller and less important than Shida (Inner) Kartli, but attractive and convenient for short trips from the capital. Its population is largely Azerbaijani, while there are also traces of German colonists, who settled in the area of Bolnisi (which they called Luxemburgi) in the 18th century and were deported to central Asia at the start of World War II, after which they went to Germany; wine in this area is more Germanic in taste than the Georgian norm. The Azerbaijanis are hard-working farmers, and you'll see women in typically Islamic leggings selling apples, pomegranates, persimmons and sweetcorn by the roadside.

MARNEULI AND BOLNISI

You're most likely to see this area on your way to or from Armenia; the traditional route to Yerevan was that built by Russian military engineers in 1834–75, but as this passes through Azerbaijan the main route is now by the A304 via Bolnisi, which is in pretty poor condition towards the border. This road is still signposted for Vanadzor and Gyumri rather than Yerevan. It's well worth stopping to see a group of churches south of Bolnisi, which are among the loveliest in the country. The A304 turns off the highway to Rustavi and Baku in the outskirts of Tbilisi, leaving the city at km12, and climbs onto the steppe, with an old fort to the right; from km20/86 it drops steeply to the village of Kumisi (where a Canadian firm is drilling for natural gas) and climbs again to Koda, site of a large army barracks. These villages are both notable for their solid houses of grey tuff, far more typical of Armenia than of Georgia. At km36/70 you'll see the huge Ageti statue on a hill to the left/east; it's a war memorial, depicting a mother handing a sword to her two small sons. From here the road drops to Marneuli, passing the 'Restaurant Original', with its English-language sign, on the way in; however this is not a tourist destination in any sense, but rather a thoroughly drab industrial town, although there is an ATM at Cholokashvilis 3.

Forking right here, the road heads southwest across a fertile valley, with a new railway parallel. At km59/59 (about an hour-and-a-quarter from Tbilisi) it reaches Bolnisi, a marginally more attractive town that stretches for 5km along the road, and may become slightly more lively with the arrival of an Australian–Georgian joint venture extracting gold from slag heaps at Soviet-era copper mines.

BOLNISI SIONI At 10km south of the town of Bolnisi, the church of Bolnisi Sioni is an outstanding example of the earliest Georgian church architecture, and the only surviving example of the original type of three-aisled basilica (without transepts). It's striking for its simplicity and calm (set in a tranquil rose-planted churchyard), and for the lovely green tuff of its western façade (added in the 17th century). The turning to Sioni is just west of km62/56, at the west end of the town

centre, marked by a sign (in Georgian only) and a defunct set of traffic lights. From here it's 7km to Sioni, an easy road to walk, although there are also buses and minibuses, mainly at peak hours.

Walking down to the bridge you'll see a few typically German houses, solidly built of stone, and a former watermill by the river. Ten minutes from the main road you'll pass the railway station and start to climb steadily to a pass 5km from Bolnisi; it's another 1km to the large village of Kvemo Bolnisi that sprawls (in a most unGermanic way) across a fertile valley. You need to fork right at the entrance to the village to bypass it; the church visible ahead on a hilltop is not Sioni but Zugrugasheni. With the village to your left, you'll pass a couple of small abandoned chapels of striking green tuff, below the bare limestone outcrops to the right. It takes 25 minutes on foot to reach the end of Kvemo Bolnisi, and then just ten more to reach the village of Sioni, where you'll find the wonderful Bolnisi Sioni church to the left.

Entering by the west door, you descend a flight of steps into the dark church; the only natural light comes from the door and from a few narrow lancet windows. It's a remarkably long church by Georgian standards, with a six-bay nave. The only frescoes are in the apse, and have faded with time; likewise the carved capitals in the nave have been damaged. The lintel over the north door (now replaced with a copy) gives the church's construction dates as AD478–93; this is the oldest inscription in the Georgian language found within Georgia itself (slightly older ones were found in Palestine). To the northeast a chapel added in the 8th century projects beyond the main apse; there's another, shorter, chapel on the church's southeastern corner. There are also the remains of ambulatories or external aisles along both sides of the church. The separate belltower or *kolokolnaya*, its steps swathed in vines, dates from 1678–88.

ZUGRUGASHENI To reach the church of Zugrugasheni, 2km away on the far side of the valley, with a car you'll have to go via Kvemo Bolnisi, but on foot you can go there directly. Turn left from the Sioni church into the village, fork left after five minutes and then turn left down a muddy track; it takes 15 minutes to reach the bridge (just after the junction from Kvemo Bolnisi) and another ten to wind up the hill to the church, strikingly set high on a hill with a high thin barrel dome to add to the effect. The nearest houses are at a collective farm further up the valley, so it's a nice spot to camp. Built in the 11th century and now disused, it's still a very impressive building, despite the metal sleeve and telegraph poles holding up one pillar. It has a two-bay nave and aisles, plus a separate deacon's nave to the north, and lateral chapels on either side of the apse. To the south a porch has been demolished. Externally there are fine carvings and high niches marking the position of the apses inside the east end. The tall narrow barrel dome, with its ornamental platform bands, is typical of the 18th century in style.

FROM BOLNISI TO THE ARMENIAN BORDER Continuing along the main road towards Armenia, at Kvesi (km68/50) there's a turning west to Pitareti and Darbazi. The church of **Pitareti** stands alone on the river Khram, by a washed-out bridge; built by Tamar's son Giorgi IV in 1213–22, it's almost square, with only a porch to the south to spoil its regularity. The plan is cruciform, with three virtually equal apses, a single-bay aisle, and a tall central drum; there are excellent carvings on the eastern façade. The church was surrounded in medieval times by a double wall, with a two-storey gatetower added in 1696. At Darbazi, reached by turning left halfway to Pitareti, are the remains of a 12–13th-century royal palace. Pitareti can also be reached by 4x4 or mountain bike from Tetri-Tskaro to the north, 59km from Tbilisi (reached by two marshrutkas per hour from Samgori metro); this was the centre of a Greek community, most of which has now emigrated. In Samshvilde, also on the Khram 4km south of Tetri-Tskaro, there's a cupola church built in AD759–77.

Just 1km further along the main road you'll pass the castle of Kvesi set on a rock to the west above the village of the same name. At km76/42, after passing through the village of Kianeti, a side road heads southeast for 3km to Kazreti, whose apartment blocks are soon very obvious; this is the terminus of the railway and the commercial centre for the upper Mashavera Valley. The road gets worse, entering a limestone valley rather like a Derbyshire dale; at km88/30 it enters Patara Dmanisi (two-and-a-quarter hours from Tbilisi), known for its cheese factory, sweetbriar jelly, walnuts, hazelnuts, and its mineral springs. Although Patara means 'Little', in fact this is the only village there is here; Didi ('Big') Dmanisi comprises the remains of a medieval fortified town, covering 13ha, on the hill above the village. In addition to the ruins of a palace and baths dating from the 13th and 14th centuries, there's a 6th-century three-nave basilica, with a narthex added by Giorgi IV in 1213–22, which was reopened in 1988. A skull of *Homo erectus* about 1.8 million years old and remains of *H. sapiens* about 200,000 years old have been found at Dmanisi, as well as Palaeolithic artefacts and the remains of extinct species of rhino, elephant, giraffe, ostrich, bear, sabre-toothed tiger, deer and cow. The site is managed by the State Museum and a visitor centre and homestays are to be provided.

The road climbs through open beech forest, and then out onto the high plateau that characterises Armenia; the first border post is at km105/13 (three hours from

11

Tbilisi), just south of the tiny village of Guguti. Unsurprisingly perhaps, the road is much better on the Armenian side.

The alternative route to Armenia is by the A310 south from Marneuli to Sadakhlo, but it's in even worse condition than the Guguti road. To begin with, cars swerve around pot-holes in the standard Georgian style, then there are alternating strips of perfect surface and stretches that have never seen asphalt, getting worse as it heads south to Sadakhlo, where you have to turn right then left. There are gaudy mosques in these Azeri-populated villages, and local buses from Marneuli to Sadakhlo. Taxis wait at the Sadakhlo border, charging GEL 35-40 to Tbilisi.

BETANIA AND MANGLISI

It's odd that in both Britain and Georgia, it's the A303 that goes west from the capital to the country's finest ancient monument, from London to Stonehenge and from Tbilisi to Vardzia. The Georgian A303 starts as Chavchavadze Avenue, passing Vake Park and the 'mountain resort suburb' of Tskhneti, before reaching the junction with the minor road from Freedom Square that winds up between Mtatsminda and Narikala as the Kojoris Gzatketsili or Kojori Highway. This passes through Kojori, 16km from Tbilisi, which, at 1,280m, was a summer resort for the Georgian nobility; to the southwest is a ruined 17th-century castle, and 1.5km to the northeast on a wooded spur of Mount Udzo is the Kabeni church, much visited by barren women. This is a dome church built in the 9th century and altered in both the 12th and 18th centuries.

At Kiketi a rough road turns right/north to reach the monastery of **Betania**, in the wooded Vere Valley, 32km from Tbilisi; its church is a masterpiece of Georgian architecture and is also famous for supposedly housing part of the Virgin Mary's robe. Set on a ridge, it's surrounded on three sides by trees, with only its high barrel dome reaching above. The monastery was founded in the 11th century, and the cruciform church was built in the 12th and 13th centuries; the frescoes were painted in 1207, and include one of just four portraits of Queen Tamar painted in her lifetime. Tourists have been robbed here, so don't go alone. Just to its west is the Darbazuli Church of St George the Triumphant (1196).

Continuing along the increasingly rough A303, at Orbeti there's a turning south to Birtvisi, site of a medieval fortress (reached by two buses a day from Tbilisi). The Birtvisi Canyon is described as a 'rock labyrinth' by the Sustainable Tourism Centre, who offer trips of one or two days' easy trekking and simple climbing, for US$50–100 each, depending on numbers (best from September to November). They also run MTB trips across the Trialeti range, starting from **Manglisi**, the next major village along the main road; it's reached by regular marshrutkas from Tbilisi, some from Victory Square and some via Kojori, running up Leonidze from Freedom Square. Here there's a lovely 11th-century church set in the trees. From Manglisi, at 1,200m, the trail climbs to 1,800m in the 6,822ha **Algetis Nature Reserve** (founded in 1965), and descends to Rkoni, 25km and five to six hours away; from here a road runs north to Ertatsminda and Kaspi (see page 135). The reserve was founded in 1965 to protect the forests of spruce (*Picea orientalis*) and Caucasian silver fir (*Abies nordmanniana*) which cover 80% of its area, as well as over 1,000 plant species and over 80 bird species.

Further to the southwest the road reaches the Trialeti Plateau, passing to the southwest of several lakes. From the first large lake, Tsalka, a three-day trekking route leads north to the Tedzami Canyon and Rkoni (see page 135). Lake Tsalka is the centre of Georgia's Greek population, still speaking Ancient Pontian Greek. This area was unpopulated as it was laid waste by every army invading from the south, but it is very fertile and ideal for cattle and potatoes; nevertheless, about a third of the population has emigrated in recent years, although Svans have come in to replace them. The A303 is a very bad road, and most traffic from Tbilisi to Akhalkalaki goes via Borjomi. At Beshtasheni, 5km north of the highway at the east end of Lake Tsalka, there are Cyclopean fortified settlements dating from the 3rd and 2nd centuries BC, with massive stone walls 6m high.

It's also worth mentioning the short excursion from Tbilisi to the village of **Digomi**, turning off the highway to Mtskheta at km8 in the modern suburb of Digomi. This village has been settled for 2,000 years, and two of its seven churches survive; to the right as you enter the village, the Church of St George dates from the late 10th or early 11th century, while the Mother of God Church, to the northwest, is older.

Red-necked grebe

Appendix I

LANGUAGE

If you have any knowledge of Russian already, you might as well concentrate on that; most older people speak Russian, and there's no prejudice against it. You can study Georgian at summer schools organised by the Centre for Georgian Studies, Tbilisi State University, Chavchavadze 1, 380028 Tbilisi (☎ *290833;* f *252501*), or at the International Centre for the Georgian Language, Gogebashvili 18 (☎ *983285;* e *rusiko@causcasus.net*). A new web-based course in Georgian is at www.ling.lu.se/education/homepages/georgian/index.html.

There are three phrase books that are of use; my favourite is the *Curzon Dictionary and Phrasebook*, by Nicholas Awde and Thea Khitarishvili (Curzon, London, 1997), which uses a transliterated version of Georgian, easy for us but unintelligible to most Georgians. The *Hippocrene Concise Dictionary* by John J Torikashvili (Hippocrene, New York, 1992) uses Georgian and Latin script. *Georgian – a learner's grammar* by G Hewitt (Routledge, London, 1996) is for students rather than travellers.

THE GEORGIAN ALPHABET
This is only a rough guide, as there are many variants, especially in handwriting.

ა	a	ი	i	ო	o	უ	u
ბ	b	ჯ	j	პ	p	ვ	v
დ	d	კ	k	რ	r	ზ	z
ე	e	ლ	l	ს	s	ჩ	ch
გ	g	მ	m	თ	t	ხ	kh
ჰ	h	ნ	n	ც	ts		

ESSENTIAL VOCABULARY

These words and phrases have been transliterated for English speakers. You will also find transliterations for German speakers, which can occasionally catch you out.

beautiful	*lamazi*	father	*mama*
big	*didi*	fine	*kargad*
bread	*puri*	food	*satch'meli*
car	*mankana*	fruit	*khili*
cheap	*ee-api*	go	*tsadi*
cheers!	*gaumarjos!*	good	*kargia*
	(response *gagimarjos*)	goodbye	*nakhvamdis*
cheese	*qu-weli*	good morning	*dila mush-wido-bisa*
closed	*dak'et'ilia*	grandfather	*papa*
cold	*tsiva*	grandmother	*bebia*
come here	*modi ak*	hello	*gamarjobat*
expensive	*ds-weeri*	home	*sakhli*

A1

hot	*tskhela*	sorry!	*bodishit! map'at'iet!*
how are you?	*rogora khar?*	thank you	*madlobt*
how many?	*ramdeni?*	very	*dsarlian*
how much?	*ra ghirs?*	warm	*tbili*
included	*shedis*	water	*ts'kali*
let's go	*tsa-vayd-et*	welcome	*mober-zandit*
mother	*deda*	what is your name?	*Ra gkvia?*
my name is …	*me mkvia …*	when?	*rodis?*
new	*akhali*	where is?	*sad aris?*
no	*ara*	who, what, which?	*romeli?*
old	*ds-weli*	yes	*diakh, ki, ho*
please	*inebet, tu sheidzleba*	you're welcome	*arapris*
small	*patara*		

NUMBERS

0	*nuli*	50	*ormots-da-ori*
1	*erti*	60	*samotsi*
2	*ori*	70	*samots-da-ti*
3	*sami*	80	*otkhmotsi*
4	*otkhi*	90	*okhmots-da-ati*
5	*khuti*	100	*asi*
6	*ekvsi*	101	*as-erti*
7	*shwidi*	200	*or-asi*
8	*rva*		
9	*tskhra*	1,000	*at-asi*
10	*ati*	10,000	*ati at-asi*
11	*tert-met'i*	100,000	*asi at-asi*
12	*tor-met'i*	one million	*milioni*
13	*tsa-met'i*		
14	*totkh-met'i*	once	*ertkhel*
15	*tkhit-met'i*	twice	*or-jer*
16	*tekvs-met'i*	first	*p'irveli*
17	*chwid-met'i*	second	*meore*
18	*tvra-met'i*	third	*mesame*
19	*tskhra-met'i*	fourth	*meotkhe*
20	*otsi*	fifth	*mekhute*
21	*ots-da-erti*	sixth	*meekvse*
30	*ots-de-ati*	tenth	*meate*
40	*ormotsi*	twentieth	*meotse*

DAYS AND TIME

Monday	*Orshabati*	Friday	*P'arask'evi*
Tuesday	*Samshabati*	Saturday	*Shabati*
Wednesday	*Otkhshabati*	Sunday	*K'wira*
Thursday	*Khutshabati*		

today	*dghes*	now	*akhla*
tomorrow	*khwal*	hour	*saati*
the day after tomorrow	*zeg*	minute	*ts'uti*
yesterday	*gushin*	in the morning	*dilit*
What time is it?	*romeli saati a?*	in the afternoon	*nashuadghevs*
It is … o'clock	*… saati a*	in the evening	*saghamos*

GEOGRAPHICAL GLOSSARY

airport	*aeroporti*	map	*r'uka*
avenue	*gamziri*	mountain	*mta*
bridge	*khidi*	river	*mdinare*
bus station	*avtobusebis sadguri*	square	*moedani*
church	*eklesia*	station	*sadguri* (also *voksal*)
gorge	*khevi*	street	*kucha*
hotel	*sastumro*	town	*kalaki*
inner	*shida*	train	*mat'arebeli*
lower	*kvemo*	upper	*zemo*

Appendix 2

FURTHER INFORMATION
BOOKS
Travellers' tales
Herodotus and Strabo both wrote about Georgia in classical times.

Anderson, Tony *Bread and Ashes: a journey through the mountains of Georgia* Vintage, 2004. A rather episodic but very atmospheric and informative account of hiking through much of the Georgian Caucasus (Anderson also edited *Conflict in the Caucasus* by Svetlana Chervonnaya – see below).

Bitov, Andrei *A Captive of the Caucasus* Weidenfeld & Nicholson/Harvill, 1993. Full of associative anecdotes, more a journey through the literary culture of Russia than through Georgia and Armenia.

Brook, Stephen *Claws of the Crab* Sinclair Stevenson, 1992/Picador, 1993.

Dumas, Alexandre the elder *Adventures in the Caucasus* (1859) Owen/Chiltern Books, 1962.

Farson, Daniel *A Dry Ship to the Mountains* Michael Joseph, 1994/Penguin, 1995. Following his father's footsteps (see following entry).

Farson, Negley *Caucasian Journey* Evans, 1951/Penguin, 1988.

Griffin, Nicholas *Caucasus: in the wake of warriors* Review, 2001. Through Georgia, Armenia and Azerbaijan on the trail of Shamil – recent (2001) but otherwise not great.

Keun, Odette *In the Land of the Golden Fleece* London, 1924.

Maclean, Fitzroy *Eastern Approaches* Cape 1949/Penguin, 2004.

Maclean, Fitzroy *To Caucasus* Cape, 1976.

Marsden, Philip *The Spirit Wrestlers* HarperCollins, 1998. A beautifully written quest in search of the surviving Doukhobors, a dissident Russian Orthodox sect, ending up in Javakheti.

Nansen, Fridthof *Through the Caucasus to the Volga* George Allen & Unwin, London, 1931.

Nasmyth, Peter *Georgia: a rebel in the Caucasus* Cassell, 1992.

Nasmyth, Peter *Georgia, in the Mountains of Poetry* Curzon/Palgrave, 1998/RoutledgeCurzon, 2001. Nasmyth's are the best books on post-Soviet Georgia.

Pereira, Michael *Across the Caucasus* Geoffrey Bles, London, 1973.

Russell, Mary *Please Don't Call it Soviet Georgia* Serpent's Tail, London, 1991.

Severin, Tim *The Jason Voyage* Arrow, 1990.

Shaw, Peter *Hole – Kidnapped in Georgia* Accent Press, 2006. A gripping account of Shaw's 2000 kidnapping ordeal, which also offers insights into the social and political background.

Steavenson, Wendell *Stories I Stole* Atlantic Books/Grove Press, 2003. An evocative view of 1990s' Georgia through the eyes of a young foreign correspondent.

Steinbeck, John *A Russian Journal* Viking, 1948/Penguin, 1999. Including 44 pages on Georgia, with photos by Robert Capa.

Thubron, Colin *Where Nights Are Longest* Atlantic Monthly Press, 1984.

History and politics
Allen, W E D *History of the Georgian People* Barnes & Noble, 1971.

Aves, Jonathan *Georgia: From Chaos to Stability* Royal Institute of International Affairs, Former Soviet South Project, 1996.

Aves, Jonathan *Paths to National Independence in Georgia 1987–90* School of Slavonic and East European Studies, London, 1991.

Aves, Jonathan *Post-Soviet Transcaucasia* Royal Institute of International Affairs Post-Soviet Business Forum, London, 1993.

Awde, N, ed. *Ancient Peoples of the Caucasus, a handbook* Curzon, 1999.

Braund, David *Georgia in Antiquity* Clarendon, 1994.

Chervonnaya, Svetlana *Conflict in the Caucasus – Georgia, Abkhazia and the Russian Shadow* Gothic Image Publications, Glastonbury UK, 1995.

Coppieters, Bruno and Legvold, Robert (eds) *Statehood and Security: Georgia after the Rose Revolution* American Academy Studies in Global Security, MIT Press, 2005.

Curtis, Glenn E (ed) *Armenia, Azerbaijan and Georgia* Bernan Lanham, Maryland, 1995.

Goldenberg, S *A Pride of Small Nations: the Caucasus and post-Soviet disorder* Zed Books, London, 1994.

Goltz, Thomas *Georgia Diary: A Chronicle of War And Political Chaos in the Post-soviet Caucasus* ME Sharpe, 2006. An entertaining and perceptive account of journalistic travels across the Caucasus.

Jones, Stephen F *Georgia – a failed democratic transition*, in *Nations & Politics in the Soviet successor states* (ed) I Bremmer, Cambridge UP, 1993.

Kleveman, Lutz *The New Great Game* Atlantic Books, 2003. A compelling account of the politicking and arm-twisting involved in extracting oil and gas from central Asia and the Caspian, and building pipelines across the Caucasus.

Lang, D M *Last Years of the Georgian Monarchy 1658–1832* Columbia UP, 1957.

Lang, D M *Modern History of Soviet Georgia* Grove Press, 1962.

Lang, D M *The Georgians* Thames & Hudson, 1966.

Sebag-Montefiore, Simon *Young Stalin* Weidenfeld and Nicholson, 2007. The prequel to the successful *Stalin: Court of the Red Tsar*. The story of his childhood in Georgia and the revolutionary exploits across the Caucasus that made him what he later became.

Shevardnadze, Eduard *The Future Belongs to Freedom* Sinclair Stevenson, 1991.

Suny, Ronald *The Making of the Georgian Nation* IB Tauris, London 1989; 2nd edition Indiana UP, 1994. Suny is also publishing a biography of the young Stalin in 2008.

van der Leeuw, Charles *Storm over the Caucasus* Curzon, London, 1998.

Waters, Chris (ed) *The State of Law in the South Caucasus* Euro-Asian Studies, Palgrave Macmillan 2005. Not just the law, but the way in which judicial, governmental, commercial and criminal interests are bound together in the Caucasus.

Wheatley, Jonathan *Georgia from National Awakening to Rose Revolution: Delayed Transition in the Former Soviet Union* Ashgate Publishing, 2005. A very academic approach to contemporary Georgian history.

Wright, J F R et al (ed) *Transcaucasian Boundaries* UCL Press, London, 1996.

The Royal Institute for International Affairs has published the following (distributed outside Britain by the Brookings Institute Press):

Coppieters, Bruno *Federalism and Conflict in the Caucasus* 2001.

Herzig, Edmund *The New Caucasus: Armenia, Azerbaijan and Georgia* 1999.

Lynch, Dov *Russian Peacekeeping Strategies in the CIS: the cases of Moldova, Georgia and Tajikistan* 1999.

Lynch, Dov *The Conflict in Abkhazia* 1998.

MacFarlane, Neil *Western Engagement in the Caucasus and Central Asia* 1999.

Literature

Lermontov, Mikhail *A Hero of our Time* Penguin, 1977. Look out also for the Nabokov translation (1958).

Pushkin, Alexander *Journey to Arzrum* (ie: Erzurum) Ardis, 1974.

Rustaveli, Shota, translated by R H Stevenson *Lord of the Panther Skin* SUNY Press, 1977.

Said, Kurban *Ali and Nino* Vintage, 2000. Set in Baku, an Azeri-Georgian *Romeo and Juliet* by a mystery author; full of romantic colour and period detail.

Wildlife guides

Flint, Vladimir *Field Guide to the Birds of Russia and the adjacent territories* Princeton UP, 1984. English, Russian and scientific names.

Gavashelishvili, Lexo et al *A Birdwatching Guide to Georgia* Buneba, 2005. Available through www.nhbs.com in Europe or Buteo Books in the Americas, an excellent guide to birding sites which covers flora and other wildlife.

Knystautas, A *Birds of Russia* Collins, 1993. Good photos, English and scientific (not Russian or Georgian) names.

Miscellaneous

Bender, Friedrich *Classic Climbs in the Caucasus* Diadem, London/Menasha Ridge, Birmingham, Alabama, 1992.

Elliott, Mark *Azerbaijan with Georgia* Trailblazer, UK; second edition 2001.

Elliott, Mark and Klass, Wil *Asia Overland* Trailblazer, UK, 1998.

Gachechildze, Revaz *The New Georgia, space, society, politics* UCL Press, London, 1995. A geography text.

Goldstein, Darra *The Georgian Feast* University of California Press, 1993.

Häberli, Katharina and Harker, Andrew *Under Eagles' Wings – Hikes, Bikes, Horseback and Skitours in Georgia* H & H Travelogue, 2005.

Holding, Nicholas *Armenia with Nagorno Karabakh* (second edition) Bradt Travel Guides, 2006.

Khutsishvili, Georgi *Tbilisi – a guide* Progress, USSR, 1981.

Kolomiets, Yury and Solovyev, Aleksey *Trekking in the Caucasus* Cicerone, 1994.

Nasmyth, Peter *Walking in the Caucasus – Georgia* MTA Publications/IB Tauris, 2006.

Rayfield, Donald *The Literature of Georgia, a history* Clarendon, 1994.

Rosen, Roger *Passport Guide to the Georgian Republic* Odyssey 3/e, 1999.

Salkeld, Audrey and Bermudez, Jose *On the Edge of Europe, mountaineering in the Caucasus* The Mountaineers, 1994.

Salkeld, Audrey and Bermudez, Jose *The Forgotten Range of Europe, an anthology of exploration in the Caucasus* Teach Yourself, 1993.

Soltes, O. *National Treasures of Georgia* Philip Wilson, London, 2001.

Wright, John *Tbilisi – a guide* W & M Press, Tbilisi, 2000. The best maps of Tbilisi, though with south at the top.

Curzon Press's Caucasus series is now published by Routledge Books (2 Park Square, Milton Park, Abingdon OX14 4RN, UK; ☏ 020 7017 6000; www.routledge.com/asianstudies):

Baddeley, J F *The Russian Conquest of the Caucasus* (reprint).

Mgaloblishvili, Tamila (ed) *Ancient Christianity in the Caucasus*.

WEBSITES

www.georgiatoday.ge The website of *Georgia Today*.

www.meggenger.com.ge The website of *The Messenger*.

www.civil.ge Detailed news from Georgia, especially relating to civil society and NGOs.

www.sarke.com The website of the *Daily News* and *Weekly Economic Review*.

www.rferl.org/reports/caucasus-report Radio Free Europe's weekly online newsletter with background analysis (see also **www.rferl.org/featuresarchive/country/georgia.html**).

www.bu.edu/iscip Academic material.

www.georgien-news.de A new weekly news magazine, in German only.

www.eurasianet.org/resource/georgia/index.shtml General resource pages.

http://georgia.usembassy.gov US government information (US embassy in Tbilisi).

www.odci.gov/cia/publications/factbook/geos/gg.html The CIA Factbook.

www.georgiaemb.org The Georgian embassy in Washington.

www.tourism.gov.ge The Georgian government's useful tourism website.

www.cenn.org The Caucasus Environmental NGO Network (CENN) website; for a round up of environmental and NGO activities.

www.amcham.ge and **www.yellowpages.ge**. For business contacts.

http://groups.yahoo.com/group/caucasus To post queries on the Caucasus Discussion List.

WIN £100 CASH!
READER QUESTIONNAIRE

Send in your completed questionnaire for the chance to win £100 cash in our regular draw

All respondents may order a Bradt guide at half the UK retail price – please complete the order form overleaf.

(Entries may be posted or faxed to us, or scanned and emailed.)

We are interested in getting feedback from our readers to help us plan future Bradt guides. Please answer ALL the questions below and return the form to us in order to qualify for an entry in our regular draw.

Have you used any other Bradt guides? If so, which titles? . . . .
. . . .

What other publishers' travel guides do you use regularly? . . . .
. . . .

Where did you buy this guidebook? . . . .

What was the main purpose of your trip to Georgia (or for what other reason did you read our guide)? eg: holiday/business/charity etc.. . . . .
. . . .

What other destinations would you like to see covered by a Bradt guide?
. . . .

Would you like to receive our catalogue/newsletters?

YES / NO (If yes, please complete details on reverse)

If yes – by post or email? . . . .

Age (circle relevant category) 16–25   26–45   46–60   60+

Male/Female (delete as appropriate)

Home country . . . .

Please send us any comments about our guide to Georgia or other Bradt Travel Guides. . . . .
. . . .
. . . .
. . . .

Bradt Travel Guides
23 High Street, Chalfont St Peter, Bucks SL9 9QE, UK
✆ +44 (0)1753 893444 f +44 (0)1753 892333
e info@bradtguides.com
www.bradtguides.com

CLAIM YOUR HALF-PRICE BRADT GUIDE!

Order Form

To order your half-price copy of a Bradt guide, and to enter our prize draw to win £100 (see overleaf), please fill in the order form below, complete the questionnaire overleaf, and send it to Bradt Travel Guides by post, fax or email.

Please send me one copy of the following guide at half the UK retail price

Title	*Retail price*	*Half price*
. . . .	. . . .	. . . .

Please send the following additional guides at full UK retail price

No	*Title*	*Retail price*	*Total*
. . .	. . . .	. . . .	. . . .
. . .	. . . .	. . . .	. . . .
. . .	. . . .	. . . .	. . . .

Sub total . . . .

Post & packing . . . .

(£1 per book UK; £2 per book Europe; £3 per book rest of world)

Total . . . .

Name . . . .

Address . . . .

Tel . . . .   Email . . . .

☐ I enclose a cheque for £ . . . . made payable to Bradt Travel Guides Ltd

☐ I would like to pay by credit card. Number: . . . .

   Expiry date: . . . / . . .   3-digit security code (on reverse of card) . . . . .

☐ Please add my name to your catalogue mailing list.

☐ I would be happy for you to use my name and comments in Bradt marketing material.

Send your order on this form, with the completed questionnaire, to:

Bradt Travel Guides GEO3
23 High Street, Chalfont St Peter, Bucks SL9 9QE
✆ +44 (0)1753 893444   f +44 (0)1753 892333
e info@bradtguides.com   www.bradtguides.com

Bradt Travel Guides

www.bradtguides.com

Africa

Africa Overland	£15.99
Benin	£14.99
Botswana: Okavango, Chobe, Northern Kalahari	£15.99
Burkina Faso	£14.99
Cape Verde Islands	£13.99
Canary Islands	£13.95
Cameroon	£13.95
Eritrea	£15.99
Ethiopia	£15.99
Gabon, São Tomé, Príncipe	£13.95
Gambia, The	£13.99
Ghana	£15.99
Johannesburg	£6.99
Kenya	£14.95
Madagascar	£15.99
Malawi	£13.99
Mali	£13.95
Mauritius, Rodrigues & Réunion	£13.99
Mozambique	£13.99
Namibia	£15.99
Niger	£14.99
Nigeria	£15.99
Rwanda	£14.99
Seychelles	£14.99
Sudan	£13.95
Tanzania, Northern	£13.99
Tanzania	£16.99
Uganda	£15.99
Zambia	£15.95
Zanzibar	£12.99

Britain and Europe

Albania	£13.99
Armenia, Nagorno Karabagh	£14.99
Azores	£12.99
Baltic Capitals: Tallinn, Riga, Vilnius, Kaliningrad	£12.99
Belarus	£14.99
Belgrade	£6.99
Bosnia & Herzegovina	£13.99
Bratislava	£6.99
Budapest	£8.99
Cork	£6.99
Croatia	£13.99
Cyprus see North Cyprus	
Czech Republic	£13.99
Dresden	£7.99
Dubrovnik	£6.99
Eccentric Britain	£13.99
Eccentric Cambridge	£6.99
Eccentric Edinburgh	£5.95
Eccentric France	£12.95
Eccentric London	£13.99
Eccentric Oxford	£5.95
Estonia	£13.99
Faroe Islands	£13.95
Georgia	£14.99
Helsinki	£7.99
Hungary	£14.99
Kiev	£7.95
Kosovo	£14.99

Krakow	£7.99
Latvia	£13.99
Lille	£6.99
Lithuania	£13.99
Ljubljana	£7.99
Macedonia	£14.99
Montenegro	£13.99
North Cyprus	£12.99
Paris, Lille & Brussels	£11.95
Riga	£6.95
River Thames, In the Footsteps of the Famous	£10.95
Serbia	£14.99
Slovakia	£14.99
Slovenia	£12.99
Spitsbergen	£14.99
Switzerland: Rail, Road, Lake	£13.99
Tallinn	£6.99
Ukraine	£14.99
Vilnius	£6.99
Zagreb	£6.99

Middle East, Asia and Australasia

China: Yunnan Province	£13.99
Great Wall of China	£13.99
Iran	£14.99
Iraq	£14.95
Kabul	£9.95
Maldives	£13.99
Mongolia	£14.95
North Korea	£13.95
Oman	£13.99
Sri Lanka	£13.99
Syria	£14.99
Tibet	£13.99
Turkmenistan	£14.99

The Americas and the Caribbean

Amazon, The	£14.99
Argentina	£15.99
Bolivia	£14.99
Cayman Islands	£12.95
Costa Rica	£13.99
Chile	£16.95
Eccentric America	£13.95
Eccentric California	£13.99
Falkland Islands	£13.95
Panama	£13.95
Peru & Bolivia: Backpacking and Trekking	£12.95
St Helena	£14.99
USA by Rail	£13.99

Wildlife

Antarctica: Guide to the Wildlife	£14.95
Arctic: Guide to the Wildlife	£15.99
Galápagos Wildlife	£15.99
Madagascar Wildlife	£14.95
Peruvian Wildlife	£15.99
Southern African Wildlife	£18.95
SriLankan Wildlife	£15.99

Health

Your Child Abroad: A Travel Health Guide	£10.95

Index

Page numbers in italics indicate maps; page numbers in bold indicate major entries